LANDS AND PEOPLES

LANDS AND PEOPLES

NORTH AMERICA

Volume 5

Grolier
INCORPORATED
NEW YORK

CONTENTS
NORTH AMERICA
Volume 5

CANADA

UNITED STATES OF AMERICA

MEXICO

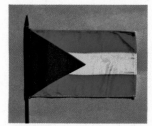

BAHAMAS

CUBA

PUERTO RICO

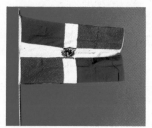

DOMINICAN REPUBLIC

HAITI

JAMAICA

BARBADOS

GRENADA

TRINIDAD AND TOBAGO

A great North American mountain peak in Canada.

NORTH AMERICA

North America is the richest continent in the world. This great wealth is due partly to the continent's vast supply of natural resources and partly to the resourcefulness of the people who live there.

The people of North America have had an amazing history. Early men came to the continent from Asia. For the most part, they failed to recognize the almost unbelievable wealth that lay hidden in the continent. It was with the coming of the Europeans in the Age of Exploration (the 15th, 16th, and 17th centuries) that the riches of North America were first uncovered and developed. The Spanish, French, and British played especially important roles in this development.

The Spaniards made use of Mexico's gold and silver. They planted wheat and started cattle ranches. They also developed sugar and tobacco plantations in the Caribbean, and started orchards of Mediterranean fruit trees—including oranges, lemons, and grapes—in California. The French built up a profitable fur trade in Canada. The British exploited the fisheries and forests of the Atlantic Provinces of Canada and of New England. They were taught to grow maize (corn) by the Indians, and they imported wheat, barley, oats, rye, and meadow grasses from England. They brought British dairy and beef cattle to North America, as well as sheep, pigs, and poultry. They also planted sugar, tobacco, and cotton in the American South.

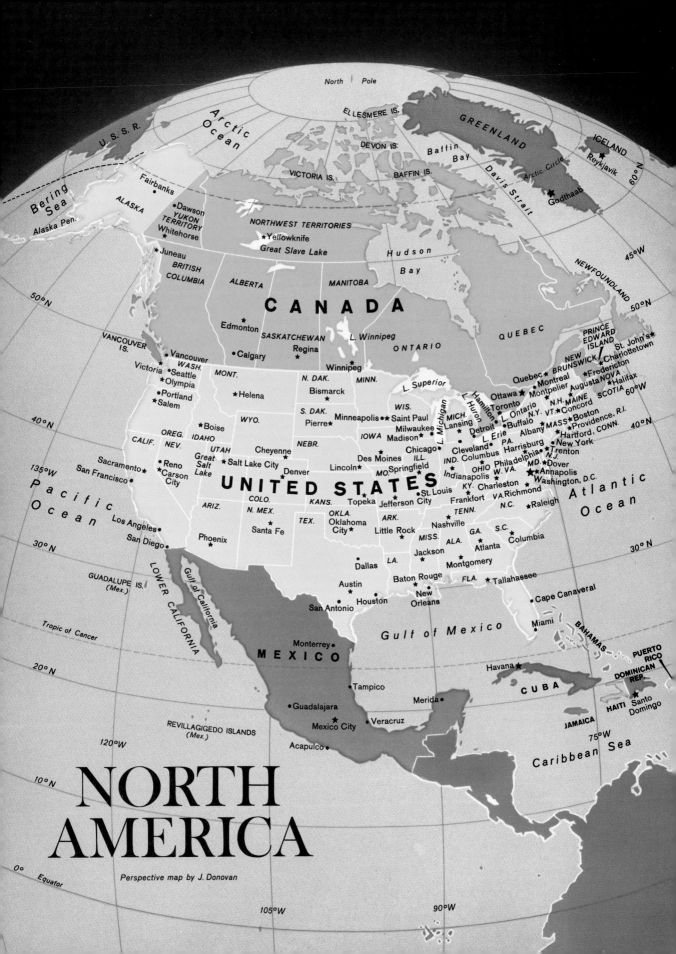

North Pole

Arctic Ocean

U.S.S.R.

ELLESMERE IS.

GREENLAND

ICELAND

Reykjavik

DEVON IS.

Baffin Bay

Arctic Circle

VICTORIA IS.

BAFFIN IS.

Davis Strait

Godthaab

60° N

Bering Sea

Fairbanks

ALASKA

Dawson

YUKON TERRITORY

Whitehorse

NORTHWEST TERRITORIES

45°W

Alaska Pen.

Yellowknife

Great Slave Lake

Hudson Bay

NEWFOUNDLAND

Juneau

BRITISH COLUMBIA

ALBERTA

MANITOBA

50° N

50° N

Edmonton

SASKATCHEWAN

L. Winnipeg

QUEBEC

PRINCE EDWARD ISLAND

St. John's

VANCOUVER IS.

Vancouver

Calgary

Regina

ONTARIO

NEW BRUNSWICK

Charlottetown

WASH.

Winnipeg

Quebec

Fredericton

NOVA SCOTIA

Victoria

Seattle

MONT.

N. DAK.

MINN.

L. Superior

Hamilton

Ottawa

Montreal

Montpelier

Augusta

Halifax

Olympia

Helena

Bismarck

WIS.

L. Michigan

Toronto

L. Ontario

N.H.

MAINE

60°W

Portland

Salem

IDAHO

S. DAK.

Minneapolis

Saint Paul

MICH.

Lansing

Detroit

L. Erie

N.Y.

VT.

Concord

Boston

40° N

Boise

WYO.

Pierre

Milwaukee

Madison

IOWA

Chicago

Cleveland

PA.

Albany

MASS.

Providence, R.I.

40° N

OREG.

NEV.

Sacramento

Reno

UTAH

Cheyenne

NEBR.

Des Moines

ILL.

Springfield

IND.

Columbus

Harrisburg

Hartford

CONN.

New York

CALIF.

Carson City

Great Salt Lake

Salt Lake City

Denver

Lincoln

MO.

St. Louis

Indianapolis

OHIO

Philadelphia

N.J.

San Francisco

135°W

COLO.

KANS.

Topeka

Jefferson City

KY.

Charleston

W. VA.

MD.

Annapolis

Dover

Pacific Ocean

Los Angeles

ARIZ.

N. MEX.

Santa Fe

OKLA.

Oklahoma City

ARK.

Little Rock

Nashville

TENN.

Frankfort

V.A.

Richmond

Washington, D.C.

Atlantic Ocean

San Diego

Phoenix

TEX.

MISS.

ALA.

GA.

S.C.

Raleigh

30° N

GUADALUPE IS. (Mex.)

Gulf of California

Dallas

LA.

Jackson

Montgomery

Atlanta

Columbia

N.C.

30° N

Tropic of Cancer

LOWER CALIFORNIA

Austin

Houston

Baton Rouge

New Orleans

FLA.

Tallahassee

Cape Canaveral

20° N

Monterrey

Gulf of Mexico

Miami

BAHAMAS

PUERTO RICO

MEXICO

Havana

CUBA

DOMINICAN REP.

Tampico

Merida

HAITI

Santo Domingo

Guadalajara

JAMAICA

75°W

REVILLAGIGEDO ISLANDS (Mex.)

Mexico City

Veracruz

120°W

Acapulco

Caribbean Sea

10° N

NORTH AMERICA

0°   Equator

Perspective map by J. Donovan

105°W

90°W

In this way the foundations were laid in colonial times for North America's economic prosperity. This prosperity increased enormously with the discovery on the continent of coal and iron, and later of oil and natural gas. The tremendous expansion of North America in the 19th and 20th centuries was built on these resources.

The geographic position of North America, lying between the Atlantic and the Pacific oceans, isolated it in the early days of European settlement. However, with the development of modern transportation, this drawback became a major asset. North American businessmen are now able to import raw materials from Africa, South America, and Australia, for instance, and to trade in the markets of the two most densely settled regions of the world—Europe and Asia.

But in the final analysis, people make geography. The initiative of the European immigrants to the New World, and later the initiative of Americans, Canadians, and Mexicans, unlocked the natural riches that produced the world's greatest agricultural and industrial belts. North Americans have grown rich because they have revolutionized the geography of their continent.

The major part of the North American continent is divided into three great nations: Canada, the United States, and Mexico. Many of the islands lying off the continent are considered part of North America. There are separate articles in this volume on the BAHAMAS, BARBADOS, BERMUDA, the CARIBBEAN SEA AND ISLANDS, CUBA, the DOMINICAN REPUBLIC, GREENLAND, GRENADA, HAITI, JAMAICA, PUERTO RICO, SAINT PIERRE AND MIQUELON, and TRINIDAD AND TOBAGO. Some geographers consider Central America a subdivision of North America. *LANDS AND PEOPLES*, however, discusses Central America in the article CENTRAL AND SOUTH AMERICA in Volume 6.

FACTS AND FIGURES

LOCATION: The mainland of North America extends from: **Latitude**—7° 12′ N to 83° 07′ N. **Longitude**—52° 37′ W (mainland) to 172° 27′ E (farthest of the Aleutian Islands).

AREA: Approximately 9,160,000 sq. mi. (23,724,400 sq. km.)—including Greenland and the Caribbean islands.

POPULATION: 290,000,000 (estimate).

CHIEF RIVERS: Missouri, Mississippi, Yukon, Rio Grande, Arkansas, Colorado, Red, Columbia, Mackenzie, Peace, Snake, Ohio, Saskatchewan, St. Lawrence.

HIGHEST POINT: Mount McKinley, 20,320 ft. (6,194 m.).

LOWEST POINT: Badwater, Death Valley, California, 282 ft. (86 m.) below sea level.

COUNTRIES AND TERRITORIES OF NORTH AMERICA

COUNTRY	AREA (sq. mi.)	(sq. km.)	POPULATION (estimate)	CAPITAL
Bahamas	5,380	13,935	190,000	Nassau
Barbados	166	430	253,000	Bridgetown
Bermuda	21	54	52,000	Hamilton
Canada	3,851,809	9,976,185	22,000,000	Ottawa
Cuba	44,218	114,524	8,250,000	Havana
Dominican Republic	18,816	48,734	4,029,000	Santo Domingo
Greenland	840,000	2,175,000	47,000	Godthaab
Grenada	133	344	100,000	St. George's
Haiti	10,714	27,750	4,674,000	Port-au-Prince
Jamaica	4,232	10,962	1,913,000	Kingston
Mexico	761,602	1,972,549	49,000,000	Mexico City
Puerto Rico	3,435	8,900	2,800,000	San Juan
Saint Pierre and Miquelon	93	241	5,225	Saint Pierre
Trinidad and Tobago	1,980	5,128	1,100,000	Port of Spain
United States of America	3,615,123	9,363,169	203,000,000	Washington, D.C.

THE NATURAL ENVIRONMENT

Geographers and geologists divide North America into a number of regions. Each of these regions has a variety of natural resources. There is a vast upland in the north called the Canadian Shield. This region is rich in deposits of iron, nickel, copper, and other metals. It is also rich in forests and waterpower. There are great Central Lowlands located in the Saskatchewan-Red River basin region; in the Great Lakes-St. Lawrence River complex; and on the plains of the Missouri, Mississippi, and Ohio rivers. These vast lowlands are rich in coal, oil, natural gas, and fertile soils that are good for growing many crops. There are mountain regions —the Appalachians on the east, the Cordilleras on the west, and the Innuitians to the north—which are rich in fuels (natural gas, coal, and oil), metals, and waterpower. And finally, there are the coastal plains of North America, which are located along the Atlantic Ocean and the Gulf of Mexico. These plains are especially rich in valuable soils, forests, oil, and natural gas.

The Canadian Shield

The physiographical makeup of North America has influenced the internal development of the continent. North America grew up by slow additions around a central core of very old, very hard rocks, called the Canadian Shield. (It is sometimes called the Laurentian Shield or the Laurentian Plateau, as well). This geological structure has been tilted up on its outer edges in the mountain ranges of Ellesmere Island and Baffin Island in Canada's Northwest Territories; in the massive dome of the Adirondacks; in the Algoman, Gogebic, Mesabi, and Cuyuna mountain ranges around the upper Great Lakes region of the United States and Canada; and in a number of low mountain ridges running eastward from Lake Athabasca and Great Bear Lake. The whole of the Shield is submerged in the center, under Hudson Bay and Foxe Basin.

The Canadian Shield is noted for its great wealth of minerals. It has two of the world's largest iron fields. They are located along the Labrador trough and around western Lake Superior. The world's largest deposits of nickel are found at Sudbury, in the southeastern portion of central Ontario. Major gold fields lie in western Quebec and eastern Ontario and in the Great Slave Lake region. One of the world's principal sources of uranium is found north of Lake Athabasca. Copper, lead, zinc, and cobalt are also found, mainly in eastern Ontario and western Quebec.

The Lowlands

There is a circle of lowlands around the Shield. The **Arctic Lowlands** are located in the Canadian archipelago, reaching to Lancaster Sound. They are broken into islands and peninsulas by the sea. East of the Shield, the lowlands are lost, except for Anticosti Island. On the south and west, the lowlands really come into their own, forming the vast plains known as the **St. Lawrence Lowlands**, the **Ohio-Great Lakes-Mississippi Lowlands**, the **Prairies** and the **Great Plains**, and to the far northwest, the **Mackenzie Lowlands**. These are the lands of the great North American rivers, which are among the most majestic in the world. Their annual floods, after the heavy winter snows have melted, have spread rich silt across much of interior North America. Where their courses have been controlled by dams and canals, they form magnificent waterways. In the early 19th century many rivers and lakes were linked by canals. The Mohawk-Lake Erie Canal and the Chicago-Illinois River Canal in the United States are notable examples of 19th-century canals that are still in use. Thus the United States developed a network of inland navigation routes unparalleled anywhere in the world, except perhaps in the Soviet Union.

The **Interior Lowlands** have the world's richest resources of coal, oil, and natural gas. These have been preserved in shallow basins mostly on the flanks of the Appalachians, Ozarks, and Rockies, but also in the heart of the Central Plains and along the edge of the Gulf coastal plain. These resources have been used to help North America in its vast industrial development and in the growth of transportation.

The Mountains

Beyond the ring of lowlands, going from the Canadian Shield outward to the oceans, are the marginal mountains, great areas of folded and altered rock that border the coasts. The oldest of these mountain ranges is the **Appalachian system**, running along the east margin of the continent from Newfoundland to Alabama, and then continuing in the south in the Ozarks and Ouachita Mountains of eastern Oklahoma and western Arkansas.

The Appalachians form three belts. There is an outer (eastern) belt, which juts into the Atlantic Ocean in New England and in Canada's Atlantic Provinces. There is a middle belt, made up of a great valley crossed by the Hudson River and parts of the Susquehanna, Shenandoah, and Coosa rivers. And, finally, there is an interior (western) belt, extending back from the Allegheny Front, or escarpment, into the low Allegheny and Cumberland plateaus. Although the Appalachians are not very high mountains—most of the ridges are from 1,200 to 2,400 feet (360–730 meters) and only a few peaks rise to over 6,000 feet (1,800 m.)—they formed an effective barrier to early settlers. The barrier was great because the Appalachian ranges, although not high, are very wide and have many ridges with narrow, zigzag valleys in between. This made travel through the mountains with pack animals and eventually wagons very difficult.

There are two major breaks, or passes, in the Appalachians, which were crucial in the exploration, settlement, and development of the United States and Canada. One of the breaks occurs at the Gulf of St. Lawrence in Canada. The other break is formed by the Hudson and Mohawk rivers in the United States. The break on the St. Lawrence led to the development of Canada's biggest city, Montreal. The Hudson-Mohawk break starts at New York City, the biggest city of the United States, and was a factor in its development. These two breaks in the Appalachian barrier eventually formed the two chief paths of immigration from the east into the interior of the North American continent.

The Appalachians have much mineral wealth, including the coalfields of the Atlantic Provinces of Canada and the much larger coal reserves of eastern and western Pennsylvania. Lead and zinc are abundant in the Canadian provinces of Newfoundland and New Brunswick. Iron ore mines were long worked at Bell Island, in Newfoundland, and they are still important in the Birmingham area of Alabama, where a large iron and steel industry has developed because of the deposit of iron ore in the vicinity. Large deposits of bauxite are worked in valleys in the region lying between the Ouachitas and the Ozarks.

6

Desert country at White Sands National Monument, New Mexico.

The swirling patterns of conservation farming in Nebraska.

The surf rushes in against the rocks on the rugged Maine coast.

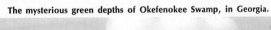

The Lone Cypress, on the Pacific Coast near Carmel, California.

Another series of marginal mountains lie in the far north. They are the **Innuitians**. The Innuitians run through the Parry Islands in the far northern reaches of Canada and continue northward through Devon Island to form the high ranges of Ellesmere Island, which point even farther north toward the North Pole. They are so remote that they have played little part in the development of North America.

This is not the case with the last series of mountains to evolve in North America, the **Western Cordilleras**. Here an enormous complex of ridges, tablelands, and basins make up one of the world's major upland areas. It consists, first, of a series of plateaus and basins, including the Yukon plateau, the upland of central British Columbia, the Columbia Mountains, the Snake River Plain, the Great Basin, and the Colorado Plateau. In this central belt there are a number of volcanoes and massive lava flows.

To the east are the **Rockies**. They start with the relatively low mountains in the Brooks Range of Alaska and the Richardson Mountains of northern Canada. In the Mackenzie Mountains they bulge out in a sprawl of arclike folds. Then in the Canadian Rockies and the Northern Rockies of the United States the mountains rise to great elevations, lifting themselves like a wall above great faults. The Rockies next continue in elliptical domes with intervening depressions. This forms the "dome and park" topography of the Central Rockies. Finally they soar up in the volcanic peaks and sharp hogbacks of the Southern Rockies and the **Eastern Sierras** (**Sierra Madre Oriental**) of Mexico.

On the far west, the **Pacific Ranges** start with the highest mountains in North America, the Alaska Range, dominated by Mount McKinley—which is 20,320 feet (6,194 m.) high. They continue through the Coast Mountains of British Columbia. Thereafter, the Pacific Ranges continue in the **Cascade** and **High Sierra** (**Sierra Nevada**) ranges. The Cascade-

Nevada system is dominated by the High Sierras. Mount Whitney—which is 14,495 feet (4,418 m.)—is the highest peak in the High Sierras. The Pacific Ranges are then continued south by the **Western Sierras (Sierra Madre Occidental)**. Finally there is the part of the **American coastal system** beginning in the beautiful volcanic mountains known as the Olympics and passing south through the Klamath Mountains (also volcanic) to the short ridges of Los Angeles and the long, spindling range extending southward to Lower (Baja) California.

The Western Cordilleras are split by great river gaps. Some of the eastward-flowing rivers start well back in the mountains and cut across the Rockies. They form passes at Peace Dam and on the Yellowhead, Kicking Horse, and Crowsnest rivers in Canada; and on the Yellowstone and North Platte rivers in the United States. Still longer, westward-flowing rivers managed to cut down through the coast mountains, often in spectacular gorges like those of the Fraser, the Columbia, and the Colorado rivers.

Through these gaps and those of the Appalachians the white man wrote a new geography of the continent. He built roads and railways to tie the Atlantic to the Pacific with bands of steel. He extended the boundaries that were to include the great east-west nations of Canada, the United States, and Mexico, carving up North America among them.

The great volume of water in the rivers and the narrowness of some of the valleys of the Cordilleras have, together, led to an increasing number of attempts to dam sections of the rivers and to use the impounded streams to generate huge quantities of electricity. Hydroelectricity has played a great part in the development of the continent.

The wealth of fuels and metals in the Cordilleras has also contributed much to the wealth of the continent. The coal, oil, and natural gas found in the Cordilleras have been very important. However, the main wealth of these ranges is in metals. Significant iron deposits occur at Vancouver Island in Canada, at Eagle Mountain, California, and at Iron Springs, Utah. The discovery of gold helped to establish settlements in the Yukon, British Columbia, and California. Large deposits of gold were also found in the Rockies in Montana and Utah and on the Colorado Plateau. Silver, first mined in the Mexican plateau, also occurs in the Colorado and British Columbia plateaus. Copper is important in the Coast Mountains of British Columbia and in both the Northern and Southern Rockies of the United States. The continent's chief source of uranium is the Colorado Plateau; lead and zinc are plentiful in southern British Columbia. All of these valuable sources of metal helped in the development of the Mountain West, an area where agriculture was difficult to establish. Mining camps were good markets, and helped the growth of both lumbering and farming.

The Coastal Plains

The last stage in the physical evolution of North America was the building out of the coastal plains, chief of which are those flanking the Atlantic and the Gulf of Mexico. Most of the Atlantic plain has been drowned (lies underwater); its outer extension forms the magnificent fishing banks stretching from New England to Newfoundland. However, from Cape Cod south, the coastal plain widens until it is 300 miles (480 kilometers) broad in Georgia. It is continued across the low, flat lime-

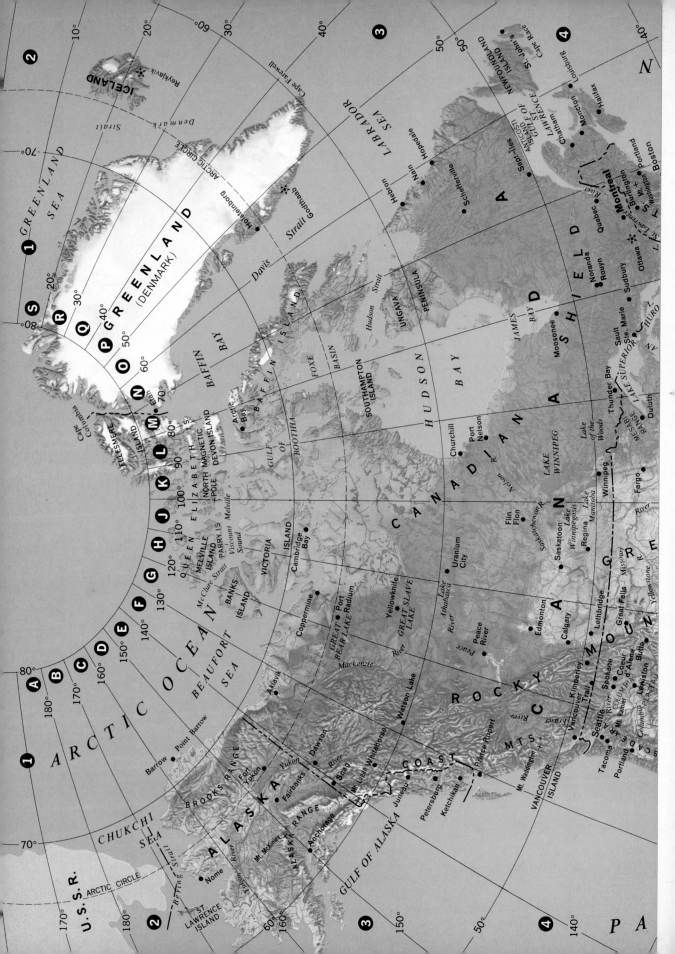

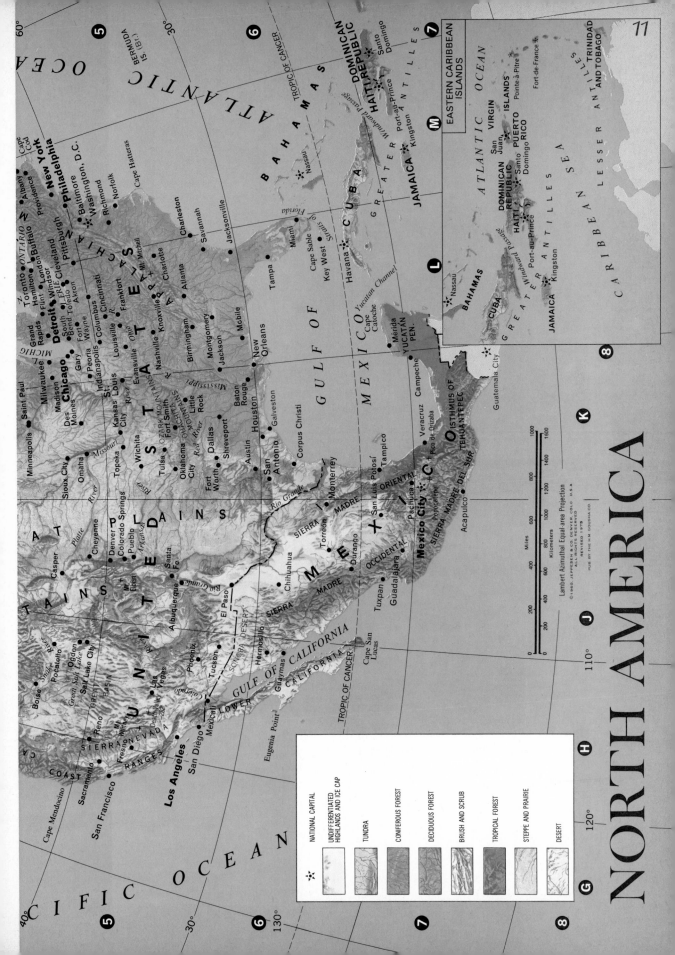

INDEX TO NORTH AMERICA MAP

stone peninsula of Florida to the lowlands of the Gulf of Mexico. Here it is divided by a great alluvial strip ending in the long, clawlike delta of the Mississippi River. The Gulf lowlands narrow again in Mexico, ending on the limestone plateau of Mexico's Yucatán Peninsula. Most of the rivers crossing the coastal plain flow down from the Appalachians in very steep-sided valleys (which are difficult to cross), then plunge in a line of water-falls over the foothills fronting the Blue Ridge Mountains. The rivers then widen out and meander slowly down to the lagoons that lie behind the great long shoreline spits and bars of areas like Cape Hatteras. Few of these rivers are easily navigable.

The coastal plains have quite a wealth of minerals. From Louisiana to southern Mexico there are extensive oil and natural gas fields. Large deposits of sulfur and salt are found along the Gulf shore of Texas and Louisiana. Florida is North America's main source of phosphate.

Glaciation

Glaciation modified the land of the United States a great deal, principally north of the confluence of the Ohio, Mississippi, and Missouri rivers. Since so much of the continent is in the high north, there was a widespread accumulation of snow and ice during the Great Ice Age. Labrador, which is still one of the snowiest parts of North America, the Rockies, and the Pacific Ranges were covered with ice to such a depth that gradually a vast ice sheet developed.

Tongues of ice moved east and southeast into the Atlantic and across the northern Appalachians. They helped to gouge out and deepen the beds of what are today the Great Lakes. Westward-moving lobes of ice pushed down the Lake Winnipeg-Red River depression and deepened the hollows now filled by lakes Athabasca, Great Slave, and Great Bear. Descending streams of ice from the Rockies joined together in huge fans across the western prairies of Canada and the Great Plains of Canada and the United States, while other glaciers, pushing down the Coast Mountains, cut the deep fiords of Alaska, British Columbia, and Washington's Puget Sound.

As the front of the ice came to a halt, masses of boulders, gravel, and sand were deposited, making the great terminal moraines, hundreds of miles long and several hundred feet high, that now dot the Central Lowland.

Perhaps the outstanding result of the Ice Age was the many large lakes it left. In its advance, the ice scooped out basins in the soft rock of the river systems that guided its expansion. When the ice retreated, it trapped water in these basins, especially where the ice blocked outlets to the sea. Then ice-front lakes developed. In other cases the basins were filled with giant masses of "dead" ice that, upon melting down, left lakes in their place. The levels of these lakes have in all cases dropped. They have left, therefore, a remarkable set of old raised beaches behind them that have been most useful for man in the building of roads and railways, in the establishment of towns, and in the development of fruit farming and truck farming.

The St. Lawrence River is the main outlet of the Great Lakes. But when ice still lay across the St. Lawrence, the Great Lakes cut overflow channels to the Mississippi and Ohio, the Susquehanna, and the Hudson rivers, and thus found outlets for their mounting waters. These old channels were filled again by the engineering efforts of men in the canal era of the early 19th century. Some of these canals are still in use—for example the canals of the Richelieu River (the St. Ours and the Chambly) in Canada and America's Erie Canal and Illinois and Michigan Canal.

Climate

Climate, which was responsible for glaciation, has been of tremendous influence in many other ways in North America. Changes in climate dominated the periods of early discovery and settlement in North America. During the Ice Age there were warm periods, known as interglacials, when the ice melted back. Even during a major advance of ice there were short times of warmth, called interstadials. Four great ice advances, known as the Nebraskan, Kansan, Illinoian, and Wisconsin, were separated by three long interglacials. Wisconsin glaciation was interrupted by several interstadials, during which men seized the opportunity to cross from Siberia into Alaska and then move southward into the empty continent. It is estimated that this journey was made 30,000 years ago. New advances of Wisconsin ice hurried their migration south and shut off fresh immigration. After most of the Wisconsin ice had dis-

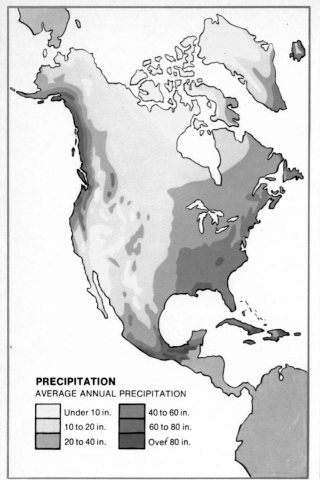

PRECIPITATION
AVERAGE ANNUAL PRECIPITATION

- Under 10 in.
- 10 to 20 in.
- 20 to 40 in.
- 40 to 60 in.
- 60 to 80 in.
- Over 80 in.

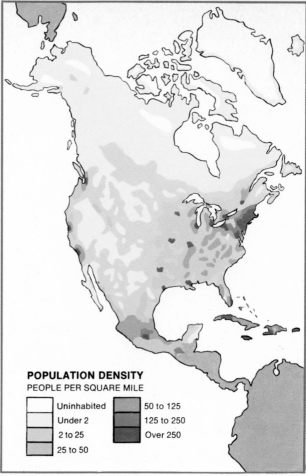

POPULATION DENSITY
PEOPLE PER SQUARE MILE

- Uninhabited
- Under 2
- 2 to 25
- 25 to 50
- 50 to 125
- 125 to 250
- Over 250

appeared there were several hundred years of cold, wet, stormy weather that must have been hard to endure. Then the weather grew much warmer—in fact, warmer than it is today. The "climatic optimum" was reached. This means that ideal conditions were present for man.

This period—more than 4,000 years ago—saw real advances in technology, and man became less primitive. In Mexico, men learned to cultivate maize and squash and thus became gardeners and village- and town-dwellers, as well as hunters and dwellers in camps. They had taken the first steps toward civilization.

At last the climate of North America as we know it today began to emerge, although there were many variations. The Little Ice Age, one of these variations, may have contributed, through increased coldness and storminess, to wiping out Viking settlements in Greenland. Early 19th-century decades were cool and stormy, later decades dry and warm. One long warm spell lasted to the mid-20th century, when glaciers in the Coast Mountains retreated.

North America now seems to be in a stable period. Although changes in climate have been minor in recent centuries, they have had tremendous importance in the settlement of semiarid lands like the Great Plains of the United States (so easily struck by drought) or the subarctic regions of Canada (so swiftly invaded by frost).

The climate of North America is dominated by four major air masses, known as the Polar Continental, the Tropical Continental, the Polar Pacific, and the Tropical Atlantic. Daily weather on the continent is created by the conflict among these air masses.

The **Polar Continental** air mass is the largest and most influential. It is cradled in the Canadian archipelago and the Hudson Bay region. By the end of October northern lands and waters are sheeted with ice. Air moving over this ice develops a huge dome of coldness, which in turn brings about a large high-pressure center. By November the polar air has spread over the Prairies and is poised on the edge of the Great Lakes. There is a rapid rush over the Appalachians to New England and New York in December. This rush is paralleled by a surge forward down the Ohio and Mississippi rivers and across the Great Plains. In late January the Polar Continental air finally comes to rest against the Ozarks. Occasional "northers," as they are known, push cold air to Florida and Louisiana in the south and across the mountains to British Columbia and California in the west. In late February the air mass begins to shrink and by June it is back in the Hudson Bay basin.

Winter also sees the **Polar Pacific** air mass grow strong. This is in association with the Aleutian low-pressure system. The waters of the North Pacific, warmed by the Kuroshio current, are much warmer than the land. The air tends to become warm and rise over this region, and therefore more air is sucked in. Consequently a great vortex of air develops, which spreads to Alaska, British Columbia, the Pacific Northwest, and northern California. A similar low-pressure system lies over Iceland and pulls in air. A part of this air, called the **Polar Atlantic** air, passes over Labrador, the Canadian Atlantic Provinces, and New England.

The **Tropical Continental** air mass comes into being in the summer over the American Southwest. Dry tropical air builds up in the Mexican basin, in Southern California, and in the Great Basin. It is strengthened by an extension of the tropical high-pressure belt in the eastern Pacific. Winds blow around the western edge of this belt from the interior of the continent out to sea so that the influence of the Pacific Ocean on the weather is nullified over most of the West. Dry, hot air also flows through the passes of the Rockies to the Great Plains.

The **Tropical Atlantic** air mass is also strongest in summer. It extends westward from the belt of high pressure between the Azores and Bermuda until, in early spring, it invades the Atlantic and Gulf coastal plains. In early summer it pours through the gap between the Appalachians and the Ozarks. Using the Mississippi Valley like a great funnel, it surges across the Central Plains to the Great Lakes. Here it breaks in two. One arm extends up the Ohio River and down the lower Great Lakes, using the Mohawk-Hudson gap across to New York and New England. Another arm reaches far into the northwest down the Red River, across the Canadian Prairies, and well down the Mackenzie Basin. Once this air mass has broken through the lower Mississippi gap, there is nothing to stop it flooding over virtually the whole of the Interior Lowlands of the continent.

On the whole, North America has a very stimulating climate with strong seasonal changes and with pronounced day-to-day changes within the seasons. The changes occur as the air masses expand or contract and as zones of conflict emerge. There are great sweeps of stormy weather when sunshine and cloud, heat and cold, wetness and dryness alternate in rapid succession. Indeed, no other continent except Europe has such stimulating and invigorating conditions.

But there is, of course, the challenge of frost in the northeast, where the Polar Continental air is cradled, and of drought in the southwest, where the Tropical Continental air is found. Actually the main challenge comes not in the areas that are permanently frost-ridden or perennially drought-stricken, but in the in-between zones, especially the northern Prairies and the Great Clay Belt of Ontario and Quebec. These areas are afflicted with frost. The Great Plains and southern Prairies are invaded by drought. This challenge has been met by "cold-farming" and "dry-farming," scientific farming methods that have been very effective, and by the breeding of frost- and drought-resistant plants. Developments like these have helped to make North American farming methods among the most efficient in the world.

Vegetation and Soil

Vegetation, soil, and climate are, of course, integral parts of physical geography. In the subarctic parts of Alaska and the Canadian north, the growth of trees ends at an altitude of about 2,000 feet (600 m.); in the Canadian Rockies, at about 8,000 feet (2,400 m.); and in the California Sierras, at 10,000 feet (3,000 m.). In the Appalachians, the dense deciduous forests (forests of trees that lose their leaves in the fall) of the valleys and lower slopes are replaced by pine forests at about 2,800 feet

Workers harvest tomatoes in the Lake Erie area of Pennsylvania.

(840 m.). The pine is, in turn, replaced by spruce at altitudes over 4,000 feet (1,200 m.). But in the northern ridges, 4,000 feet is usually the limit for tree growth.

Physical geography affects vegetation in other ways, too. The Cordilleras stop the rain from reaching the interior. Therefore a difference develops between dense, wet, coniferous forests (forests of cone-bearing, primarily evergreen trees) on the Pacific slopes and the much thinner mixed forests of the interior uplands, with yellow and ponderosa pine and balsam, poplar, and birch.

In the main, vegetation reflects climate. When the first men came to the continent, most of North America, lying in the temperate latitudes and under the influence of two great oceans, was covered with forest. There were two exceptions. The north and northeast of the continent was one exception. This area was permanently dominated by Polar Continental air and was treeless, with vegetation consisting of mosses, heath, and grass. This kind of vegetation is called tundra. The western interior and southwest was the other exception. In this region there was a Tropical Continental climate and the land was largely grassland, desert scrub, and desert.

Forests. The forests can be divided into northern, western, and eastern types. The northern forest is the only North American forest to stretch all the way across the continent. The interior grasslands split the western from the eastern division. The northern forest extends much farther north on the Pacific coast than it does along Hudson Bay and the Atlantic. This is because of the influence of the mild, moist Polar Pacific air, which brings long growing seasons well into Alaska. Hudson Bay and the Atlantic region are under the quite different influence of the Polar Continental air, which covers much of the land with frost, snow, and ice for many months a year.

The northern forest is mainly coniferous, although it also includes willow, alder, balsam, and birch. There are enormous stands of one or two types of spruce or pine, growing to heights of 20 to 30 feet (6–9 m.). The trees are very close together and there is little underbrush. Timber is cut in large areas of the forest for use in the manufacture of pulp and paper products. However, in the remoter parts of the forest—the home of many fur-bearing animals, including beaver, muskrat, mink, marten, squirrel, and fox—the fur trade is of chief economic importance.

The western forest merges with the northern forest in the Pacific Northwest. Here western trees like the Sitka spruce are mixed with the northern white spruce. But from Sitka south, the forest, though still largely coniferous, changes. It is made up of much larger trees and is denser and more luxuriant. Dense stands of tall Douglas fir, western hemlock, western cedar, and, in California, sequoia provide some of the best timber in the world for construction purposes. The trees grow to heights of 100 to more than 200 feet (30–60 m.).

The eastern forest is much broader than the western, extending from the Missouri River to the Atlantic coast. The eastern forest differs from the northern and western types in being mainly deciduous, although in the Appalachian region and on belts of sandy soil it is still coniferous. The deciduous trees form great latitudinal zones, based on the increasing warmth of the climate from north to south. Maple, beech, elm, and white oak grow in the St. Lawrence basin and New England. In the Ohio basin and the mid-Atlantic coastal plain, the zone consists of hickory and red oak. Walnut, butternut, and red and black oak grow along the lower Mississippi and on the southern Atlantic coastal plain. The fourth area, along the Gulf coast plain and in Florida, has the live oak, the Kentucky coffee tree, the tupelo, the papaw, and the southern swamp cypress. Palmetto palms and coastal mangroves are also common.

The southern pineries form a major exception to the generally deciduous nature of the eastern forests. Here tall, slender loblolly and longleaf pines flourish on the old sandy shores left stranded high and dry as the Atlantic coast plain rose slowly out of the sea after the retreat of the glacier. These pineries are one of the last great timber and pulpwood reserves left in the eastern United States.

The Grasslands.   Grasslands replace forests in the drier inland part of the continent. The grasslands lie roughly west of the Ozarks and the Missouri River and south of the South Saskatchewan River. They extend to the Pacific Ranges, except at higher elevations where forests grow. In the dry, deeper basins the grasslands change to mesquite bush and sagebrush.

When the white man came to the eastern and northern parts of the grasslands—to the Missouri, Red, and Saskatchewan river valleys—he found tall grass as high as a man's waist. This was soon plowed up for wheat farming. West of the tall grasslands, through most of the Great Plains, and on the rims of the Great Basin, the Columbia Plateau, and the Great Valley of California, was shortgrass prairie. The prairie made excellent rangeland for grazing livestock.

Soils.   The soils of North America vary according to vegetation and climate. North America has a wide range of soils, from those of arctic tundras to those of tropical jungles. (The soils also vary according to the physical and chemical changes man has induced through fertilizers.) The tundras of Alaska and northern Canada have thin, washed-out soils, which are permanently frozen under a shallow "active" layer of about 9 inches (23 centimeters). In the summer this active layer thaws out. Since much of the water from the thaw cannot drain away, the soil often becomes waterlogged and very acid.

Grasslands and desert scrub have soils known as pedocals. Many of the drier ones are also saline (salty). The soils that developed under the tall grasses are black because they have a rich upper layer of rotted material. They are suited to growing a wide range of grain crops.

Under the short grasses there is less humus, so that the color changes from chocolate to light brown. At the same time, with a semiarid (fairly dry) climate, there is much more evaporation of moisture, and alkaline salts are brought close to the surface. Where the vegetation is really scanty, consisting of bunchgrass and mesquite or sagebrush (with lots of bare spots in between), there is relatively little humus. In this kind of area, the soil is very light brown—sometimes nearly yellow—in color.

The vast majority of North American soils are humid pedalfers. These are soils that, thanks to the humidity, have developed deposits of aluminum hydroxides and iron oxides. Such soils range all the way from subarctic types in Alaska and northern Canada to tropical types in the Mexican rain forests. The northern soils have a moderate depth of humus from pine needles and rotted trunks and tree roots. This is washed down by water from melting snows and also by early summer rains.

In the warm temperate areas like the southern United States and California, high summer temperatures, along with considerable soil moisture, have led to strong oxidation of the iron elements in the soil. Because of this the soil is often reddish in appearance.

Finally, in the very hot and also wet parts of southern coastal Mexico, there is a deeply weathered red soil. Where the topsoil is worn away by erosion, the land is not at all fertile. But where topsoil has been retained, the land is good for growing tree crops, sugarcane, or rice.

THE MAN-MADE ENVIRONMENT

Coming into North America, man found a wonderful range of soils, vegetation, metals and fuels, climate, drainage, and terrain to help him. He had, in fact, come on one of the richest of all homes. Man's use of the land gradually changed the natural environment into a man-made environment.

Indians and Eskimo

The ancestors of the American Indians and the Eskimo began to change the face of North America simply by coming there. About 30,000 years ago they migrated from areas in northeastern Siberia. They had primitive tools and did not know how to use many of the resources they came to possess. Some of these early people settled in basins isolated among the western mountains. They continued to lead very simple lives, hardly improving on the simple tools they brought with them. This is possibly one reason why the Paiute Indians, for instance, sought the refuge of mountain basins and of deserts, where they could live their lives unmolested and unchanged. Here they roamed as collectors of wild seeds and berries and as hunters of small game like gophers

A team of huskies draws an Eskimo sled through the northern snows.

A lone oil rig represents the future of the continental north.

Glen Canyon Dam in the desert country of the American Southwest.

An Ohio steel plant, part of the Great Lakes industrial complex.

A fishing village in Nova Scotia, port for inshore fishermen.

and rabbits. They had digging sticks to dig out succulent roots and grubs and darts and small bows and arrows to shoot game. These early people lived in temporary shelters of branches and leaves woven into huts. They had few possessions because they had to travel, following game from winter pastures in the basins to summer pastures on the hills. They made virtually no impact on the land, adapting themselves to existing conditions.

The peoples who took to fishing were more successful. They lived either in Alaska and the Canadian Arctic (ancestors of the Eskimo) or in present-day British Columbia and the states of Washington and Oregon (ancestors of the Pacific coast Indians).

Although the early Eskimo lived in a very cold and inhospitable region, they had one advantage—there were plentiful supplies of fish and of fish-eating mammals like walrus, seal, and bear. Therefore, even if they had to fight hard against many odds, they could usually get plenty to eat and were able to dress themselves in thick, warm clothes made of fur. Their ice houses, too, were very snug inside.

The Eskimo were very adept at designing highly specialized and highly efficient tools, like ice-drillers, adzes for shaping bone, bone needles for sewing up skins, bone fishhooks, harpoons, and spear-throwers. They also made good sleds from whalebone or driftwood, and kayaks as well. Their heavy skin parkas, skin trousers, and high boots, or mukluks, were serviceable clothes that have since been copied by many people working in arctic or alpine lands.

However, the harshness of Eskimo life and the need to be constantly on the move to follow the seasonal migrations of game meant that they never grew in population and never built permanent villages or towns. Their lives were simple, usually giving them enough to live, but not enough to live well. They did not alter their environment to any great extent.

The Indian fishermen of the Pacific coast were, by contrast, much better off and made a much greater impact on the land. Living off the teeming salmon runs of the great fiords of the west (a diet they supplemented with deer and other wildlife from the forest), they had plenty of food. This probably accounted for the growth in their population. To house their increasing numbers they built large villages of big, well-made houses. These were constructed of logs and planks cut from the abundant forests. The houses were filled with wooden furniture, bark matting and containers, and blankets made of skins. They dug canoes out of the giant fir trees. These canoes carried men out to the rich halibut and seal fisheries off the islands.

With security and even a certain amount of wealth, the fishermen developed art and music. They are also noted for their magnificently carved and colored totem poles. The Pacific coast Indians cleared away parts of the forest, established trails, and had sites for permanent settlements. They laid the foundation for many modern west-coast towns and roads. Unfortunately, their influence was restricted to the coast by the lofty mountains that lie behind it.

Across the mountains lived the main hunting peoples of the continent. The hunters of the northern forests and of the grassy prairies depended to such an extent on game that few of them practiced agriculture. The hunters of the eastern forests, on the other hand, used a primitive form of agriculture to give them a richer diet and greater security. They tended to advance further and did more to change their environment.

The hunters of the northern forest lived on enormous herds of caribou or hunted deer and moose. On the whole there was plenty of game, and people did not lack food, except in the depth of winter. These hunters made remarkably good use of the birch tree. They made birch-bark canoes and covered their tipis with birch bark; they made bark containers and used birch bark instead of paper for their rudimentary writing. They dressed in deerskin shirts and trousers and wore elk-skin moccasins. They did not change the forest very much, but they did have sites used repeatedly for their camps, and they knew all the worthwhile rivers and river portages. Many of their portage routes were followed by white men and were turned into roads and canals.

The hunters of the interior grasslands were more successful, perhaps mainly because they lived off huge herds of buffalo in the Canadian Prairies and the Great Plains. Here the Blackfeet, the Mandan, and other plains tribes hunted the buffalo in great drives, stampeding them and shooting down the panic-stricken animals with bow and arrow. Sometimes they killed hundreds of buffalo by frightening them into stampeding off cliffs. The abrupt escarpments of the Great Plains were ideal for this. Buffalo meat was dried and stored for lean times or long journeys. Buffalo skins were made into tents, blankets, and cloaks. The people of the prairies and plains lived fairly well, but they had few permanent settlements since they had to follow the migrating herds. By firing the grasses to stampede herds, or simply to keep down bushes and thus maintain the grazing lands, the Indians did a lot to change the natural vegetation of their portion of North America. They were responsible for a widespread reduction of woodland and the considerable enlargement of areas under grass.

The hunters of the eastern forest—from the Iroquois of Lake Ontario and the Finger Lakes to the Creek and Cherokee of the southern plains— got their food supply not only from killing deer, bear, and turkey, but from growing maize, beans, and squash in little plots and fruit trees in small orchards. Thus they had a much greater variety of food than most other Indian tribes. This gave them both security and a certain amount of wealth. Since they planted crops, they had permanent villages. Some of these villages grew into small towns, with rows of houses and with walls of pointed logs for protection. Population grew. The arts of weaving, pottery, and metalwork flourished. Political federations of tribes were organized into leagues that provided protection from hostile tribes and eventually from the whites. There was also a certain amount of trade.

The Indians of the eastern forest, however, only verged on a civilized life. They had no domestic animals. They had not invented the plow or the wheeled vehicle. And their methods of producing food were still primitive and wasteful. From time to time they exhausted the soil and had to move on to a new settlement. Nevertheless, the people of the eastern forest did clear quite a lot of timber, and their larger villages were permanent. They cut trails through the woods, and above all, they introduced maize (the Indian name for corn) and tobacco into the Mississippi-Great Lakes lowlands and the coast plains.

It was the farmers and city-dwellers of Mexico and Guatemala who made the great step forward to a settled, civilized way of life. This occurred among the Pueblo Indians of present-day New Mexico and among the still more advanced Maya, Toltecs, and Aztecs of Mexico. The success of the pueblo-dwellers lay in irrigation. By using the streams that had spread out small well-watered fans at the mouths of western canyons, and then channeling the water to fields of maize and squash, they were able to get a regular supply of food. They did not have to depend on the risky, seasonal business of hunting. Hence they could build permanent settlements and devote much time to religion and the arts.

In the Valley of Mexico, at the southern end of the Mexican plateau, several civilizations grew up. The oldest was flourishing about 4,000 years ago. These ancient people of Mexico first discovered how to cultivate maize, one of the great agricultural gifts to mankind. They later became good weavers and potters, and they built permanent cities with temples. However, most of their settlements are lost to us, as they were buried by lava flows.

About the 3rd century A.D. the early people of the Mexican plateau were more than matched in achievement by the Maya, who developed their civilization primarily in the forests of Guatemala. They cleared the forest to plant fields of maize, potatoes, squash, and tomatoes. This rich agriculture supported large cities with great temples. Later, between A.D. 500 and 700, the center of Mayan civilization shifted to the Yucatán Peninsula. Here, too, the Maya cleared the woodland for fields. Mayan power declined after the 10th century to give way to the Toltec civilization of the Mexican plateau. The Toltecs had great temples decorated with splendid pillars and plumed serpents.

Finally the Aztecs became the dominant people of Mexico. Their capital, Tenochtitlán, now Mexico City, was founded in 1325. Although they were progressive in many respects, the Aztecs spent the greater part of their wealth on temples. They did not develop inventions to increase the comfort and well-being of the ordinary man. Thus, their skill in working metals was used mainly for making gold and silver ornaments for nobles and high priests. They did not use iron, like the Europeans, to produce the kind of ironware needed in kitchens and mills and on the kinds of plows and carts that helped greatly to improve the standard of living in Europe at approximately the same time. The Aztecs transformed their own immediate environment by replacing woodland and grassland with cultivated fields. But they did not carry the blessings of their culture to the rest of Mexico. They did not have the love of exploration, the zeal for science and invention, or the power to organize trade and make the most of their gains. Consequently, when the Spanish conquistadores arrived in Mexico in the 16th century, the Aztec empire fell.

Spanish North America

From its beginnings, Spanish North America was strongly influenced by past traditions. When they came to North America in the 16th century, the Spaniards had just finished a long and bitter war with the Moors, in which their religious zeal was matched by military skill. They came to North America led by priests and soldiers. In trying to Christianize the Indians, the Spaniards occupied the temple sites of the Indian religions, pulled down the temples, and replaced them with churches. They established Spanish-style cities with great Catholic churches dominating the central plazas.

City or town life was dominant in Spanish America from the first. The Spaniards would sometimes reshape an existing Indian town, as was the case with Mexico City. In other instances they would build new towns or cities. This was frequently the case in areas where the Aztecs lived in small villages. In other parts of Mexico, there were groups of nomadic Indians. The Spaniards tried to change their nomadic ways. They persuaded them to live in new towns and to work the land around the towns as farmers. Spanish soldiers were granted large estates, provided they built a town with a church on their estate and did their part in developing the countryside. They developed huge private estates or haciendas, which they worked with Indian labor.

The hacienda usually centered on a great house. There was usually a church, a school, foremen's houses, and a workers' village on the estate. Haciendas sometimes had several outlying villages as well. These great estates were run on highly disciplined, almost military lines. Many haciendas developed wheat farming and the extensive grazing of cattle and sheep. This was the same pattern as that developed on the great estates of Spain. In the coastal regions of Spanish America, the Spaniards developed sugar plantations, and on the slopes of the hills behind, plantations of coffee and cacao.

Although Spanish expansion was fast, Spanish immigration was slow. The Spaniards first used the island of Hispaniola (now divided between Haiti and the Dominican Republic) as their main port of entry. From there, Spanish colonists went to Mexico, Guatemala, Cuba, and Florida— and of course to other parts of Central and South America. They also occupied the Mississippi Delta. But when the main center of Spanish life shifted to Mexico, Spain began to find it difficult to occupy and rule the distant areas around the Gulf of Mexico.

The Spanish struck inland to the Rio Grande and then upriver into northern Mexico and present-day Texas and New Mexico. Then they used the Gulf of California to reach the mouth of the Colorado River. Their shipping routes along the Pacific coast of South, Central, and North America led them to California. They established missions as well as great ranching haciendas in California. These frontier posts were separated from the southern settled part of Mexico by the Mexican and Sonora deserts; so California, too, was difficult to administer.

Had the Spanish adopted a policy of giving free land to colonists in North America—as the British did—they might have tempted many more Spaniards to settle in their New World territories. With many loyal Spaniards as colonists, Spain might have been able to preserve even the outermost parts of its North American empire, instead of losing these areas to the United States. But many Spaniards who might have been tempted to brave the hazards of colonization in the New World were not going to move from Spain to become tied to great landowners like those at home. Consequently the Spaniards relied increasingly on Indian labor.

The Spaniards did not usually enslave the Indians (unless they rebelled, in which case they were sent to work in the mines). The landowners used them like Spanish peasants. They gave them houses and small plots of land and some village commons. In return for this, they secured their labor to work the rest of the hacienda. Gradually many Spaniards married Indian women, and the mestizo evolved, a person of mixed Spanish and Indian blood.

26

The twinkling lights of New York—symbol of the modern age.

The central plaza of Guadalajara, Mexico, with its splashing fountain, is built in the traditional Spanish-colonial style.

Beacon Hill, Boston, once the heart of British North America.

Jackson Square, New Orleans, retains the French colonial spirit.

Although the Spaniards were city-dwellers, they were traders, not manufacturers. Mexico inherited this tradition. Most of Mexico's wealth, until fairly recently, came from trading primary products, chiefly from its mines, its haciendas, and its farms.

Mexico's mines have been particularly valuable. The Western Sierras are noted for gold, copper, lead, and zinc, particularly in the Chihuahua district. The Eastern Sierras have fairly large deposits of coal near Monterrey, which are not far from deposits of iron—hence Monterrey's iron and steel industry. Across the southern central plateau, between the Salinas basin to the north and the Mexican basin to the south, lies a volcanic area that is very rich in silver, lead, and copper. The Gulf Coast plain has substantial oil fields at Tampico and at Tuxpan. Mexico's mineral resources are therefore considerable.

Yet agriculture is the occupation of almost half of the Mexican people. In the last 50 years many of the haciendas and much of the Church's land has been broken up into small farms. Most of the old village commons (village-owned lands used by everyone) have been subdivided. Small farmers have been subsidized to produce cash crops for the foreign market. Mexican cotton, hemp, vegetables, sugar, bananas, and coffee now have a wide sale in Europe and in the rest of North America.

With the aid of American and European capital and technology, Mexico has recently developed many industries, whose production includes iron and steel at Monterrey, petrochemicals at Veracruz, and textiles and leather goods at Mexico City. A wide range of other consumer articles are also made in Mexico City. These developments, and the change from old-style Spanish architecture to contemporary American- and European-style architecture, have made Mexico increasingly like its big northern neighbor in appearance and way of life.

Mexico City in particular is like many large cities in the United States. It has broad avenues laid out in a grid pattern, with a bustling central business district and sprawling residential suburbs, clusters of huge skyscrapers, and big industries on the outskirts of the city. It also has race courses, motor-racing tracks, golf and country clubs, and a large, busy airport. Cars are everywhere, and the subsequent problems of parking them and of getting into and out of the city with the daily rush of commuters are typically American. Thus, while relics of the old Spanish life are found everywhere, Mexico has made itself a thoroughly up-to-date American country.

The Main Regions of Mexico. The geography of Mexico—especially the climate and the soil—has affected the development of the main regions of the country. The dominant geographical feature is the Central Plateau. This is flanked on west, east, and south by the Sierras. Off western Mexico is the peninsula of Lower California. In the east is the coastal plain of the Gulf of Mexico and the Yucatán Peninsula. The least populous area of Mexico is Lower California. This region has both mountains and coastal terraces. There is some ranching, copper mining, and commercial fishing in Lower California. And cotton is grown—with the aid of irrigation—around Mexicali.

The mainland coast of the Gulf of California forms the Sonora desert. Irrigation is used on some river deltas in this area for growing cotton, wheat, rice, and winter vegetables.

Deep gorges are cut into the Western Sierras by these rivers, so that the mountains are difficult to use. Small towns have grown up around the copper mines of the area. The Eastern Sierras are much better developed. Here the land is more suitable for farming and the region is close to populated areas of the United States. The greatest wealth of the Eastern Sierras, however, comes from high-grade bituminous coal. The Southern Sierras (Sierra Madre del Sur) are high, broad, and deeply cut by rivers. These mountains have wet, stormy summers and, in the main, are not profitable. But there are many small farms in the valleys that form part of the *tierra templada,* or temperate zone. Acapulco on the southern Pacific coast—in the *tierra caliente* (hot zone)—is a well-known resort town.

Across the Isthmus of Tehuantepec, mountains continue in the Chiapas region. The valley of Chiapas, a deep rift in the highlands, has coffee and cacao plantations. Above the tree line, high pastures support cattle ranching. Farther north the land slopes down to the low plateau of Yucatán Peninsula, fringed by the Gulf coastal plain. This is the land of the Maya, who still live there on small farms. There is cattle ranching in the interior of the Yucatán Peninsula. The northern, drier parts of the Yucatán are used for growing henequen (tropical hemp).

Farther north, the Gulf coast, fringing the mainland, is wetter and more productive. This is the *tierra caliente.* It is Mexico's best land for growing maize (corn). In addition, a wide variety of tropical fruits and, on the western hill slopes, fine coffee are grown here. Rice and sugar are grown in the swampier lowlands. Tampico, center of the Mexican oil in-

Mexican Indians in Chihuahua plant corn in the traditional way.

dustry, and Veracruz, Mexico's chief port, are the main cities of the hot zone. South of these cities is the Papaloápam power and irrigation complex.

The chief region of Mexico has developed on the Central Plateau, the country's main geological structure. It is the biggest area of the *tierra templada,* with an average annual temperature of 60 degrees Fahrenheit (16 degrees Celsius) in Mexico City. The central part of the region is very rich in metals. Silver has been mined at Zacatecas since 1548. Durango produces most of Mexico's iron, as well as gold, silver, and copper. The mineral belt divides the plateau in two. To the north is a series of rather low basins—about 4,000 feet (1,200 m.) above sea level—which are mostly desert. The southern plateau is much higher—5,000 to 8,000 feet (1,500–2,400 m.)—and culminates in the highest peaks in Mexico. The great volcano of Popocatepetl is 17,890 feet (5,453 m.) high. The climate here is more temperate and humid, and the land is fertile.

The northern part of the plateau is the center of Mexico's main irrigation system. Cotton is the main crop, along with alfalfa. Alfalfa is fed to cattle on the large cattle ranches that take up most of the land area.

The southern part of the plateau is Mexico's most fully developed region. Although it includes only 14 percent of the country's area, half the population lives there. The southern plateau saw the rise of the Toltec and Aztec empires. The Spanish found ancient cities and agricultural areas there when they conquered Mexico in 1521. The plateau is really a group of basins—the Puebla, Toluca, Guanajuato, Jalisco, Aguascalientes, Morelos, and Mexico basins. Mexico basin (known as the Valley of Mexico) is the greatest of them and supports the capital city of more than 3,000,000 people. Wheat and beans are the chief food crops. Maguey, a plant that is grown for the manufacture of pulque, a popular Mexican alcoholic beverage, is also grown here. And there are large herds of dairy and beef cattle. However, industry is much more important than agriculture on the southern plateau. Puebla is Mexico's chief textile town; Guadalajara has many agricultural industries; Mexico City has a wide range of manufacturing, including textiles, shoes, food products, and petrochemicals. Its main importance, however, is as a financial and shopping center and, of course, as the center of government and administration for the whole country.

French North America

The French empire in North America was once very extensive. It reached from Louisburg in Nova Scotia, to Quebec on the St. Lawrence River, to Detroit on the Great Lakes, and to New Orleans on the Mississippi Delta. But like the Spanish, the French overreached themselves. They lost much of their empire—first to the British and later to the United States.

Because of their difficulties with Protestantism in their own Roman Catholic homeland, the French were especially determined to set up a strong Roman Catholic Church in Canada. The Church was full of missionary zeal, and missionaries did much to carry French influence to the Great Lakes, Hudson Bay, and the Mississippi River.

The French missions, established by explorer-priests in the wilderness, were not like the Spanish missions of Mexico and California. The French missionaries made no attempt to control great stretches of land, nor did they try to convince the Indians to give up hunting and take up farming. And they certainly did not try to make the Indians into town- or city-dwellers. More often than not, the French missions were simply shrines in the forest or mission stations from which priests went out to preach to the Indians. The missions did sometimes set up protected reservations where Indians could come and live in times of trouble. For example, Hurons or converted Iroquois sometimes sought mission protection against those Iroquois who remained warlike.

But the French missions did not make a great impact on the land. It was not until the French peasant arrived in North America that the French church became a positive factor in shaping the cultural geography of the continent. When French settlers began arriving, the Church divided up the settled areas into bishoprics and parishes. Parish churches, nunneries, schools, and almshouses were set up. Eventually the civil authorities used the Church units for their administrative divisions. In fact, the local mayor and council would often meet in the church hall, have the priest act as their clerk, and spend part of their taxes on the church school. To this day the Roman Catholic Church is very powerful in Quebec.

In order to encourage settlement the French Crown divided the land it had acquired from the Indians into estates, or *seigneuries*. The *seigneurs* who were granted the land were required to keep their tenants trained in the use of weapons and to give their loyal support to the French Crown in time of war. They were also required to pay certain dues to keep up the colonial government. The landlords in their turn divided up their *seigneuries* into tenant farms and obtained rents from their tenants. They collected taxes called *cens* on the frontage of each lot and taxes called *rentes* on the total acreage of the lot. To minimize these taxes the tenants took as narrow a frontage for their farms as possible. This narrow breadth was compensated for by great length. Hence the French system of strip farms came into being in French North America. The farmhouses were very close to each other, almost like houses on a village street, while their fields stretched out behind. This pattern may still be seen along the St. Lawrence River today. The *seigneuries* were broken up in the mid-19th century when the tenants were able to get loans to buy their farms. French Canada, therefore, still has a rural population engaged in small-scale farming and small villages served by a few market towns dominated by large churches or, in some cases, cathedrals.

However, cities dominate Quebec province, and Montreal dominates the cities. One out of three people in Quebec lives in greater Montreal. This is a very great concentration of population. It is due to a long history of commercial and industrial enterprise. Montreal was the center of the French fur trade. It took the initiative in building the St. Lawrence canals and was the headquarters of the Canadian Pacific Railway, which built a transcontinental line from Montreal to Vancouver, with a connecting line to Saint John, New Brunswick. Montreal became the major eastern terminal for prairie wheat. The main stock exchange in Canada was developed there, and this city came to influence Canadian financial development. It was an early center of both French and English universities and therefore became a focus for science and the arts as well as commerce. Eventually Montreal started large-scale industries, including engineering and petrochemicals, flour making, brewing, and the making of fur coats and other clothing.

British North America

This vast domain came into being at a time when there was a growing division in Britain between King and Parliament and between the Established (Anglican) Church and the Puritans and other Protestant groups. Consequently two ideas lay behind the settlement of North America. The King was determined to rule in the colonies even if he could not rule as he wished at home. He kept colonial affairs in his own hands, and he gave great grants of land to his favorites or to those who asked for and received his personal charter. Some of the grantees were English aristocrats, and some were merchants who had formed exploration and trading companies. Other people, from all walks of life, chose to go to North America so they could enjoy religious freedom. The King's grantees and chartered companies tended to establish large estates and trading towns. The Puritans developed farming townships and mill towns.

The first estates were granted in Newfoundland, Nova Scotia, and Virginia. Experience soon showed that Virginia and the other southern colonies were much more suitable to farming than the northern colonies. There was a broad coastal plain in the south that was absent in the north. The south had long, moist summers and short, mild winters. The north, on the other hand, had long, bitter winters and short, cool, stormy summers. Consequently it was in Virginia and farther south that most of the large landholders took up their grants. Fortunately they found a lucrative cash crop in tobacco, which had suddenly become popular in Europe. Great manorial estates soon sprang up along the many creeks of the southern Tidewater. Fine manor houses were built for the landowners. Near the big house there was often a mill, the factor's house, the houses of those who helped run the estate (overseers, for instance), and then, some distance away, the huts of the estate workers. Some large plantations also had a schoolhouse and a chapel.

At first, indentured labor from Britain was used to work the southern plantations. The indentured field hands were usually poor people who agreed to work for a master for 2 to 7 years in return for their passage and keep. Then they were free to make their own way in the colonies. Unfortunately, there never seemed to be enough of this labor. Many men ran away before they had finished their term, and most of them were quite unsuited to life on the tobacco plantations. Consequently, the planters began to use Negro slaves imported from Africa. Slavery was one of the unhappiest institutions Britain brought to the new land. It was a development that would create problems for America for generations to come.

The planters soon built up nearly self-sufficient communities. Those with access to the coast even did their own exporting and importing. As a result relatively few middlemen were needed. For this reason, the South failed to produce a strong middle class, such as that in the North. Furthermore, since its wealth depended on the sale of primary produce—tobacco, cotton, sugar, hemp, lumber, and turpentine—there was little need to develop manufacturing. The South relied on buying manufactured goods from Britain or New England in return for its sale of cotton and tobacco. Town life was not strongly developed. Southern towns were mainly trading and residential centers, not hubs of industry.

By contrast, the North soon developed industry and trade as its principal occupations. This was due in part to the difficulty of farming in

A graceful symbol of the life of the Old South—an 1849
plantation house with tall columns and shady galleries.

A reminder of New England's rural past—a covered bridge.

the rocky, cold, and stormy land. However, it was also due to the skills brought over by English settlers, including mill owners, craftsmen, and apprentices. Fortunately the northern coast was full of deepwater inlets that made good harbors. There was also ample waterpower available because of fast-running streams and waterfalls. Forests were at hand, and so timber was available for building ships and for making articles of trade. However, natural resources were limited. The North made its money by importing raw materials from the southern states and the West Indies— cotton, hemp, sugar, and cacao—and turning these into household goods for sale throughout America and Western Europe.

The Middle Atlantic states had elements of both northern and southern ways. The Dutch, in what was to become New York State, had developed the patroonship system of large estates, in which the patroons, or estate owners, controlled waterfront areas. A Dutch patroon in the Hudson Valley, for instance, could build a trading town on the Hudson River from which to develop his holdings inland. In Pennsylvania, William Penn was granted an enormous amount of land, part of which he tried to rent out to tenant farmers, part of which he sold. In his plans for Philadelphia, large town lots were to be left for the town houses of country estate owners. Nevertheless, in both colonies family business and factories were encouraged.

Increasingly, Philadelphia and New York turned to trade, finance, and industry. New York in particular forged ahead as the port of entry to the Hudson-Mohawk gap, the principal commercial route from the coast to the interior. In the canal era, the Hudson-Mohawk gap was used in building the Erie Canal from Albany on the Hudson to Buffalo on Lake Erie. In the age of railroads, the New York Central Railroad was built through this gap. In this way New York came to command the cheapest and most direct access to the most important prospective markets in North America—the Great Lakes and the Ohio-Mississippi-Missouri plains.

The rivalry of Britain and France over North America was keen from the beginning. British possessions—including the colonies of Newfoundland and Nova Scotia—surrounded Quebec. As British power replaced Dutch power in New York, the British challenged French interests in the Hudson-Champlain gap and across the Lake Ontario-Mohawk gap. In 1763, at the end of the French and Indian War, Quebec passed to the British. For a short time Britain dominated the continent.

Britain, however, made the serious error of enlarging Quebec to include all the land south of the Great Lakes to the Ohio and Mississippi rivers. This land was also claimed by Virginia, Georgia, the Carolinas, and some of the New England colonies. As a result, when Britain lost the Revolutionary War, the United States was able to take over this vast southern projection of British North America. In fact, there was even pressure in the new United States to take over what is now southern Ontario as well. However, the claims on Ontario were probably an American error, for they made those North Americans who remained loyal to the British Crown even more determined to keep the land north of the Great Lakes and the St. Lawrence River.

Loyalists streamed into the eastern townships of Quebec and the valleys and coasts of present-day New Brunswick, Nova Scotia, and Prince Edward Island during and after the American Revolution. American pressure also served to bring the aims of the Loyalists and the French together in Quebec. Neither group wanted to be American. This relationship was further advanced by British recognition of the French language, law, and church in Quebec. Thus Britain established the binational system in Canada—a unique scheme that was to be both the chief problem and chief pride of Canada—two nations within one state.

Both nations—French and English—respected the rights of the Indians. The Canadian Indians were not pushed into isolated reservation areas as were the Indians of the United States. They were granted prime reservation areas, many established quite close to major Canadian cities. However, most of the Indian hunting grounds were taken away.

Having committed itself to a policy of having solidly French, Loyalist, or Indian areas in Canada, the British had, more or less, to accept the desire of other peoples to settle in solid blocs. There were German communities in Nova Scotia, Ontario, and Manitoba. There were colonies, or groups, of Icelanders in Manitoba and many colonies of Ukrainians in the Canadian Prairies. In fact, the prairie region became a patchwork quilt of ethnic blocs. As a consequence, Canada widened its idea of a state or nation from a bicultural to a multicultural one.

Britain long dominated the economy and the political development of British North America. Britain bought Canadian lumber, wheat, meat, leather—and later iron and nickel. It sold Canada its manufactured goods. Britain still buys a lot of wheat, lumber, wood pulp, and metals from Canada. However, it does not sell as many manufactured goods as before, since Canada has built up its own flourishing industries. Politically, Britain made the basic border treaties for Canada—for instance, the Red River, Maine, and Oregon treaties. In 1867 Great Britain ratified the proposal to unite the separate self-governing provinces and colonies of British North America to form one nation—the Dominion of Canada.

After independence, Canada adopted a national policy of protecting its own infant industries from British and American competition. Although Canada continued to be a major producer of primary products—selling lumber, oil, natural gas, and metals to Britain and the United States—it went a long way toward satisfying its own needs for manufactured goods.

Canada's main regions are the Atlantic Provinces (Newfoundland and Labrador, Nova Scotia, New Brunswick, and Prince Edward Island), the Central Provinces (Quebec and Ontario), the Prairie Provinces (Manitoba, Saskatchewan, and Alberta), British Columbia, and the Yukon and Northwest Territories.

The **Atlantic Provinces** have developed mainly on the basis of the Appalachians. However, they include in the Gulf of St. Lawrence a portion of the Great Lakes-St. Lawrence Lowland and a valuable part of the Canadian Shield. The Appalachians sweep west and east of the New Brunswick and central Newfoundland uplands. They contain small but valuable coalfields in northern Nova Scotia and, in the uplands, significant amounts of lead and zinc. The Appalachians there are mainly a forested area; the region's chief exports are wood pulp and newsprint. The St. John and Annapolis valleys and the lowlands of Prince Edward Island provide a limited but quite rich production of dairy products, apples, and potatoes. The Labrador plateau shares with Quebec the Ungava iron field and much waterpower. The many islands and peninsulas of the Atlantic Provinces provide ports for commercial fishermen fishing the famous Newfoundland and Nova Scotia banks and the waters of the Gulf of St. Lawrence. The Atlantic Provinces rely on selling the goods of farms, forests, fisheries, and mines, and have little manufacturing. Their principal towns are transportation and marketing centers. Saint John, New Brunswick, and Halifax, Nova Scotia, have a special importance. They are Canada's principal ice-free ports open to the Atlantic trade in winter.

The **Central Provinces** are by far Canada's wealthiest and most populous provinces. They have almost 60 percent of all Canada's population and make about 80 percent of all Canadian manufactured goods. This is partly due to their central position; they are able to get raw materials from and sell to both east and west. The prosperity of the Central Provinces is also based on the use of the St. Lawrence Seaway, one of the great trading routes of the continent, connecting the Canadian and United States heartlands with the Atlantic.

Both Quebec and Ontario share the fertility of the St. Lawrence-Great Lakes lowlands. There are fine dairy, beef, fruit, and tobacco farms and productive truck farming. Both provinces share in the gold and copper of the Canadian Shield. Ontario also has important nickel, uranium, cobalt, lead, and zinc mines. The shield provides further vast quantities of hydroelectricity and very extensive forests.

Montreal and Toronto dominate the Central Provinces. Montreal is especially active as a great railway terminus and port for oceangoing ships. Toronto is a center of industry. Toronto is, in addition, Ontario's provincial capital. Unlike the Atlantic Provinces, the Central Provinces have developed a number of cities of varying sizes—including Quebec City, Ottawa, Hamilton, London, and Windsor as well as Montreal and Toronto. These cities form Canada's manufacturing belt. Ottawa, Canada's capital, was chosen to help unite Canada's French-speaking and English-speaking citizens, since both French and British settlers came to the Ottawa Valley.

The Prairie Provinces and British Columbia form western Canada, and although they are very different, they tend to complement each other in their needs and in their developments. The **Prairie Provinces** are made up mainly of the Interior Lowlands of the continent. The lowlands are forested in the north. They form a great wheat and mixed-farm belt in the central portion and in the southeast, where the tallgrass prairie used to be found. And there is ranching in the southwestern portion of the lowlands, which was once shortgrass prairie. The greatest wealth of the Prairie Provinces comes from wheat and meat. Mineral wealth, however, is rapidly increasing. Coal was important in early railroad days, but has declined since the development of diesel fuel. Oil and natural gas are extremely important and are pumped to Vancouver and Seattle, Washington, in the west and to Toronto and Montreal in the east. Copper, zinc, and nickel are also mined in the region. The Prairie Provinces are rapidly becoming urbanized with the development of the flour and meat-packing industries and the manufacture of petrochemicals and forest and mining products. Winnipeg is the place where all routes from eastern and western Canada meet.

British Columbia is the most varied region in Canada. Since it is very mountainous, it does not have much room for agriculture. However, its deep, sheltered valleys are famous for their fruit and vegetable farms. Since the Prairie Provinces cannot grow fruit because of their severe winters, they are a major market for British Columbia. More than half of the province is forest, most of it along the west coast, which has a very wet and mild climate that is ideal for trees. Dense forests of giant firs and cedars have given rise to a major lumber industry, British Columbia's major source of income. The mountains are rich in fuels, metals, and waterpower. The Rockies, or their foothills, have oil and coal. The interior plateau was the site of the British Columbia gold rush in the 19th century. Gold is still mined there, but the region is now famous primarily for its yield of copper, lead, and zinc. Copper, gold, and iron are mined in the Coast Mountains and on Vancouver Island.

Although it has a wealth of natural resources, the province has few manufacturers. Vancouver dominates the province as a transportation, marketing, and finance center. It ranks third in Canada (after Ontario and Quebec) as a manufacturing center. The provincial capital is an administrative city, Victoria, on Vancouver Island.

The northern territories (including the **Northwest Territories** and the **Yukon**) are still very empty and undeveloped. This is due to their harsh climate and to their distance from markets. It is not due to a lack of resources. There are iron, copper, and nickel in Keewatin and gold, lead, zinc, oil, and coal in the Mackenzie territory and the Yukon. The region is a great storehouse of minerals. The Mackenzie plains have some potential for agriculture, and some of the vast belt of forest could be useful. But the north awaits the time when the world needs more of its kind of products and can afford to pay the high costs of getting them out from such distant and difficult territories.

The United States

The United States took control of a large section of British North America after the Revolutionary War. Although it remained English-speaking and largely Protestant and based its legal practice on English law, the United States became a unique and distinct nation.

Peoples of all nationalities, races, and creeds were welcomed to the new United States. Roman Catholics and Jews came; people from all parts of Europe flocked in. Eventually people came from all parts of the world, and all of these people became loyal Americans, each group contributing something from its past to the future of America. The United States insisted, in a sense, on a break from former allegiances and an identification with an American way of life. People did not, by and large, live in tight national or religious blocs or colonies as they did in Canada. (The Mormons were one exception.) America stressed the settlement of new areas by individual families. Individual enterprise, individual responsibility, and the part played by the individual within the nation were all important ideals for Americans.

Unlike Canada, which is a state made up of two nations, the United States became a nation made up of many states. From the beginning, the federal government encouraged and helped to make possible the rise of a single nation. It insisted on certain federal rights. It pressed for internal improvements, such as roads and canals, to provide a national framework for development. An American system of tariff protection (protective taxes on foreign goods) was adopted to build up American industry. All this had its impact on geography. For these policies of the United States Government did make the growth of transportation and communications, of cities and industries, very rapid.

In early days, the mountain belts formed barriers to development. However, the James, Potomac, and Hudson rivers provided gaps in the mountains that allowed the building of toll roads and later of railways. Americans were able to build railways to the Pacific because early travel across the Rockies was first made possible by the Missouri-Columbia, Yellowstone-Snake, North Platte-Snake, South Platte-Colorado, and Arkansas-Rio Grande breaks, or gaps, in the Rockies. The Erie Canal linked the Hudson River and the Great Lakes; the Miami and Wabash canals linked the Great Lakes and the Ohio; and the canal at Chicago, called the Illinois and Michigan Canal, linked the Great Lakes with the huge Mississippi system.

This tremendous network of water and rail routes (and later airways) helped the United States to make use of its remarkable natural resources. The late 18th and early 19th centuries saw New England as the factory for America; New York and the other Middle Atlantic states, the transportation and commercial centers; the Midwest, America's breadbasket; and the South, the source of cotton, the raw material for much of America's clothing. This simple specialization became more and more complex. The American manufacturing belt linked the Middle Atlantic states with New England and then extended to the southern Great Lakes region. The Midwest and the South remained predominantly agricultural, but both developed industries based on that agriculture. The Mountain West, which was at first devoted to trapping, ranching, and mining, swiftly became agricultural as well, through irrigation. The Pacific West, which grew through primary products like lumber, gold, oil, wheat, and fruit, underwent an industrial revolution. It became the main target for migration within the United States. In other words, the United States has made great strides toward developing each of its regions, and this is one reason why it has such a high standard of living.

Although the country has vast resources, it has vast demands as well. Consequently the United States imports a lot of raw materials. From the beginning America has played a large part in developing international trade, and its influence abroad has affected the geography not only of its neighbors in North America, but also of the rest of the Americas, of Western Europe, and even of Asia. Africa and Southeast Asia, as they have become independent of Britain, France, and the Netherlands, have come to share more trade with America. The United States has abandoned its former highly nationalistic American system in favor of a strongly international policy. This has been backed up with treaty alliances, which have greatly extended the impact of America on geography. The United States has become a two-ocean as well as a continental power.

The chief geographical and economic regions of the United States are: the American manufacturing belt; the agricultural Midwest; the South; the Mountain West; and the Far West, including Alaska and Hawaii.

The American Manufacturing Belt. This vital area is located on the shortest route to Europe and dominates the interior of the continent. It has spread across four main structures: the Atlantic coast plain, the

Appalachians, the Great Lakes-St. Lawrence lowland, and parts of the Canadian Shield.

The Atlantic coast plain has remarkable bays or estuaries that provide excellent harbors for shipping. The Appalachians have forests as well as waterpower, coal, and oil. The Great Lakes-St. Lawrence lowland has exceptionally rich soil for agriculture, a wealth of waterpower, and two great outlets to the sea—the Hudson-Mohawk river system and the St. Lawrence Seaway. The parts of the Canadian Shield controlled by the United States—areas located in the Adirondacks and the Superior upland—are rich in iron ore and wood. These four regions and their resources were linked by the New York State Barge Canal and canals from the Great Lakes to the Ohio and the Mississippi rivers. They were also linked by major railways, by highways, and later by a network of airways.

Thus a fantastic concentration of resources and routes was at hand, a concentration unknown perhaps in any other part of the world except Western Europe or in the central and southern portions of the Soviet Union. Early industries located on the eastern edge of the Appalachians used available waterpower to operate their machinery. They used raw materials brought in from the South and from the West Indies. They produced woolen and cotton goods and forest products; they cured fish; and they manufactured a wide variety of tools and machines. The Ohio-Great Lakes connections were developed to get coal from Pennsylvania and West Virginia to the Great Lakes and iron ore from the Superior upland to the manufacturing towns. Pittsburgh, Youngstown, Cleveland, Detroit, Gary, Chicago, Buffalo, and Duluth—all of these towns and cities developed large iron and steel works, which in turn used coal to heat their furnaces. They became centers for making farm machinery and transportation equipment—including tractors, cars, trains, and lake boats. The manufacture of electric appliances and of chemical and rubber goods eventually developed there, too.

New York State's Hudson River valley was a key to progress.

The coastal and the interior industrial areas were tied into this complex by the Mohawk gap. Key cities in this area were Rochester, Syracuse, Troy, and Schenectady. There are flour and feed mills there; and electrical and chemical goods, textiles, and precision implements are manufactured.

The whole American manufacturing belt has a dense population made up of many ethnic groups. People have come to the manufacturing belt from rural areas, especially the South. This migration has included both blacks and whites. Most people in the region now live in big cities. Huge metropolitan areas have developed. These often spread far into the country, absorbing smaller towns and villages. Along the Atlantic coast, these complexes of cities and suburbs virtually touch each other. They include the Boston area, the New York area, Philadelphia, Baltimore, and Washington. Another congregation of cities occurs in the upper Ohio River around Pittsburgh. Still another has developed along Lake Erie, the Niagara River, and Lake St. Clair. This giant city includes Cleveland, Detroit, and Buffalo. Yet another cluster of cities has grown up around southern Lake Michigan, dominated by Chicago.

All of these vast urban areas have congestion at the center and expansion at the edges. All of them have tightly packed centers of offices, shops, and hotels reaching ever higher in clots of skyscrapers. They all have traffic problems. And they all have suburbs sprawling far out into the countryside, where groups of single-family houses are taking up the best farmland. All have massive redevelopment programs to help bring new life and better facilities to the hearts of the cities.

The Midwest. This huge region reaches from the Appalachians to the Rockies and from the Great Lakes to the Ozarks. This is the geographical heartland of the continent. It is an area of vast plains inter-

Combines harvest the legendary North American wheat crop.

A typical stretch of Midwestern farmland, located in Ohio.

rupted only by low scarps or ridges that step down from the Cumberland Plateau or climb up the Missouri Coteau to the Great Plains and the foothills of the Rockies. A system of navigable rivers running north to south (which are linked by canals to the lakes) and a meshwork of east–west roads and railways have helped the marketing of produce and the distribution of machines, seed, fertilizers, and other necessities in the region. The enormous market provided by the manufacturing belt, and the ease with which overseas markets can be reached by shipping on the Mohawk-Hudson river system, the St. Lawrence Seaway, or the Mississippi have helped to develop trade enormously.

The Midwest has, because of these and other advantages, become the most productive agricultural area in the Western Hemisphere. On the plains and terraces of the north, in a climate suited to growing silage corn, hay, alfalfa, and oats, the American dairy belt has emerged. It supplies the nearby manufacturing cities with milk and butter. Cheese is also produced here for sale all over the country. Fruit is grown in more sheltered areas, such as the eastern shore area of Michigan. Southward, the climate is distinctly warmer, with a July average of 75 to 78 degrees F. (24–27 degrees C.).

Corn comes into its own in the southern portion of the Midwest and is grown in a belt going from Ohio through Indiana and Illinois to Iowa and Nebraska. This corn is raised mainly as feed for livestock. Some farms specialize in the growth and sale of corn. Others, perhaps with some hilly land suited to pasture, keep beef cattle or hogs and grow corn to fatten their own stock. Oats, hay, and winter wheat are grown in rotation, mainly for feed. Corn is also made into whiskey, especially in Indiana and Kentucky. South of the Ohio and the Missouri rivers, where there are about 200 days free of frost each year, tobacco and cotton are the chief money-making crops. Here the Midwest merges into the South.

To the west, on the Great Plains, spring wheat is grown in the short growing season of the Dakotas, and winter wheat and oats are raised in the longer growing season of Nebraska. Farther west still, in the semiarid regions, with less than 15 inches (38 cm.) of rain a year, is America's cattle empire. This is the area of shortgrass rangeland. Cattle ranchers still ship a lot of young beef east for fattening, but increasingly they are fattening their own stock on lucerne (alfalfa) grown by irrigation and on barley, which is brought in.

The main cities of the region are located at the principal junctions of its major railroads, highways, and water routes. The agricultural products of the region are gathered together and marketed in these cities. Cincinnati, on the Ohio (once the hog capital of the world); Indianapolis, in the heart of the Corn Belt; St. Louis, the great wholesale center for the mid-Mississippi and Missouri region; Minneapolis-St. Paul, the wheat metropolis; and Denver, the service center for the high plains, are typical midwestern market centers. All of these cities have big railway yards and trucking terminals, large wholesale agencies, big office and shopping centers, hotels for conventions, and a number of industries using local agricultural products.

The South.   This is a region of contrasts. One finds the humid plains of Florida and the dry plateaus of Texas, the high Smokies and the low-lying land of the Mississippi Delta. One sees the old manorial homes of Virginia and the tenant shacks of depressed areas in the Ozarks. There is iron and steel in Alabama and oil in Oklahoma. It is difficult, at first glance, to see how the South can be spoken of as one region. Historically, however, it grew and held together as the rural South, an agricultural area concerned mainly with farming. It was the land of cotton and tobacco plantations. It was a black South, where slaves were used, and an Anglo-Saxon South with a remarkably homogeneous white population. These factors are still important, though much less so than they once were.

The South today is much less dependent on cotton than it once was. The southern coast plains are now a major truck farming and poultry belt. The fattening of livestock for market on the Piedmont and mixed farming on the interior plateaus (with more emphasis on the growing of grain than on the growing of cotton) have become widespread.

Again, the role of the Negro is not as prominent a factor in the agricultural economy of the South as it once was. Many Negroes have moved north or to the Far West. Moreover, federal legislation is breaking down racial segregation and employment barriers. Those Negroes remaining in the South are no longer restricted to specific kinds of work. Slowly northerners are migrating South, bringing people of different ethnic backgrounds. Finally, industry is springing up everywhere. Although the South is still, theoretically, rural, cities like Miami, Atlanta, Houston, and Dallas are growing swiftly.

The federal government has established rocket centers in the South; in fact, the whole rocketry industry is now located mainly in the South, from Florida to Texas. Moreover the South is using its power potential, as in the Tennessee Valley, for industry. Oil and natural gas production are also being developed. Textile, pulp and paper, cement, electrochemical, and petrochemical industries are springing up to make a new urban and industrial South. There are no giant cities as yet, but Richmond, Virginia; Atlanta, Georgia; Birmingham, Alabama; and Houston,

The top of North America—towering Mount McKinley in Alaska.

Texas, have a potential for becoming giants. They are increasingly important manufacturing and trading centers. New Orleans keeps its prominence as a great trading port, and Miami is the chief tourist and residential center of the new South.

The Mountain West. This almost legendary region is the least populated part of the United States, for obvious reasons. It is made up of high mountains, plateaus, and basins. Most of the basins are semidesert. However, this region also has distinct assets.

The mountains and plateaus are rich in minerals. There is gold, copper, silver, lead, and zinc. There are also large iron deposits in the region. Utah is now one of the main mining centers of the continent. The mountains are high enough for large, and in some cases permanent, snow fields, which feed rivers that flow even across arid land. A significant part of the arid land has been irrigated, and as a result irrigation-based farming has revolutionized agriculture in the area. Once again, Utah is a main irrigation center. Consequently, Salt Lake City, with mines and irrigated farms nearby, is the main city of the region.

Few other cities of the Mountain West have grown to any notable size, yet life in the region is still city centered, as more and more services are called for by the mining and ranching communities. The Mountain West has a youthful population, which is a great asset for the future.

The Far West. This is America's most rapidly growing region. Since it was the last area to be developed, it benefited from all previous advances. American settlers started ranching, farming, and prospecting while the northern part of the region was still in dispute with Britain. Great waves of settlers traveled the Oregon, California, and Santa Fe trails. A few years after oxcarts and stagecoaches had creaked and bumped their way west, the railroads came. San Francisco, Seattle, and Los Angeles had barely started developing into major cities when the automobile was invented. The automobile had just begun to have an impact on the western cities when airplanes arrived. Indeed, the stress on transportation made the Far West. Ocean routes connected it with the Far East and, through the Panama Canal, with the Atlantic. Thus it came to have a surprisingly good location, in spite of being at the "end of the trail." This "end" was a new beginning.

America succeeded Spain as the chief power in the Pacific, fell heir to Guam and the Philippines, annexed Hawaii, and bought Alaska. In the 19th century this tremendous extension of American influence allowed the Pacific Northwest and California to gain markets and influence that extended outward for thousands of miles.

And of course they had things to trade. The Far West is quite a rich area. In the north, it has a mild, wet climate, ideally suited to forests. There are Sitka spruce and coast pine in Alaska, and Douglas fir, western cedar, and redwood in Washington, Oregon, and northern California. These are among the best pulp and lumber forests in the world. Their products are bought abroad and in the eastern United States.

Early pioneers made farming important in the Far West. There is a large wheat-growing area in the central Columbia basin, with flour mills at Spokane and Portland. The Willamette Valley and Puget Sound lowland have fine dairy farms, apple orchards, pea farms, and many other kinds of farms. The Great Valley of California, with a wet winter and a dry, hot summer, has been ideal for growing fruits and vegetables and for cotton as well. Cotton is grown in California with the aid of a remarkable irrigation system fed from the snowcapped Klamaths and High Sierras. California made good use of refrigerator ships, trains, and trucks

The beautiful and fertile Willamette Valley of Oregon.

to ship its oranges, grapes, prunes, and other fruits throughout North America and to Western Europe.

The sunny climate that was so well suited to maturing and drying fruit had a lot to do with the founding of two famous California industries: motion pictures and airplanes. In the early days of both industries it was essential to have steady, sunny weather—for shooting film or testing planes. Both industries now sell their products throughout the world. The impact of the Hollywood film has probably carried American culture into more cities and villages around the globe than anything else.

It was gold that really developed California, however, and also put Alaska on the map. The famous California and Yukon gold rushes brought in thousands of immigrants who stayed on even after the mines closed. Both areas still have gold mining, but copper, lead, and zinc are more important today.

More important still is the "black gold," or petroleum, of southern California. Natural gas is now also produced at Los Angeles and near San Francisco. The development of hydroelectricity has been spectacular in the Columbia and lower Colorado valleys. This wealth of fuel and power has helped in the rise of the great petrochemical, electrometallurgical and electrochemical industries in the Los Angeles, San Francisco, and Seattle regions. Seattle is also important as the hub of America's great salmon, halibut, and seal fisheries. These are the three largest of a whole galaxy of cities of the Far West. Even though much of the wealth of the Far West comes from fishing, farming, forestry, and mining, it is mostly centered in (since it is serviced from) large cities.

Los Angeles is now the third largest city in the United States and has the second largest metropolitan area. It has an especially impressive service area in terms of finance, wholesaling, transport, and, above all, radio and television communications. San Francisco is the oldest trading

Golden Gate Bridge crosses from Marin County to San Francisco.

center in the Far West. However, its rail and port facilities are largely at Oakland, across the bay. It still serves as the chief business center for the Great Valley. Seattle is the heart of the Puget Sound region. It is a center for the processing and manufacturing of wood products, food, chemicals, and machinery. It is also the hub for transportation industries.

Part of the attraction of the Far West is its great tourist value, with spectacular scenery and a lovely climate. This attraction is especially strong in Hawaii, "the gem of the Pacific." Many visitors return to the Far West to retire, and California vies with Florida as a retirement center. Climate, scenery, good food, fine shops and places of recreation, and plentiful residential sites are among the chief assets of the Far West. California is the most rapidly expanding state in the United States.

CONTINENT OF CONTRASTS

North America is a continent of strong contrasts and real challenge, of vast resources and great opportunity. It was late in being settled by the Indians and in being discovered by Europeans. The early civilizations of North America developed in great geographical isolation, and so the continent did not, for many years, have a wide influence in the world as a whole. When the white man did arrive in North America to colonize, he found the continent comparatively empty and undeveloped. But since he came with centuries of European know-how behind him, he was able to make a quick and effective use of the land.

The Spaniards were more concerned with Central and South America than with the north. Their base in Mexico was cut off from most of North America by desert. Because of this, they lost their hold on Texas and California. However, they did a great deal to transform Mexico into a Latin landscape, reminiscent of the Mediterranean countries. The French spread themselves widely, but too thinly, and were not able to consolidate their holdings. These holdings were taken over by the British, who, however, very wisely left a French-Canadian way of life to develop, which adds distinction to Canadian life as a whole. Canada is an attempt at a bicultural, multiracial state. It tries to preserve a balance between its different elements. Its main problems have been the lack of a habitable north and the presence to the south of the powerful United States.

The Americans took over from the British in the 13 colonies of the Atlantic coast. They forged a nation that expanded beyond the Appalachians, took over the rich heartland of the continent in the Great Lakes and Ohio-Mississippi plains, crossed the Rockies, and established itself firmly on the Pacific coast. The vital interests of the United States extend today from Western Europe to Asia.

Together with Canada and Mexico, the United States has developed the resources of the continent and of the flanking oceans enormously. This development has led to often strong regional differences on the continent, which contribute variety to life. It has also led to an over-all standard of living that is the highest of all the continents of the world.

In all of these developments, geography has played an important part as people have come to challenge the handicaps and make the most of the opportunities of North America.

J. WREFORD WATSON, University of Edinburgh
Author, *North America: Its Countries and Regions*

Eskimo gather ice to melt for drinking water.

ARCTIC

The Greeks, who first observed that the stars had their orbits about a fixed pole in the heavens, named the north polar regions Arktos, for the constellation of the Bear. The south polar region is called the Antarctic because it is anti—or opposite—the Arctic.

The north and south polar regions, long the goal of courageous explorers, are alike in some respects but different in others. The Arctic Ocean, with the North Pole in its approximate center, is surrounded by the landmasses of Europe, Asia, North America, and the large island of Greenland. Antarctica, with the South Pole in its approximate center, is a landmass surrounded by the Pacific, Atlantic, and Indian oceans. Both areas are known for extremely cold temperatures, ice, and isolation from the mainstream of civilization.

In 1909 two Americans, Admiral Robert Peary and an associate, Matthew Henson, became the first men to reach the North Pole. Peary traveled by ship to Ellesmere Island and then by dog team over the ice of the Arctic Ocean to reach his goal. He made a sounding of the ocean and determined its depth to be about 10,000 feet (3,000 meters). (The Antarctic continent, on the other hand, was estimated to rise over 10,000 feet

ARCTIC

Perspective map by J. Donovan

AFRICA

EUROPE

AZORES

TROPIC OF CANCER

30°W

20°N

45°W

15°W

Atlantic Ocean

60°W

40°N

CAPE BRETON IS
Grand Banks

London
Copenhagen
Karlskrona
DENMARK
Stockholm
Oslo
NORWAY
SWEDEN
FINLAND
Lapland

30°E

North Sea
Shetland Isls.
Faeroe Isls.
Jan Mayen Is.

GREAT BRITAIN

IRELAND

ICELAND
Reykjavik

50°N

30°W

Greenland

Grand Banks

50°N

Godthaab

New York
Washington, D.C.

December limit of
pack ice

Denmark Strait

Norwegian Sea

0°

Greenland Sea

Ice Cap
11,190 ft.

GREENLAND
(Den.)

Davis Strait

Frobisher Bay

Labrador

Ottawa

90°W

Moscow

UNION OF SOVIET SOCIALIST REPUBLICS

Archangel
Kola Peninsula
Murmansk

Arctic Ocean

Barents Sea

NOVAYA ZEMLYA

Kara Sea

SPITSBERGEN
(Nor.)

Peary Land

Cape Sheridan

ELLESMERE IS.

Smith Sound

Thule

Jones Sound

Lancaster Sound

Baffin Bay

BAFFIN ISLAND

Hudson Bay

Churchill

75°E

SEVERNAYA ZEMLYA

Cape Columbia

North Pole

Permanent pack ice

North Magnetic Pole
(1962)

MELVILLE ISLAND

VICTORIA ISLAND

Coppermine

CANADA

UNITED STATES

90°E

Siberia

Norilsk
Dudinka
Yenisei River

Laptev Sea

NEW SIBERIAN ISLANDS

120°E

135°E

East Siberian Sea

105°W

120°W

BANKS IS.

Arctic Ocean

Beaufort Sea

Inuvik
Aklavik
Coppermine

90°W

Seattle

Yakutsk

MONGOLIAN PEOPLE'S REPUBLIC

ARCTIC CIRCLE

Kolyma River

Chukchi Sea

Barrow
ALASKA
(U.S.)
Fairbanks

Gulf of Alaska

150°E

CHINA

SAKHALIN
Sea of Okhotsk
Kamchatka Peninsula

Bering Strait
Nome

St. Lawrence I.

Bering Sea

135°W

JAPAN
KURILE IS.

ALEUTIAN ISLANDS

150°W

180°

165°E

Pacific Ocean

HAWAII (U.S.)
Pearl Harbor
(Naval Base)

35°W

above sea level by Roald Amundsen, the first man to reach the South Pole.)

The Arctic is generally defined as the area north of 66° 30′ North latitude, or roughly the area north of the Arctic Circle. Within the boundaries of the Arctic and sub-Arctic there are forests and animals, fish, and birds, which support a population of about 1,000,000. Extremely valuable deposits of oil, coal, and minerals have been discovered in the region.

When civilization first developed in the Northern Hemisphere men moved east and west to a belt of temperate climate and environment. To the north was cold; to the south was heat. The growth of the population, opportunities for trade, and just plain curiosity finally led men to cross the imaginary barriers that had kept them from the extreme northern and southern portions of the globe. The Arctic was the first of these extreme points to be explored, since it was closer to the settled regions of the world.

THE FIRST ARCTIC EXPLORERS

The first polar explorer of whom we have a record was Pytheas, a Greek mathematician, scientist, and navigator of the 4th century B.C. He dreamed of the unknown that lay west and north of the Strait of Gibraltar. A thirst for travel, knowledge, and science lured Pytheas; commerce enabled him to quench it. The merchants of Marseilles (now in France), who were greedy for more profits in minerals, furs, and brocades, were convinced by Pytheas that these materials could be obtained cheaply at their source. The merchants agreed to provide Pytheas with ships and men for his expedition.

About 330 B.C. Pytheas sailed through the strait on the first recorded voyage to the north polar region. The ships traveled up along the west coast of Europe and crossed the Channel to England. During this time Pytheas observed the tides of the ocean and is credited with being the first Greek to establish the relationship between lunar attraction and the tides. Pytheas circumnavigated England, explored the interior, and satisfied his commercial backers with lucrative trading.

While he was in England, Pytheas learned of a land to the north that was said to be surrounded by ice. His curiosity drove him northward to discover whether land really did exist in the icy north. As he traveled, at a place called Thule (which most authorities believe was in Iceland, although it is now the name of a town in Greenland), Pytheas encountered a dense fog, which he described as "a molluscous substance, in which earth, air, and sea mingled and in which the universe is suspended." Pytheas was convinced that he had reached the point where the earth ended. Actually he was enveloped in what modern explorers call a whiteout and aircraft pilots say is "like flying in a milk bowl." It is an atmospheric condition peculiar to the polar regions, in which the ice or snow surface and the air seem to blend together.

There is no record of any polar explorers after Pytheas until the 9th century A.D., when Irish monks—perhaps fleeing a war—set sail in small hide-covered boats called coracles. These brave monks may have been the first explorers to reach the Faeroe Islands, Jan Mayen Island, Iceland, and possibly even Greenland. The monks were on shore to welcome the first Viking explorers when their dragon-prowed longboats reached Iceland.

Huskies are part of the team at an Arctic weather station.

The Vikings were a hardy people who played a dominant role in probing the Arctic regions in the 9th and 10th centuries. One of the most colorful and famous was Eric the Red, who was born in Norway about A.D. 950. When he was about 20, he is believed to have committed two murders that forced him to flee to Iceland. There he married and settled down to farm some land.

Unfortunately his violent nature led him into a quarrel. He killed again and was declared an outlaw. He formed an expedition and sailed westward with his family in search of new land. About 982 he discovered the land now known as Greenland and founded two small colonies on its southwest coast. Here Eric was more fortunate. He lived out his life on a farm with his family and remained at peace with his neighbors. The colonies of Greenland, with a population of about 2,500, survived for about 4 centuries and then vanished. (It has been suggested that the colonies died out because of a plague or a massacre by the Eskimo, or as the result of generations of malnutrition.) By about 1400 the exploration and colonization of Greenland had ended.

Even the small amount of knowledge that had been gained about the Arctic resulted in the production of new maps, which excited the imagination and interest of scientists, explorers, and others who dreamed of the enormous wealth they could gain if they found a shorter sea route to Cathay, as China was called in the Middle Ages. The conquest of the Northwest and Northeast Passages, as these sea routes were called, and the honor of being the first to reach the North Pole were the new challenges in the Arctic.

IN SEARCH OF THE NORTHWEST PASSAGE

Sir Martin Frobisher, an English naval officer, navigator, and explorer, led three expeditions in search of the Northwest Passage to Cathay. In 1576, with a small fleet of three ships and 35 men, he sailed via the Shetland Islands for his destination. One of the ships was lost in rough weather, another ship deserted. Frobisher pressed on in his ship, skirted Labrador, and sailed into what he believed was a strait. The strait later proved to be a bay and was named for Frobisher.

The first expedition was notable mainly for being the first to sight Greenland since the disappearance of the Viking colonies. Frobisher's ships brought back cargoes of black ore that was believed to contain gold. Sadly, the black ore contained nothing more valuable than iron pyrites—fool's gold. The Cathay Company, which had financed Frobisher's expeditions, went bankrupt. Frobisher was ruined financially, but Queen Elizabeth I held him in such high esteem that she promoted him to admiral in the Navy. Although Frobisher had not found the Northwest Passage and the expeditions were financial failures, his reports created even more interest in the Arctic region.

Further English expeditions helped expand men's knowledge of the Arctic sea lanes, but the difficulties of navigating in uncertain weather, through partly charted waters that were often blocked by ice floes and huge, menacing icebergs, took their toll of men and ships.

In April, 1610, Henry Hudson sailed from England under the auspices of the Muscovy Company. During that summer he explored and charted

A Canadian camp set up to study the polar ice at the edge of North America.

the coast and islands of Hudson Bay. But Hudson tarried too long and his ship became locked in ice for the winter. During this period of privation and suffering, part of the crew mutinied. Hudson, his son John, and five loyal sailors were bound and set adrift in a boat without arms, food, fresh water, or navigational instruments. They disappeared and nothing was ever seen or heard of them again.

Another English navigator, William Baffin, became convinced that Hudson Bay was a blind alley as far as the search for the Northwest Passage was concerned. He shifted his research operations northward. In 1616 he reached the point on the west coast of Greenland now known as Thule. He explored Davis Strait and discovered Smith Sound, Lancaster Sound, and Jones Sound. At last the search for the seaway was in the right latitude. Although Baffin had made the deepest penetration westward through the North American continent, he believed that due to ice and the depth of the water, the Northwest Passage would never become a commercial seaway.

Throughout the 17th and 18th centuries the whaling industry flourished in the waters of the Arctic. The skillful, secretive captains of the whaling ships learned much about the polar region, but they did not speak or write about their discoveries for fear that others would trespass on their hunting grounds.

At the beginning of the 19th century the Royal Geographic Society of England put new pressure on the Admiralty to conquer the phantom waterway—the Northwest Passage. The Admiralty complied by appointing a distinguished naval officer, Sir John Franklin, to command an expedition consisting of the ships *Erebus* and *Terror*. The ships, which took along enough provisions for a 3-year voyage, sailed from England in May, 1845, with specific orders concerning the courses to be taken in order to sail from Baffin Bay in the west to the Beaufort Sea in the east. Two years passed without word from Franklin or his men.

Three years after Franklin had set sail, England and the United States began the most extensive search and rescue operations in polar history. Huge rewards were offered for help in solving the mystery of the ships that had disappeared. In the course of the next 9 years, 39 expeditions were launched at a cost of over $5,000,000. The whole of England waited for news of the lost fleet, and a popular song described the explorer's widow's eagerness to have the search go on:

> And to bring him back to a land of life,
> Where once again I would be his wife . . .
> I would give all the wealth I ere shall have
> But I think, alas, he has found a grave.

The mystery was solved at last when records were found that proved that the entire company of the expedition had perished. It was a terrible tale of ships locked in the ice, of scurvy, starvation, and death. A handful of men from Franklin's expedition had managed to survive a little longer than the others by taking shelter with Eskimo, from whom they learned how to live in the Arctic. But they were impatient for the sight of a less desolate landscape and set out on foot across the frozen waste and died.

Franklin's records and charts did show a way to navigate the Northwest Passage. Further maps and information that were gained by the rescue teams helped produce a comprehensive picture of the area. The

Northwest Passage finally was successfully navigated by the great Norwegian polar explorer Roald Amundsen between 1903 and 1906. He made the passage in the *Gjöa*, a ship so small that it could carry only a crew of six. Amundsen's long voyage gave him much valuable information about clothing, sledging, and the use of Arctic dogs that was of immense value to him when he set out to conquer the South Pole.

THE NORTHEAST PASSAGE TO TRADE

The exploration and charting of the Northeast Passage, from the North Sea to the Pacific across the icy seas north of Europe and Asia, differed from its counterpart on the opposite side of the Arctic Ocean. The Northwest Passage had been probed only from the east, while the Northeast Passage was approached by ship from east and west and overland through Siberia, the northern Asiatic part of the Soviet Union.

The Company of Merchant Adventurers, an association of English foreign traders, contributed considerably to the exploration and development of the Arctic. This private company, whose members were all subjects of the English Crown, enjoyed a monopoly on trade in certain areas of the world.

In 1553 the Company organized an expedition of three ships for the purpose of exploring and charting the Northeast Passage and "for the discovery of regions, dominions, islands, and places unknown." Sir Hugh Willoughby was placed in command of a fleet of three ships. Richard Chancellor, who was made pilot of the expedition, was placed in command of one of the ships. When the ships of the fleet were driven apart by a storm, Willoughby and his two ships proceeded to northern Russia and anchored on the Kola Peninsula. The following year Russian fishermen found the two ships and the dead bodies of the entire crews. Chancellor waited 7 days at the rendezvous point where he had been supposed to meet Willoughby, then proceeded in his ship to Archangel. Czar Ivan IV (Ivan the Terrible) learned of Chancellor's arrival and invited him to the court at Moscow. The Englishman traveled 1,500 miles (2,400 kilometers) overland to the capital, where he was greeted hospitably and was able to arrange a favorable trade treaty. The treaty resulted in the formation of the Muscovy Company and began 20 years of profitable trade between Russia and England.

England's chief rivals in the race for supremacy on the seas and in commerce were the Dutch, who also hoped to establish trade relations with the Russians. In the late 16th century Oliver Brunel, the Dutch emissary, established friendly relations with the wild, warlike Cossacks, whose leader Ermak Timofeev had laid claim to the vast area of Siberia in the name of the czar. Brunel's party accomplished little in the search for the waterway, but he was highly successful in trade. Willem Barents, the most successful of the Dutch explorers, believed that ships would encounter less ice north of the island of Novaya Zemlya (north of Russia) than in the strait between that island and the mainland. He explored and charted Novaya Zemlya (1594–95) and discovered Barents Island and Spitsbergen (1596). During the winter of 1596–97 Barents' ship was frozen in the ice, and Barents and many of his men died. Only a few of his companions reached Kola, in Lapland, and were rescued. Further exploration lapsed for about a decade, but the profitable trade with the Russians continued.

These are Eskimo children of the Arctic.

Czar Peter I (Peter the Great) of Russia believed in the Northeast Passage and saw that its conquest for commercial use was vital to the development of his country. Much knowledge was gained of the northern coast of Russia from the Cossacks, who had led the conquest of Siberia. It was a Cossack, Semeon Dezhnev, who in the early 17th century sailed eastward from the entrance of the Kolyma River, through the ice of the Siberian Sea, and then through Bering Strait and into the Pacific Ocean. This feat must have been unknown to Peter I, because before he died in 1725, he ordered a massive survey of the entire north coast of Russia and the conquest of the Northeast Passage. Vitus Bering, a Danish navigator who had served in the Russian Navy for 20 years, was appointed by the Czar to command this colossal undertaking.

Bering established his headquarters for planning in St. Petersburg, and picked Yakutsk in east Siberia as the assembly point for all the material required for a base to build ships. This material would be transported 5,000 miles (8,000 km.) overland to the port of Okhotsk on the Sea of Okhotsk in Russia's far east, where the base would be established to build his fleet of ships. Completed, the ships would sail across the Sea of Okhotsk to Kamchatka. A glance at the map of the Arctic Ocean and Russia will reveal that this was a herculean task.

Bering and his men toiled for 3 years in St. Petersburg, Yakutsk, and Okhotsk. In the summer of 1728 he sailed north in his newly constructed ship, the *Gabriel*. He explored the northeastern coast of Asia and dis-

Inuvik in Canada's Northwest Territories—a government-planned and -run village.

covered Saint Lawrence Island and the Diomede Islands. He had crossed the strait that now bears his name without seeing the North American coast. Five years after his departure from St. Petersburg in 1725, he returned home to make his report to the Admiralty College of Russia. His report was examined for 2 years, and then Bering was informed that he would not be paid his salary because he had not accomplished his mission to "sail until he met an European Establishment." Influential friends persuaded Empress Anne to continue the investigations originally ordered by Peter I. Vitus Bering was adequately rewarded for his past efforts and continued to direct the plan of exploration and conquest. Bering gave 15 years of his life to this project and then died at his post in 1741 after his ship ran aground on the coast of a deserted island.

Bering's exploration, which had helped extend men's knowledge of the geography of northeast Asia and northwest America, stimulated Russia's Great Northern Expedition. The Siberian coast on the Arctic Ocean was to be charted and colonized in order to support the Northeast Passage. Men and material were poured into the project without regard for the enormous cost or loss of life. The endeavor was successful.

Baron Nils Nordenskjöld, the first man to cross the Northeast Passage, was born in Finland in the early 19th century. At a dinner party shortly after his graduation from the university, he offered a toast that was misinterpreted by the Russian Governor-General of Finland, who banished him from the country. In 1857 Nordenskjöld settled in Stockholm, and Sweden became his adopted country. Nordenskjöld, backed financially by Oscar Dickson, a wealthy merchant from Goteborg, became Sweden's leading polar explorer. In 1878, after he had participated in several Arctic expeditions, the King of Sweden appointed him commander of an expedition, with orders to conquer the passage that had been the goal of explorers for over 3 centuries.

Nordenskjöld's fleet consisted of his flagship, the *Vega,* and two supporting ships. The expedition sailed from Karlskrona on June 22, 1878, and arrived at the mouth of the Yenisei River on August 6. There the supporting ships dispersed to carry on their assigned tasks of exploration and trade along the coast and inland on the rivers. The *Vega* continued eastward with good ice conditions and weather until it became beset in heavy ice near Bering Strait, where it was forced to spend the winter. The following summer brought favorable weather conditions that permitted the *Vega* to complete its short voyage to the Pacific Ocean. The ship reached Yokohama, Japan, on September 2, 1879, and returned home via the Suez Canal.

With proof that the Northeast Passage existed, the Russians accelerated their program of developing this seaway. In 1932 they formed a government department, the Chief Administration of the Northern Sea Route, known in Russian as Glavsermorput. Glavsermorput created a vast organization consisting of a fleet of icebreakers and ice cargo ships, networks of communication and meteorological stations, an aircraft ice reconnaissance force, and a hydrographic service. The Arctic Institute of

Shrimp boats in the harbor at Christianshaab, Greenland.

Leningrad poured in teams of scientists and technicians by land, sea, and air to solve the unknown problems.

During World War II immense quantities of American war materials were sent to the Soviet Union from both entrances of the Northeast Passage. Since 1944 the Northeast Passage has been the Soviet Union's private domain for commercial and military operations.

OVER, UNDER, AND AT THE NORTH POLE

The North Pole remained the third basic goal for explorers to achieve in the conquest of the Arctic. The assaults on the seaways to the Orient across the Arctic regions resulted in an accumulation of information on geography, weather, and living conditions, which was available to those seeking the honor of being the first to reach the North Pole.

In 1891 the Philadelphia Academy of Natural Sciences appointed Robert Peary of the United States Navy to command a polar expedition to investigate Greenland. The "polar bug" bit him, and he devoted most of the next quarter century to the exploration of the Arctic. His greatest desire was to be the first man to reach the North Pole, and he was determined to do it. Peary made several expeditions to the Arctic region, and as a result he made important observations of the land, peoples, and climate of the far north. Peary's careful study of Eskimo methods of building igloos and using sled dogs was especially valuable to him and to later explorers.

In 1908 Peary sailed from the United States in the *Roosevelt* for Cape Sheridan, where he set up his winter quarters. The following spring he established a number of depots along his proposed route, and on March 1 his party departed from Cape Columbia at the northern edge of Ellesmere Island, 413 nautical miles (478 mi.; 769 km.) from the Pole. They traveled by dog sledges over the ice of the Arctic Ocean toward their destination. At prearranged points, sections of the supporting parties returned to their base. Admiral Peary, a Negro crewman, Matthew Henson, and four Eskimo continued the journey and became the first men to reach the North Pole on April 6, 1909. They had survived the hardships of sub-zero weather and the hazards of traveling across ice floes and over ridges of ice that often reached more than 50 feet (15 m.) in height. Peary's goal had been won, but when he returned home he found that his title of first man at the Pole was being challenged by an anthropologist, Dr. Frederick Cook, who claimed he had reached the North Pole a year ahead of Peary. The dispute raged on, but today Peary is generally accepted as having been the first to reach the top of the world.

It was natural that men should seek a faster and easier way of traveling over the polar areas than by trudging behind a dog sledge or forcing a ship through the ice floes. So they took to the air. Salomon August Andrée, a Swedish scientist and aeronaut, departed from Spitsbergen with two companions on July 11, 1897, in a balloon, the *Eagle,* for the North Pole. Andrée and his men were airborne in the *Eagle* 66 hours and then, in violent weather, the balloon crashed on the ice. Thirty-three years passed before their bodies, with their diaries, were found on White Island northeast of Spitsbergen.

After World War I several nations sponsored aerial flights that fanned out over the Arctic regions. Rear Admiral Richard E. Byrd, an

American naval officer, aviator, and explorer, became the first man to fly over both the North and South poles. On May 9, 1926, Byrd, with Floyd Bennett as copilot, took off from Spitsbergen and arrived at the North Pole without any serious trouble. He circled the Pole and then returned triumphantly to his base at Spitsbergen. Two days later Roald Amundsen and Lincoln Ellsworth departed from the same base in the dirigible *Norge* for Alaska via the North Pole. Colonel Umberto Nobile, the Italian who designed the dirigible, acted as pilot. Over the North Pole they dropped the flags of the United States, Norway, and Italy. They arrived safely in Alaska 72 hours after takeoff, having traveled 3,393 miles (5,459 km.) across the Arctic Ocean from Europe to the United States. For Peary and his crew an advance of 25 miles (40 km.) a day had been considered a cause for celebration.

Sir George Hubert Wilkins, an Australian polar explorer, also distinguished himself in polar flying both north and south, and then became convinced that he could travel to the North Pole in a submarine under the ice. In 1931 he organized an expedition to accomplish this in the submarine *Nautilus* (one of a series of submarines of that name), but the craft was not equal to the task, and in November of that year it sank in a Norwegian fiord. Admiral Cruzen of the United States Navy included a submarine in the Task Force that established weather bases in the Arctic in 1946, during which time the underwater craft probed several miles under the ice. This was followed by more under-ice operations by the United States Navy's submarines *Carp,* in 1948, and *Redfish,* in 1952.

The nuclear submarine U.S.S. "Whale" surfaces in the Arctic Ocean.

A new power source and several new devices convinced the United States Navy that it could operate its submarine fleet under the ice of the Arctic Ocean. The new power source was nuclear energy. Among the new devices was the topside fathometer to measure distance under ice. An inertia guidance system was also available to permit accurate navigation without the aid of stars, sun, or radio stations. The United States Navy then prepared plans to send the modern nuclear-powered submarine *Nautilus* to the North Pole in the summer of 1958.

The *Nautilus* departed from Pearl Harbor, Hawaii, on July 22, 1958, submerged, and then proceeded silently on its epic journey. It sailed north through the Bering Sea, and then proceeded at various depths and speeds to the North Pole. It was under the ice at the North Pole on Sunday, August 3, 1958. The vessel then proceeded south between Greenland and Spitsbergen and thence to Portland, England, where it landed 21 days and 8,146 miles (13,107 km.) after its departure from Hawaii. It was a tremendous accomplishment, but the commanding officer, Commander William R. Anderson, described it by stating, "It was like the New Jersey Turnpike once we got started."

A group of four British explorers became the first men ever to walk across the polar ice cap in 1968–69. Their 477-day trip, which took them across 3,620 miles (5,825 km.) of frozen waste, was full of dangers, including confrontations with fearless polar bears. The team leader, Wally Herbert, said the walk "seemed like conquering a horizontal Everest." In spite of modern technology, Arctic exploration is still exciting and sometimes dangerous.

HOW THE PEOPLE OF THE ARCTIC LIVE

From the description of the Garden of Eden in the Old Testament one can assume that it definitely was not located in the polar regions. One cannot imagine tribes of people migrating to this inhospitable Arctic region by choice. Groups driven from neighboring continents, however, have settled in the Arctic, including the Lapps, Samoyeds (now called Nentsi), Chukchi, Ostyak, Koryak, Yukaghir, and Tungus. In general, their characteristics are the same, and with some exceptions, due to differences in terrain, they have been forced to lead similar lives in order to survive. These were the people that the explorers of the white race met in their search for a short water route to Cathay and when they undertook their races to the North Pole.

Fishing in the rivers and seas provided an abundance of halibut, cod, salmon, and haddock. The highly prized seal provided material for a variety of needs. The lean meat of the seal and part of the fat provided food for men and dogs; the blubber supplied light in winter and heat for cooking and shelters; boots and boats were made from the skins; and the intestines made excellent waterproof garments. To hunt the wily seal the Eskimo used a harpoon and stalked his prey in a kayak, a watertight sealskin boat in which the sailor, clad in a sealskin suit, was laced into the cockpit. With a double-headed paddle he could handle the craft with great dexterity.

Meat forms a large portion of the Arctic man's diet. An Eskimo may eat as much as 20 pounds (9 kilograms) a day of lean meat plus a large amount of blubber. This provides him with a layer of fat that helps keep him warm and allows him to go for days without eating. To hunt the rein-

Young Lapps at Hammerfest, 300 miles (480 km.) north of the Arctic Circle.

deer, caribou, musk-oxen, and foxes that provide the Eskimo with food and clothing, he needs transportation. Next to the kayak in importance for hunting is the Eskimo's sledge and dogs. The original sledges were made of wooden frames covered by sealskin. The Arctic dogs used to pull the sledges were at first half-domesticated wolves. Careful breeding produced the Eskimo, Ostyak, and Samoyed sledge dog. The Eskimo dogs, weighing 50 to 70 pounds (23–32 kg.), have broad chests and powerful shoulders and resist the cold with a coat of thick hair. As the nomadic Arctic tribes intermingled, so did the dogs, which resulted in a mongrel sledge dog. Today, if one were to ask a dweller of the far north what an Eskimo dog is, the answer would probably be, "Any dog that belongs to an Eskimo."

In addition to food, clothing, and transportation the Eskimo and his dogs needed shelter. This was a simple matter for a dog, who just spun around in the snow to make a hole and then settled down into it. The drifting snow would cover him like a blanket, except for a small hole the dog's nose kept open for breathing. The Eskimo made his house with whatever material he could find—driftwood, sod, stones, sealskin, or blocks of snow for the well-known igloo.

Vilhjalmur Stefansson, the Arctic explorer and author, stressed in his speeches and writings that the vegetation of the Arctic was a garden compared to the moss and lichens that clung to the rocks of the Antarctic. There are hundreds of flowering plants and more than a score of ferns that come to life in the summer. The tundra of the northern land areas supports such plants as saxifrage, bluegrass, heather, poppy, blue-bell, cat's paw, dandelion, and edible mushrooms. In the subarctic taiga zone there are forests of towering trees such as spruce, fir, and cotton-wood, all of great economic value. The growing season lasts for only a short time, from a few days to 3 months. But in some areas the long summer days of sunlight compensate for the short period of growth.

The Eskimo Today.   The Eskimo family is a close-knit group. Parental authority is absolute. Several families form a tribe led by a chief who is appointed, usually for his prowess as a hunter. The languages spoken by the people of the Arctic regions are simple. One word usually suffices for a sentence. From Siberia to Greenland the language is uniform, due to complete isolation from civilization and the lack of a written language.

Well-intentioned but misguided settlers and traders influenced Eskimo in some areas to adopt the wooden frame house. The white man's method of heating a house with wood and coal was contrary to the natives' methods of preserving natural warmth in an abode well-covered with sod and with a long tunnel entrance open to fresh air. Some scientists believe that the change of housing may have made the Eskimo more susceptible to tuberculosis and other respiratory diseases that the white man introduced into the region. In addition, as the white man pushed into the Arctic in recent times, the Eskimo have often suffered from exposure to diseases that were new to them, such as smallpox and measles.

THE ARCTIC TODAY

Two giant nations, with different ideologies, confront one another across the ice of the Arctic Ocean. Both are developing their economic and military strength in that area.

The Soviet Union has developed the Northeast Passage to a much greater degree than the United States has its counterpart across the Canadian Arctic. Soviet ships ply their trade east and west in the passage and into the interior of the country on its big rivers. Siberia, once a dumping ground for political prisoners, also has attracted millions of people because of its mineral wealth. An industrial empire has been created to mine the gold, nickel, uranium, copper, diamonds, coal, cobalt, and lead that have been discovered there. Development of farming and the breeding of animals, particularly of reindeer herds, has been speeded up to provide food. Housing has been designed to cope satisfactorily with the environment, and huge dams have been constructed to provide power, heat, and light. Murmansk, the seaport on the Kola Gulf of the Barents Sea, the terminus of the Northeast Passage, has grown to have a population of about 275,000. Norilsk is a booming city of 127,000 and there are several cities of more than 50,000. The people earn relatively good salaries, live in large apartment houses, and enjoy good schools, hospitals, music, and sometimes television.

Canada and the United States started the orderly development of their northern regions about 25 years later than the Russians. It was not until recent years that these countries found it necessary to probe north to replenish their oil and mineral stocks and to expand their living areas. The Northwest Passage has not yet proved as satisfactory for commercial shipping as the oil and mineral companies would like. In the summer of

The S.S. "Manhattan" was the first commercial ship to cross the Northwest Passage.

1969 the S.S. *Manhattan* became the first commercial ship to complete the difficult passage, which gave promise that the route might be useful in the future.

Reports of some scientists that the amount of ice in the Arctic is being reduced each year are promising for commercial shipping. It is not known whether this warming of the Arctic region is a temporary or permanent trend. Measurements of ice and temperatures have not been recorded over a long enough period to be certain. If the ice disappeared it would be a boon to shipping in the polar routes, but some scientists say it could also be a disaster for mankind. The winds blowing over the ice-free waters of the Arctic Ocean would pick up moisture that would result in an increase of snowfall on the land areas, and thus start another ice age.

Military operations of the Soviet Union and the United States have increased the population of the northern regions. Roughly one third of the Americans living in Alaska are military personnel or their dependents. About 7,000 men are stationed at the United States Air Force Base at Thule, Greenland. Both countries have erected radar stations that dot the Arctic Circle. Air bases support the aircraft, which are equipped for cold weather flying. Soviet and American aviators have operated successfully from ice islands. Submarines equipped with missiles loaded with nuclear warheads lurk under the ice pack of the Arctic Ocean. These submarines are capable of surfacing anywhere in the pack by rising horizontally like a whale that breaks the ice with its back.

The North Pole has been crossed under the ice, on the ice, by balloons and aircraft, and by spacecraft. It is man's fervent prayer that it will never be crossed by missiles launched in anger.

GEORGE J. DUFEK, Rear Admiral, United States Navy (Ret.)
Director, The Mariners Museum, Newport News, Virginia

CANADA: AN INTRODUCTION

by Lester B. PEARSON
Former Prime Minister of Canada

Canada, my country, means many things to me.

First, of course, the land itself: vast and varied in its splendor and magnificence; mountain peaks reaching into blue sky; waving grain on the limitless prairie; the once lonely northland; the beauty of lake and stream and forest; the flaming glory of autumn leaves and the birth of spring from snow and sun.

But Canada means far more than this. It means people: those who are already deeply rooted in its soil and its history; those who in recent years have come across the ocean to share in and help shape our future. Canada means men and women at work and at play; men praying, men thinking, men doing, men dreaming. It means a country, strong and developing, with many problems but with great opportunities, moving forward in faith and hope, with confidence but without conceit.

Some countries have too much geography and not enough history; some, the reverse. Canada has enough of both geography and history. Together they have been the vital factors in the nation's development.

Canada is the second largest country in the world. It is a land to challenge man as well as to captivate him. It is still a largely undeveloped country, with great resources still untapped. Many of these great resources lie hidden in the far reaches of the Canadian North. Not long ago northern Canada was thought to be a frozen wasteland: remote, forbidding, and impossible for development or settlement on any substantial scale. Canadians know better now. "Go North" has replaced "Go West" as the call to adventure—and achievement.

The Impact of Geography

The movement of people to the Canadian North and the opening up of the historic Northwest Passage by air and by sea have made clear the importance of our position on the map between the two superpowers (the United States and the Soviet Union) who, we now realize, are both our neighbors.

Canada, which has become a great industrial nation as well as a source of raw materials, is on the threshold of a northern expansion that may become as important to our political and economic future as the opening of the Canadian West was in the 19th and early 20th centuries. At the present time, however, our policies, our problems, and our interests remain centered on the welfare of the vast majority of our 22,000,000 people who live in a narrow belt of land of 200 miles (320 kilometers) or so along the 3,000-mile-long (4,800 km.) boundary with our southern neighbor. With that neighbor, the United States, we have an especially close and friendly relationship. However, it is a relationship made up of both attraction and anxiety.

Canada's growth in a narrow, east–west band across a great continent has been called a ribbon development. This ribbon development explains in part the kinds of political, geographical, and economic problems that had to be overcome in the building of the Canadian nation. That we have overcome these difficulties represents the triumph of faith over doubt; of national feeling over regional interest; of politics—in the broad sense—over geography. For Canada, the natural economic and geographic lines of development run north to south. However, to build a great nation our forefathers knew they had to develop their portion of North America east to west, across a whole continent. To carry out this decision required both determination and imagination.

The Atlantic Provinces are, for instance, a geographical unit. They are separated, at least in part, from the rest of Canada by a northern extension of the New England states of the United States. Forest, rock, and river cut off the central, industrial provinces of Quebec and Ontario— also adjoining American states—from Canada's Prairie Provinces. The Prairie Provinces, in turn, were a geographic and economic northern extension of the North Central United States. The Rocky Mountains gave British Columbia a feeling of "splendid isolation." This province had its natural lines of contact and development down the Pacific coast of the United States and out across the Pacific Ocean toward the Orient.

It is understandable that the pull of regionalism has remained strong in Canada. The wonder is that we have been so successful in overcoming it. This has been one of the great national achievements of modern times: the steady progress from widely separated dependent colonies, to coast-to-coast Confederation, and to the proud sovereign nation of today.

Neighbor to the South

There are inevitably many economic, cultural, and political pressures exerted on the modern Canadian nation by its neighbor, the United States. These pressures, which have been persistent but not unfriendly, have resulted, for one thing, in billions of dollars of United States private investment in Canada.

Canada, in fact, with its great and varied resources, is becoming a major source of supply for the United States of those raw materials that are becoming depleted or scarce in the United States. United States investment has resulted in a pace and pattern of economic growth in Canada that would not have been possible otherwise. It has helped to bring about a great increase in the volume of our international trade. The combination of great resources, an industrious and enterprising people, social and political stability, and huge foreign investment has made Canada a strong modern country with an impressive gross national product and one of the very highest per capita incomes in the world.

Our huge foreign investment, however, has had other results that made us anxious about our future as a separate and independent nation. How can Canadians help but worry about maintaining their own Canadian destiny when more than 60 percent of our manufacturing is controlled outside Canada? Most of this control is exerted by firms in the United States. Our problem here is how to prevent American participation in our development from leading to control and absorption of Canada by the United States. I am confident that Canada can solve this very real problem. And I am confident that it can solve it without falling back on narrow, restrictive economic nationalism, which would cut off vital foreign investment in our future.

This United States economic pressure on our independent Canadian status is complicated by other United States influences—cultural and not so cultural. The impact of the United States on the Canadian way of life is intensified by the ease of exchange and communication, in all its forms, between the peoples of the two countries. Indeed, in many respects our way of life in Canada is almost indistinguishable—except in French-speaking Canada—from that of Americans. Many Canadians rightly worry about this sameness as a greater threat to Canadian identity than close economic and financial relationships—and an even more difficult threat to deal with. This problem of national identity, too, can be solved by a healthy national pride in our land and in our Canadian heritage. This pride must show itself in political and social action worthy of that heritage. Our national pride and strength will enable us to build a strong and united Canadian Confederation. We will be able to do this, however, only if we understand the circumstances and the lessons of our history.

The Legacy of the Past

It was the French and the English who explored and took over—often in ways that are cause for shame rather than satisfaction—the land of Canada from the Indians and the Eskimo. After they controlled the land, the English and the French fought each other for dominance in Canada. The English were victorious. Canada became a British colony. However, it became a unique colony in which the French were not submerged, but retained their own language, traditions, and culture. The position of the French language, tradition, and culture in Canadian life was recognized when we became a confederation of British North American colonies in 1867, by terms of the British North America Act.

During the subsequent years, gradually, without bloodshed, and through political and peaceful evolution, Canada became an independent nation, but one that by its own free will retained the British monarch as its head of state. Queen Elizabeth II of the United Kingdom is also Queen of Canada. And Canada became a member of that association of free states that grew out of the British Empire and is now known as the Commonwealth of Nations.

Since the Canadian Confederation recognized two languages and cultural groups, English and French, Canada is, in that sense, dual in origin. But we are also—and this is important—multiracial in our growth. The population of Canada is now roughly one-third Anglo-Saxon in origin, one-third French, and one-third other ethnic stocks. This dual origin and racial variety are important factors in our present position and in our future development. They mean that the unity of Canada cannot be based on uniformity or on the doctrine of the melting pot.

The day has long since passed when the French-speaking minority of Canada could be absorbed by the English-speaking majority. Especially in recent years, the French-speaking people of Quebec—who are a minority in Canada but a large majority in the province of Quebec—have insisted on their full right to retain a separate language, culture, and traditions within the Canadian Confederation. If we are to keep united and strong, this right must be recognized by the majority in a manner that will enable French-speaking Canadians to feel that they are full partners and equal citizens—in opportunity and in responsibility—with all other Canadians. Only in this way can there be national unity in Canada. More and more Canadians are coming to realize this fact. The conversion of this understanding into political and constitutional action in a new federal system is a major, perhaps the major, domestic problem for Canada. This problem of national unity can be solved, and I am confident it will be. But the solution of the problem requires the rejection of extreme views on both sides.

Most of our political and constitutional evolution has revolved around federal-provincial relations, including the special situation of one province, Quebec. There have been problems in such relations from the very beginning of our history. This is normal in a federation. In solving these problems we must now take into consideration the new spirit of progressive nationalism in Quebec. This new spirit was brought about by what has been called the Quiet Revolution. This revolution has underlined Quebec's unique position in Canada.

The Future

I repeat my faith in Canada's ability to overcome its governmental problems. For this, there will have to be new constitutional arrangements, a new federalism appropriate for our times. This complex series of problems is being worked out by the democratic method of discussion and negotiation between provincial governments and the federal government.

Meanwhile Canada forges ahead economically, in the extension of social justice and welfare, and in the building of a good society. There is much still to be done. The progress made and the results achieved often serve to make us more conscious of imperfection and failure; of the magnitude and complexity of the challenge as well as the exciting promise of new opportunities. We are an affluent society, which makes the poverty that still exists among us all the more intolerable. We are trying to become a just society, but in a new and modern world that makes it essential to re-examine old ideas and old institutions. We have to grow. But we must also ensure that the profit—economic and social —of this growth will be fairly distributed among all our people. In short, we must balance economic growth and social justice.

Our international policies have reflected this hope for the future, especially since World War II. We have accepted international responsibilities and play an active part at the United Nations, in the North Atlantic Treaty Organization (NATO), and elsewhere in international affairs. We have believed in the necessity of collective action for collective security. We have insisted that while arms may be needed for security, arms alone will never produce a creative peace. So we have joined other nations in the search for peace and security for all men, and we have been glad to take on international commitments to that end.

Believing as we do in international co-operation both for peace and for economic and social progress, it gives a Canadian deep satisfaction to hear one of the most distinguished of French editors, Claude Julien of *Le Monde,* say, as he did recently,

> Canada enjoys throughout the world the trust . . . of a great many peoples. . . . It has served the cause of peace throughout the world as no other country has been able to do with the means available to it.

This tribute is too generous, but I hope that we will deserve it by the way we manage our domestic problems and our foreign relations in the years ahead.

Canada's federal Parliament Building in Ottawa.

CANADA

Canada, the largest country in North America and the second largest country in the world, is a confederation of 10 provinces and two territories.

The present Canadian nation was born with the passage of the British North America Act by the British Parliament in 1867. The British North America Act united the three British North American Provinces—Canada (Ontario plus Quebec), New Brunswick, and Nova Scotia—into the Dominion of Canada. This confederation was subsequently expanded, as other provinces joined the original four. Canada's stature steadily increased among the nations of the world, and the British gave this fact formal recognition in 1931, with the passage of the Statute of Westminster. Parliament thereby ratified Canada's status as a nation fully equal with Britain in the Commonwealth of Nations. Officially Canada is still a constitutional monarchy ruled by the British monarch.

The Parliament of Canada, based in Ottawa, is the nation's chief governing body. The Parliament consists of the House of Commons and the Senate. The House of Commons initiates legislation. The Senate has a generally advisory function. Members of the House of Commons are popularly elected, and senators are appointed by the governor-general (the Queen's representative in Canada) on the advice of the prime minister. The prime minister, the nation's chief political officer, is the head of the largest party in the House of Commons.

Each of the provinces has its own, one-house legislature. The chief executive in each province, the premier, is head of the largest party in the provincial legislature.

CANADA

INDEX TO CANADA MAP

Country Capital
Provincial Capital
UNDIFFERENTIATED HIGHLANDS AND ICE CAP
TUNDRA
CONIFEROUS FOREST
DECIDUOUS FOREST
STEPPE (SHORT GRASS)

FACTS AND FIGURES

CANADA is the official name of the country.

CAPITAL: Ottawa, Ontario.

LOCATION: Northern North America. **Latitude**—41° 43′ N to 83° 07′ N. **Longitude**—52° 37′ W to 141° W.

AREA: 3,851,809 sq. mi. (9,976,185 sq. km.).

PHYSICAL FEATURES: Highest point—Mount Logan, Yukon Territory (19,850 ft.; 6,050 m.). **Lowest point**—sea level. **Chief rivers**—St. Lawrence, Mackenzie-Peace, Yukon, Nelson, Saskatchewan, Churchill, Fraser. **Major lakes**—Great Slave, Great Bear, Athabasca, Winnipeg, Superior, Huron, Erie, Ontario.

POPULATION: 22,000,000 (estimate).

LANGUAGE: English, French.

RELIGION: Protestant, Roman Catholic.

GOVERNMENT: Constitutional monarchy. **Head of state**—British monarch represented by governor-general. **Head of government**—prime minister. **Legislature**—parliament consisting of senate and house of commons. **International co-operation**—United Nations, Commonwealth of Nations, North Atlantic Treaty Organization (NATO), Organization for Economic Co-operation and Development (OECD).

CHIEF CITIES: Montreal, Toronto, Vancouver, Winnipeg, Ottawa, Hamilton, Quebec City, Edmonton, Halifax, Calgary.

ECONOMY: Chief minerals—petroleum and natural gas, copper, nickel, iron ore, zinc, asbestos, coal, gold, lead. **Chief agricultural products**—wheat, cattle, dairy products, hogs, poultry, tobacco, oats, potatoes, barley. **Industries and products**—machinery and transport equipment, pulp and paper, petroleum refining, meat-packing, wood products, textiles, cement. **Chief exports**—newsprint paper, motor vehicles and parts, wheat, crude petroleum and natural gas, lumber, wood pulp, copper, aluminum. **Chief imports**—motor vehicles and parts, machinery, petroleum and petroleum products, aircraft, steel, electrical equipment.

MONETARY UNIT: Canadian dollar.

NATIONAL HOLIDAY: July 1, Dominion Day.

NATIONAL ANTHEMS: "God Save the Queen"; "O Canada."

MOTTO: *A Mari usque ad Mare* ("From Sea to Sea").

NATIONAL SYMBOL: Maple leaf.

CHRONOLOGY OF CANADIAN HISTORY

1000 Vikings make their first landings in North America, probably in Newfoundland and on Nova Scotia.

1497 John Cabot lands on east coast of Canada.

1534 Cartier discovers Gulf of St. Lawrence.

1604 Samuel de Champlain (Father of New France) and Sieur de Monts found colony (Acadia) at mouth of St. Croix River, New Brunswick.

1608 Champlain founds city of Quebec.

1642 French missionaries found Montreal (Ville Marie).

1670 Hudson's Bay Company (British) gets charter to fur-trading rights around Hudson Bay.

1689–1763 Series of wars result in British conquest of New France.

1774 In Quebec Act, Britain grants French Canadians freedom to practice their religion and retain their language, laws, and customs.

1791 The province of Quebec is divided into Upper Canada (now Ontario) and Lower Canada (Quebec).

1793 Alexander Mackenzie becomes first white man to cross the continent north of Mexico.

1812 Lord Selkirk's pioneers found colony at present site of Winnipeg, beginning settlement of West.

1837–1838 Rebellions break out in Upper and Lower Canada.

1839 Governor-General Lord Durham urges self-government for Canada.

1840 Union Act joins Upper and Lower Canada under single government.

1848 United Canada wins self-government.

1849 Vancouver Island becomes British crown colony.

1858 British Columbia becomes a colony.

1864 Canadian representatives meet at Quebec to plan Confederation.

1866 Vancouver Island and British Columbia united as British Columbia.

1867 British North America Act establishes the Dominion of Canada, a confederation of four provinces—Quebec, Ontario, New Brunswick, and Nova Scotia.

1869–1870 Canada buys St. Rupert's Land and Northwest Territories from Hudson's Bay Company.

1869 Canada's take-over of Red River valley region sparks first rebellion of métis (French-Indians), led by Louis Riel.

1870 Métis revolt put down; Manitoba joins Confederation as fifth province.

1871 British Columbia becomes sixth province.

1873 Prince Edward Island joins Dominion (seventh province).

1885 Completion of Canadian Pacific Railway, spanning continent; Riel, leading second métis revolt in Saskatchewan, is defeated and executed.

1905 Alberta and Saskatchewan become eighth and ninth provinces.

1926 Crisis over governor-general's power leads to clarification of Canadian-British relationship and greater Canadian autonomy.

1931 British Parliament passes Statute of Westminster.

1939–1945 World War II involves Canadian forces all over the world.

1945 Canada builds first nuclear reactor outside United States (Chalk River, Ontario).

1949 With Newfoundland joining as 10th province, Canada assumes its present form.

1954–1959 Canada and United States co-operate to build St. Lawrence Seaway.

1962 At Rolphton, Ontario, first Canadian nuclear power plant begins operations; Trans-Canada Highway completed.

1965 Canada adopts its new flag—red maple leaf.

1967 Expo 67, World's Fair at Montreal, signals Canadian celebration of first centennial of Confederation.

1973 Canada becomes one of four members of commission to oversee Vietnam ceasefire; resigns later that year.

1975 Canada begins the first stage (use of Celsius scale) of conversion to metric system.

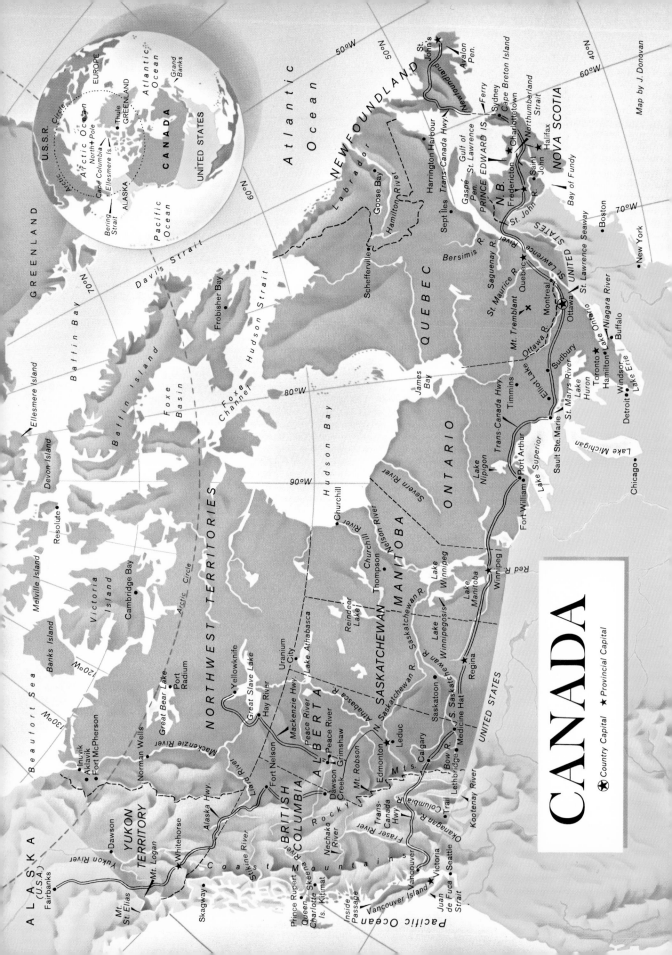

CANADA

⊛ Country Capital   ★ Provincial Capital

Map by J. Donovan

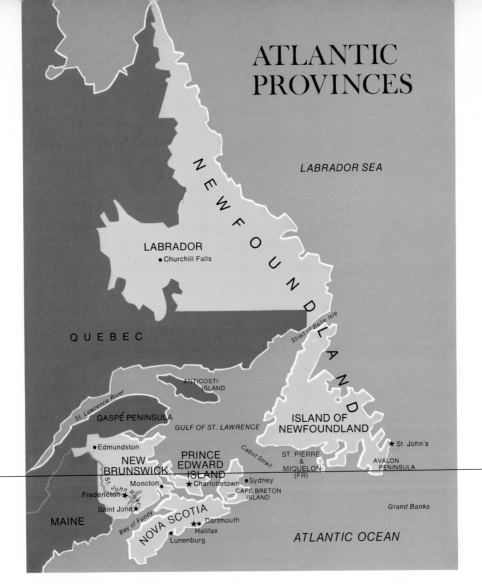

ATLANTIC
PROVINCES

LABRADOR SEA

NEWFOUNDLAND

LABRADOR
• Churchill Falls

QUEBEC

Strait of Belle Isle

ANTICOSTI
ISLAND

St. Lawrence River

GASPÉ PENINSULA

GULF OF ST. LAWRENCE

ISLAND OF
NEWFOUNDLAND

★ St John's

• Edmundston

Cabot Strait

ST. PIERRE
&
MIQUELON
(FR)

AVALON
PENINSULA

NEW
BRUNSWICK

PRINCE
EDWARD
ISLAND

• Sydney

Moncton

★ Charlottetown

St. John River

CAPE BRETON
ISLAND

Fredericton ★

Saint John •

Grand Banks

MAINE

Bay of Fundy

NOVA SCOTIA

★ • Dartmouth

Halifax

• Lunenburg

ATLANTIC OCEAN

ATLANTIC PROVINCES

The Atlantic Provinces, Canada's four smallest provinces, are located on the Gulf of St. Lawrence, the great bay at the mouth of the St. Lawrence River. There are four Atlantic Provinces: Newfoundland and Labrador (or simply Newfoundland), Nova Scotia, New Brunswick, and Prince Edward Island. The last three areas were known for many years as the Maritime Provinces. When Newfoundland became part of Canada in 1949, the name Atlantic Provinces came into use to refer to all four of these eastern Canadian provinces.

Although the Atlantic Provinces are Canada's four smallest political divisions, their combined area is almost as large as France. About 2,000,000 people live in this vast region, and large areas remain a wilderness of forests and lakes or of cold, sparsely vegetated land. The largest expanse of wilderness is found in Newfoundland and Labrador, which is about three times the size of the other three provinces combined. But with the exception of tiny Prince Edward Island, all the provinces have substantial uninhabited or virtually uninhabited areas. The regional economy is primitive in the sense that it is still closely tied to the land and sea. But this is also one of Canada's longest-settled areas, a region of lively customs and traditions.

Land and Sea

Except for Prince Edward Island and parts of Nova Scotia, the soil in the Atlantic Provinces is largely rocky and unproductive. As a result, comparatively little farming goes on there. The greater sources of provincial wealth are mines, forests, and factories—and, of course, the sea. For a long time the economy of the Atlantic Provinces was bound up almost entirely with the sea. This is no longer the case, but settlement in the Atlantic Provinces is still concentrated along the coast, where the climate also happens to be most equable. The largest cities are located on the coast, as well as the scores of small, picturesque fishing villages for which the provinces are famous.

Inshore and Offshore. Even today, when fishing has diminished in relative economic importance, thousands of men still get up at four in the morning, pull on their oilskins, and head out. These are the so-called inshore fishermen, who set their traps or nets or lines within 15 miles (24 kilometers) of shore. They use small, open boats, which are 30–40 feet (9–12 meters) long. Lobsters are the mainstay of these inshore fishermen. They also catch quantities of cod, scallops, herring, and salmon before returning to their home port each afternoon.

Farther out to sea, 50 miles (80 km.) or more from shore, are the offshore fisheries. Here trawlers, large fishing boats of up to several hundred feet (about 100 m.), operate. This is the area of the Grand Banks, one of the great fishing regions of the world, attracting fishing fleets from the United States and Europe as well as Canada. The Grand Banks are relatively elevated portions of the great underwater plateau known as the continental shelf. The largest and most fished-in of the banks, Grand Bank, which is larger than the state of Maine, is located to the southeast of Newfoundland island. Many other banks surround the three maritime provinces in the Atlantic Ocean and the Gulf of St. Lawrence. The waters of the Grand Banks are relatively shallow. They range from about 150 to 600 feet (45–180 m.) deep. An abundant growth of plankton and other basic sea life attracts great schools of fish to the area. Cod, haddock, flounder, and herring are the main catch here. Billions of pounds of fish are caught on the Grand Banks every year; about a third of the catch is caught by Canadian trawlers.

New Currents, Old Tides. Despite the excellence of the fishery, fishing does not provide a good living for many of the fishermen of the Atlantic Provinces. The number of fishermen has declined considerably in the 20th century, particularly since World War II. Even so, there remain too many fishermen to be supported by the low prices that generally prevail in the international fish market.

Many fishermen would be more than happy to give up their hard seafaring life if they could find some other way of making a living. But this has been one of the continuing problems in the Atlantic Provinces for fishermen and non-fishermen alike: a scarcity of economic opportunity and the lack of economic development. Many people have left the provinces for central and western Canada in search of jobs.

The provincial and national governments have combated that trend by trying to attract new industries to the Atlantic Provinces. And recently there have been some impressive results. In the late 1960's, for example, construction was begun on several mammoth coastal oil refineries to refine petroleum brought by transoceanic tankers all the way from the Middle East. Throughout the Atlantic Provinces things are changing, as new industries and business ventures are established and new schools, hospitals, and roads are built. But the sense of the past remains strong here, too, which is why this is one of the more colorful parts of Canada.

NEWFOUNDLAND AND LABRADOR

This province was called simply Newfoundland for a long time, and it is still called that by many people. But in 1964 the provincial assembly decided to give the province's region of Labrador equal status and voted to call the province by the joint name of Newfoundland and Labrador. Actually, Labrador, which is separated from the island of Newfoundland by the 10–15 mile (16–24 km.) width of the Strait of Belle Isle, constitutes more than 70 percent of the total provincial land area. Some of the most important economic developments in the Atlantic region are taking place in Labrador. One such development is the construction of one of the largest hydroelectric plants in North America, at Churchill Falls. And astonishingly large deposits of iron ore have been discovered in western Labrador. These major developments notwithstanding, the region is still largely a cold, forbidding wilderness, and more than 95 percent of the province's more than 500,000 people live on the island of Newfoundland. Even there settlement is sparse in the interior, a region of forests, lakes, bogs, and also of great stone-littered areas known as barrens, where almost nothing but gray reindeer moss grows.

An oceangoing freighter leaves St. John's harbor, Newfoundland.

ATLANTIC PROVINCES

NEWFOUNDLAND AND LABRADOR is the name of the province.

CAPITAL: St. John's, Newfoundland.

MAJOR CITY: St. John's, Newfoundland.

AREA: 156,185 sq. mi. (404,520 sq. km.).

POPULATION: 540,000 (estimate).

PHYSICAL FEATURES: Highest point—Cirque Mountain, Labrador (5,160 ft.; 1,713 m.). **Lowest point**—sea level. **Major rivers**—Exploits, Humber (Newfoundland); Churchill (Labrador). **Major lakes**—Grand, Red Indian (Newfoundland); Melville (Labrador).

PROVINCIAL MOTTO: *Quaerite prime regnum Dei* ("Seek ye first the kingdom of God").

NEW BRUNSWICK is the name of the province.

CAPITAL: Fredericton.

MAJOR CITY: Saint John.

AREA: 28,354 sq. mi. (73,437 sq. km.).

POPULATION: 660,000 (estimate).

PHYSICAL FEATURES: Highest point—Mt. Carleton (2,690 ft.; 820 m.). **Lowest point**—sea level. **Major rivers**—St. John. **Major lakes**—Grand Lake.

NOVA SCOTIA is the name of the province.

CAPITAL: Halifax.

MAJOR CITIES: Halifax, Dartmouth, Sydney.

AREA: 21,425 sq. mi. (55,491 sq. km.).

POPULATION: 800,000 (estimate).

PHYSICAL FEATURES: Highest point—1,000 feet (305 m.). **Lowest point**—sea level. **Major rivers**—St. Mary's, Mersey. **Major lakes**—Bras d'Or, Ainslie.

PROVINCIAL MOTTO: *Munit haec et altera vincit* ("One defends and the other conquers").

PRINCE EDWARD ISLAND is the name of the province.

CAPITAL: Charlottetown.

MAJOR CITY: Charlottetown.

AREA: 2,184 sq. mi. (5,656 sq. km.).

POPULATION: 120,000 (estimate).

PHYSICAL FEATURES: Highest point—450 ft. (136 m.). **Lowest point**—sea level.

PROVINCIAL MOTTO: *Parva sub ingenti* ("The small under the protection of the great").

A Seafaring Province

The overwhelming majority of Newfoundland's population lives along the island's indented coastline. The greatest concentrations are on the Avalon Peninsula in the southwest, where winters are relatively mild. St. John's, Newfoundland's capital and largest city (with a population in its metropolitan area of over 130,000 people), is located on the Avalon Peninsula. It is a busy commercial center, built around an excellent harbor. The steep sides and narrow entrance of the harbor give shelter from all winds. Fishermen have been frequenting the harbor since the 16th century, when European fleets came to lay out their catch of cod to dry and to repair their ships. Today the Canadian trawlers that fish Grand Bank operate principally out of St. John's harbor, to which they bring great quantities of cod and other fish to be processed in the city's factories.

Newfoundlanders are the most seafaring of all Canadians, the province boasting more fishermen than any other. However, the chief source of provincial wealth is not the fishery, but the iron mines of Labrador, which provide more than one third of the iron ore produced in Canada. Newfoundland's forests are the province's second most valuable resource, providing the raw material for the tons of newsprint (cheap paper used in newspapers) produced there every year. Corner Brook, in the western part of the island, is the leading center for the manufacture of newsprint and other wood and paper products.

As for the fishermen, they are having to adapt themselves to changing times. Many are giving up their small, open boats to join the crews of large, well-equipped trawlers or to seek work in new industries. Increasingly, they are moving from small, outlying fishing villages (called "outports") to larger towns and cities where jobs are available and also where schools, hospitals, and other services are accessible.

Economic changes notwithstanding, the heart of the province, as expressed in its folk songs, still belongs to the romance of seafaring. One such folk song, perhaps the most popular, is "On the Squid Jigging Ground," a merry ballad that gets its title from the catching (or "jigging") of squid for bait. It is still likely to be heard wherever Newfoundlanders gather, at home or abroad.

History

The small Beothuk Indian tribe inhabited the region before the first Europeans arrived. There is evidence that the Beothuk lived in Newfoundland and Labrador for thousands of years before finally becoming extinct in the 19th century. But the European fishermen who came here, many of whom were from Western Europe, were less than enthusiastic about hazarding Newfoundland's harsh winters. For a long time, Europeans came to fish without establishing permanent settlements.

The first Europeans to visit were probably Norsemen who ventured across the North Atlantic from Iceland and Greenland about A.D. 1000. Virtual proof of their presence was uncovered in 1963, when traces of various building structures were excavated at L'Anse aux Meadows at the northern tip of the island. This small community, which apparently was occupied for only a short time, may very well have been founded by the famous Norse explorer Leif Ericson himself.

The European usually credited with being the first to explore Newfoundland, as well as other parts of the Atlantic Provinces, is John Cabot. He arrived at the head of an English expedition in 1497. But very probably Europeans were fishing the Grand Banks earlier in the century. Fishing fleets from Spain, Portugal, England, and France were active in the region in the 16th century. The first ships arrived in the spring and the last departed late in the year, before ice clogged the surrounding seas. Outposts were established, but no permanent settlements.

In 1583 Sir Humphrey Gilbert formally laid claim to Newfoundland for himself and England, having previously received a patent for colonization from Queen Elizabeth I. Gilbert died soon thereafter. Newfoundland remained the province of the offshore fishermen, who actually obstructed settlement of the region, fearing that it would interfere with their own onshore rights. By the middle of the 18th century the island had only about 3,400 permanent settlers. Most of these oldest settlers were from southern Ireland and southwestern England. To this day, Newfoundlanders in isolated fishing villages still speak with the accents and even with the archaic vocabulary of those places as they were centuries ago.

In the 19th century the island's population finally began to increase more rapidly, reaching 130,000 by 1855. In that year, the people of Newfoundland colony were granted responsible government, which meant that they could make their own laws, subject to British approval. This government decided not to join the Canadian Confederation when it was formed in 1867. On subsequent occasions, Newfoundland wanted to join the Confederation but failed to gain membership. It finally became a province of Canada on March 31, 1949.

NOVA SCOTIA

Nova Scotia means "new Scotland" in Latin. In 1621 King James I of England chartered Sir William Alexander, a Scotsman, to colonize the area in North America that the French then called Acadia (or Acadie). In the charter, which was written in Latin, the land was called Nova Scotia. This name honored Alexander and the Scottish colonists who founded the first British settlement in the region. Today, nearly two thirds of the population is made up of people of Scottish and English descent. There are also Irish, Germans, and other peoples. To a large degree the different peoples of Nova Scotia have remained culturally distinct, maintaining the lively and varied traditions for which the province is known.

Acadia

French colonists were the first Europeans to settle Nova Scotia (part of Acadia). The colonists were called Acadians. But the first known inhabitants of the region were the Micmac, an Indian people who believed in a god or superman named Glooscap, who was said to have made the world, to have created the first Indians from an ash tree, and to live in a wigwam among the clouds. The Micmac still live in Nova Scotia.

In 1605, the French made the first permanent settlement in Canada at Port Royal, a few miles away from present-day Annapolis Royal. The French gave the name Acadia to Port Royal and the various subsequent French settlements on the Atlantic coast. The boundaries of Acadia were never clearly defined but were probably intended to include the Atlantic Provinces as well as parts of Maine and Quebec. The largest Acadian settlements were on the northern part of the Nova Scotia peninsula in the rich farm country of the Annapolis River valley and in the lands adjoining the Minas Basin. The British countered with their own claims and with smaller, less successful Scottish settlements. In the course of

Halifax, Nova Scotia, the leading port of the Atlantic Provinces.

the 17th century, while Britain and France jockeyed for control of North America, Acadia changed hands several times. It was at last granted formally to Great Britain under the terms of the Treaty of Utrecht (1713), which ended Queen Anne's War, the second of the four French and Indian wars.

The French Acadians continued to live in their old settlements, but did not forswear their French allegiance. In time this became intolerable to the British, and in 1755 many of the Acadians, who must have numbered about 10,000 to 14,000, were expelled from their land and from the region entirely. This is the heartrending story told in the famous poem *Evangeline* by the American poet Henry Wadsworth Longfellow. Some of the Acadians escaped expulsion by hiding out, and some who did leave the peninsula later returned. Today about 80,000 Acadians live in Nova Scotia, principally in the southern part of Cape Breton Island and in western Nova Scotia. Most are bilingual, speaking both French and English. The Acadians have annual festivals in which boys and girls wear the costumes of French colonial days and sing old French songs. Often these gatherings include Cajun visitors from Louisiana, descendants of the Acadian deportees who settled there long ago.

Bluenoses and Highlanders

About the time the Acadians were deported, 200 German and Swiss families settled at Lunenburg on the Atlantic coast. In the 19th and 20th centuries Lunenburg became one of the most celebrated shipbuilding towns in North America, famous for its shapely wooden fishing schooners.

On the northern shore, the excellent farmlands left by the Acadians were quickly occupied by immigrants from New England, and by 1775 about two thirds of the colonial population of about 18,000 consisted of New Englanders. After the American Revolution, there was an additional large influx of United Empire Loyalists, Americans who had remained loyal to Britain despite the Revolution. A substantial part of the colony's émigré Americans had relatives in the United States, particularly New England, and this remains the case among Nova Scotians today. New Englanders applied the affectionate nickname Bluenoses to their cousins in Nova Scotia, imagining, mistakenly, that the climate was forever bleak and cold and that therefore their noses turned blue with the cold. Actually the more populous coastal regions of the Atlantic Provinces, which get the warming benefit of the Gulf Stream, are only slightly colder in winter than Boston, Massachusetts. But Nova Scotians continue to be called Bluenoses today and, in fact, accept the nickname with pride.

In the first half of the 19th century, a great era of shipbuilding and commercial growth, about 50,000 Scots and Irishmen arrived in Nova Scotia. Most of the immigrants were from the Scottish Highlands. They settled principally on Cape Breton Island and in the counties of Antigonish and Pictou in the eastern part of the peninsula. The ancient Gaelic language these first settlers spoke can still be heard on Cape Breton Island today. There are still annual gatherings with competitions in Highland dancing to the tune of bagpipes and in the singing of folk songs in Gaelic.

The Land

In 1867 Nova Scotia became one of the four original provinces to join the Canadian Confederation. The population has about doubled since that time, and today it is almost 800,000, making Nova Scotia the most populous of the Atlantic Provinces.

The province consists of the Nova Scotia peninsula and of nearby Cape Breton Island, which is connected to the mainland by a stone causeway. Together these two masses of land look like a lobster on the map. (Lobsters, as a matter of fact, are the mainstay of the Nova Scotian fishery.) The terrain of the province (as well as that of neighboring New Brunswick) is rugged and irregular, but not mountainous. There are rich, flat, and rolling farmlands in the Bay of Fundy region. These are the lands once occupied by the Acadians. Fruit farming and dairying are now the principal agricultural pursuits of Nova Scotia. Cape Breton Island has some fairly extensive coal mines, which are of less economic importance now than they once were. Otherwise, outside the settled coastal regions Nova Scotia consists mainly of forests. These forests are still the province of the lumbermen and also of the Canadian and American sportsmen who come to hunt and fish. Nova Scotians love the outdoors and hold annual competitions in shooting, canoe racing, and log chopping. They also compete at birling, a sport that gets its name from an old Scottish word meaning "spin." In birling, two men or boys jump on a floating log and make it spin with rapid movements of their feet, until one loses his footing and is "birled" off.

Cities. Nova Scotia is the most urbanized and industrialized of the Atlantic Provinces. More than 400,000 people, or about 60 percent of the provincial population, live in towns and cities. The greatest concentration is in the provincial capital of Halifax, its twin city Dartmouth (across Halifax harbor), and the surrounding metropolitan area. Halifax was founded by the British in 1749 as a kind of counterweight to the Acadian settlements near the northern coast. Today Halifax handles more commerce by far than any other city in the Atlantic Provinces. It is an important base for the Canadian Navy, and it is also a building center. Leading industries in the twin cities include food and fish processing, oil refining, and defense industries. Dalhousie University, the largest institution of higher learning in Nova Scotia, is located in Halifax.

NEW BRUNSWICK

New Brunswick is known for its forests and loggers, just as Newfoundland is known for its fishery and fishermen. Beginning in the early 19th century, the dense New Brunswick forests became the basis for a great shipbuilding industry along the coast.

In New Brunswick lumbermen of legendary skills toiled to get the great logs to sawmills and shipyards, without the benefit of railroads or motor trucks. The region's numerous rivers and streams were used to carry great rafts of logs to the sawmills. In inaccessible parts of the province, today's loggers still use the rivers and streams to carry logs. Originally the loggers worked at felling timber all winter, and then in the spring would come the drive to the mills, down rivers and streams swollen by melting ice and snow. A high degree of skill and ingenuity was required to keep the logs moving and to prevent jams. The work

A paper mill in Saint John, New Brunswick, operates near the famous reversing falls of the St. John River.

of shepherding the big logs was also very dangerous. One of the best loggers' folk songs, "The Jam on Gerry's Rock," tells about the death of some New Brunswick lumbermen in a drive of long ago.

The Economy Today

By the 1870's the New Brunswick forests were fairly well depleted. In addition, the building of wooden ships was in decline. By that time, most of the loggers had moved to the United States, where they played a notable part in the westward march of the American lumbermen. The forest subsequently grew back, and today forest-based industries, especially pulp and paper manufacturing, play a major role in the provincial economy. About 87 percent of the province is still forest.

About 3 or 4 percent of New Brunswick is productive farmland, about the same percentage as in Nova Scotia. Potatoes are grown in quantity in the valley of the St. John River. Dairying is an important industry in the Kennebecasis River valley, near the southern coast. In northeastern New Brunswick, around Bathurst and Newcastle, large deposits of lead, copper, zinc, and silver were uncovered shortly after World War II. They now constitute the core of a mining industry that has surpassed the province's agricultural production in value.

Cities. Saint John is an old and conservative-minded city, with a population (in its metropolitan area) of over 100,000 people. It is, after Halifax, the leading commercial city in the Atlantic Provinces. Like

Halifax, its port is ice-free all year. As a terminus of the Canadian Pacific Railway, the city thrives on the transshipment of wheat and manufactured products for export from the Canadian interior. Busy, noisy Moncton, with a population of about 48,000, is a hub city, in which railway lines converge and through which goods are distributed to different parts of the Atlantic Provinces. Fredericton, the provincial capital and home of the University of New Brunswick, is located about 60 miles (97 km.) up the St. John River from Saint John. It has a population of about 24,000.

Fantastic Fundy

New Brunswick has two very different coastlines, separated by the neck of the Nova Scotia peninsula (or the Isthmus of Chignecto, as this neck of land is properly called). The east coast, which faces the Gulf of St. Lawrence, is generally flat and low-lying and is known for the quaintness of its Acadian fishing villages. The southern coast has a steep rock face and is known for its extraordinarily deep tides and great, rushing tidal currents. The depth and strength of the tides here derive from the fact that this coast faces the Bay of Fundy. Ocean tides increase greatly in pressure and depth as they are funneled into this narrow, 100-mile-long (160 km.) Bay of Fundy. When the moon exerts its greatest pull, tides may rise and fall more than 50 feet (15 m.) in parts of the

Inshore fishermen catch cod and sardines in fish traps like this.

bay, meaning that the water will be more than 50 feet deeper at high tide than at low tide. These large fluctuations produce some remarkable spectacles in New Brunswick. One is the reversing falls near the mouth of the St. John River. As the tide rises, the river is thrust back by the saltwater up a series of rocky ledges, like a waterfall or rapids in reverse. Another remarkable phenomenon occurs at the mouth of the Petitcodiac River, near the end of the bay, where the tides reach about their greatest height. At high tide, a wall of water several feet high may be seen rushing over the shallow water up the river, a tidal bore that may reach all the way to Moncton, about 15 miles (24 km.) upstream.

Provincial History

The history of New Brunswick is similar in many ways to that of Nova Scotia, of which New Brunswick was, in fact, a part until 1784. Long ago, the region was the hunting ground of the Micmac and Malecite Indian tribes. Members of both tribes still live in the province. Initial colonization was by French Acadians, several thousand of whom were living in the region by the middle of the 18th century. As in Nova Scotia, some Acadians escaped deportation in 1755 by hiding in the woods, and others were deported and later returned. Today the province has the largest Acadian population in Canada. Also, a large number of French-descended inhabitants have moved to New Brunswick at one time or another from Quebec. Altogether about 40 percent of the province's more than 600,000 people are of French descent.

The first substantial British settlement in New Brunswick occurred in the period following the conclusion of the French and Indian War in 1763. Several thousand New Englanders and Yorkshire farmers from England came to settle principally in the lower St. John Valley. A much larger immigration took place after the American Revolution, when United Empire Loyalists, or British sympathizers, moved into the St. John Valley from Saint John to Fredericton. Many descendants of the Loyalists still live in the province. New Brunswick never had as large a Scottish immigration as Nova Scotia, but many Irish immigrants settled in the province in the 19th century. The province was one of the four original members of the Canadian Confederation.

PRINCE EDWARD ISLAND

Prince Edward Island is by far the smallest of the Atlantic Provinces. It has a total area of 2,184 square miles (5,657 square kilometers) and is only about one tenth the size of the second smallest Canadian province, Nova Scotia. With a population of more than 100,000, Prince Edward Island has the greatest population density of any Canadian province.

The island lies in a bight, or bay, within the Gulf of St. Lawrence. It is half surrounded by the shorelines of Nova Scotia and New Brunswick. Because Prince Edward Island is enclosed in this way, the Indians called it Abegweit, which means "sheltered in the sea." The French called the island Île Saint Jean. Canadians today often shorten the island's name to P.E.I. Islanders themselves simply call it the Island.

The first settlers were French Acadians, most of whom were expelled by the British during the French and Indian War. The island was formally ceded to Great Britain by France at the end of the war, in 1763. It was settled subsequently by Irishmen and Scots. The British named the island Prince Edward Island in 1799. It was named in honor of Prince Edward Augustus, Duke of Kent, who was the son of King George III and commander of British forces in North America. The little capital was called Charlottetown in honor of Prince Edward's mother, Queen Charlotte Sophia. It was at Charlottetown that delegates from the Canadian provinces first met in 1864 to consider confederation. A fine modern theater-and-arts center commemorates that meeting today. Prince Edward Island became a province of Canada in 1873.

The island has few hills of any size. There is some woodland, but most of the island's deep red soil is cultivated or used for pasture. Thus its nickname is Garden of the Gulf. Potatoes, dairy products, cattle, and pigs are the most important agricultural products. There is a profitable lobster fishery, and the oysters of Malpeque Bay on the northern shore are considered by some people to be the best to be had anywhere in the world.

Prince Edward Island—like two other famous islands, Great Britain and Ireland—has a reputation for friendliness and hospitality and also for a love of horses and horse racing. The island is a favorite summer resort for inland Canadians, who frequent the northern shore, with its long beaches of fine sand the color of cocoa. The island is well-known abroad from the children's book *Anne of Green Gables*. The home of its author, Lucy Maud Montgomery, at Cavendish on the north shore, may be seen by visitors to Prince Edward National Park.

THOMAS H. RADDALL, Author, *Halifax, Warden of the North*

A stretch of rich farmland on Prince Edward Island.

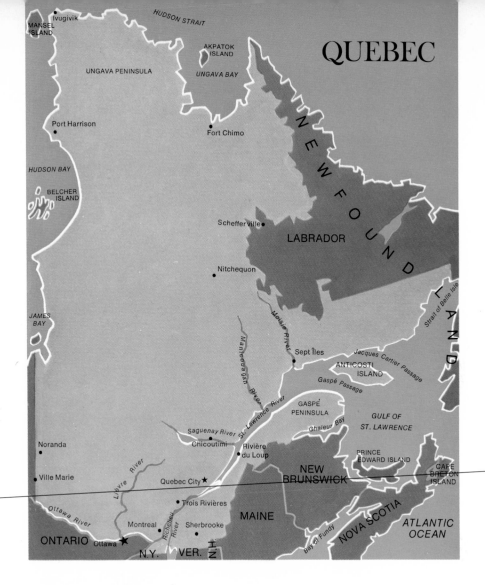

QUEBEC

Quebec is the largest of the 10 provinces of Canada and the second most populous. But to the French-speaking people of Quebec their province is only a small island in a vast sea of more than 200,000,000 English-speaking North Americans in the United States and Canada.

Quebeckers tend to think of themselves as different from everyone else. This feeling of uniqueness is found among the English-speaking minority in Quebec, too. English Quebeckers—who constitute roughly 12 percent of the province's population—can identify with the large English-Canadian majority in the rest of Canada. But in their own province they are a small minority. Even the many French-speaking Indians in Quebec are likely to feel unique. Being French-speaking, they may actually find it difficult to communicate with English-speaking Indians in other parts of North America.

For more than 2 centuries the *Québecois,* as the French-speaking citizen of Quebec is called, has tried fiercely to preserve the language,

FACTS AND FIGURES

CAPITAL: Quebec City.

MAJOR CITIES: Montreal, Quebec City.

AREA: 594,860 sq. mi. (1,504,669 sq. km.).

POPULATION: 6,000,000 (estimate).

PHYSICAL FEATURES: Highest point—Mt. Jacques Cartier (4,160 ft.; 1,268 m.). **Lowest point**—sea level. **Major rivers**—St. Lawrence, Ottawa, Koksoak, Outardes, Fort George, Saguenay. **Major lakes**—Mistassini, Clearwater, Minto, St. John, Bienville, Payne, Abitibi, Allard, Timiskaming.

PROVINCIAL MOTTO: *Je me souviens* ("I remember").

customs, culture, and religion that set him off from the majority of Canadians. Today the Québecois is no longer content merely to preserve his centuries-old heritage. He wants to expand and enhance his culture. The Québecois has begun to demand a larger share of Canada's national wealth and more influence in the affairs of Quebec and of Canada as a whole. He has grown more assertive. In the 1960's some Québecois even talked of seceding from Canada and establishing Quebec as an independent or semi-independent state. At the same time, the Québecois considers himself the most authentic of Canadians. He speaks of himself as *canadien.* The others, the majority of Canadian citizens, are only *les anglais,* "the English."

HISTORY

Je me souviens ("I remember") is the official motto of Quebec province. And in recalling his people's role in the building of Canada, the Québecois has a great deal to remember. He remembers with pride the great explorer from northern France, Jacques Cartier. In 1534 and 1535 Cartier became the first European to explore the St. Lawrence River valley extensively. He was the first European to penetrate to the two great Indian settlements in the region—Stadacona, at the site of present-day Quebec City, and, largest of all, Hochelaga, at the site of present-day Montreal. In the early 17th century another Frenchman, Samuel de Champlain, made invaluable explorations of the Atlantic coast, the northern United States, and the Canadian interior, particularly the St. Lawrence and Ottawa river valleys. No other man did more to explore, map, and generally encourage settlement in this vast region. In 1608 Champlain was instrumental in the establishment of the first French settlement in the Canadian interior, at the site of present-day Quebec City.

The Québecois remembers that his French ancestors were the first Europeans to farm the Canadian soil. It was France that provided the first missionaries to risk their lives among hostile Indians and the explorers and fur traders to blaze paths into the Canadian interior. In 1642 another Frenchman, Paul de Chomedey, Sieur de Maisonneuve, founded the settlement of Ville Marie just below the famous—and treacherous—Lachine Rapids of the St. Lawrence River. In time this small outpost for fur traders and missionaries became the big, bustling city of Montreal, Canada's greatest metropolis.

An Abandoned People

By the middle of the 18th century the population of Canada consisted of between 55,000 and 65,000 French Canadians. They lived in the lowlands bordering the St. Lawrence River between Quebec City and Montreal. The *habitants,* as they were called, were predominantly

Long, narrow Quebec farms stretch back from the St. Lawrence.

farmers. Their farms fronted on a river or a road and were long and narrow, placing the farmhouses relatively close together. This pattern is still evident in the Quebec countryside. The *habitants* were a close-knit and deeply religious people. Families were large, and by the middle of the 18th century most families had already been in Canada for several generations. They were already a breed unto themselves, with their own special interests and a uniquely austere and pious devotion to their Roman Catholic faith.

Then came the Seven Years War (1756–1763), in which Great Britain took control of Canada from France. It is possible that the French could have prevented a British victory if they had been willing to make more than the most minimal effort to defend their colony. But France was too busy warring against its enemies in Europe to supply Canada with the necessary men and supplies. In 1759 the British delivered the decisive stroke against New France, as French Canada was then called. An armed force under the command of General James Wolfe captured Quebec City from combined French and Canadian forces under the command of the French general Louis Joseph de Montcalm. The following year the French colonial government surrendered to the British.

In 1763, under the terms of the Treaty of Paris, French Canada (which then meant Quebec) was formally ceded to Britain. By that time all of the French civil administrators as well as the principal landowners and businessmen had returned to France forever. Of the leaders of New

France, only the Roman Catholic clergy remained behind. Because of this they became even more important to the peasant farmers of Quebec —who were largely illiterate—than they had been before.

A Static Society

Despite the imposition of British rule the life of the Québecois remained much the same as it had been under French rule. In 1774 the British Parliament passed the Quebec Act, which gave official sanction to the Roman Catholic religion of the French Quebeckers, permitted the former French civil law to be reinstated, and in general provided a favorable situation for the survival of the traditional Québecois way of life. And survive it did, largely unchanged for the better part of 200 years. The Québecois remained rooted in the past while the world around him changed. By the middle of the 19th century French Canadians no longer constituted a majority of the population of Canada, although they still remained a majority in Quebec.

The Québecois lacked either the desire, the temperament, or the training to compete with the British newcomer for the wealth of Canada's growing economy. Because of the high birthrate in Quebec, many Québecois migrated to other parts of Canada or to the New England states of the United States to find new farmland and jobs. Those who remained in Quebec remained as small farmers, set up small businesses, or migrated to the towns and cities, where they generally worked at unskilled or semiskilled jobs for low wages. A sizable number of Québecois did enter the professions. Clergy were in abundance, and it was a rare family that did not include a priest or nun.

The Roman Catholic Church in Quebec had an importance that went far beyond the performance of religious functions. The clergy were the largest group of French-speaking people in Canada with any degree of higher education. Until quite recently the Roman Catholic and Protestant churches had complete control of public education in Quebec. The Roman Catholic role in public education was dominant because the vast majority of students attended Roman Catholic schools. In the more distant past, Roman Catholic priests and nuns would often act as doctors, and more often than not, priests would even oversee business arrangements between French-speaking farmers or traders and English-speaking merchants.

In the schools and universities under Roman Catholic control, education in Quebec became strongly oriented toward theology, classical studies, law, and medicine. On the other hand technology, business, and science were largely ignored by the French Canadians and became a virtual monopoly of the English Canadians. Thus, it was not surprising to find that in a province with a population that was overwhelmingly French Canadian, almost all large businesses and industries were owned and managed by English Canadians, as well as by outside British and American interests.

Today all of this is changing. By general agreement something important took place in Quebec in the 1960's. What happened is now known as the Quiet Revolution, and it has set Quebec on a new course within the Canadian Confederation. No one knows as yet where it will lead. One thing is now certain: the winds of change are blowing strongly in Quebec and things will never be as they were.

The Quiet Revolution

What is the Quiet Revolution? It is really two things, or has two aspects. First it is a revolution against English Canada—the central government in Ottawa as well as English-Canadian power in Quebec province itself. Second, and just as important, it is a revolution in the traditional Quebec way of life, a rebellion against the stagnation of the past.

In part, Quebec's dispute with English Canada has been a simple case of friction between a provincial government and the federal government. In the 1960's, for example, it was charged that Quebec received back from the federal government only a fraction of the money in benefits and services that it paid in taxes. This is the kind of dispute that continually arises between provincial governments and Ottawa. Similar disputes arise between state and federal governments in the United States. In Quebec, however, this kind of natural dispute is greatly aggravated by long-standing grievances and tensions between French Canada and English Canada.

The fact is that more than a century after confederation with British Canada, the French Quebeckers still consider themselves to be only second-class citizens of Canada. Quebec elects a sizable block of members to Parliament, and several of Canada's prime ministers have been Québécois. In fact, the colorful and dynamic Pierre Elliott Trudeau, elected in 1968, is one. But beyond these elected offices, Quebeckers feel discriminated against in most other phases of national life. Thus, in the early 1960's, Quebec nationalists were pointing out embarrassing facts like these: that of 17 directors of the Bank of Canada, only one was French Canadian; that of 17 vice-presidents of the Canadian National Railways, not one was French Canadian; that there was no French Canadian among the top officials of the federal ministry of forestry, although Quebec has about one fourth of Canada's usable forests.

The grievances of the Québécois against British Canada have not always been as tangible as "who holds what job." One great cause of resentment among the French Canadians of Quebec is that so many of them speak English, while only a small percentage of British Canadians speak French. Issues like these are emotionally charged. Resentments of all kinds have built up for hundreds of years, and feelings run deep.

The majority of Québécois are almost certainly looking for a strong Quebec within the Canadian Confederation, but they are also very proud of their French-Canadian heritage. There is a small, yet vigorous, group among them who want Quebec to pull out of Canada entirely and go it alone. Originally known as *les séparatistes,* they have more recently preferred to be called *indépendantistes.* The *indépendantistes* are very active, and their influence on the existing political parties cannot be overestimated.

The Revolution Within. Perhaps even more important than the revolution against British Canada has been the revolution within the traditional institutions of French Quebec itself. In very large part the great changes that have occurred in Quebec stemmed originally from two developments. The first was the death in 1959 of Maurice Duplessis, the Conservative premier of Quebec who ruled the province with an exceptionally firm hand through most of the 1940's and 1950's. Following his death in 1959, the slogan "It's time for a change" became the watchword of Quebec politics. Another major factor in the revolution in Quebec was the enormous liberalization that took place within the Roman Catholic Church during the reign of Pope John XXIII (1958–63). Indeed Quebec's powerful and once ultraconservative Roman Catholic Church has become an important force for reform and change within the province.

Perhaps nowhere have the effects of the Quiet Revolution been so evident as in the field of public education, where an enormous overhaul of the existing system has taken place—with the approval of the Roman Catholic and Protestant churches. For the first time in the history of Quebec, education has come under provincial as well as religious control. Children in Quebec's public schools still receive religious instruction. Schools are still administered by Roman Catholic and Protestant boards. The schools themselves are either Roman Catholic schools conducted primarily in French (although there are a number conducting classes in English, especially in Montreal and Quebec City), or Protestant schools, conducted in English. However, over-all direction of the system is now in the hands of the Ministry of Education, which was first created in 1964.

Through the ministry, the provincial government has put a new emphasis on science, mathematics, technology, and business, in a system traditionally dominated by classics and theology. The idea has been to make education more practical, more relevant to modern life. A massive program of adult education has been undertaken, with particular emphasis on advanced technology. Quebeckers have become education-conscious as never before, and universities in the province are finding it difficult to cope with all their applications. Everywhere there is a sense of urgency, the collective effort of a people in a hurry to get somewhere through education.

THE PEOPLE

The new Québecois is still unique on the continent, but in a different way. He is no longer the isolated figure he once was. In fact, in his everyday life he is faced with the challenge of blending three civilizations, North American, Anglo-Saxon, and French. The Québecois functions in an atmosphere of North American comfort, and he demands the same high standard of living that prevails in much of the United States and Canada. He has come to respect the practicality and talent for organization of the English Canadian and increasingly strives for them. But finally he is the product of his French heritage. The new Québecois is even more determined than were his forefathers to preserve his French language and culture.

In the past French Canadians had large families and relied heavily on this tradition for survival as a group. Today the tradition of the large family has gone forever. That it has disappeared is in itself a sign of the Québecois' new confidence that he can not only survive but also maintain his identity in a country where he is greatly outnumbered. The Québecois gained enormous confidence from the success of Montreal's Expo 67, the great international world's fair held in Montreal in 1967. Expo 67 drew world attention to him as nothing before. The Québecois knows it might never have been accomplished without English-Canadian know-how, but he also knows that his artistic touch and creativity were important factors in making Expo one of the most praised and successful world exhibitions ever held.

Today the Québecois has found new ways to express his French language and culture. One outcome of the Quiet Revolution has been a new movement to maintain cultural links with the French-speaking nations of the world. This kind of activity has caused uneasiness in Ottawa, where it is felt that only the central government should be involved in international relations. As a result Quebec and Ottawa have been working to form joint delegations to the various conferences of French-speaking nations that are held throughout the world.

Another offshoot of the Quiet Revolution has been the emergence of the *chansonnier* on Quebec's cultural scene. *Chansonniers* (literally, "songsters") are a new breed of entertainers, who can best be described as modern-day troubadours. *Chansonniers* write and sing their own songs, which are in French. Their songs are about Quebec, its people, climate, cities, rivers, and lakes. Of course there are also many songs about love. Priding themselves on having created a truly Canadian form of music, the *chansonniers* are immensely popular within Quebec itself but are virtually unknown throughout the rest of Canada. This is another symptom of Canada's cultural disunity.

From Farm to City.   Traditionally the French Canadians of Quebec were a people of the soil. Farming was a living, a way of life, and, even more, an ideal, the very best way of life. In today's rapidly changing Quebec, life on the farms and in rural areas has probably changed least. There are no crowds, no mass transportation systems, no rushing to beat the clock. The rural Quebecker will probably go more out of his way

Quebec's country villages look much as they did 100 years ago.

than his city cousin to help a stranger. Families are still very close-knit, and the people are still deeply attached to their Roman Catholic faith. The big church with the tall steeple still dominates the landscape, and *le curé,* the country priest, still commands the respect and reverence he has always enjoyed. This is no longer necessarily true in the bigger cities, where the young French Canadian is inclined to blame Quebec's clergy for having contributed to making his forefathers endure many generations of inequality.

But the Quebec farmer is changing too. With progress and mechanization the peasant farmer, with his old horse-drawn plow, has given way to the agricultural businessman, who operates larger, more productive farms. With increased use of farm machinery, less farm labor is needed, and there has been a long-term exodus from the country to the cities of the province.

CITIES

Quebec's urban population has exceeded its rural population for over 50 years now. Today more than 70 percent of all Quebeckers live in urban areas. In the cities life is more hectic and less constrained; it is freer and easier. The Church does not play the dominant role in social life that it does in the country. Girls are more smartly dressed.

The Québecois loves to eat, and the big cities, Montreal especially, are known for their fine restaurants. Most of the better-known restaurants specialize in French cuisine, which tends to be more elaborate than traditional French-Canadian fare. As a matter of fact, hearty pea soup with pork is the dish for which Quebec is known. Pork is also the basis for many other traditional dishes, which include *tourtière* (a tasty pork pie), *ragoût de pattes* (pigs' feet stew), and *cretons,* which are slices of a kind of pork loaf (resembling head cheese), served cold.

Montreal.   This is Canada's largest city and the largest city in the world (after Paris) in which French is the predominant language. The population within Montreal's city limits is about 1,250,000, and the population of the entire metropolitan area is more than twice that.

Situated more than 1,000 miles (1,600 kilometers) from the Atlantic Ocean, but right on the St. Lawrence Seaway, Montreal is one of the busiest ports in the world. Along the waterfront are huge grain elevators, warehouses, oil tanks, and refineries. Crude oil brought into Montreal by tanker from Venezuela and the Middle East is refined and then transported as fuel oil, gasoline, and other products to various parts of Canada. Wheat comes in from the vast Canadian prairies. Montreal is one of the great wheat-shipping ports of the world.

Montreal is also one of the great industrial centers of Canada, turning out products of all kinds. Most of the big companies operating in Quebec have their main provincial offices in Montreal. Big factories belch their smoke out over the city, which, like many of the great urban centers in North America, has lately developed an air pollution problem.

Montreal is a cosmopolitan, sophisticated city. Two thirds of its population is French Canadian, and, in addition, most of the province's English-speaking population lives in or about Montreal. Many immigrants from the European continent have also settled here, including Italians, Germans, Greeks, and latter-day French immigrants. There are also a sizable number of Americans. But basically there are two distinct com-

The lights of Montreal's skyline are reflected in the river. This exciting modern city has become a symbol of Quebec's hopes for the future and a source of great pride for all Canadians.

munities in Montreal, with English Canadians concentrated in the western end of the city and the majority of the French living on the east side. The English community is on the whole quite prosperous. English Canadians still control most of the executive and managerial positions in Montreal's big businesses. English Canadian, British, and American money has done a lot to make Montreal the dynamic modern metropolis it is today. The French-speaking majority, for their part, would like to see their city become more French. Montreal has been the center of the Quebec independence movement and of protest marches and student unrest.

Quebec City.   About 150 miles (240 km.) northeast of Montreal on the St. Lawrence River is the provincial capital, Quebec City. Population within the city limits is about 186,000, and the population of the metropolitan area is about 480,000. Quebec is often called the most picturesque city on the continent.

A walk through Quebec's old, winding streets is a walk through the history of French Canada. The pace of life is more relaxed here than in bustling Montreal. Career opportunities are not as plentiful or impressive, but in compensation there is Old World charm in a setting of North American comfort.

Quebec is more a French city than Montreal. Only 5 percent of the population is of British descent, but English Quebeckers have their own

Quebec City, the provincial capital, has a unique charm.

schools and churches, an English-language television channel and radio station, and an English daily newspaper.

Other Cities. **Sherbrooke**, about 80 miles (130 km.) due east of Montreal, is called the Queen of the Eastern Townships. It has a population of about 80,000 and is an important manufacturing center for textiles and women's clothing, among other things. It is also the home of the University of Sherbrooke, a Roman Catholic institution established in 1954.

Trois Rivières (Three Rivers), about halfway between Montreal and Quebec on the St. Lawrence, is one of Canada's oldest settlements. Founded as a fur trading post in 1634, today it has a population of about 56,000 and is a major center for the manufacture of newsprint, the paper used in the production of newspapers.

Chicoutimi, with about 35,000 people, is the leading city of the Saguenay Valley, which is the greatest aluminum-producing region in Canada.

THE LAND

The Quebec of today, with its modern cities, its increasingly mechanized farms, and its quickening pace of life, is a far cry from the Quebec that Britain conquered more than 200 years ago. But in one way, as a glance at the map of the province makes clear, Quebec has not changed substantially. The vast majority of the people still live relatively near the St. Lawrence River. With a total area of almost 600,000 square miles (1,554,000 square kilometers), Quebec is big enough to accommodate half a dozen of the countries of Western Europe quite comfortably. This is a province where the land still dwarfs the people.

As in colonial days, most farming, commerce, and industry are still concentrated in the region known as the St. Lawrence Lowland, a tri-

In winter skiers flock to the snowy slopes of the Laurentians.

A group of rugged Quebec loggers work fast to prevent a jam.

angular-shaped basin with one apex in the area of Quebec City, a second around Montreal, and a third near Sherbrooke. But in large part, the industries of the St. Lawrence Lowland are dependent on the resources of less heavily settled or virtually unsettled parts of Quebec.

The natural resources are found in the Appalachian region, the Quebec Highlands, which occupy most of the area south and east of the St. Lawrence River, and in the vast Canadian, or Laurentian, Shield, which occupies approximately the northern five sixths of the province. The vast forests of these regions support a great amount of lumbering, and the lumber is the basis for Quebec's large paper and pulp industry. There is evidence of immense mineral deposits in the area that have scarcely been tapped. The rugged Gaspé Peninsula jutting out in the Atlantic Ocean has substantial copper reserves, which have only begun to be mined. And creating great excitement are the discoveries and the anticipation of future discoveries of minerals north of the 52nd parallel in that vast area known as New Quebec. Already some of the richest deposits of iron in the world have been located in New Quebec. Elsewhere throughout the province deposits of nickel, lead, silver, gold, granite, zinc, graphite, and other minerals are attracting foreign investment. In addition, some of the largest asbestos mines in the world are located in the Eastern Townships region, southeast of Montreal.

Perhaps the Canadian Shield's greatest gift to Quebec is hydroelectricity. The rivers that go tumbling through the Shield power huge turbines that light homes and keep machines running all over Quebec. The provincial government has been developing its hydroelectric resources at a staggering rate, and today Quebec produces more generated power per person than any other region in the world. And development continues. The 1960's saw the completion of the spectacular Daniel Johnson Dam, the highest multiple arch dam in the world. Rising high in the Canadian Shield, some 255 miles (410 km.) up the Manicouagan River, it creates a reservoir of 800 square miles (2,100 sq. km.) when full; this is one of the world's largest man-made reservoirs. For the future the Quebec Government has contracted for the bulk of the power from the huge Churchill Falls project, which was recently completed in neighboring Labrador. Projects like these help provide the cheap electricity vital for industrial expansion in Quebec.

Today agriculture remains an important part of Quebec's economy. Dairy farming is the source of most agricultural revenue, and also important are livestock raising, sugar beet and tobacco cultivation, and maple sugar and syrup production. With the increasing use of farm machinery, farm workers now constitute less than 10 percent of Quebec's total labor force. Farming itself, as a matter of fact, accounts for only 5 percent of the total production of Quebec's economy every year. But it is also the basis for the food and beverage processing industry, which is the province's largest industry. Paper and allied industries as a group are the province's second largest industry.

Of all the Canadian provinces Quebec is the most changing, the most talked about, the most different, and the most proud of its difference. It has its growing pains, and, quite naturally, the people of Quebec wonder at times how their province will eventually fit into the Canadian picture.

JO OUELLET, Editor, *The Quebecker*

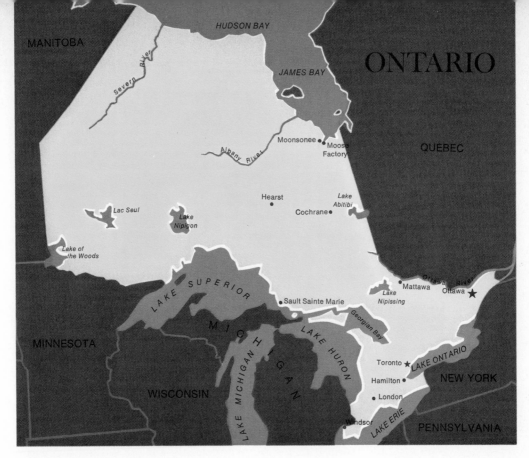

ONTARIO

ONTARIO

Both historically and geographically, Ontario is the heartland of Canada. It is the senior member of the Canadian family and site of the federal capital, Ottawa. A network of water highways connects Ontario with its prosperous neighbor to the south, the United States, and with the trade routes of the world. Because of these factors and because of its great size, wealth, productivity, and central location, Ontario holds a key position among the provinces.

Ontario is home to about a third of Canada's people, and this population of more than 8,000,000 is expected to double by 1985. It is lavishly supplied with raw materials, abundant water for transportation and low-cost power, fertile farmlands, minerals, renewable forests, valuable markets nearby for its raw materials and manufactured products, impressive scenery, and facilities for outdoor sports. War and rebellion have not scarred the land. Aside from a few skirmishes in 1812, Ontarians have lived in peace at home for more than 2 centuries. All these factors combine to make Ontario the base on which so much of modern Canada has been built.

THE LAND

Ontario's physical dimensions are on the grand scale: it is 1,300 highway miles (2,090 kilometers) from east to west and more than 1,000 miles (1,600 km.) from north to south. Its total area is 412,582 square

---

FACTS AND FIGURES

CAPITAL: Toronto.
MAJOR CITIES: Toronto, Hamilton, Ottawa, London, Windsor.
AREA: 412,582 sq. mi. (1,068,589 sq. km.).
POPULATION: 8,000,000 (estimate).
PHYSICAL FEATURES: Highest point—Ogidaki Moun-

tain (2,183 ft.; 665 m.). **Lowest point**—sea level. **Major rivers**—St. Lawrence, Albany, Severn, Ottawa. **Major lakes**—Nipigon, Lake of the Woods, Seul, Nipissing, Abitibi.

PROVINCIAL MOTTO: *Ut incepit fidelis sic permanet* ("As loyal she began so she remains").

---

miles (1,068,589 square kilometers). The province is so wide that it has two time zones—1,000 miles (1,600 km.) in the Eastern Time Zone and 300 miles (480 km.) in the Central Time Zone. People traveling from the Quebec border in the east to the western province of Manitoba must adjust their watches before they get to the western border. The St. Lawrence River and four of the Great Lakes form the southern boundary, giving Ontario a freshwater coastline of 2,362 miles (3,800 km.). On the north is a 680-mile (1,094 km.) saltwater coastline.

Ontario may be divided into two distinct regions, northern and southern Ontario. There are great contrasts between the two: rattlesnakes, peaches, grapes, wild swamp orchids, and tobacco farms in the south; reindeer moss and polar bears in the far north. Northern Ontario has seven eighths of the territory and one tenth of the people of the province. More than half of it is a low, rocky plateau that was gouged and twisted by the glaciers of the Ice Age. Because of this glacial action Ontario has more than 250,000 lakes. It is part of the Canadian Shield, a pre-Cambrian geological formation that is extremely rich in minerals. Rolling plains run south and west from the Shield. (Details about the Canadian Shield can be found in the article on NORTH AMERICA.)

The dividing line usually recognized between northern and southern Ontario extends from Mattawa on the Ottawa River through Lake Nipissing and along the French River to Georgian Bay. In addition to this watery boundary, southern Ontario is surrounded by lakes Ontario, Erie, and Huron, making it, in effect, almost an island. Its outstanding geological feature is the Niagara Escarpment, a cliff or plateau that extends from Niagara Falls west and north for about 250 miles (400 km.). Since it is sheltered by the Niagara Escarpment from severe cold weather, the Niagara Peninsula is one of the world's great fruit-growing areas.

Such a vast range of latitude means great variations in climate. The Upper Great Lakes area is very cold in winter. So is the north in general. The peach farmer in Niagara shudders when he hears the temperature readings from northern Ontario. Temperatures in Cochrane, 500 miles (800 km.) north of Toronto, vary from 12 degrees Fahrenheit to –9 degrees F. (–11 degrees Celsius to –23 degrees C.) in January. In contrast Windsor, Ontario's fourth largest city, located just south of Detroit across the international border, has a January temperature range of 32 degrees F. to 20 degrees F. (0 degrees C. to –7 degrees C.).

Ontarians call their extreme south the Banana Belt because the climate along the Lower Great Lakes is much milder than it is in Canada's Prairie Provinces or in many parts of the northern United States. The large bodies of water minimize abrupt changes of temperature between seasons or between night and day. Where Ontario dips lowest, it is farther south, for instance, than northern California in the United States. Naturally this pleasant southern region is where most Ontarians prefer to live.

"Ontario" is an Indian word meaning "beautiful lake," a most appropriate name. Nineteen percent of the province's surface area is water. Its climate, history, business, and pleasure have all been crucially affected by its lakes and rivers. Today Ontario's thousands of northern lakes serve as a wonderland for pleasure-seekers and a hunting ground for prospectors, who have long searched the Canadian Shield for precious metals. The great rivers that cross Ontario served in the beginning to bring explorers and fur traders into the heart of the New World and thus made possible the conquest of the North American continent.

HISTORY

The region that is now Ontario was originally inhabited by Eskimo and Indians. It was discovered and explored mainly by the French, settled largely by colonists from the newly independent United States, and expanded by the British. Later it was brought to its present growth and prosperity by Canadians of Italian, Ukrainian, Jewish, Polish, German, Dutch, Icelandic, Greek, Czech, Hungarian, and Asian backgrounds. Its original people, the Indians, numbered 50,000 in 1969, giving Ontario the largest Indian population of any Canadian province.

The exploration and settlement of Ontario followed its vast network of waterways. The first white man to explore the region was Samuel de Champlain, in 1613 and 1615. All of the original exploration along freshwater routes was done by the French. They built their earliest forts at portages on the water trails of the great fur trade.

Saltwater exploration, on the other hand, was in British hands. The first British settlement was far north, at Moose Factory, on James Bay. This was a Hudson's Bay Company post, started just after King Charles II had bestowed upon the Hudson's Bay Company of fur traders the magnificent gift of a quarter of a continent. That is, the King granted the company the watershed of all the rivers that flowed into Hudson Bay. This disregard for the claims of the French aroused extreme hostility among French fur traders, who had, after all, reached Ontario first. For many decades the territory between Hudson Bay on the north and the French forts along the Great Lakes on the south was fiercely disputed.

The struggle for the New World became part of the Seven Years War between France and Britain (1756–63). The North American phase of the war was called the French and Indian War. In a decisive battle at Quebec (1759), Britain's General James Wolfe defeated the French commander, Louis Joseph, Marquis de Montcalm, although Wolfe himself died in the battle and Montcalm was seriously wounded and died the next day. The British victory not only made the territory that is now southern Ontario British, it also freed the British colonies farther south, in what is now the United States, to rebel against the mother country. As strange as this sounds, many historians believe that it was, in part, fear of the French in Canada interfering in their affairs that had prevented the American colonies from rebelling earlier.

When the United States of America was created by the American Revolution, thousands of citizens in the new nation preferred to remain under British rule. They flooded northward. Called Tories in the United States and United Empire Loyalists in Ontario, they gave Ontario the peculiar distinction of having its first major wave of immigrants come from North America—not from Europe.

Shortly after their arrival, the Loyalists made it clear that they did not care to live under the seignorial landholding system and French civil law of Quebec. So it was decided to detach the part of Quebec that lay west of the Ottawa River and from it form a separate province called the Province of Upper Canada. The new province was created by the Constitutional Act of 1791 and included most of what is now southern Ontario. During the War of 1812 between Britain and the United States, there were skirmishes and battles between British and American soldiers along the borders of southern Ontario. But most of the American immigrants had little interest in their former country's quarrel with Britain.

Canada became a self-governing British dominion as a result of Confederation in 1867. Confederation united four provinces—Nova Scotia, New Brunswick, Quebec (Lower Canada), and the province that had been Upper Canada. The new, greatly extended province took back its original name, Ontario. Since Confederation, Ontario's growth has been peaceful —and spectacular.

One of the first requirements under Confederation was the ambitious project of building a railway from coast to coast. In 1885 the project was completed, binding the huge, sprawling land into a single nation. The railroad's completion helped make Ontario the heartland of Canada. With untapped riches beneath its soil and agricultural wealth spreading across its plains, the province flourished. In the 20th century immigration constantly increased its population and the growing labor force unlocked its wealth.

GOVERNMENT

Ontario is governed under the parliamentary system. The system includes a legislative assembly of 117 seats, an executive council (cabinet), and a lieutenant governor whose functions are largely ceremonial. Real executive power is in the hands of the Cabinet and the premier, or provincial prime minister. This provincial office should not be confused with that of the federal prime minister, head of the confederated Canadian Government. The premier of Ontario is the leader of his party. He and his cabinet members are drawn from the majority party in the legislature, which means that all cabinet officers must stand for election before appointment and represent the winning party. The legislature is elected by popular vote of all citizens 18 and over.

Ontarians refer to their premier and his Cabinet as "the government." In the parliamentary system the executive and legislative leadership is always of the same party and stands for the same policies. The government can be put out of power if it loses a vote of confidence in the legislature. If the premier wishes to test popular support of his policies, he may call for a general election at any time. Either he and his party are returned to power, in which case the premier remains in office, or they are defeated by the opposing party, and "the government falls." This means that the winning party forms a new Cabinet. In any case, 5 years is the maximum time that any provincial government can remain in power without going to the people for a fresh mandate. This system is very flexible and democratic, making it impossible for a government that lacks support in the legislative assembly to stay in power for a fixed term, imposing its policies on the country against the judgment and general wishes of the electorate.

The traditional parties in Ontario are the Progressive Conservatives and the Liberals. In recent years two other parties have emerged, the New Democratic Party and the Social Credit Party. The Communist Party is legal in Ontario and has occasionally elected a member or two to the legislature. The legislature meets in Toronto. Ontarians also elect representatives to the federal government at Ottawa.

THE ECONOMY

Ontario's gross provincial product exceeds $29,000,000,000, which means that the province earns 40 percent of the Canadian national income. Ontarians have the highest average personal incomes in Canada, too. The province itself is the richest market in the country, and in addition it is located near heavily populated parts of the United States. Ontario's factories, rising to the challenge of these markets, produce half of Canada's manufactured goods. A quarter of the work force is engaged in manufacturing. Ontario turns out 80 percent of Canada's steel, a quarter of its pulp and paper and agricultural products, and most of its automobiles, rubber, and electrical goods. The list of products includes cigarettes, canned goods, outboard motors, textiles, pulp and paper, furs, plastics, locomotives, books, prefabricated homes, chemicals, drugs, synthetic fabrics, packaged goods, furniture, electronic equipment, petroleum products, clothing, and processed foods. Ontario's factories also turn out combines, harvesters, tractors, and tilling equipment, earning many millions of dollars annually in export sales. Aircraft made in Toronto accounts for most of the Canadian aviation industry's exports to countries all over the world. Airplanes such as the Beaver, Caribou, Buffalo, and Twin Otter, tailored for Canadian bush operations with short takeoffs and landings, are very popular in other countries.

But manufacturing is not Ontario's only source of income. The province is rich in timber, minerals, and agricultural resources. Ontario still has immense forests. Pulp for newsprint accounts for over half the value

This flourishing tobacco farm is located in southern Ontario.

of forest production. The bulk of it is exported to the United States. Many of the great daily newspapers in the United States were once part of evergreen trees growing in the sweeping forests of Ontario. To protect this great forest heritage, the government operates a fleet of 40 planes to spot forest fires. These planes aid ground forces, because it is easier to spot fires in their early stages from the air. These planes are equipped to attack fires with water bombs.

Ontario's greatest treasure chest is in its attic. Minerals funnel down from the north. The Canadian Shield is unbelievably rich in nickel, copper, asbestos, iron ore, gold, uranium, platinum, cobalt, zinc, silver, and sulfur. Even more exciting to Ontarians is the knowledge that they have barely begun to tap their hidden wealth.

Ontario produces 57 percent of the world's nickel. It also possesses the largest known deposits of uranium on earth. Many vital hardening metals are dug from Ontario rock. Mining towns are scattered throughout the rock country. New model communities keep springing up wherever new discoveries are made. The most important nonmetallic mineral is salt. Ontario can supply almost all the salt Canada needs.

Ontario lacks coal, oil, and natural gas. It imports coal from the United States, just south of the lower Great Lakes, while oil and gas come by pipeline from the Canadian Prairies. This lack is balanced by intensive development of waterpower. Ontario Hydro, a state-owned utility, is one of the world's great hydroelectric undertakings, with a current generating capacity of 11,300,000 kilowatts. Generating stations near Niagara Falls alone have a capacity of 2,000,000 kilowatts. Ontario Hydro has, in recent years, pioneered in the development of thermal (steam-electric) generating plants using (most recently) nuclear energy.

Efficient, modern farming methods have made it possible for fewer people to plant, tend, and harvest Ontario's crops. This means that more people can go to the cities and work in industry. Only 7 percent of Ontario's people live on farms. However, mechanization of farms has developed to such an extent that a farmer today can feed himself and 39 nonfarmers.

Major agricultural areas are in the southwestern and central regions and in the valleys of the St. Lawrence and Ottawa rivers. Hardier crops can be grown quite far north in the Cochrane Clay Belt. In eastern farms dairying and livestock raising are dominant.

Visitors from the United States are often amazed when they see the extensive vineyards and tobacco fields of southern Ontario. In North America only California exceeds Ontario in the production of wine. Most vineyards are in the Niagara Peninsula. Fruits of all kinds grow on the peninsula and along the shores of Lake Erie.

Southwestern Ontario is famous for tobacco, the province's largest cash crop. The tobacco grown here supplies almost all of Canada's market and is exported to many countries. Migrant tobacco pickers come from as far away as Kentucky, Virginia, and the Carolinas to harvest the crops. The region also has an intensive market-vegetable production, especially in corn, tomatoes, onions, sugar beets, and soybeans.

CITIES

The major cities of Ontario are in the southern part of the province. They include Toronto, the provincial capital and the second largest city

Toronto's impressive City Hall symbolizes Ontario's future.

in Canada; Ottawa, the federal capital; and Hamilton, Windsor, and London, which are manufacturing and agricultural centers. (Toronto and Ottawa are also manufacturing centers.)

Major cities have not yet developed in northern Ontario. However, centers like Thunder Bay, Sudbury, Sault Ste. Marie, Timmins, and Kirkland Lake may one day become major cities. They are also involved in the great businesses of the north: lumber, paper production, shipping, mining, and steel production. As the north develops, these cities will inevitably grow in size and importance. (Separate discussions of Toronto, Ottawa, and Hamilton appear in CANADIAN CITIES.)

Toronto, with a population in its metropolitan area of more than 2,600,000 people, in many ways dominates the life of the province. This is not true just because of the city's size and its role as provincial capital. Toronto is dominant because it enters into almost every aspect of the province's life. It is a major port because of its location on the St. Lawrence Seaway. It is an industrial and manufacturing center because, in part, of its easy access to both raw materials and markets. It is a financial and business center for all of Canada. And, perhaps most important of all, it is a leading educational and cultural center.

Ottawa, the federal capital of Canada and the residence of the governor-general, has a population in the city proper of over 300,000 people and in its metropolitan area of over 600,000. Situated literally at

The changing of the guard in front of Parliament in Ottawa.

the Ontario-Quebec border (and with a significant French-speaking population of its own), Ottawa represents Canada's historic desire to join together its English and French traditions.

The federal Parliament buildings, standing on a cliff above the Ottawa River, are a familiar sight to visitors from all over the world.

Hamilton, close to Ottawa in size, is one of Canada's most important industrial centers. Its excellent location on Lake Ontario long ago made it an important Great Lakes port; its position was even further improved by the development of the St. Lawrence Seaway, which made it accessible to oceangoing ships. **Windsor**, another important industrial center, lies just across the Detroit River from Detroit, Michigan. Good relations between the United States and Canada have made international border-crossing a daily event for many Americans and Canadians in the adjoining cities.

London, lying inland from Lake Erie, is situated in the heart of one of North America's richest agricultural areas. It has become an industrial city as well as a center for the marketing of agricultural products.

TRANSPORTATION

Means of transportation in Ontario vary widely, from motorized freight canoes, snowmobiles, and tractor trains in the north, to the immense railroad and harbor facilities of the south. Historically, rivers and lakes provided Ontario's first highways. Even today waterways continue to provide a cheap and direct means of transportation. The St. Lawrence Seaway brings oceangoing vessels from the Atlantic to Ontario's ports. A proposed saltwater port at Moosonee in James Bay would give Ontario direct shipping to Europe by way of the northern route. Major ports on the continental waterways of the Great Lakes handle cargo by the millions of tons.

The Welland Canal is a vital link in the St. Lawrence Seaway.

The showplace of the inland ocean system is Niagara Falls. The power and beauty of the great cataract are shared by the United States and Canada. Millions of visitors come to marvel, and many stay in the hotels and tourist facilities on the Canadian side of the Falls, where the view is especially spectacular. Niagara's statistics are dazzling: 15,000,000 cubic feet of water per minute tumble over the two precipices—the American Falls and the Canadian Horseshoe Falls.

Shipping bypasses the falls by means of a canal. When a freighter goes around Niagara Falls, it climbs "stairs" to get from Ontario to Lake Erie. The ship is lifted from one level to the next higher level by canal operators raising the water level in the locks. To someone standing in a nearby peach orchard, this presents a strange sight: a salt-stained, ocean-going freighter, moving along the canal, seems to drift above the treetops and through the orchard.

Ontario is served by three east–west interprovincial railroads. The province also has one north–south rail line, the Ontario Northland Railway, which has its northern terminus at Moosonee on James Bay. Trains on this line, which stop at mileposts to pick up prospectors or drop off hunters, fishermen, and sightseers, have helped to open up the mines and the paper industry in the Abitibi region and elsewhere. The Algoma Central runs through rich resource country, from Sault Ste. Marie to Hearst, in northwestern Ontario. New lines are built as new resources are discovered and new industries are developed to exploit them.

Railways also serve city-dwellers. Government-owned, high speed "GO" trains bring commuters into Toronto from outlying suburbs to the east and the west. Toronto's subway system is also being extended.

Air travel has been vital to Ontario since the beginnings of the air age. The province now has many airports, water-landing facilities, and countless thousands of lakes where small aircraft can land. Air transportation makes it possible to reach remote spots that were once accessible only on foot or by pack train.

Ontario has 23,000 miles (37,000 km.) of paved highway, including the longest toll-free superhighway in North America and the longest stretch of 12-lane freeway in the world. The province is considered a leader in highway development. Major highways link Ontario with New York, Michigan, and Minnesota.

EDUCATION

Ontario places such a high priority on the education of its citizens that it spends almost half its annual budget on its extensive school system. The province has both a department of education and a department of university affairs. School is free and compulsory for children up to the age of 16. Children in remote villages of the north sometimes go to school in railway school cars. These cars are mobile classrooms that are moved from place to place and set up for regularly scheduled classes on railway sidings near the communities they serve. High schools in Ontario have one more grade than American high schools do. The high school graduate in Ontario has completed the 13th grade. His education is roughly equivalent to that of the American student who has just finished his first year of college.

There are 16 degree-granting universities in Ontario. Total university enrollment is over 103,000. There are also community colleges of applied arts and technology, teachers colleges, nursing schools, and countless technical schools. University scholarships and student loans are available for students with good academic standing.

These handsome buildings are part of the University of Toronto.

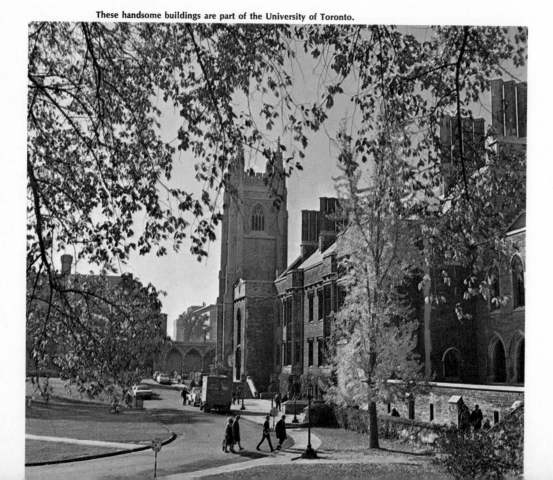

Of the universities, the largest and oldest is the University of Toronto, which includes three autonomous universities, three theological colleges, and one graduate college. The University of Toronto has a present enrollment of just over 20,000 full-time students.

LEISURE

Most of the people of the province live in southern Ontario. They don't stay at home on pleasant summer weekends if they can help it. "Going to the cottage" or "going to the lake" somewhere to the north is a way of life for all who can manage it.

Sometimes vacationers go to the parks, 100 of them provincial, three maintained by the federal government. However, the whole northland is still one gigantic park, with thousands of lakes and hundreds of rivers. Under the new pressures of growing population, conservation of Ontario's vast wilderness has become an important consideration.

Canadians naturally take to water and snow. In fine weather the sound of the outboard motor resounds through the north, where waterways offer long and sheltered trips. The Indian names of Ontario's northern vacation areas have the lyrical sound of talking waterfalls: Manitoulin, Nipigon, Wawa, Agawa, Kawartha, Nipissing, Moosonee, Hurricanaw, and Abitibi. In winter the whine of the snowmobile takes the place of the throb of the outboard motor. The fast, lightweight snowmobile is helping to open up the north in many practical ways. It is also the newest plaything for many Ontarians.

Curling, a game that is related to bowling but uses granite stones slid over the ice, is immensely popular. It is enjoyed by people of all

Curling is one of the most popular sports in Canada.

ages. In smaller towns, local curling clubs frequently serve as general social centers. People follow curling competitions with the furious interest that Americans devote to baseball and football. In most towns the hockey arena is located near the curling rink. Hockey is Canada's unofficial national sport. Ontario youngsters play hockey from the time they are little the way boys in the United States play sandlot baseball.

THE ARTS

Ontario's cultural institutions are almost as much a part of its educational system as its schools. The provincial government gives an increasing amount of aid to museums, art galleries, and libraries. Private organizations, of course, also offer support to cultural institutions. The museums in Toronto, Ottawa, and London are particularly outstanding. The Royal Ontario Museum in Toronto is superb. The new Centennial Science Centre in Toronto has attracted international acclaim.

There are thousands of drama groups, choirs, orchestras, bands, art clubs, and galleries in Ontario. Music is the most popular of the performing arts. Competitive festivals are held throughout the province, while the best of the international shows and artists, both popular and classical, tour Ontario. They are brought to Toronto by the O'Keefe Centre, the Royal Alexandra Theatre, and to Ottawa by the National Arts Centre. The Stratford Shakespearean Festival is world-famous.

Much of Ontario's cultural excitement centers in Toronto. The city is home to the Toronto Symphony, the National Ballet Company, the St. Lawrence Centre for the Arts, the Canadian Folk Arts Council, the Canadian Opera Company, and the National Youth Orchestra. Toronto supports two legitimate theaters plus numerous playhouses and little theaters. It is a big production center for television, radio, films, and popular music. Because Toronto is the largest English-speaking Canadian city, it has become the publishing center for English-speaking Canada.

The Canadian folk arts festivals, held across Canada, have their headquarters in Toronto. Each year they stage the National Folk Arts Festival —one of the largest and most professionally staged folk spectacles on the continent.

Toronto also holds an annual Metro International Caravan, where citizens can visit and discover 33 different cultures. The pavilion of each ethnic group in the metropolitan area presents its own atmosphere, food, crafts, and performing arts. "Eat and shop around the world, at home" is the slogan. Shuttling buses link the different halls, which is why Toronto gives the name "Caravan" to this world tour in miniature. It expresses vividly the new Ontario mosaic of peoples. Half of all the immigrants coming to Canada settle in Ontario.

Because of its resources, its productivity, and its cultural, social, and governmental developments, Ontario will continue to be the foundation of Canada's development. It is one of the fastest growing areas anywhere in the world. The development of new technologies, new mineral discoveries, and expanding world markets indicate an enormous and rapid economic growth in the future for Ontario. This promise is of great importance for all Canada, for in many ways Ontario may be the key to Canada's future.

JOHN FISHER, President, John Fisher Enterprises Limited
Former Commissioner, Canadian Centennial Commission

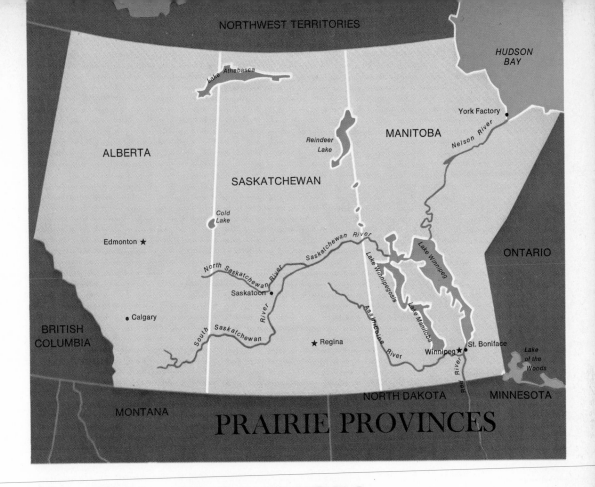

NORTHWEST TERRITORIES

HUDSON
BAY

Lake Athabasca

York Factory

Nelson River

*Reindeer
Lake*

MANITOBA

ALBERTA

SASKATCHEWAN

*Cold
Lake*

Edmonton ★

ONTARIO

North Saskatchewan River

Saskatchewan River

Lake Winnipeg

Saskatoon

Lake Winnipegosis

• Calgary

South Saskatchewan

Lake Manitoba

BRITISH
COLUMBIA

Assiniboine River

★ Regina

Winnipeg ★ St. Boniface

*Lake
of the
Woods*

Red River

NORTH DAKOTA

MINNESOTA

MONTANA

PRAIRIE PROVINCES

PRAIRIE PROVINCES

Early in the 20th century, the Canadian Government advertised in foreign newspapers: "Canada has free land." In 1905 the German Government hotly protested this practice, declaring: ". . . the attempt to lure our fellow countrymen to this desert subarctic is to be denounced as criminal." But the Germans and other Europeans kept coming anyway. So did Americans, for by 1905 the frontier was passing in the United States, and the best land was already claimed. Until 1914 hundreds of thousands of immigrants poured in from Eastern Canada, Britain, Germany, Poland, and Russia, riding the long colonial trains that chuffed across Lake Superior's northern shore into the Canadian West. The immigrants did not seem to care that they had little or no farming experience, that they were ill-prepared to face life on the frontier, or that temperatures in many areas were searing hot or below zero. "Free land!" was the cry.

The best free land was mostly in the prairies, due north of Minnesota, North Dakota, and Montana. "Prairie" comes from the French word meaning "meadow." A belt of fertile grasslands, rising progressively in steppes toward the west, covered the southern half of the Prairie Provinces of Manitoba, Saskatchewan, and Alberta and gave them their nickname. For a $10 registration fee a man could get 160 acres (395 hectares) plus the chance to acquire another 160 acres later.

PRAIRIE PROVINCES

ALBERTA is the name of the province.
CAPITAL: Edmonton.
MAJOR CITIES: Edmonton, Calgary.
AREA: 255,285 sq. mi. (661,288 sq. km.).
POPULATION: 1,700,000 (estimate).
PHYSICAL FEATURES: Highest point—Mount Columbia (12,294 ft.; 3,747 m.). **Lowest point**—Fort Smith (576 ft.; 176 m.). **Major rivers**—Athabasca, Pembina, Peace, Hay, North and South Saskatchewan, Red Deer. **Major lakes**—Athabasca, Claire, Lesser Slave.

MANITOBA is the name of the province.
CAPITAL: Winnipeg.
MAJOR CITY: Winnipeg.
AREA: 251,000 sq. mi. (650,090 sq. km.).

POPULATION: 1,000,000 (estimate).
PHYSICAL FEATURES: Highest point—Baldy Mountain (2,727 ft.; 831 m.). **Lowest point**—sea level. **Major rivers**—Assiniboine, Nelson, Churchill, Red, Winnipeg. **Major lakes**—Winnipeg, Winnipegosis, Manitoba.

SASKATCHEWAN is the name of the province.
CAPITAL: Regina.
MAJOR CITIES: Regina, Saskatoon.
AREA: 251,700 sq. mi. (651,903 sq. km.).
POPULATION: 900,000 (estimate).
PHYSICAL FEATURES: Highest point—Cypress Hills (4,546 ft.; 1,386 m.). **Lowest point**—Lake Athabasca (699 ft.; 213 m.). **Major rivers**—North and South Saskatchewan, Churchill, Qu'Appelle, Souris, Assiniboine. **Major lakes**—Athabasca, Reindeer.

This was the boom period of western growth. In 1891 only 5 percent of Canada's 4,800,000 people lived west of Ontario; 30 years later, it was 28 percent. Now about a sixth of Canada's population live in the three Prairie Provinces—over 1,700,000 in Alberta, and about 1,000,000 each in Saskatchewan and Manitoba.

The growth of the Prairie Provinces changed Canada in important ways. It expanded and strengthened the Canadian economy enormously, for the region became one of the world's greatest wheat-growing centers. It still holds much of the untapped freshwater resources of the North American continent. Increasingly it is proving to be a valuable source of mineral wealth—crude oil, natural gas, uranium, and potash—all vital to Canada's expanding industrial development.

The settlement of the prairies also broadened the whole sense of what it meant to be a Canadian. It created new activities and opportunities. Immigrants brought new languages and customs into a land that had previously been overwhelmingly dominated by persons of British and French descent. The New Canadians, as they were called, became an important force in the life of the nation.

New Canadians

The term "New Canadian" can refer to any immigrant to Canada, but it usually means immigrants whose mother tongue is neither English nor French. New Canadians in the Prairie Provinces have generally come from Europe, although the Chinese played an important role in construction of the Western railroads. The greatest influx of New Canadians started around the beginning of the 20th century. Immigration rose to a peak in 1914, came to a standstill during World War I, and then resumed at a reduced rate in the 1920's. It nearly came to a halt during the Depression of the 1930's but picked up again after World War II. Many immigrants were displaced persons who had lost their homes in the war. As an underpopulated country, Canada urgently needed immigrants and has always been kind to them. Immigration continues today, but with the recent increase in use of farm machinery the farm population has declined. Most New Canadians who go west now migrate to the cities.

In Manitoba and Alberta about 45 percent of the people are either descendants of immigrants or immigrants themselves. In Saskatchewan the figure is even higher, about 50 percent. Germans and Ukrainians are the largest ethnic groups, but there are many others, including Scandinavians, Russians, Austrians, Italians, Poles, Icelanders, and even some Frenchmen (from France, not Quebec).

The Pioneers Arrive. Early in the 20th century when immigration was at its height, it is said that in Winnipeg, Manitoba, as many as 70 languages could be heard on the city's streets. Of these English was probably not the most common. Many immigrants were waiting for a chance to get into the United States. Others stayed in Winnipeg, and a great many more moved out into the open prairies.

On the prairie, the settler found himself in a land of overwhelming emptiness—a huge sea of grass stretching toward the horizon. Typically he built a hut of sod, for there were few trees, set his plow against the virgin prairie grass, and settled down with his family to a life of harsh isolation. But many from Central and Eastern Europe broke this pattern and formed group settlements. Instead of living on individual farms, they clustered in small villages like those they had left behind in Europe. From this center they went out to work their lands.

The Canadian Mosaic. In time changes came to the block settlements of the West. Villages have been modernized, landholdings have been reorganized and consolidated, and life styles have become more Canadian. But even today parts of the West have a definite European look. Reflecting the Eastern European immigration, the prairies are dotted with the onion-domed Orthodox churches common in Eastern Europe. Where Frenchmen settled, for instance along the Red River below Winnipeg, one finds the narrow, deep farms reminiscent of the French countryside or of Quebec. Often farmhouses are close together, forming a kind of rural street. Whole towns are still inhabited by ethnic groups that keep up their old customs and beliefs. The Icelandic colony, Gimli (Paradise), on Lake Winnipeg, famous for its literature, is an example

A Ukrainian church in Manitoba, a piece of the Canadian mosaic.

of such a town. Perhaps the most clannish of New Canadians are the Doukhobors, an intensely religious sect from Russia that came originally to Saskatchewan.

Aside from groups like these, most New Canadians have become very much a part of the mainstream of Canadian life. Yet they also make a conscious effort to hold onto their own special ways. There is a stress on ethnic pride, speaking the mother tongue, and wearing the national costumes. Visitors from the United States are surprised at how many second-generation New Canadians, with parents born in Canada, still speak the language of their European grandparents. Of course New Canadians speak English, too, and attend English-speaking public schools.

Canadians use the word "mosaic" to describe the individuality of the nation's immigrant groups. They contrast this mosaic with the melting pot tradition of Americanization in the United States, which aims to make all newcomers typical Americans.

The Land

What kind of land did the homesteaders find? The eastern third of the Prairie Provinces is covered by a great half-horseshoe of land curving down from the Arctic southeastward around Hudson Bay. This is the Laurentian, or Canadian, Shield, a treasure-house of forests and water-power, sprinkled with thousands of lakes that are linked by countless streams. To the south the Shield is edged by a belt of parklands, woods, and fields that merge still farther south into the prairies. Almost all homesteaders settled on the fertile prairies. There, hundreds of miles of shimmering wheat fields have given this part of Canada the title Granary of the Western World.

Yet the German Government was not far wrong when it described these Canadian prairies as "desert subarctic." The climate of the prairies is blisteringly hot in summer and devastatingly cold in winter. In Winnipeg, Manitoba, temperatures have been known to fall to –54 degrees Fahrenheit (–47 degrees Celsius)—bitter cold even for Canada—and sum-

A western Indian woman gathers wild rice in the traditional way.

mer temperatures have gone as high as 108 degrees F. (42 degrees C.). In Regina, capital of Saskatchewan, the extreme range has been from –56 degrees F. (–48 degrees C.) to 110 degrees F. (43 degrees C.). Prairie weather is highly variable and unpredictable as well. There are no nearby oceans to moderate extremes of hot or cold, or mountains to block the air masses that sweep across the steppes from north to south. Temperatures may rise or fall 50 degrees in a matter of hours. Early or late winter can bring tornadoes, and midwinter brings blizzards. In late summer a sudden frost can destroy a wheat crop and wipe out a year's work. During the growing season there is the danger of droughts.

The vagaries of climate have brought incalculable grief to the farmers. By far the worst time was the 1930's, an era still recalled with horror in the West. Part of the problem was that there were too many farms, and too much grassland had been plowed up and cultivated. The 1930's had been preceded by periods of good rainfall and high wheat and beef prices, encouraging farm expansion. Optimistically, farmers bought land and machinery, planted heavily, and increased their livestock.

Then in the 1930's the prairies suffered year after year of parching drought. With much of the natural grass cover plowed away, the soil had little to bind it. The land was devastated by wind erosion, like the Dust Bowl in the United States that suffered the same fate at that time. Mile after mile of wheat fields was transformed into dunes of windblown topsoil. At the same time, because of the worldwide economic depression, farmers could not even get a good price for the little they managed to raise. Thousands of farmers went into bankruptcy.

Prairie farmers learned some terrible lessons from the disaster. Today they know the limits of their land. They know the rainy fertile regions where a good living can be made from a small farm, and the risky areas where even 1,000 acres (2,500 hectares) might not be enough. The farmers, as well as the federal government in Ottawa, have realized that they must not overburden the land. Programs have been developed to provide irrigation and promote conservation and wise use of the land.

Beautiful Lake Louise, Alberta, is cradled in the Rockies.

Grain elevators rise at a railroad siding on the vast prairies.

Economy

Today only Saskatchewan is predominantly agricultural. In Manitoba and Alberta, agriculture accounts for a fourth or a fifth of the total value of provincial production, but in Saskatchewan it still accounts for more than half. Even there, however, manufacturing is growing and mineral production has increased enormously in the past 10 years. Saskatchewan's potash deposits could keep the world's underdeveloped areas in fertilizer for many years, and there is also a wealth of oil and natural gas. Northern Saskatchewan is a place of deep woods, where both lumbering and the tourist industry prosper.

Nevertheless, grain is still the mainstay. The province's 86,000 farms, averaging 780 acres (1,900 hectares), make up a third of Canada's farmland. Wheat farming requires large acreages and lends itself to a high degree of mechanization. So farming has become big business, and the value of a farmer's land and equipment may run into several hundred thousand dollars. Yet he still has to worry about the demand for wheat on the international market. If the crop is good throughout the world, prices decline. The Canadian Wheat Board, an agency of the federal government, guarantees a minimum price per bushel, but may not be able to do this for the entire crop. Then the farmer has to store his wheat until demand increases. It can happen that a farmer with nearly $100,000 worth of land, equipment, and stored wheat can have little actual cash in hand. As a result many farmers are diversifying.

The same pattern applies also in the provinces on either side of Saskatchewan—Manitoba and Alberta. There cattle ranching vies with wheat farming, and many other economic activities—food processing, distribution of supplies and equipment, transportation of produce—depend directly on farming.

Manitoba, settled earlier than other western provinces, is the transitional province between East and West. It is a land of lakes, including the biggest lake in the Prairie Provinces. It is the most industrialized of the Prairie Provinces and the most richly endowed with hydroelectric resources. The second largest nickel-mining and -processing center in the world is at Thompson. Whiteshell, northeast of Winnipeg, is the site of Canada's second nuclear research center.

Extraction of oil and natural gas is vital to the wealth and security of Alberta. The sight of oil wells being drilled, completed wells pumping, and great refineries and tanks is a constant reminder to Albertans of the value of their "black gold." Manufacturing is also of growing importance. In western Alberta, the prairies give way to the Rocky Mountains. The spectacular peaks rising beyond the oil derricks remind Albertans of another kind of value: the overwhelming beauty of their land. Of the territory set aside by Canada to be preserved in a state of nature, over half is in Alberta, including 5 national parks and 43 provincial parks. Banff National Park and the serene splendor of Lake Louise, reflecting snowcapped peaks, draw visitors from all over the world.

Politics

Prairie people traditionally distrust the East. By "the East" they mean Ontario and Quebec, Canada's centers of wealth and power, and Ottawa, seat of the federal government. It is a widely held western opinion that the East governs Canada at the expense of the West. Prairie farmers complain about government farm policies. They often express their antagonism by electing politicians who are outside the two mainstream parties of Canada, the Liberals and the Progressive Conservatives. For instance, the Social Credit Party, a minor party that has never formed a national government, once controlled Alberta's government.

Socialism and Co-operatives.   Another minor party that has profited from anti-East sentiment is the New Democratic Party, Canada's socialist party. The idea of collective ownership has long had considerable appeal in the Prairie Provinces. Farmers realized that they were going to have to band together to prevent abuses by powerful grain storage operators and by the railroads. So they formed marketing co-operatives. Today co-operatives remain a distinctive part of life in the Prairie Provinces. In Saskatchewan almost all farmers belong to the Saskatchewan Wheat Pool, the largest primary grain-handling organization in the world.

In politics, the mildly socialist Cooperative Commonwealth Federation (CCF) held power in Saskatchewan between 1944 and 1964. In that year socialist rule came to an end when the New Democratic Party (NDP), successor to the CCF, lost to the Liberals. But the NDP still remains strong in Saskatchewan, and in 1969 it became the governing party in Manitoba. In Alberta, on the other hand, where the Social Credit Party governed for over 30 years, the Progressive Conservatives are now in control.

Socialized Medicine.   One of the important accomplishments of the CCF-NDP during its 20 years of uninterrupted rule in Saskatchewan was to institute the first system of socialized medicine in North America. State-financed hospitalization began in 1947, and a program of complete medical care followed in 1962. The latter plan was highly controversial. When it went into effect on July 1, 1962, most Saskatchewan doctors immediately shut their offices and engaged in what amounted to a strike. After 23 days the strike was settled. When the Liberal Party came to power, the plan had proved itself so completely that there was no possibility the program would be abolished.

Cities

There are still millions of unclaimed acres available for cultivation in the Prairie Provinces—probably twice the area now being cultivated. But most of this land is in the frigid, sparsely populated north. Today most newcomers tend to avoid the north and gravitate instead to the cities. Although about half the population of Saskatchewan is still rural, in Manitoba and Alberta two thirds of the people are city-dwellers.

Winnipeg, Manitoba's capital, began as a natural traffic crossroads, located as it is at the junction of the Red and Assiniboine rivers. It still plays that pivotal role. All the chief railways, roads, and flight lines of the Prairie Provinces converge on Winnipeg. Agricultural products from the prairies are processed there and shipped east. Farmers order machinery and supplies through Winnipeg concerns. It is the financial and manufacturing center of the prairies.

Winnipeg has a lustrous cultural history, due in part to its rich ethnic mix. Its attractions include art galleries, a symphony orchestra, the Royal Winnipeg Ballet, one of the world's largest music festivals, and the University of Manitoba, headquarters of the province's network of affiliated universities. About 540,000 people live in Winnipeg and its suburbs, making it one of the largest cities in Canada.

Regina, capital of Saskatchewan, is located in the heart of the wheat fields. It provides goods and services for the surrounding farm population and serves as an important shipping center. To the north is the province's other principal city, **Saskatoon**, home of the University of Saskatchewan, which also has a branch in Regina.

Alberta also has two major cities—Calgary in the south and Edmonton in the north. **Calgary**, at the foot of the Rockies, is a sprawling, prosperous, bustling place. It is a city of sawmills, flour mills, meat-packing

Regina is the attractive provincial capital of Saskatchewan.

plants, oil refineries, locomotive shops, and brick and cement works. It is also a university town, site of the University of Calgary. The city is famous for its annual Calgary Exhibition and Stampede, a giant rodeo.

Edmonton is called the gateway to the north because it is the hub of roads and rail lines that fan out northwards. Like Calgary, it is a manufacturing town. It is also the provincial capital and home of the University of Alberta.

History

The first Europeans in the Prairie Provinces were fur traders, both French and English. The Hudson's Bay Company charter of 1670 gave that British company control over all the land around Hudson Bay. A trading post, York Factory, was soon established where the Nelson River empties into Hudson Bay. The French penetrated the West by the rivers of the southern prairies. In 1733 they founded Fort Rouge at the junction of the Red and Assiniboine rivers, where Winnipeg now stands.

Throughout the 18th century competition between French and British traders spurred exploration. In 1754 a Hudson's Bay Company man, Anthony Henday, crossed the South Saskatchewan River near present-day Saskatoon. He continued west into Alberta and became the first white man to explore that region. In 1763, when Britain defeated France in the French and Indian War, France gave up all claims on the Canadian mainland. A new fur trade competition resulted between British companies— the Hudson's Bay Company and the North West Company, formed by independent traders in 1783.

Out of this competition came the heroic feat of Alexander Mackenzie, a Northwester. To advance his company's interests, he set forth in 1789 to find the fabled Northwest Passage, which legend claimed would unite the Atlantic and Pacific Oceans. He followed a great river (later to be named the Mackenzie after him), but to his chagrin it emptied into the Arctic. Four years later, in 1793, he struggled across the Rockies to the Pacific.

Early Settlement. Slowly settlement followed the fur trade. In 1812 Thomas Douglas, Lord Selkirk, a Hudson's Bay Company shareholder, brought a small group of Scottish Highlanders to settle at the site of present-day Winnipeg. In 1815 the pioneers, numbering about 200, came under attack from Northwesters and their allies, the métis (people of mixed French and Indian stock). Another attack broke up the colony the next year, but it was rebuilt. In 1821 the feuding fur trading companies were merged as Hudson's Bay Company. With peace restored, farmers and ranchers began moving in.

The Riel Rebellions. On the whole, the Prairie Provinces were won from the grudging hand of nature, rather than by men fighting men. The bloody Indian wars so common in the United States were largely alien to the Canadian prairies. The outstanding exceptions to this peaceful progress are the Red River Rebellion of 1870 and the Rebellion of 1885. Together they are called the Riel Rebellions, after Louis Riel who led them. He was a métis, son of a French trapper and an Indian woman.

Fighting began in December, 1869, when Riel, with the backing of his fellow métis, forcibly took over the government of the Red River region, the only settled area, from the representatives of the Canadian federal government. His actions were sparked in part by developments in the East. Canada had become a nation with the passage of the British North America Act in 1867, which united the four eastern provinces as the Dominion of Canada. Two years later Canada bought the vast western lands of the Hudson's Bay Company. The métis feared a federal take-over of their hunting grounds and rose to prevent it.

After about 6 months, federal troops forced Riel to flee. Before he fled, he had helped bring about the creation of Manitoba as a province with the same rights of self-government as other Canadian provinces. About 12,000 people lived in the entire huge expanse of the first western province admitted to the Dominion in 1870. (Saskatchewan and Alberta did not become provinces until 1905.)

The defeated métis drifted westward into Saskatchewan. But the transcontinental railroad, begun in the 1870's, pushed into Saskatchewan in the early 20th century with homesteaders following close behind. The railroad was a triumph for Canada. Nothing else could have tied the enormous underpopulated land together as it did. Along the railroad, towns turned into cities overnight, and villages sprang up around water tanks, while fortunes were made and lost in real estate speculations. But the métis viewed this development with severe misgivings. Again they feared that the federal government would let white men take over their hunting lands. In 1885 they once more called for Riel.

During the uprising the Indians and métis raided small settlements, and there were several massacres of white settlers. But federal troops soon checked the fighting and captured Riel. He stood trial for treason at Regina and was hanged. His execution sparked an uproar, for he had become a symbol of minority rights.

Later History.   Except for the Riel Rebellions, the winning of the Canadian West was almost free of Indian fighting. The law moved in early, with the establishment of the North West Mounted Police (later the Royal Canadian Mounted Police) in 1874. The Mounties, called the Friendly Force, had a superior record for fairness to Indians and helpfulness to isolated settlers. Friction was also eased by the fact that when the greatest settler rush came in the 20th century, the Indians were already accustomed to white men through their contact with railroad builders. In fact, western Canada became a sanctuary for tribes being driven out of the United States.

At first the white men's infectious diseases, to which Indians had no immunity, badly decimated the native population. In recent years, however, the Indian population has been increasing again. Health is improving thanks to new health care facilities and government programs. Education and job opportunities for Indians are also getting better. In 1960 Indians were given the right to vote. Today a new spirit is alive in the tribes—a growing demand, especially among young Indians, for a more important voice in their country's affairs.

The Prairie Provinces are growing up, becoming more urbanized, more modernized, more industrialized. But this is still the West. The work of young prairie writers and artists still reflects the broad plains, the pioneer farmers that conquered them, and the mosaic of races and nationalities that populate them. And even as the prairie winds still sweep across the wheat fields, the winds of change are blowing in the turbulent politics of provincial capitals and tribal councils.

BARRY BROADFOOT, *The Vancouver Sun*

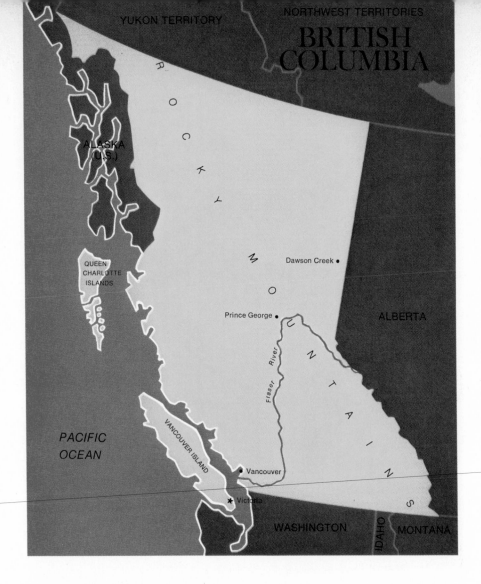

BRITISH COLUMBIA

British Columbia, Canada's Pacific coast province, is called B.C. for short. Some people half-jokingly claim that the initials stand for British California. Indeed, the climate of the southern coastal region where most British Columbians live resembles California's climate far more than it resembles the climate of the rest of Canada. About half of the province's over 2,000,000 people live in and around the city of Vancouver. Here the mean temperature in January is 37.2 degrees Fahrenheit (1.8 degrees Celsius), indicating that in the coldest month the average daily temperature is above freezing. However, winter brings the rain and fog typical of the coastal sections of the Pacific Northwest.

Eighty miles (130 kilometers) away, across the Strait of Georgia, is B.C.'s other major city—Victoria, the provincial capital. Here winters are still pleasanter. Victoria nestles on a protected harbor in the southeast corner of Vancouver Island, guarded from Pacific storms by the island's mountains. Its low rainfall, about 27 inches (70 centimeters) a year, is

FACTS AND FIGURES

BRITISH COLUMBIA is the name of the province.
CAPITAL: Victoria.
MAJOR CITIES: Vancouver, Victoria.
AREA: 366,255 sq. mi. (938,600 sq. km.).
POPULATION: 2,400,000 (estimate).

PHYSICAL FEATURES: Highest point—Mount Fairweather (15,300 ft.; 4,663 m.). **Lowest point**—sea level. **Major rivers**—Fraser, Columbia, Peace, Liard. **Major lakes**—Atlin, Babine, Okanagan, Kootenay. **PROVINCIAL MOTTO:** *Splendor sine occasu* ("Splendor without end").

just enough to preserve its famous green lawns and superb gardens. Roses bloom in January, for the temperature drops to freezing only about 20 days in the year. Victoria is warmer in winter than many cities in the southern United States.

Yet summers in the Vancouver-Victoria area are cool and sunny, with average July temperatures in the low 60's F. (below 20 degrees C.). No wonder many Americans and Canadians keep vacation cottages on the Gulf Islands or the twisting shoreline of the Strait.

There are two reasons for the beguiling weather. First, the Japanese Current tempers the climate of the whole Pacific coast, including B.C., while Vancouver Island acts as a buffer against the lashing rains that may bring an average annual precipitation of over 200 inches (510 cm.) on the west coast of the island. Second, the mountains that rise precipitously from the coast block the extremely hot or cold continental air currents blowing from the prairies and the British Columbian interior.

Perhaps it is climate that makes coastal British Columbians different from other Canadians. They are less threatened by the elements, so life is freer and people tend to express themselves as individuals. Or perhaps it is because they migrated there in the first place seeking freedom and escape from the harsh weather of other provinces. At any rate, Vancouver has a reputation for being an unorthodox place. And a British Columbian writer, Roderick Haig-Brown, says, ". . . some visitors claim Vancouver Islanders are the world's strangest, but then they do not know the people of the islands between Vancouver Island and the mainland."

He feels, however, that the people of the Cariboo and the Kootenays in the interior are strange too, and their weather is far different. Climatically B.C. is a land of extreme contrasts: at Dawson Creek the thermometer may reach –50 degrees F. (–10 degrees C.) in winter, while in summer Kamloops may swelter in heat. On the west coast of Vancouver Island, Henderson Lake averages 264 inches (670 cm.) of rain a year. Yet the Thompson Valley, between eastern mountain ranges, is sagebrush country, with less than 7 inches (10 cm.).

THE LAND

The most striking feature of British Columbia is its mountains. The vast 500-mile-wide (800 km.) belt of mountains, known as the Western Cordillera, consists of four regions. Along the coast and running about 100 miles (160 km.) inland are the rugged Coast Mountains, with many peaks over 10,000 feet (3,000 meters). Next come the Interior Uplands, a rough drought-stricken plateau that provides most of the province's ranching land. In the eastern half of British Columbia are the Columbia Mountains and finally, on the Alberta boundary, the Rocky Mountains.

About two thirds of British Columbia's people live in the Vancouver-Victoria region in the southwestern corner of the province. The rest of the province, which is the largest province in the West, has a sparse

A stretch of the Trans-Canada Highway in scenic Rogers Pass.

population. The population is scattered along the Fraser, Peace, Thompson, and Columbia river valleys, over the Cariboo rangelands, and through the Okanagan Valley in the southern interior. Much of it is savage-looking, breathtakingly beautiful country. Flying over it, a visitor must be keen-eyed to spot the arable lands—strips of green along rivers or narrow lakes winding between ranges. The largest green strip is the Fraser Valley in the south, about 100 miles (160 km.) long and 5 to 20 miles (8–32 km.) wide.

   The Fraser, one of the West's major rivers, has been described by

The rushing waters of the Fraser River go over Robson Falls.

Canadian novelist Hugh McLennan in these terms: "You look down the steep trench—in many places you look down thousands of feet—and you see the intruder. . . . It flows with cataract force for more than six hundred miles with only a few interludes of relative quiet. In a sense the Fraser does not flow at all: it seethes along with whirlpools so fierce that a log going down it may circle the same spot for days as though caught in a liquid merry-go-round." Only in its last 60 miles or so (100 km.), before it enters the Pacific at Vancouver, is the river finally tamed. The lower part of the Fraser River valley is one of the province's best agricultural areas, devoted mainly to dairy farming.

But comparatively little of British Columbia is farmland. The heart of the province's wealth lies in its immense mountain forests, particularly the dense stands of Douglas fir, western hemlock, and western cedar of the Coast Mountains. The strong wood of these trees provides some of the best timber for construction purposes in the world. Lumbering, saw-mills, and plants making paper and other allied wood products provide British Columbia with its most important industry.

Mining is important, too. British Columbia leads all the provinces in the production of lead. However, the most valuable mineral is copper. Copper mining has grown rapidly, and petroleum, natural gas, and zinc are also extracted in sizable quantities.

British Columbian waters are part of the world's largest salmon fishery, an area that also takes in the coastal waters of the American Northwest. Though salmon is king, many other kinds of fish are caught commercially or by sportsmen who crowd the province in season hoping for spectacular catches.

Agriculture is less important than mining but by no means insignificant. Ranching and dairy farming are the major sources of farm income. The province also produces an abundance of fruit.

British Columbia is rich in waterpower. Two great hydroelectric developments on the Peace and Columbia rivers insure a continuing power

Rafts of logs await processing at a pulp mill in Port Alberni.

supply for manufacturing, mining, and fast-growing cities. Shipbuilding and supplying the needs of boating enthusiasts are prosperous industries. The province had its first $1,000,000,000 budget in 1969.

THE PEOPLE

The original British Columbians were Indians. The coastal tribes, especially, were noted for their magnificently carved totem poles, their complex culture, and their fishing prowess. Among them were the fierce Haida who used to raid rival tribes' settlements along the coast in 70-man canoes. Much of their culture was destroyed when the white man came, but today the people of the salmon are coming back to their position of tribal leadership. Use of Indian themes by artists adds to the new sense of Indian pride. More than 45,000 Indians now live in B.C.

Two thirds of the province's people are of British descent. Scottish fur traders and English pioneers were the principal early settlers. Scandinavians came second, and there was a sprinkling of Germans, Dutch, and French. Like most Pacific Coast regions, British Columbia received a large influx of immigrants from Asia, beginning with the Chinese who worked on the transcontinental railroad. Vancouver has one of the largest Chinese communities in North America. Generally, assimilation of ethnic groups has gone along rather peacefully. Nearly three fourths of the population is Canadian-born.

The most clannish of the province's New Canadians are the Doukhobors, a deeply religious sect that came originally from Russia to Saskatchewan and later moved in large numbers to the Grand Forks and West Kootenay districts of B.C. Staunchly pacifist, some Doukhobors have refused to take any oath of allegiance to Canada, serve in the Canadian armed forces, or even send their children to school. This has caused friction, especially between the government and the most dissident group, the Sons of Freedom. While they are few in number, the Doukhobors, like the Indians, are a challenge to British Columbia's ability to handle the problems of minority groups.

British Columbians of the Vancouver-Victoria region feel very close to their neighbors across the border. They think nothing of taking the 4–5 hour drive to Seattle, Washington. Seattle is more than a place to visit. British Columbians feel at home there, and in the states of the Pacific Northwest in general. The feeling of closeness across the border is probably greater there than in any other part of Canada except the Atlantic Provinces, where many Canadians have relatives in New England. At times of extreme discontent with the ruling powers far away in eastern Canada, a minority of British Columbians have even favored joining the United States as a state.

The majority, however, are proud to be Canadians. Like the rest of their countrymen, they are more interested in hockey than in baseball, and their views on international issues are distinctly Canadian rather than American. But they share with other Western Canadians a distrust of the East, Canada's power centers in Quebec and Ontario, where most large Canadian corporations have their headquarters. They feel easterners and the people who run the federal government at Ottawa do not understand their special problems. They like to vote for one party in federal elections and a different one in provincial elections. Perhaps as an expression of antagonism for the East, they often turn their backs on the mainstream parties, the Liberals and Progressive Conservatives, and put their provincial government in the hands of the Social Credit Party. Although this minor party has never controlled the federal government, it has governed British Columbia for many years. It is a relatively conservative party. At the other extreme, the socialist New Democratic Party remains strong in B.C.

British Columbians are enthusiastic lovers of outdoor sports—boating, fishing, hiking, tennis, and golf in good weather, hockey and curling in the winter. Vancouver is the boating capital of Canada. For thousands of visitors it is also the gateway to the playground of Vancouver Island, the balmy coastlands to the north, or the fisherman's paradise of lakes and streams in the interior.

Although British Columbia is a young, pioneering land, it is in many ways technologically advanced. There is an excellent highway network, and railroads have thousands of miles of track. Railroads, airlines, and, since 1962, the Trans-Canada Highway—which makes it possible to drive from one end of Canada to the other without entering the United States —have ended the isolation once characteristic of the province. Within B.C., airlines reach into most areas, even isolated Indian communities.

Artists and writers gravitate to Vancouver and Vancouver Island. The arts have tended to be regional, based on the westerner's involvement with his magnificent land and its pioneering history. Presently new avant-garde techniques and ideas are finding great favor with an active group of young artists centered mainly in Vancouver.

Cities

Vancouver is the largest city in the Canadian West and among the largest in Canada. It is not only the focus of economic activity in the province, but also the shipping center through which lumber, fish, manufactured goods, and the enormous wheat crop of the Prairie Provinces are funneled to the Orient and the rest of the world.

Vancouver owes its pre-eminence as much to its large natural harbor as to its climate. When it was incorporated in 1886, the "city" consisted of a few muddy streets and wooden shacks, a saloon, and a sawmill in a rain forest. The city council met in a tent. But Vancouver was an open door between the great markets of Asia and the wealth of the Canadian West, so it became a major port. Today it is also headquarters for lumber and food processing, and for mining, construction, and other companies. Much shopping is done through Vancouver mail-order houses.

About 425,000 people live in the city itself, with another 650,000 in the surrounding suburbs. Ringed by snowcapped mountains and the sea, it is a place of fine residential areas, theaters, and art galleries. There is also a symphony orchestra and an opera company. It is the seat of Simon Fraser University and the University of British Columbia. Stanley Park, with its tangle of rain forest and its beaches, is among the largest and most delightful city parks in the world.

If Vancouver is a tourist center, tourists are even more important to the provincial capital, **Victoria**. A city of almost 200,000, it accommodates some 500,000 visitors a year. Playing host to them and taking care of government administration are the city's main businesses. Victoria is a small jewel of a city, proud of its gardens, the flower baskets decorating its streets, its ivy-covered Parliament Building, and its growing University

Vancouver, the province's biggest city, is a modern metropolis.

Victoria, the capital, is bedecked with hanging flower baskets.

of Victoria. Many protected inlets nearby make it a boater's paradise. It is a favorite retirement spot for Canadians who are tired of enduring 6 months of winter.

HISTORY

White men first approached British Columbia from the sea. In 1778 the famous Captain James Cook of Britain's Royal Navy took shelter at Nootka Sound on the large island that would later be named for one of his young officers, George Vancouver. Vancouver returned in 1792 and sailed completely around the island. In 1793 he summered near Bella Coola on the mainland, unaware that the first explorer to reach the Pacific from the east would shortly emerge near that very place. When Alexander Mackenzie of the North West Fur Company made his heroic transcontinental crossing, reaching the coast just after Vancouver sailed away, neither man knew of the other's exploit.

In 1805 another Northwester, Simon Fraser, founded the first trading post in British Columbia. Three years later he explored the great river that bears his name, a stream first discovered by Mackenzie in 1793. Hudson's Bay Company men were beginning to explore the Columbia River. The two companies were merged under the name Hudson's Bay Company in 1821. In 1843, an officer of the company, James Douglas, founded Fort Victoria (later Victoria) on Vancouver Island. England granted the island to the company on condition that a settlement be established there. Douglas was named governor of Vancouver Island.

Suddenly in 1858 Victoria turned into a boom town. It was the outfitting post for thousands of Americans, Canadians, and Australians on their way to the Fraser River gold strikes. England established the colony of British Columbia on the mainland and appointed Douglas governor of that colony, too. Gold strikes laid the basis for permanent settlement of the mainland interior, while coal discoveries at Nanaimo on Vancouver Island began the spread of settlement north from Victoria.

In 1867 the British North America Act created the independent Dominion of Canada, composed of the four eastern provinces. On the coast the two colonies merged as British Columbia, with Victoria as capital. British Columbia was not at all sure it wanted to affiliate with the remote provinces in the East. People debated alternatives: should they remain a British crown colony? Loyalty to England ran higher there than in the rest of Canada. Or should they ask for admission to the United States? Many settlers were American gold prospectors.

Canada countered these threats of secession with the promise of a transcontinental railroad linking B.C. to the East. On this condition, British Columbia consented to become the sixth province of Canada in 1871. At that time its population consisted of about 9,000 white men and perhaps three times as many Indians.

True to its promise, Canada built the railroad. In 1885 westbound workers met eastbound construction gangs from Vancouver in a canyon in British Columbia, and they drove the spike that tied East and West together. At the western terminus Vancouver, city of shacks and tents, was on its way to becoming Canada's western portal on the world, and thus growing to be the metropolis of shining towers, snarling traffic, and impressive houses nestling along the shore that it is today.

BARRY BROADFOOT, *The Vancouver Sun*

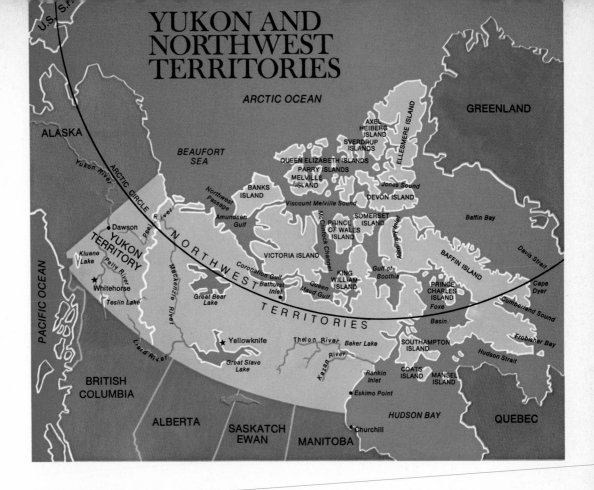

ARCTIC OCEAN

GREENLAND

ALASKA

BEAUFORT
SEA

AXEL
HEIBERG
ISLAND
SVERDRUP
ISLANDS

ELLESMERE ISLAND

QUEEN ELIZABETH ISLANDS
PARRY ISLANDS
MELVILLE
ISLAND

Jones Sound

DEVON ISLAND

BANKS
ISLAND

Northwest
Passage

Viscount Melville Sound

Baffin Bay

Amundsen
Gulf

SOMERSET
ISLAND

PRINCE
OF WALES
ISLAND

Admiralty Inlet

BAFFIN ISLAND

Davis Strait

Dawson

YUKON
TERRITORY

VICTORIA ISLAND

Coronation Gulf

McClintock Channel

KING
WILLIAM
ISLAND

Gulf of
Boothia

Cape
Dyer

Kluane
Lake

Pelly River

Bathurst
Inlet

Queen
Maud Gulf

PRINCE
CHARLES
ISLAND

Cumberland Sound

Whitehorse

Mackenzie River

Great Bear
Lake

Foxe
Basin

Teslin Lake

Yellowknife

Thelon River

Baker Lake

SOUTHAMPTON
ISLAND

Frobisher Bay

Liard River

Great Slave
Lake

Kazan River

Rankin
Inlet

COATS
ISLAND

MANSEL
ISLAND

Hudson Strait

BRITISH
COLUMBIA

Eskimo Point

HUDSON BAY

QUEBEC

ALBERTA

SASKATCH
EWAN

MANITOBA

Churchill

U.S.S.R.

Yukon River

ARCTIC CIRCLE

Peel River

PACIFIC OCEAN

NORTHWEST TERRITORIES

YUKON AND
NORTHWEST TERRITORIES

The Canadian North, consisting of the Yukon and the Northwest Territories, covers an area that is larger than many of the major countries of the world—and yet the entire population of this vast region could fit comfortably into a single small city.

With 1,511,979 square miles (3,915,327 square kilometers) of territory, the Canadian North covers more than 40 percent of the land area and a great deal of the freshwater area of Canada. The entire region is half the size the United States was before Hawaii and Alaska were admitted to the Union. And yet only about 60,000 people live there—one person to every 30 square miles (78 sq. km.). About 15,000 of these northern Canadians are Eskimo; less than 10,000 are Indians. Of the remainder of the population, many are Europeans working in missions or trading posts. Only a relatively small minority of the inhabitants of the Canadian North are native-born, white Canadians.

The Canadian North, which officially begins at 60 degrees north latitude and stretches to the northern tip of Ellesmere Island at 83 degrees, is far from being the monotonous, uniform land many people imagine it to be. The only uniform feature of the region is the ice and snow that cover it for most of the year. The section of the Northwest

---

YUKON AND NORTHWEST TERRITORIES

YUKON TERRITORY is the official name.
CAPITAL: Whitehorse.
AREA: 207,076 sq. mi. (536,327 sq. km.).
POPULATION: 19,000 (estimate).
PHYSICAL FEATURES: Highest point—Mount Logan (19,850 ft.; 6,050 m.). **Lowest point**—sea level. **Major rivers**—Yukon, Klondike, Pelly, Lewes, Peel. **Major lakes**—Teslin, Kluane, Aishihik, Kusawa.

NORTHWEST TERRITORIES is the official name.
CAPITAL: Yellowknife.
AREA: 1,304,903 sq. mi. (3,379,000 sq. km.).
POPULATION: 38,000 (estimate).
PHYSICAL FEATURES: Highest point—Mount Sir James McBrien (9,049 ft.; 2,758 m.). **Lowest point**—sea level. **Major rivers**—Mackenzie, Arctic Red, Great Bear, Liard, Hay, Slave, Coppermine, Thelon, Kazan. **Major lakes**—Great Bear, Great Slave.

Territories called the Barren Lands (or Barren Grounds), which stretches west of Hudson Bay and north to the Arctic Ocean, is a vast treeless plain. In contrast, there are mountain ranges on the islands of the Arctic Archipelago that rise to 9,000 feet (2,700 meters). In the Yukon Territory, the elevation reaches 19,850 feet (6,050 m.) at Mount Logan—the tallest mountain peak in Canada.

THE LAND

The most important division in the Canadian North is between the Arctic and the sub-Arctic regions. Strictly speaking, the Arctic Circle neatly cuts off the top of the world just above 66 degrees north latitude. However, the real division between Arctic and sub-Arctic is a climatic and ecological division, not a geographic one. The true Arctic begins where trees no longer grow except as stunted bushes in sheltered ravines. This dividing line does not go straight from east to west. At the Mackenzie delta, 69 degrees north and well within the Arctic Circle, the trees still grow. The tree line slopes fairly steadily southeastward until it reaches Hudson Bay at Churchill, 10 degrees farther south. At this point, stunted conifers (primarily cone-bearing evergreens), bare on one side because of the northeasterly wind, mark the division between the taiga (the northern forest) and the tundra (the vast treeless Barren Lands of the north).

Although the Barren Lands are tundra, and therefore treeless, they are not truly barren. In this region the southern vegetation of the Canadian North gives way to a spongy mat of giant lichen interwoven with a great variety of tiny shrubs. Although no cultivated crops will grow on the tundra because of the coldness and shortness of the summers, there is plentiful animal and plant life. There is a tiny amount of precipitation in the area. It rarely exceeds 10 inches (25 centimeters) a year and is often less. The Barren Lands would indeed be a desert if it were not for the permafrost (a permanently frozen layer of soil below the surface). The permafrost extends many feet downward, seals the ground from below, and keeps the surface moist after it thaws.

In summer the great rivers—such as the Mackenzie, Yukon, Thelon, and Kazan—flow freely through the Arctic North. For a brief season the land is brilliant and loud with life.

Some 800 different kinds of plants grow in the Canadian Arctic. Many of the plants are minuscule, but they sprout quickly in the spring as soon as the snow has melted. In a brief space of time, the Arctic plants cover the tundra, and during the long summer days they form a brilliant carpet of tiny flowers. Until the snows return in September, the Arctic (particularly for one who looks carefully at the ground) is full of color.

Yellowknife, Northwest Territories, is on Great Slave Lake.
The buildings in the foreground are part of a gold refinery.

The rocks are covered with green and orange patterns of map lichen. The region's miniature berry plants turn orange and purple in the fall.

Few land mammals and just as few birds pass the winter in the Arctic. (The musk-ox, the polar bear, the fox, and the hare are among the hardy animals that do stay.) But as the snow melts, the air fills with insects and migrant animals flood in. The caribou—hundreds of thousands in a single herd—march out of the taiga to graze on the lichens of the Barren Lands. No less than 75 species of birds, including the Arctic tern, come to breed beside the northern lakes. The Arctic terns are the most remarkable of all migratory birds. Each year the terns fly about 12,000 miles (19,300 kilometers) to breed—from summer in the Antarctic to another summer, this time in the Arctic. In the seas and channels between the mainland and the great Arctic islands live many marine mammals, including the walrus; the white whale, or beluga; the narwhal; and several species of seals.

Neither the fauna nor the flora of the sub-Arctic woodlands are as distinctive as those of the Arctic tundra. The Yukon is really an extension of the Western Cordillera. The forests of the Northwest Territories reach without interruption to north of the Great Lakes. Although there are some birds and plants peculiar to the northern woodlands, the mammals of this region are usually similar to those found farther south. However, the special breed of wood bison in the Northwest Territories is considerably larger than the bison of the plains.

THE PEOPLE

The life of the people of the Canadian Arctic was for countless generations as distinctive as its animal and plant life. South of the tree-line, in the sub-Arctic, lived the northern Indians—Dog-Rib, Wood

Igloos are built beside modern houses in this Eskimo village.

Cree, Hare, Slave, Kutchin, and other tribes. The life of these people was adapted to hunting in the forest, and they rarely ventured onto the open tundra. North of the treeline lived the Eskimo, who feared the forest. Many Indians still live in the northern forests and many Eskimo still live on the tundra, but their way of life has changed radically in recent years.

Traditional Eskimo Life.   In prehistoric times the Eskimo developed a highly specialized way of life adapted to existence in a land where the climate was rigorous and food was scarce. Many of their inventions were admirably suited to their way of life. They built the kayak, a light and easily maneuverable skin-covered boat, and the igloo, a house of snow blocks and ice windows built in the shape of a geodesic dome. This ingenuity extended to their hunting tools and hunting methods, some of them highly sophisticated. They found artistic expression in their remarkable sculptures in soapstone, whalebone, and walrus ivory.

The Eskimo were divided into two groups. One group roamed the Barren Lands. Their way of life depended on hunting the migrating caribou, which provided food, clothing, and summer tents. The other group lived on the seashores and islands of the Arctic Ocean. Their way of life depended on the hunting of seals and other marine animals.

Before the white men came, the Eskimo lived according to very simple social patterns. They had no tribal institutions, no chiefs, no formal government of any kind. The scarcity of food forced them to hunt and travel in extended family groups rather than bands, and leadership fell to the best hunter or to the man feared for his powers as a shaman, or medicine man. Only at festival times in summer, when food was abundant, would the Eskimo gather in large numbers. Lying and theft appear to have been unknown among them. There was no word for war in their language. They treated their women well and were kind to those of their children who survived. However, in times of hardship some Eskimo children were killed in infancy to prevent starvation of family groups. Life in the North, for all the ingenuity with which the Eskimo had adapted their lives, was hard and perilous. And yet they remained a good-natured and cheerful people.

HISTORY

Europeans reached the Canadian North before they found their way to any other part of the American continent. In the 11th century Norsemen sailed from Greenland, landed on Baffin Island, and met the Eskimo living there. The Norse colonies in Greenland vanished inexplicably during the late Middle Ages. The first Europeans to enter the northern reaches of the continent after this were seamen and adventurers who came from England, beginning in the 16th century. They came to seek a northern water route connecting the Atlantic and the Pacific, by which they could reach the riches of Cathay (China). This was called the Northwest Passage. The first of these English seafarers was Martin Frobisher, who came to the North in 1576. He explored Baffin Island, sailing into the bay on the island's south coast that was to be named after him.

Many of the adventurers who followed Frobisher were also seeking the legendary Northwest Passage. Adventurers persisted in this search until a Northwest Passage was finally completed by the Norwegian explorer Roald Amundsen in 1906, exactly 330 years after Frobisher's voyage. The long procession of explorers who came to the North had very little effect on the lives of the Eskimo and Indians of the region. In fact, some of the explorers—men like John Rae in the 19th century and

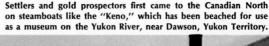

Settlers and gold prospectors first came to the Canadian North on steamboats like the "Keno," which has been beached for use as a museum on the Yukon River, near Dawson, Yukon Territory.

This Arctic oil refinery is located on the Mackenzie River.

Vilhjalmur Stefansson in the 20th century—actually adopted the Eskimo way of life and lived off the land that they explored.

The first European settlements in the Canadian North were the fur-trading posts that the Hudson's Bay Company established, beginning in 1670, around the bay whose name they borrowed. Some of the original posts are still in use. The fur traders were followed by the whalers, who established their first shore stations in 1840 and employed many Eskimo. The whaling era lasted until 1906, when a substitute material for whale-bone in ladies' corsets was invented and the industry collapsed almost overnight.

Gold Rush

During the early centuries of European contact, from 1670 to 1870, the whole of the northern mainland of what is now Canada was the province of the fur traders. The fur traders held a charter from King Charles II of England entitling them to this vast area as well as the whole of the Canadian Prairies. After Canada became a nation in 1867, it acquired the territories of the Hudson's Bay Company and renamed them the Northwest Territories. In 1880 Britain transferred the Arctic Archipelago to Canada. The prairie region of the Northwest Territories was administered by the North West Mounted Police until 1905, when it was transformed into the provinces of Saskatchewan and Alberta, with the 60th parallel marking off the 1,000,000 and more square miles (more than 2,500,000 sq. km.) that still constituted the Northwest Territories.

The Canadian Government did not become truly involved in the administration of any part of the Northwest Territories north of 60 degrees until the discovery of gold in the Klondike River region in 1897. The gold strike was made in the westernmost part of the Northwest Territories in the region bordering on Alaska—the Yukon. (The Yukon was named for the great Yukon River, which runs through the region. The Klondike is a tributary of the Yukon.) The gold rush that followed the strike on the Klondike brought some 30,000 white men into the Yukon region. The North West Mounted Police arrived at Dawson City to establish Canadian governmental authority. In 1898 the Yukon became a separate territory, and so it has remained. It is governed today by an elective council, with a government-appointed commissioner holding executive authority.

The real Arctic regions were left to fur traders and to the missionaries (who began to arrive in the 1890's) until the early years of the 20th century. At that time representatives of the Canadian Government appeared, once again in the form of the North West Mounted Police. The Mounties combined every function of law-keeping and administration. The first Mounted Police post in the Arctic was established in 1903. From that time on, the Mounties made regular trips by boat and sled over the tundra and through the Arctic Archipelago to establish Canadian law and to demonstrate Canadian sovereignty over the region.

Modern Eskimo Life

A little religion, a little law, a few trade goods—until the period after World War I this was the only way in which the life of the Eskimo was generally affected by the Canadian Government. White men in the North adapted their way of life to local Indian and Eskimo ways, rather than the reverse. The modernization of the North began with the introduction of the radio and the airplane. These two developments completely changed a world where formerly the only communication had been by kayak and dogsled. In the years between World War I and World War II, bush pilots established mail services and brought in prospectors, which led to the opening of the first Arctic mines. But the 1940's were the crucial times in the destruction of the old Stone Age pattern of northern living.

Eskimo children play on the tundra near their village on the Arctic Sea. A communications station, part of the northern warning system, is seen on the promontory in the background.

In the late 1940's and continuing into the 1950's American and Canadian soldiers and technicians established their northern warning systems (radar and communication systems to warn of approaching enemy aircraft). The very presence of outsiders in their land involved the Eskimo in modern life. In that decade also, the sale of rifles to the Eskimo of the Barren Lands led to the rapid reduction of the herds of caribou. By the end of the 1940's the Eskimo of the Barren Lands were doomed unless drastic relief was given. Many died. The survivors were brought to places on the edge of Hudson Bay tidewater—Rankin Inlet, Eskimo Point, and Baker Lake, for instance—to start a settled village life remote from their nomadic past. About one seventh of the Eskimo were taken farther south to be cured of active tuberculosis, which they had contracted from the white man since they had no natural resistance to the disease. This disaster marked the virtual end of the Eskimo culture in the Canadian Arctic.

In 1953 the Canadian Government, awakening to a sense of its responsibility to the peoples of the North, established the Department of Northern Affairs. A flood of civil servants and teachers entered the North —in the ratio of one government worker to every eight or 10 Eskimo— to set up a welfare system. However, the system, perhaps inevitably, was forced to ignore the traditional patterns of Eskimo life in its attempt to bring modern ways and advantages to the people. Hunting was supplanted by other jobs—and by compensation from the welfare system— as a means of existence. English was used in the schools. Boys, at the age when they would normally be accompanying their fathers on hunting trips, were sent instead to boarding schools. The Eskimo language, rich in hunting terms, shrank as the Eskimo's breadth of experience narrowed. The traditional songs and drum dances were abandoned until only old men performed them. Even Eskimo sculpture has declined in quality because of commercialization.

THE FUTURE

Perhaps inevitably, the old life of the North is ending. An attempt is being made, through education, to create a northern society in which Eskimo, Indians, and other Canadians will be equal. As a result of this policy, the Eskimo have experienced a great deal of change in their lives within a short period of time. Many Eskimo have become confused and disturbed by their progress, within a decade or so, from a Stone Age world to a world of airplanes and bulldozers.

Economically, life in the Canadian North is largely dependent on the money that the Canadian Government spends there. The fur trade has declined because of the competition of synthetic fabrics and of ranch-bred furs. The lack of soil on the glacier-scraped land prevents the development of short-summer farming or even of a considerable forest industry.

Tourism and mining remain the potential assets of the Canadian North, but neither has been developed fully. In the 1950's the exploitation of the mineral and scenic resources of the North was one of the great issues of Canadian politics. Today the emphasis on conservation has made Canadians more inclined to think of the North's natural resources as wealth to be held in reserve for future progress. The slow pace of development in the Arctic is likely to continue for many years.

GEORGE WOODCOCK, University of British Columbia

CANADIAN CITIES

Because Canada is such a vast country, many people think of it as basically a rural or even frontier nation. In fact, about three out of four Canadians live in what the Canadian census defines as "urban areas." Some of these areas include fairly small towns and villages. Even so, well over half the people of Canada live in towns or cities with populations of over 30,000. And urbanization is a continuing trend. The greatest population increases in the past few decades have occurred in urban areas. Young Canadians are leaving small towns and flocking to the big cities. Almost all new immigrants to Canada are settling in the big cities.

Like the United States, Canada is increasingly a nation of city-dwellers. For the moment, Canadian cities are not yet suffering the urban crisis that has engulfed many cities in the United States. Hopefully, problems of slums, urban sprawl, housing, pollution, and transportation can be dealt with there while they remain manageable. What is clear is that Canada's cities will continue to grow in importance both nationally and in the entire North American picture.

Montreal

Montreal is Canada's largest and most cosmopolitan city. The languages predominantly spoken there are French and English. However, many other languages are heard in Montreal, where large numbers of immigrants from abroad settle. About 65 percent of the population is French-speaking, and there is a vigorous and influential English-speaking minority. Theatrical productions in both languages flourish in Montreal. Of the city's four universities, two are French-language and two are English-language. McGill University, an English-language school and the largest university in the province, is an internationally recognized center for advanced study and research in many fields. The University of Montreal is the largest French-language university outside of France.

Montreal occupies part of a 30-mile-long (48 kilometers) island in

Dominion Square in Montreal, with the Cruciform Building (upper left) nearby.

the St. Lawrence River about 500 miles (805 km.) southwest of where the river empties into the Gulf of St. Lawrence. The city is built around a big hill known as Mount Royal, the upper slopes of which are occupied by the rolling meadows and woods of Mount Royal Park. There is a beautiful view from there of the city, the shoreline, and, in the distance to the north, the foothills of the Laurentian Mountains. It is a view, too, that has been changing with the recent building boom in Montreal.

One of the more interesting building developments in Montreal, though, is not visible from Mount Royal. This is the extensive underground complex of pedestrian promenades and tunnels that have been built under the city's busy downtown streets. Along these promenades, sheltered from ice and snow, are scores of shops and boutiques, restaurants, bars, and theaters. Escalators provide access to a complex of office buildings, the most famous of which is Place Ville Marie, also called the Cruciform Building. Indeed, this cross-shaped skyscraper now overshadows Mount Royal as Montreal's most prominent landmark.

Another feature recently added to the city's landscape is Man and His World, a permanent display in which scores of foreign countries operate pavilions. The 1967 Universal and International Exposition (Expo 67) was so successful that Montreal decided to retain much of it as a permanent feature of the city. Man and His World includes science buildings and museums, restaurants and nightclubs from around the world, an aquarium, a marina, and an exciting midway.

In addition to all the new construction, Montreal has many traditional sights of interest. There is the stately old Roman Catholic church of Notre Dame, downtown in the Place d'Armes. Notre Dame is so huge that there is seating capacity for 5,000 people, with standing room for 2,000 more. Southwest of Mount Royal stands the imposing domed

Oratory of Saint Joseph, a Roman Catholic shrine. Of considerable interest, too, is the old quarter of Montreal, in the eastern part of the city, where some buildings date from the 17th and 18th centuries.

The first permanent settlement at Montreal dates from 1642, when Ville Marie de Montréal was established by a small group of French colonists led by Paul de Chomedey, Sieur de Maisonneuve. For a long time the settlement grew very slowly. The first period of substantial development came in the first half of the 19th century and paralleled the expansion of shipping on the St. Lawrence and Great Lakes during that era. In 1844 Montreal was made the capital of Canada. But in 1849 hostility between the British and French communities culminated in the burning down of the parliament buildings, and the capital was moved.

Montreal has continued to grow in the 20th century. In recent decades it has entered into what very well may be its golden age, an era that has seen the completion of the St. Lawrence Seaway and the creation of the immensely successful Expo 67. Further recognition of the city's new international status came when Montreal was designated the site of the summer Olympics for 1976.

Toronto

In the 1960's, people were saying of Montreal, *Montréal ça bouge*— "Montreal, it's moving." Very much the same sort of thing was being said of Toronto as the 1970's began.

This big, thriving city on the northwest shore of Lake Ontario was the scene of a project that was called the largest single downtown development ever undertaken in North America. The project, which began to come off the drawing boards in the early 1970's, includes plans for a massive development of Toronto's waterfront and railroad terminal area. Plans also call for a communications center, to include a TV broadcasting and production center, as well as convention and hotel facilities, six office towers, and apartment buildings with space for 20,000 occupants. All this was an expansion of a building boom that descended on Toronto in the 1960's and that included the construction of what is perhaps now the city's most celebrated building, the new city hall.

Toronto is a great business center, the home of Canada's most important stock exchange. It is the headquarters of the nation's English-language publishing and printing business, export center for many products, and a manufacturing hub for iron and steel, meat-packing, and food products. Toronto is also the provincial capital of Ontario. Perhaps most important, it is one of Canada's leading educational and cultural centers. The University of Toronto is the nation's largest university, and the Royal Ontario Museum is noted for its Oriental collections. Toronto is the home of the National Ballet of Canada. The Toronto Symphony Orchestra has an excellent reputation among music lovers. On another cultural level, Toronto plays host to the Canadian National Exhibition, a great industrial and agricultural fair, every year in late summer.

POPULATION ESTIMATES FOR METROPOLITAN AREAS

Montreal	2,700,000	Hamilton	500,000
Toronto	2,600,000	Edmonton	500,000
Vancouver	1,000,000	Quebec City	480,000
Ottawa	600,000	Calgary	400,000
Winnipeg	540,000	Halifax	223,000

Toronto's skyline, from Lake Ontario.

The first settlement in the area of Toronto was made by French fur traders, who built a trading post there in about 1720 and subsequently built a fort as well. The smoking ruins of the fort fell into British hands during the Seven Years War (1756–63). The British purchased the land surrounding the old fort from the local Indians in 1787, and in 1793 Toronto was selected as the capital of the recently created province of Upper Canada. It was renamed York in honor of the Duke of York.

During the War of 1812, the government buildings were burned by the Americans. It was in retaliation for this act that the British set fire to the White House in Washington. In 1834, the city was incorporated under its original name of Toronto (a Huron word meaning "place of meeting"). After Confederation in 1867, the city began to spread out and to absorb neighboring communities. By 1954 Toronto and a number of surrounding communities formed a metropolitan supergovernment that may well come to serve as a model for other North American cities seeking to improve co-ordination between city and suburban governments. Metro, as it is called, is responsible for police, water supply and sewerage, public transportation, welfare, and other services.

Vancouver

Vancouver is the biggest city in the Canadian West, Canada's leading Pacific port, and the gateway to one of the most popular resort areas in the nation. It is located across the Strait of Georgia from Vancouver Island to which it is connected by ferry. To the north, across Burrard Inlet, the snowcapped Coast Mountains form a spectacular backdrop to the city. An arm of the Fraser River forms the city's southern boundary.

With its mild temperatures both in winter and summer and its abundant rainfall, Vancouver is a gardener's delight. The city's residential areas have long been noted for their beautifully landscaped houses. Recently high-rise apartment buildings and modern skyscrapers have also been built.

In Vancouver the snowcapped Coast Mountains are only a short distance away.

Vancouver has what it claims is the second largest Chinese district, after New York's, in North America. It also has Stanley Park, a 900-acre (400 hectares) park that is known across the continent as a meeting place for young people. The University of British Columbia is located just west of the city on a headland overlooking the Strait of Georgia.

Named for Captain George Vancouver, who explored the area in 1792, the present city evolved from a small settlement of sawmills, known as Granville, that came into being in the 1860's. Vancouver was incorporated as a city in 1886, a year after the completion of the Canadian Pacific Railway, Canada's first transcontinental railroad.

Features of Vancouver's cultural life include an art gallery, a symphony society, and the annual International Festival of the Arts. The festival, which consists of dramatic and musical productions of all kinds, has drawn major performing companies from all over the world.

Winnipeg

Winnipeg is the largest city of the Prairie Provinces and the capital of Manitoba. It is located at the eastern end of the Canadian wheat belt and owes much of its importance to its position as a major grain market.

Winnipeg stands where the eastward-flowing Assiniboine River joins the northward-running Red River. The Red River formed much of the eastern boundary of the city until the boundary was extended to include St. Boniface, the French-speaking city on the opposite bank.

The first settlement in the Winnipeg area was a fur-trading post called Fort Rouge established by the Frenchman Pierre Gaultier de Varennes, Sieur de La Vérendrye, in 1738. The British fur-trading company called the North West Company built Fort Gibraltar in the area in 1804. Fort Gibraltar was subsequently destroyed and a new post, Fort Garry, was built on the same site after the North West Company merged with its former rival the Hudson's Bay Company in 1821. In the end several posts called Fort Garry were built in the Winnipeg area. Meanwhile, a

The Legislative Building in Winnipeg houses Manitoba's provincial legislature.

group of Scottish settlers had set up a little colony in the area (the Red River Settlement) in 1812, and this colony was the nucleus of what would eventually be the city of Winnipeg. (The name, incidentally, comes from the Cree Indian word *win-nipiy,* meaning "murky water," a reference to the brownish color of the city's rivers.) Winnipeg was incorporated as a city in 1873.

Winnipeg boasts one of Canada's finest ballet companies (called the Royal Winnipeg Ballet) and a symphony orchestra. A music festival is held there every spring. The University of Manitoba is in suburban Fort Garry, while the University of Winnipeg is in the city itself.

Ottawa

Ottawa, the federal capital of Canada, is on the southern shore of the Ottawa River where that river is joined by the Gatineau and Rideau rivers. The nation's Parliament Buildings occupy a promontory overlooking the river. Dominating the group of buildings is the famous 300-foot (90 meters) Peace Tower, with its 53-bell carillon and chamber memorializing the more than 100,000 Canadians who died in World War I and World War II. At the extreme eastern end of the city is Government House, or Rideau Hall, the residence of the governor-general of Canada. The official residences of the prime minister and opposition leader are also located in Ottawa.

As the nation's capital, Ottawa is the site of the National Museum, a research institution with collections of many kinds; the National Art Gallery; and the National Library and Public Archives of Canada; and the

National Arts Centre for operas, plays, and concerts. This attractive city also has two universities, Carleton University (English-speaking) and the bilingual (English- and French-speaking) University of Ottawa. More than a third of the inhabitants of the Ottawa area are of French descent.

Nicholas Sparks, who was Irish by birth, is regarded as the founder of Ottawa. After working for a few years at a settlement on the north shore of the Ottawa River, he purchased, in 1821, a tract of land on the south shore that comprised much of what became downtown Ottawa. Only a few more settlers had arrived by 1826, when a group of Royal Engineers came to construct the Rideau Canal as a military bypass of the St. Lawrence River route to Lake Ontario. The canal, never used for military purposes, is now used only by pleasure craft. The community was then called Bytown, after Colonel By, the engineer in charge of building the canal. Bytown grew to be a prosperous lumber town, with many sawmills and gristmills. In 1855 it was incorporated as the city of Ottawa, a name derived from that of a local Indian tribe. Because of its central location in Canada, Ottawa was chosen as the Canadian capital in 1857. Construction of the Parliament Buildings was begun in 1859. In 1916 most of the Centre Block was destroyed by fire, but was soon reconstructed to nearly its original appearance.

Hamilton

Hamilton, at the western end of Lake Ontario, is known as the Pittsburgh of Canada because of the concentration of iron and steel industries there. Hamilton has one of Canada's busiest ports, with large quantities of iron ore, coal, and limestone being shipped in, put through the mills,

Ottawa, the nation's capital. View is from the Rideau Canal toward Peace Tower.

and shipped out again in the form of finished iron and steel products, which are the city's major manufactures.

Among places of exceptional interest in Hamilton are the large, open-air markets behind city hall and the city's vast Royal Botanical Gardens. McMaster University is adjacent to the Botanical Gardens. A massive project in the late 1960's transformed downtown Hamilton.

The area around Hamilton was first explored by the great French explorer Robert Cavelier, Sieur de La Salle, in 1669. The first settlers, United Empire Loyalists, arrived in the vicinity in 1778. The city was named for George Hamilton, who bought a tract of land on which the settlement was built. Hamilton was incorporated in 1846.

Quebec City

Travelers are often heard to say that Quebec is one of the most beautiful cities in North America. This historic capital of the province of Quebec is partly perched on a plateau of solid rock rising some 330 feet (100 m.) above the St. Lawrence River. The river curves its way around this natural citadel. A picturesque boardwalk skirting the promontory offers visitors a breathtaking view of the river and of the Laurentian Mountains a few miles to the north. A prominent feature of Upper Town, as this part of the city is called, is the Chateau Frontenac, a magnificent hotel in the style of a French castle. Nearby is the Citadel, a huge stone fortress composed of some 25 buildings, built by the British in the 1820's. A large part of Upper Town, in fact, is surrounded by thick granite walls, some portions built during the French regime. Just outside the city walls are the Plains of Abraham, where in 1759 the British administered the decisive blow leading to the end of the French control of Canada. Today the battlefield is a scenic 235-acre (95 hectares) park.

Many tourists come to this cradle of French civilization in North America every summer. Tourists come in winter, too, when snow changes Quebec, with its winding streets and steep hills, into a picture-book city. Every winter there is a mammoth carnival.

Winter in Quebec City. An ice palace fronts the Chateau Frontenac.

In addition to its importance as a historic city, Quebec serves as capital of the province of Quebec. It is also a fairly important industrial center and port. The historic buildings in the old sections of town retain their interest in the shadow of modern buildings. The narrow winding streets lead out to modern expressways. Population growth has pushed the city east and west along the banks of the St. Lawrence and toward the foothills of the Laurentians. In suburban Ste. Foy is the new campus of Laval University, Canada's oldest French-speaking university.

Edmonton

Edmonton, the capital of Alberta, lies along the banks of the North Saskatchewan River, which winds through the city in a deep gorge. Like Winnipeg, Edmonton is a city of broad streets and numerous parks. The University of Alberta is in Edmonton. The city has been a beneficiary of the Alberta oil boom of the past decades, and there has been a considerable amount of building.

The first settlement in the area was Fort Edmonton, a fur-trading post established downriver by the Hudson's Bay Company. Edmonton's present site was sparsely inhabited until the end of the 19th century, when it served as a supply base for prospectors on their way to the Klondike gold rush. Edmonton was incorporated as a city in 1904. But its real growth began a year later when the city was chosen as the capital of the newly created province of Alberta and, at the same time, became a terminus of the Canadian Northern Railway.

Calgary

Calgary, in southern Alberta at the junction of the Bow and Elbow rivers, is surrounded by prairies and rangelands that merge into the foothills of the Rocky Mountains. On a clear day the Rockies themselves are visible from high points around the city. Calgary is internationally famous for its annual rodeo, called the Calgary Exhibition and Stampede.

Fort Brisebois, an outpost of the North West Mounted Police, was

Oil-rich Edmonton, in the middle of prairie country.

Halifax, the Atlantic Provinces' major city.

renamed Fort Calgary in 1876, a year after it was founded. When the Canadian Pacific Railway reached Calgary in 1883, ranchers and homesteaders began to stream into the area. Calgary was incorporated as a city in 1893. With its stockyards and meat-packing plants, it gained fame as a cow town. The discovery of natural gas and oil in the area in the 20th century has further bolstered the city's economy.

Calgary is the home of the Southern Alberta Institute of Technology and of the University of Calgary. On St. George's Island in the Bow River is a zoo and also a dinosaur park.

Halifax

Halifax is the capital of Nova Scotia, the largest city in the Atlantic Provinces, and one of Canada's major seaports. A channel separates it from the neighboring city of Dartmouth, to which it is connected by bridges. Shipyards line Halifax's waterfront. An outstanding landmark in the business district is Province House, built in 1818. It is a fine example of Georgian architecture. Province House still houses the provincial legislature. Another landmark, St. Paul's Church, completed in 1750, is the oldest Anglican church in Canada. Halifax is the home of four universities, Dalhousie, the provincial university and largest, King's College, St. Mary's, and Mount St. Vincent.

Founded by the British as a military and naval post in 1749, Halifax occupied a strategic position during the struggle between the British and French for control of North America. On Citadel Hill, now a national historic park, stands a massive, star-shaped fortress that was rebuilt several times in the settlement's early history. Its inhabitants are called Haligonians. Halifax was an important naval base and assembly point for troop shipments during World War I and World War II.

Reviewed by J. CROMWELL YOUNG, Executive Editor, *Encyclopedia Canadiana*

SAINT PIERRE AND MIQUELON

"Those islands that are as French as can be," was how former French President Charles de Gaulle referred to Saint Pierre and Miquelon on July 20, 1967. He made the statement during a visit to the islands—the first visit ever made there by a French head of state. Saint Pierre and Miquelon are tiny islands about 13 miles (21 kilometers) off the southern coast of Newfoundland. They are the last remnant of the once great French empire in Canada. French is still spoken in Canada, but the residents of Saint Pierre and Miquelon are truly French, for these islands remain an overseas territory of France.

The visitor to Saint Pierre, the principal town of the island of Saint Pierre and territorial capital, could well believe himself to be in a small French town. The fishermen wear the blue denim trousers and berets favored by French workingmen. The shops, the hotels, and the long loaves of bread the women carry from the bakery are all reminiscent of

The seafaring men of Saint Pierre carry model ships and banners to the harbor in the annual ceremony of the blessing of the fleet.

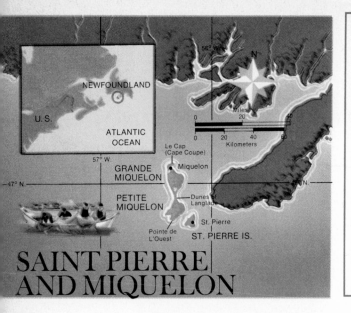

SAINT PIERRE AND MIQUELON

FACTS AND FIGURES

CAPITAL: Saint Pierre.

LOCATION: Atlantic Ocean off southern coast of Newfoundland. **Latitude**—46° 45′ N to 47° 7′ N. **Longitude**—56° 05′ W to 56° 25′ W.

AREA: 93 sq. mi. (241 sq. km.).

PHYSICAL FEATURES: Highest point—in northern Miquelon, 815 ft. (248 m.). **Lowest point**—sea level.

POPULATION: 5,225 (estimate).

LANGUAGE: French.

RELIGION: Roman Catholic.

GOVERNMENT: Overseas territory of France. **Head of government**—French-appointed governor. **Legislature**—general council.

ECONOMY: Industries and products—cod fishing and cod products. **Chief export**—cod products. **Chief imports**—most consumer goods, including clothing, fuel, foodstuffs, and machinery.

MONETARY UNIT: French franc.

France. About 4,300 of the approximately 5,200 residents of Saint Pierre and Miquelon live in the town of Saint Pierre. It is the territory's major commercial port, and since most of the islanders are fishermen, they must live near the harbor where their boats are moored. The remaining islanders live either in outlying sections of Saint Pierre island or on Miquelon, the other major island. Miquelon is sometimes considered to be two islands. Miquelon proper lies to the north and is connected by the Dunes of Langlade to Langlade, the southern portion of the island, which lies closest to Saint Pierre. There are also a number of tiny islets in the territory. All of the islands are rocky and bleak, supporting almost no farming. The islanders have always depended on the rich fisheries of the Grand Banks for their livelihood. Cod and cod products are the islands' chief exports. There is also a growing tourist trade, attracted by the islands' unusual atmosphere and the possibility of duty-free shopping.

History and Government

Men are believed to have been fishing the waters near Saint Pierre and Miquelon for many centuries. French claims to the islands date from the 16th century, and by the early 17th century there were a few settlers on the islands, most of them from the Basque country of France and Spain. The greatest wave of settlers came in 1763, after the British expelled the French colonists from Acadia, as the Atlantic coastal region of Canada was then called. Most of the present inhabitants of the islands are descendants of these exiled Acadians. Although Great Britain did have possession of the islands for more than 70 years in the 18th and early 19th centuries, Saint Pierre and Miquelon have been continuously French since 1814.

As a territory of France, the islands are administered by a governor appointed in Paris, by his personal advisory council (privy council), and by a 14-man elected general council. A referendum was held in 1958, and the islanders voted to remain a territory of France in preference to independence.

Reviewed by PRESS AND INFORMATION SERVICE OF THE FRENCH EMBASSY, New York

GREENLAND

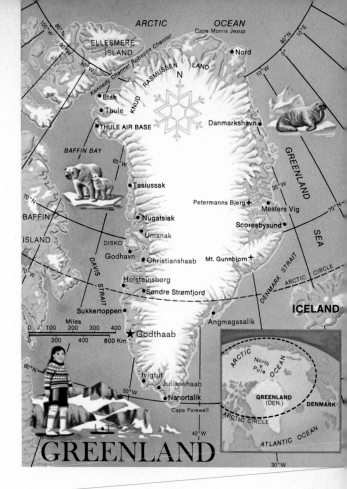

It was Eric the Red, the famous Norse explorer, who named Greenland. After being expelled from Iceland in A.D. 981, Eric spent several years exploring the great and hitherto unknown island lying about 175 miles (280 kilometers) west of Iceland. He eventually tried to establish a settlement there. Calling the island Greenland was salesmanship on Eric's part. He thought the name would attract settlers from Iceland. Actually, the southwestern part of the island settled by Eric the Red and his followers is one of the few "green" parts of Greenland. Most of the island, 80 percent or more, is covered by an enormous ice cap that constitutes one of the most forbidding stretches of polar land known to man. Only the island's ice-free coastal areas are habitable, and even there life has always been hard and uncertain. Until the 20th century most Greenlanders lived primitive, nomadic lives, depending to a large extent on seal hunting for their existence. Today most of the people live in permanent homes, have jobs, and are becoming used to such modern conveniences as sewing machines, radios, and motorboats. Even so, the average European or American is still likely to find life on Greenland fairly primitive.

The Land

Because it is located in the far north, Greenland is distorted on the familiar Mercator projection maps to appear as large as North America. Although Greenland is not actually that large, it is, in fact, the largest island in the world. Its total land area, about 840,000 square miles (2,175,000 square kilometers), makes it about as large as all of the United States east of the Mississippi River. From Cape Morris Jesup—the northernmost point of land in the world—to Cape Farewell, at Greenland's southern tip, it is about 1,650 miles (2,670 km.), a distance greater than that from Winnipeg, Canada, to the southern tip of Texas. About 47,000 people live in this great expanse, fewer people than may live within a few blocks of a large European or American city.

The vast stretches of Greenland's interior are covered by the Inland Ice, a gargantuan, dome-shaped accumulation of ice and snow of more than 700,000 square miles (1,800,000 sq. km.). Estimates of the thickness of the Inland Ice go to 2 miles (3 km.) and even more. The Inland Ice is girded by great, craggy mountains, with the highest peak reaching over 12,000 feet (3,700 meters). The pressure from its own weight is constantly pushing the ice cap outward in the form of glaciers. Squeezing through the coastal valleys, the glaciers break off, or "calve," sending great icebergs thundering into Greenland's fiords. These icebergs, as well as the frequent fogs and severe storms of the area, constitute major hazards to shipping around Greenland.

The Inland Ice restricts settlements to the coast. Even on the ice-free stretch of the coast of southwestern Greenland, men seem dwarfed by the land, the steep mountains, and the deep fiords. None of the settlements is very large; Godthaab, the largest town and capital, has a population of about 6,000 people. Water is scarce in this generally rugged, bare, and rocky terrain, and there are no forests of any size. Almost all wood must be imported. The sheltered valleys support farming—principally sheep farming—but the size of herds is limited by the relatively small amount of fodder that can be produced on the land. There is some mining of cryolite (used in making soda and aluminum) and of coal. Greenlanders must, therefore, depend largely on the sea for their living.

The People

Greenland is an integral political part of Denmark, but most Greenlanders are of mixed Eskimo and European descent. One may therefore encounter people who have blonde hair, blue eyes, and at the same time, the distinctly Mongoloid features of the Eskimo.

It is generally assumed that the Eskimo came to Greenland more than 1,000 years ago, having crossed over from the mainland of North America. The first known European settlers, led by Eric the Red, encountered relics of Eskimo settlements, but not the Eskimo themselves. Possibly they had migrated from the island at that time, or perhaps they were living in northern or eastern Greenland. The Norsemen settled in southwestern Greenland, principally in two major settlements near present-day Godthaab and Julianehaab. The settlements survived, and during the 11th and 12th centuries the population may have risen to about 9,000 settlers of European—principally Norwegian—descent. The Europeans raised cattle, hunted, and traded with Europe. In the 16th century, the settlers disappeared, but no one is quite sure what happened to them. The last written record of the Norsemen is a marriage license issued in 1408. Archeological evidence has been found, however, to indicate the survival of Norsemen to the 16th century.

History

For centuries the Greenland Eskimo lived in their traditional nomadic way. Then, in 1721, Hans Egede, a Norwegian Lutheran missionary spon-

A group of Eskimo stroll down a main street in Godthaab.

sored by the King of Denmark, established a small settlement on the west coast of Greenland. His mission was to renew the ties to Christianity of whatever Norsemen might remain in Greenland. Finding that there were no more Norsemen, Egede devoted himself to introducing both Christianity and Scandinavian civilization to the Eskimo. About the same time, Danish traders came to western Greenland. Missionaries and educators learned the native Eskimo dialect and taught the Eskimo to read and write. In the course of the 19th century, illiteracy was virtually abolished in Greenland. The native Eskimo tongue remains the predominant language on the island even today.

The greatest changes in the Greenlanders' way of life have taken place in the 20th century. Beginning about 1917, the gradual warming of Greenland's coastal waters drove the seal north and brought in cod. The Eskimo kayak is giving way to the motorized fishing boat, and fish-processing plants have been built in almost every town. Social, political, and economic ties with Denmark have been strengthened. In 1953 Greenland, which had been a colony of Denmark, became fully integrated politically with the mother country. Today Greenlanders enjoy all the rights of Danish citizenship.

Since World War II, Greenland has assumed importance as an outpost of Western defense. The United States has built large military airfields in Søndre Strømfjord and Thule, as well as a complete defense system at Thule. There are also a number of American Distant Early Warning (DEW line) stations in Greenland.

Reviewed by ULLA CHRISTIANSEN, Danish Information Office, New York

UNITED STATES: AN INTRODUCTION

by Henry Steele COMMAGER
Author, The American Mind

Those men who won American independence and launched the new United States had a very special conception of history and of America's place in history. They were familiar enough with the past—especially the classical past—and with the lessons of history. But they did not believe that America was shackled by that past or bound by those lessons. While the new nation was not to be exempt from history, neither was it the prisoner of history. It was the special glory of America that it was to launch a new era in history, that it was to embark upon a series of experiments that had no precedent in the past. Here, in this New World, man was to have a second chance. Here, in this great historical laboratory, it might be possible to work out the laws of history—not of past history, but of future. Here could be traced the interaction between heredity and environment—the heredity that of the past; the environment that of vast and varied and rich new land. Here it would be possible to discover whether man was capable of governing himself; whether he could create a civilization not only materially rich but intellectually and morally rich, a civilization that would be prosperous, free, humane, and just. For here, in the most favorable environment ever granted mankind, men could work out their destiny free from those ancient tyrannies that had plagued them from the beginning of recorded history: the tyranny of the despot and of the state, the tyranny of ignorance and poverty and plague and war. Here, for the first time, it might be possible to show what man was really capable of.

For George Washington and Thomas Jefferson and Tom Paine and many of the other Founding Fathers, the American people now had a heaven-sent opportunity to triumph over the past and to mold the future. That was what Washington meant when he wrote that "the Foundation of our Empire was not laid in the gloomy age of Ignorance and Superstition, but at an Epoch when the Rights of Mankind were better understood and more clearly defined than at any former period, the researches of the human mind after social happiness . . . carried to a great extent, and the Treasures of knowledge, acquired by the labours of Philosophers, Sages and Legislatures . . . laid open for our use." That is what Jefferson meant when he wrote of America that "this whole chapter in the history of man is new. The great extent of our territory is new. Its sparse population is new. The mighty wave of public opinion which has rolled over it is new." This is what the French philosopher-statesman Turgot meant when he wrote of Americans that "This people is the hope of the Human Race." Perhaps Tom Paine put it more dramatically than anyone: the American, he said, was a new Adam in a new Paradise.

A Well-Favored Land

All the conditions were favorable—all perhaps, but the presence in the new nation of the hateful institution of Negro slavery. Americans occupied the richest territory that had ever been open to any people—a territory that was still virgin land. There was land enough, said Jefferson in his first Inaugural Address, "for our descendants to the thousandth and thousandth generation." Americans had a benign government which did not "take from the mouth of labor the bread it has earned." They enjoyed immunity from the wars of the Old World. They had religious freedom. They were an enlightened people with the highest standards of literacy anywhere in the world. They cherished science and education, made important contributions to both, and made the benefits of both available to all men alike, or, at least, all who were free. Thanks to a century and a half of experience in self-government, they were more mature politically than any other people on the globe.

They created a nation—something no other people had ever done before, for heretofore nations had not been "created" but had grown. They confronted squarely the problem of tyranny in government, and managed to fix curbs on governmental power: the written Constitution, the separation of powers, checks and balances, the Bill of Rights, and judicial review among them. They even invented the modern political party to enable men to make their governmental mechanisms work and help democracy function. All of these great political inventions are still working pretty much as they were originally designed to work.

Philosophically, too, the new principles and institutions appeared to work. The principle that men make government and that all the powers of government derive from the people did not bring about political upheavals, but, on the whole, order and tranquility. The principle of the independence of Church from the State did not lead to a decline in religion or a breakdown in morals; the churches flourished and the moral standards were quite as high as those elsewhere. The principle of the supremacy of the civil to the military authority was faithfully observed— even during the Civil War—without any danger to the safety of the republic. The greatest mixture of peoples and languages in modern national history went into the melting pot, although the melting pot did not melt everything and everybody down to a single product. Finally, if democracy did not produce a society where everyone was equal, it produced one where there were no legal distinctions between classes, and except for Negroes, few other distinctions that talent and energy could not overcome. For almost a century slavery cast its dark shadow across the whole of the American scene. Even after slavery had been abolished, racial prejudice and the exploitation of blacks by whites persisted. This was, and is, the greatest failure of American democracy. It is a failure which the new generation of Americans can—and must—overcome.

The Growth of the Country

In the area of growth, too, history seemed to justify the optimism of the Founding Fathers. By the thousand and then by the million, immigrants came to the new nation that beckoned across the Atlantic. Wave after wave they came, settling into the cities along the Atlantic seaboard, swarming out onto the prairies and the plains, creating new commonwealths, but merging, too, in the great web of American society. Within the lifetime of those who had seen George Washington inaugurated as the first President of the United States, Oregon and California were admitted to the Union. That was how fast the new nation expanded and grew. By the end of the 19th century the United States had become the leading industrial nation of the world, the leader, too, in agriculture, transportation, and finance.

No wonder that Americans of the 19th century congratulated themselves that better than any other people they had justified faith in progress. No wonder they took for granted that the "pursuit of happiness was carried on here under Providential auspices and with Providential blessing, and that many new states, as they came into the Union, guaranteed to their citizens in their Constitutions not only the right to pursue happiness, but to obtain it!" Nor is it surprising that again and again throughout their history Americans should revive that sense of destiny which had first sustained the Puritans and then the Founding Fathers in their struggle for independence and nation-making. In the 19th century that sense of mission took the form of Manifest Destiny, and was invoked to justify the Mexican War and to rationalize the war to liberate Cuba from Spanish rule; in the 20th century, it took the form of a crusade "to make the world safe for democracy."

Changing America

Yet, inevitably, history caught up with the Americans. Or perhaps we might say that in time the forces of heredity—that is, of history—and human nature proved more powerful than those of environment. With the passing years the United States became more and more like the nations of western Europe—and these came to be more and more like the United States. All were troubled by the same large problems; all were being transformed by technology and science; all were caught up in world as well as domestic problems; all, eventually, were involved in global wars. By the middle of the 20th century, Jefferson's America was, superficially, almost unrecognizable. It had been transformed from a rural to an urban nation; from an agricultural to an industrial. It had abandoned isolation for globalism. It had changed from a classless society to one that was flawed by great extremes of wealth and poverty and by tensions between ethnic and racial groups. It had used up many of those fabulous resources designed to last to the thousandth generation. It had lost whatever "innocence" had distinguished it from the Old World, as it had given up its repugnance to the military and become the world's leading military power.

Thus over a span of two centuries the United States had lost or forfeited many of its advantages. Yet, the American nation, for all the problems that glare upon her from every corner of the horizon, is still immensely strong in will, in power, in resources and in resourcefulness. It is still relatively safe from attack, except by atomic weapons which no power dares to use. It still cherishes religious freedom and other freedoms as well, for though there are storm clouds on the horizon, the Bill of Rights is respected. Americans have, over the years, created a distinctive style of life, one rooted in older civilizations, to be sure, but full of energy and ingenuity and originality, and contributing more and more to the world of literature, the arts, and science.

There is nothing certain in history. Most of the great civilizations of the past have declined or disappeared, as many of the great empires of our own civilization have disappeared. That may be our fate too, for we are not exempt from history. It remains for the next generation, and its successors, to make sure that this will not be so.

"The Declaration of Independence" (1786–96), oil painting by John Trumbull. Yale University Art Gallery.

UNITED STATES

American historians have never agreed on what caused the spectacular development of their country. Some have sincerely believed that a love of freedom motivated much of the early development of the United States. Other historians have cited the desire for adventure, the lust for gold and land, or the itch to get more "elbow room" as reasons for the nation's expansion and growth. Surely it requires a multitude of personalities and motivations to conquer a wilderness of continental size, and it is likely that all these motives played a part.

Discovery

A taste for adventure drove the Vikings of Scandinavia to seek out new lands. They were intrepid seamen. Appearing out of the north about A.D. 1000, they were the first white men known to have reached North America. The Vikings probably made their initial landings on the coasts of Newfoundland, Cape Breton Island, or Nova Scotia.

Vinland, as the Norsemen named the new North American continent, slumbered untouched by further European exploration for almost 5 centuries before a Genoese sea captain, Christopher Columbus, sailing under the Spanish flag, rediscovered the New World. For Columbus, landfall came none too soon: his 3 small ships were easily tossed in heavy seas, and many of the crewmen, clinging to the superstition that the earth was flat, feared that at any moment they might tumble with their ships over the "edge" into dark oblivion. They were beginning to contemplate mutiny. Finally, one evening, they saw land on the horizon.

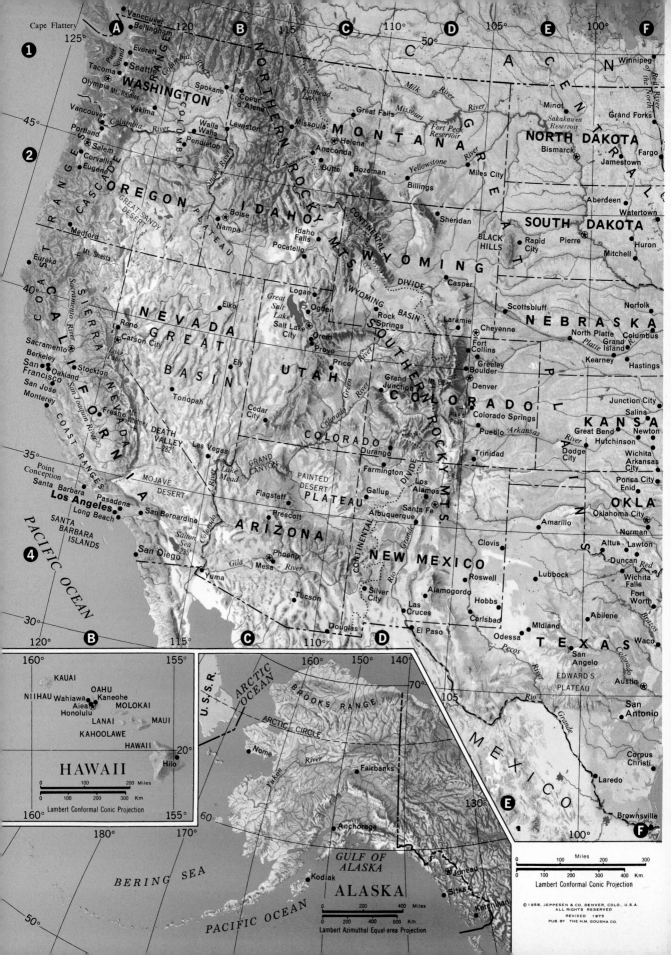

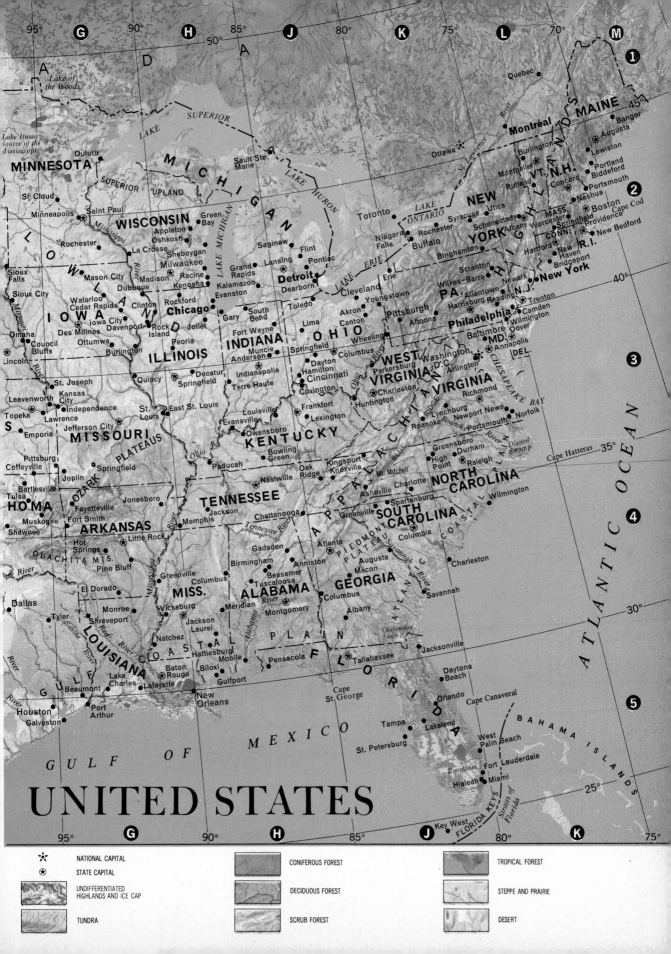

UNITED STATES

Lake of the Woods
Lake Itasca Source of the Mississippi

CANADA

95° G 90° H 85° J 80° K 75° L 70° M

Quebec

1

LAKE SUPERIOR

Montréal MAINE 45°

MINNESOTA
Duluth
Sault Ste. Marie
MICHIGAN
Ottawa
St. Lawrence River
Bangor
Augusta
Lewiston
Burlington
Montpelier VT. N.H. Portland
Concord Biddeford

2

St. Cloud
Minneapolis
Saint Paul
SUPERIOR UPLAND
LAKE HURON
Toronto
LAKE ONTARIO
Rutland Nashua Portsmouth
NEW Syracuse Utica Boston Cape Cod
WISCONSIN
Green Bay
LAKE MICHIGAN
Saginaw
Niagara Falls
Rochester
YORK Schenectady Albany Worcester MASS. Springfield Providence
Appleton
Oshkosh
Flint
Pontiac
Buffalo
Binghamton Scranton CONN. Hartford New Bedford
La Crosse
Sheboygan
Lansing
Erie
Wilkes-Barre New Haven R.I.
Bridgeport

Sioux Falls
Rochester
Madison Racine
Grand Rapids
Kalamazoo
LAKE ERIE
Cleveland
Youngstown
PA.
Allentown
Newark New York 40°
Mason City
Milwaukee
Evanston
Toledo
Akron
Pittsburgh
Altoona
Harrisburg Reading Trenton
N.J.

Sioux City
Dubuque
Kenosha
Gary
South Bend
Canton
Camden
Waterloo
Clinton
Rockford
Fort Wayne
Lima
OHIO
Wheeling
Philadelphia Wilmington
Cedar Rapids
Chicago
WEST Washington Baltimore Dover
IOWA
Joliet
INDIANA
Springfield
Columbus
VIRGINIA
D.C. MD. Annapolis
3
Omaha
Des Moines
Davenport
Peoria
Muncie
Dayton
Parkersburg
Arlington DEL.
Council Bluffs
Ottumwa
Rock Island
ILLINOIS
Anderson
Hamilton Cincinnati
VIRGINIA
CHESAPEAKE BAY
Lincoln
Burlington
Indianapolis
Terre Haute
Covington
Charleston
Richmond

St. Joseph
Quincy
Decatur
Springfield
Frankfort
Huntington
Lynchburg
Newport News
Kansas City
East St. Louis
Louisville
Lexington
Roanoke Portsmouth
Leavenworth
Independence
St. Louis
Evansville
KENTUCKY
BLUE RIDGE
Norfolk
Lawrence
Jefferson City
Owensboro
Greensboro Durham
Cape Hatteras 35°
Topeka
MISSOURI
Bowling Green
High Point
Raleigh
S
Emporia
PLATEAUS
Paducah
Oak Ridge Kingsport
Point
Dismal Swamp
Springfield
Ohio R.
Nashville
Knoxville
Mt. Mitchell
NORTH

Pittsburg
Joplin
OZARK
Nashville
Charlotte
CAROLINA
Wilmington
Coffeyville
Asheville
Spartanburg
4
Bartlesville
Jonesboro
TENNESSEE
Greenville
SOUTH
Tulsa
Jackson
Chattanooga
PIEDMONT
Columbia
HOMA
Fayetteville
ARKANSAS
Memphis
Tennessee River
Greenville
CAROLINA
Muskogee
Fort Smith
APPALACHIAN
COASTAL
Shawnee
Gadsden
PLATEAU
Columbia
Hot Springs
Atlanta
Augusta
Charleston
Little Rock
Birmingham
Anniston
Macon
OUACHITA MTS.
Pine Bluff
Bessemer
GEORGIA
Savannah
El Dorado
Greenville
Columbus
Tuscaloosa
Columbus
Monroe
MISS.
ALABAMA
Albany
Dallas
Tyler
Shreveport
Vicksburg
Jackson
Montgomery
30°
Natchez
Meridian
ATL.

LOUISIANA
Laurel
PLAIN
FLORIDA
Jacksonville
Hattiesburg
Mobile
Okefenokee Swamp
Beaumont
Lake Charles
Baton Rouge
Biloxi
Pensacola
Tallahassee
Daytona Beach
Houston
Port Arthur
Lafayette
Gulfport
Galveston
New Orleans
Cape St. George
Orlando
Cape Canaveral
5
GULF
Tampa
Lakeland
BAHAMA ISLANDS
St. Petersburg
West Palm Beach
MEXICO
Everglades
Fort Lauderdale
Hialeah Miami
ATLANTIC OCEAN
GULF OF MEXICO
Key West FLORIDA KEYS Straits of Florida
95° G 90° H 85° J 80° K 75°

	NATIONAL CAPITAL		CONIFEROUS FOREST		TROPICAL FOREST
	STATE CAPITAL		DECIDUOUS FOREST		STEPPE AND PRAIRIE
	UNDIFFERENTIATED HIGHLANDS AND ICE CAP		SCRUB FOREST		DESERT
	TUNDRA				

INDEX TO UNITED STATES MAP

The next day they saw sandpipers and green reeds in the water. The crewmen danced on the decks of their ships. On Friday, October 12, 1492, Columbus waded ashore on an island the local Indians called Guanahani (San Salvador Island in the Bahamas) and claimed possession of the land for King Ferdinand and Queen Isabella of Spain. Luck favored Columbus. For years the Indians had believed that a ship would appear bearing a white god. When the Spaniards arrived, they were treated with great respect.

The Spaniards, too, could be misled by fantasies. After many centuries of fighting the Moors, Spain tottered on the brink of bankruptcy. Therefore, the Spanish will-o'-the-wisp was the fabulous legend of the Seven Cities of Cibola, where the streets were paved with gold. Of course, no one could really say where Cibola was.

One day in 1536 Spanish slave hunters came upon a small group of Spaniards accompanied by a single black man. The leader of this bedraggled party, which had escaped from a shipwreck off the coast of Texas, was Álvar Núñez Cabeza de Vaca. Cabeza de Vaca practically hypnotized his fellow Spaniards with his tales of Indians shooting arrows tipped with emeralds and of fabulous treasures in the legendary Cibola.

Hernando de Soto, who had served with Pizarro in the conquest of Peru, was fascinated by the yarns of Cabeza de Vaca and apparently believed everything he heard. The King of Spain appointed De Soto governor of Cuba, with permission to conquer all of the unknown land north of the Gulf of Mexico. But De Soto had almost phenomenal bad luck. Instead of finding the shining towers of the Seven Cities, he encountered a vicious little war with the Choctaw members of the Creek Confederacy in present-day Alabama.

De Soto searched the banks of the Yazoo River, one of the tributaries of the Mississippi, for gold, and, finding none, pressed on to the Mississippi the following spring. He died of "the fevers" in May, 1542. He never found great treasures.

In the late 16th and early 17th centuries, exploration of the New World attracted adventurers from many other countries—including Britain, France, the Netherlands, Sweden, and Denmark. Lured by the vast profits that could be won by exchanging trinkets for valuable fur pelts, companies chartered by these nations built trading posts and forts. The French voyageurs even ventured by canoe along rivers into the interior, trading with the Indians as they went. Most of the explorers and most of the investors who financed their expeditions still believed there was a great treasure to be found. Others, like Henry Hudson, sought out another legend—the Northwest Passage, a fabled water channel through

"The Rocky Mountains—Emigrants Crossing the Plains" (1866), **lithograph by Currier and Ives. Collection of Roy King.**

the North American continent to the Pacific and on to Asia beyond. In the 19th century explorers finally learned that the Northwest Passage did not exist as they imagined it.

Settlement

In 1607 captains Christopher Newport, John Ratcliffe, and Bartholomew Gosnold turned their ships between Cape Henry and Cape Charles and steered up the James River to the site where they planned Jamestown, the first permanent English colony in the New World. A more miserable setting for a town could hardly be imagined: the land was swampy and alive with mosquitoes.

To their bitter disappointment, the gentlemen adventurers found no gold nuggets in New World forests. They had to become farmers or starve. Jamestown would probably have collapsed had not John Rolfe brought a strain of Caribbean tobacco with him that grew easily in the rich Virginia soil. This New World plant was in great demand in England and proved to be the financial base for the precarious beginnings of the future United States.

The Pilgrims who sailed from England aboard the Mayflower in 1620 were supposed to reinforce the Virginia Company claims on the North American coast. Their ship found safe harbor at a place called Plymouth, above the northern curve of Cape Cod. The Mayflower immigrants were the first to seek the New World for motives other than adventure or greed, for they were, in fact, pilgrims who had endured religious persecution in the Old World. They were the prototype of a long line of refugees who came to America in search of liberty. It was this longing for religious freedom that drove them to brave the hazards of the North Atlantic in their tiny craft. A larger migration to New England (Massachusetts Bay) followed in 1630, motivated by the same zeal for liberty to worship in accordance with the stern Puritan conscience.

FACTS AND FIGURES

UNITED STATES OF AMERICA is the official name of the country.

CAPITAL: Washington, D.C.

LOCATION: Forty-nine states and the District of Columbia are on the continent of North America. Hawaii, the 50th state, is in the North Pacific Ocean. **Latitude**—24° 33′ N to 49° N (without Alaska and Hawaii). **Longitude**—66° 57′ W to 124° 45′ W (without Alaska and Hawaii). **Latitude**—24° 33′ N to 71° 23′ N (without Hawaii). **Longitude**—66° 57′ W to 172° 27′ E (without Hawaii).

AREA: 3,615,123 sq. mi. (9,363,169 sq. km.).

PHYSICAL FEATURES: Highest point—Mount McKinley, Alaska (20,320 ft.; 6,194 m.). **Lowest point**—Badwater, Death Valley, California, 282 ft. (86 m.) below sea level. **Chief rivers**—Missouri, Mississippi, Arkansas, Red, Rio Grande, Columbia, Colorado, Yukon. **Major lakes**—Huron, Ontario, Michigan, Erie, Superior, Great Salt, Iliamna.

POPULATION: 203,000,000 (1970 census).

LANGUAGE: English.

RELIGION: Protestant, Roman Catholic, Jewish.

GOVERNMENT: Federal union of 50 states. **Head of government**—president. **Legislature**—Congress (Senate, House of Representatives). **International co-**operation—United Nations, Organization of American States (OAS), North Atlantic Treaty Organization (NATO), Southeast Asia Treaty Organization (SEATO), Organization for Economic Co-operation and Development (OECD).

CHIEF CITIES: New York City, Chicago, Los Angeles, Philadelphia, San Francisco, Detroit, Pittsburgh, St. Louis, Washington, D.C., New Orleans, Boston, Houston.

ECONOMY: Chief minerals—coal, petroleum and natural gas, copper, iron ore, sand and gravel, stone. **Chief agricultural products**—wheat, corn, cattle, hogs, dairy products, cotton, soybeans, tobacco. **Industries and products**—food processing, transportation equipment, machinery, electrical equipment, chemical products, iron and steel. **Chief exports**—machinery and transport equipment, chemicals, wheat and other grains, soybeans, tobacco, precision instruments. **Chief imports**—machinery and transport equipment, petroleum and petroleum products, paper and paper products, clothing, meat, coffee.

MONETARY UNIT: U.S. dollar.

NATIONAL HOLIDAY: July 4, Independence Day.

NATIONAL ANTHEM: "The Star-Spangled Banner."

MOTTO: In God We Trust.

NATIONAL SYMBOL: Bald eagle.

"Midnight Ride of Paul Revere" (1931), oil painting by Grant Wood. The Metropolitan Museum of Art, New York City, Arthur H. Hearn Fund, 1950. Courtesy of Associated American Artists, New York.

Of course once the English colonists gained the "safety" of the New World, they frowned upon anyone who dissented from their strict beliefs. This led other English settlers to strike out for Rhode Island.

But with the exception of the New Englanders, most original settlers were not particularly interested in freedom or the rights of man. As a rule they were driven far more by the desire for wealth. It was primarily this motivation that brought about success in colonization on the extensive scale preceding the American Revolution. In the late 17th century the English swept away Dutch government control of New York and of other scattered settlements reaching to the upper part of Chesapeake Bay. The English came to command the Atlantic Coast of North America from the French holdings north of Massachusetts to the Spanish claims south of the Carolinas. The claims of the Indians, the original inhabitants of the whole continent, were sometimes settled by payment of token sums and trinkets; more often they were ignored or settled in blood.

Meanwhile French voyageurs and priests explored the northern interior of North America in search of furs. Under the leadership of Father Jacques Marquette and Louis Jolliet, who carried their canoes across portages to the Wisconsin River and from there paddled on to the Mississippi, the French made a serious bid to offset the commercial claims of the British.

The French eventually lost their great North American empire to the British. However, the British were themselves to face trouble with their colonial offspring.

Revolution

Among the rebels stood many towering figures—Benjamin Franklin, Thomas Jefferson, Patrick Henry, John Adams, Thomas Paine, and numerous other revolutionaries—but none with head held higher than George Washington of Virginia.

As a young man, Washington became a favorite of Lord Fairfax, the great Virginia landowner, who sent him on surveying jobs into the northern and western uplands of Virginia. He emerged as an experienced explorer and later became a colonel of the Virginia Militia. As an officer he tried to avoid a war with the French and the Indians.

The ill-starred French and Indian wars, which Washington tried to avert, were fought—and many battles were lost as badly as Washington had predicted they would be, because the British had no understanding of Indian warfare. Following his role in these wars Washington went on to become an influential figure in Virginia's House of Burgesses.

When the French and Indian War, the concluding war of the series, ended in 1763, the British controlled Canada, too. Their holdings in the New World were now so vast that they tried to pay much closer attention to their American colonies. The "attention" took the form of new controls and taxes, which were soon interpreted by some colonists as a threat to their liberties. When the British closed the port of Boston and issued decrees concerning the quartering of troops in private houses in Boston, Washington saw clearly the tragedy that was casting a shadow across the land. In April, 1775, shots rang out at Lexington and Concord. On July 4, 1776, representatives of the thirteen colonies gathered at Philadelphia to declare that the "United States of America" was an independent nation.

The hard struggle began in earnest. Washington, commanding the bedraggled militia that miraculously defeated the professional Redcoat armies, was most astonished at the sacrifices people suffered for the sake of those personal freedoms that they believed were God-given. The desperate determination that comes from fighting for one's own territory against an invader more than made up for the poverty and amateurishness of the American volunteers.

But if the British could not defeat the Americans, there was for a time considerable question whether the Americans would defeat themselves. The newborn country staggered under a system of government called the Articles of Confederation. Each ex-colony was so jealous of its freedom that it wished to function almost as a separate nation (which is what "state" meant) and resisted giving power to any central authority. States were allowed to levy taxes and borrow money.

Predictably, the worst happened. Currency became valueless, giving rise to the saying, "Not worth a Continental." Farmers owed money to merchants, who, in turn, owed it to bankers. Almost everyone owed taxes to his state. Now that Americans had their hard-won "victory," foreign nations began to reckon how many months it would take for the United States of America to fall apart.

The Constitution

In 1787 the states convened a Constitutional Convention in Philadelphia, where their representatives buckled down to the formidable task of forging a workable government.

A later president, Woodrow Wilson, called George Washington "the heart and soul" of that Constitutional Convention. Walking the streets of Philadelphia in the blazing summer of 1787, Washington was equally polite to convention members under the age of 30 and to wispy-haired old Benjamin Franklin from Philadelphia. Washington knew the varying and, at times, competing interests that these delegates represented. His wartime experiences had taught him much about the new country.

FACTS ABOUT THE 50 STATES

STATE	ABBR.	CAPITAL	AREA (sq. mi.)	(sq. km.)	RANK IN AREA	POPULATION (1970 census)	RANK IN POP.	NICKNAME	ADMITTED TO UNION
Alabama	Ala.	Montgomery	51,609	133,667	29	3,444,165	21	Heart of Dixie	1819
Alaska	——	Juneau	586,412	1,518,807	1	302,173	50	The Great Land (not official)	1959
Arizona	Ariz.	Phoenix	113,909	295,025	6	1,772,482	33	Grand Canyon State	1912
Arkansas	Ark.	Little Rock	53,104	137,540	27	1,923,295	32	Land of Opportunity	1836
California	Calif.	Sacramento	158,693	411,015	3	19,953,134	1	Golden State	1850
Colorado	Colo.	Denver	104,247	270,000	8	2,207,259	30	Centennial State	1876
Connecticut	Conn.	Hartford	5,009	12,973	48	3,032,217	24	Constitution State	1788
Delaware	Del.	Dover	2,057	5,328	49	548,104	46	The First State	1787
Florida	Fla.	Tallahassee	58,560	151,670	22	6,789,443	9	Sunshine State	1845
Georgia	Ga.	Atlanta	58,876	152,489	21	4,589,575	15	Peach State (not official)	1788
Hawaii	——	Honolulu	6,450	16,706	47	769,913	40	Aloha State	1959
Idaho	Ida.	Boise	83,557	216,413	13	713,008	42	Gem of the Mountains	1890
Illinois	Ill.	Springfield	56,400	146,076	24	11,113,976	5	Land of Lincoln	1818
Indiana	Ind.	Indianapolis	36,291	93,994	38	5,193,669	11	Hoosier State	1816
Iowa	Io.	Des Moines	56,290	145,791	25	2,825,041	25	Hawkeye State	1846
Kansas	Kans.	Topeka	82,264	213,064	14	2,249,071	28	Sunflower State	1861
Kentucky	Ky.	Frankfort	40,395	104,623	37	3,219,311	23	Bluegrass State	1792
Louisiana	La.	Baton Rouge	48,523	125,675	31	3,643,180	20	Pelican State	1812
Maine	Me.	Augusta	33,215	86,027	39	993,663	38	Pine Tree State	1820
Maryland	Md.	Annapolis	10,577	27,394	42	3,922,399	18	Old Line State	1788
Massachusetts	Mass.	Boston	8,257	21,386	45	5,689,170	10	Bay State	1788
Michigan	Mich.	Lansing	58,216	150,780	23	8,875,083	7	Water-Winter Wonderland	1837
Minnesota	Minn.	Saint Paul	84,068	217,736	12	3,805,069	19	Gopher State	1858
Mississippi	Miss.	Jackson	47,716	123,585	32	2,216,912	29	Magnolia State	1817
Missouri	Mo.	Jefferson City	69,686	180,487	19	4,677,399	13	"Show Me" State	1821
Montana	Mont.	Helena	147,138	381,088	4	694,409	43	Treasure State	1889
Nebraska	Nebr.	Lincoln	77,227	200,018	15	1,483,791	35	Cornhusker State	1867
Nevada	Nev.	Carson City	110,540	286,299	7	488,738	47	Silver State	1864
New Hampshire	N.H.	Concord	9,304	24,097	44	737,681	41	Granite State	1788
New Jersey	N.J.	Trenton	7,836	20,295	46	7,168,164	8	Garden State	1787
New Mexico	N. Mex.	Santa Fe	121,666	315,115	5	1,016,000	37	Land of Enchantment	1912
New York	N.Y.	Albany	49,576	128,402	30	18,241,266	2	Empire State	1788
North Carolina	N.C.	Raleigh	52,586	136,198	28	5,082,059	12	Tarheel State	1789
North Dakota	N. Dak.	Bismarck	70,665	183,023	17	617,761	45	Flickertail State	1889
Ohio	——	Columbus	41,222	106,765	35	10,652,017	6	Buckeye State	1803
Oklahoma	Okla.	Oklahoma City	69,919	181,090	18	2,559,253	27	Sooner State	1907
Oregon	Oreg.	Salem	96,981	251,181	10	2,091,385	31	Beaver State	1859
Pennsylvania	Pa.	Harrisburg	45,333	117,412	33	11,793,909	3	Keystone State	1787
Rhode Island	R.I.	Providence	1,214	3,144	50	949,723	39	Little Rhody	1790
South Carolina	S.C.	Columbia	31,055	80,432	40	2,590,516	26	Palmetto State	1788
South Dakota	S. Dak.	Pierre	77,047	199,552	16	666,257	44	Sunshine State	1889
Tennessee	Tenn.	Nashville	42,244	109,412	34	3,924,164	17	Volunteer State	1796
Texas	Tex.	Austin	267,338	692,406	2	11,196,730	4	Lone Star State	1845
Utah	——	Salt Lake City	84,916	219,933	11	1,059,273	36	Beehive State	1896
Vermont	Vt.	Montpelier	9,609	24,887	43	444,732	48	Green Mountain State	1791
Virginia	Va.	Richmond	40,817	105,716	36	4,648,494	14	Old Dominion	1788
Washington	Wash.	Olympia	68,192	176,617	20	3,409,169	22	Evergreen State	1889
West Virginia	W. Va.	Charleston	24,181	62,629	41	1,744,237	34	Mountain State	1863
Wisconsin	Wis.	Madison	56,154	145,439	26	4,417,933	16	Badger State	1848
Wyoming	Wyo.	Cheyenne	97,914	253,598	9	332,416	49	Equality State	1890

CHRONOLOGY OF UNITED STATES HISTORY

1492	Columbus lands in the New World.
1607	Founding of first permanent English colony, Jamestown, Virginia.
1775	Battles of Lexington and Concord signal beginning of American Revolution; Second Continental Congress meets.
1776	July 4, Declaration of Independence adopted at Philadelphia.
1781	British surrender at Yorktown, Virginia; U.S. becomes self-governing.
1787	Congress passes Northwest Ordinance; Constitutional Convention meets at Philadelphia.
1789	Government under Constitution begins; Washington is first president.
1791	Bill of Rights added to United States Constitution.
1803	United States buys Louisiana Territory from France.
1804–1806	Lewis and Clark Expedition crosses North America.
1812–1814	War of 1812.
1819	Florida ceded to the United States by Spain.
1820	Missouri Compromise.
1825	Erie Canal opened.
1836	Texas revolts against Mexico, gains independence as a nation.
1842	Great westward migration to Oregon begins.
1845	United States annexes Texas.
1846	United States-British border dispute settled, making Oregon a United States territory; Mexican War begins.
1848	Mexican War ends with United States acquiring from Mexico territory that included New Mexico, Arizona, Colorado, Utah, Nevada, Wyoming, and California. Gold Rush to California begins.
1850	California admitted to Union as free state, as part of Compromise of 1850.
1860	Abraham Lincoln elected president; South Carolina secedes from the Union.
1861	Firing on Fort Sumter begins Civil War.
1862	Homestead Act grants free land to settlers.
1863	Emancipation Proclamation frees slaves.
1865	Civil War ends; Lincoln assassinated; 13th Amendment to U.S. Constitution abolishes slavery.
1867	U.S. buys Alaska from Russia.
1869	"Golden Spike" ceremony marks completion of transcontinental railroad.
1898	Spanish-American War; United States gains Philippines, Puerto Rico, Guam.
1914	Panama Canal opens, linking Atlantic and Pacific.
1917	United States enters World War I.
1920	19th Amendment gives women right to vote.
1929	Stock market crash; Depression begins.
1933	New Deal begins, with Congress passing acts aimed at recovery from Depression.
1941	Japanese attack on Pearl Harbor, December 7, signals United States declaration of war on the Axis powers and entrance into World War II.
1945	United States drops first atomic bomb on Hiroshima; United States and 49 other nations sign United Nations Charter in San Francisco; World War II ends.
1950–1953	Korean War.
1954	Supreme Court declares racial segregation in public schools unconstitutional.
1959	Alaska and Hawaii admitted to Union.
1963	Assassination of President John F. Kennedy; Lyndon Johnson becomes president.
1964	Civil Rights Act passed.
1964–1973	United States involvement in war in Southeast Asia.
1969	First men land on the moon.
1973	Cease-fire agreement signed ending U.S. involvement in Vietnam.
1974	President Richard M. Nixon resigns; Vice-President Gerald R. Ford becomes president.
1975	United States prepares for its 1976 Bicentennial.

Washington's wit, his charm, and his obvious goodness of personality softened many an argument, outside the convention meetings, that might have grown even more acrimonious behind the locked doors of Convention Hall when the Convention was in session. When their work was finally done, the delegates had not only written a new Constitution, but had created a new kind of government.

That Constitution, now one of the oldest written constitutions still in use, cut boldly through legal tangles that many statesmen had considered hopeless. It granted the central government the power to tax, to coin money, and to maintain armed forces. It created a federal court system crowned by a supreme court. To solve the nearly insuperable conflict between those who wanted representation by states and those who demanded representation based on population, it created a legislature of two houses: in the upper house (Senate) the states were equal, each with two representatives, but in the lower house (House of Representatives) the people were directly represented, giving the largest states the biggest delegate body.

By June, 1788, the required 9 states had ratified the Constitution and it became law. George Washington was elected first president of the new country. However, many Americans were still fearful that the liberation they had fought for might be snatched away by the more centralized powers under the Constitution. Therefore, in 1791 the Bill of Rights (the first ten amendments to the United States Constitution) made clear what the rights and freedoms of the United States people would be.

Opening the West

At first the land at the disposal of the United States seemed inexhaustible, especially after a monumental addition in 1803. In that year President Thomas Jefferson (not at all certain that he acted within his Constitutional rights) authorized his representative, James Monroe, to buy "Louisiana" from Napoleon. The Louisiana Purchase gave the United States title to all the remaining North American land claimed by France, land that covered perhaps 828,000 square miles (2,145,000 square kilometers).

An exploring expedition was organized, charged, in part, with investigating the extent of the new territory, much of which had never been seen by white men. The party was headed by Captain Meriwether Lewis, the President's private secretary, and William Clark, younger brother of the famous Indian fighter George Rogers Clark.

That spring (1804) Lewis and Clark started by flatboat up the Missouri River. By late autumn they had traveled 1,600 miles (2,575 kilometers) and had penetrated to the approximate site of present-day Bismarck, North Dakota, where they spent the winter.

As they penetrated farther into the West, fabulous sights met their eyes. And yet at the same time their journey disproved many legends

"Fur Traders Descending the Missouri" (1844?), oil painting by George Caleb Bingham. The Metropolitan Museum of Art, New York City. Morris K. Jessup Fund, 1933.

that people had believed for centuries. Their explorations laid to rest forever the dream that men could find a continuous navigable water passage cutting across the United States.

More than anything else the Lewis and Clark Expedition demonstrated that Americans were capable of crossing, perhaps someday conquering, this vast expanse of empire. Lewis and Clark crossed the Rockies in September, 1805; in November they saw at last the crashing surf of the Pacific Ocean. Returning the following spring, they divided into two parties for part of the trip, one traveling the Missouri and the other the Yellowstone, in search of less arduous passes through the Rockies. When the expedition reached St. Louis on September 23, 1806, the weary explorers had journeyed 9,000 miles (14,500 km.).

The Mountain Men

Far too little remembered, far too little revered are the mountain men. They first appeared in the 1820's, seeking beaver pelts when beaver hats were in fashion for men both in the United States and in Europe. Above the timberline of the Rockies, they trudged through ravines where no white man's foot had ever trod before.

Kit Carson was of this breed. So was Joseph Reddeford Walker, who, clutching a rifle in one hand and a Bible in the other, may have been the first white man to behold the beauty of the Yosemite region. Another famous Bible-toter, Jedediah Smith, discovered passes through the fortress wall of the Sierra Nevada Mountains; and Jim Bridger was the first to come upon the Great Salt Lake.

A onetime saddler's apprentice, Kit Carson drifted into the fur trade between St. Louis and "Touse," as the natives pronounced Taos, New Mexico, in those days. At the age of 19, Kit began to build his legendary reputation as a frontiersman and guide. From then on almost everyone— hunters seeking pelts, parties organized to kill buffalo herds, missionaries migrating to convert the Indians—tried to get Kit to help them. He served as guide to explorers, especially John C. Frémont, the Pathfinder, and to homesteaders from many countries.

During the first half of the 19th century something mysterious was taking place, something like the gradual shaping of a great wave. An expedition under Zebulon M. Pike (for whom was named Colorado's great peak) made many valuable discoveries. In the 1830's missionaries started westward. The Methodists reached "the Oregon country" and established a mission in 1835.

Before another decade had passed Kit Carson stood and watched endless trains of prairie schooners spreading their clouds of dust along the Santa Fe Trail, the Oregon Trail, and the California Trail. After 1848 additional hordes pressed across the Rockies to join the California Gold Rush. The West Coast's sudden population explosion demanded new means of communication. Now occasionally a horseman swept by, waving his hat to Kit or some other mountain man, playing his brief role: rider for the Pony Express. Already other men "sot" the posts and strung the coast-to-coast telegraph wires that spelled death for such enterprises as the Pony Express. Then came expeditions of a new kind—surveyors plotting the best course for the transcontinental railroad that would bring additional thousands of homesteaders taking advantage of the Homestead Act of 1862. The "golden spike" completing the railroad link was driven in 1869, 2 years after the United States reached farther still and bought Alaska from Russia. About this time there were other dust clouds, this time on north–south trails as Texas cowboys drove their herds of longhorns to railhead cow towns for sale.

For all the westering peoples, mountain men and homesteaders and cowboys, there were troubles peculiar to the frontier. There were Indian raids and rattlesnakes in the front yard. Barns and houses burned. Drought cracked the soil until it looked as if it had been cloven by earthquakes. Lightning bolted out of grayish summer skies, and prairie fires rolled like a sea of molten waves. In forested areas of the Northwest a man's back ached from clearing a field where the trees grew so thickly he could scarcely thrust his hand between them. Considering all this, it seemed the government helped little—but, on the other hand, it was too far away to interfere much with a man's freedom. The pioneers stayed and conquered and grew into a proud people.

Did they make America, or did the land itself make them? Geography certainly played a vital role in the development of the nation.

The Land

It is now almost 1,000 years since the Vikings beached their tiny craft on Vinland's shores; the modern explorers soaring among the clouds can view the country coast to coast in hours, about as long as it took a mountain man to hunt down a grizzly bear.

As it is hard to describe the glitter of precious gems, it is even harder to find words for the beauty of a city seen from the air at night. The surrounding countryside is like a black velvet pillow, and it is impossible to guess the location of forests, rivers, swamps, and farms. Then the jewel, the city, suddenly appears on the horizon. Perhaps by daylight it might have seemed no more than an ugly jumble of old factories and smoking chimneys, but dressed in a shining web of lights it takes on breathtaking splendor. Flying lower, one can see the highway lights and the corner street lamps start to form twinkling patterns. Sometimes the houses of the city are banked on hillsides, shedding the glow from their windows on lawns and driveways. Other houses give shape to the river valleys.

By daylight a different America appears. Most viewers are startled to find how much of the nation still remains forest and mountain and farmland. The country is a checkerboard of varying squares of yellow and green. There are fields of corn, of rye, of winter wheat—of any vegetable you wish to name. Cows graze in meadows, or, in Montana, chew their cuds while standing slantwise on steep mountainsides. The gentle valleys, their streams sparkling in the sunlight, drain the land. Many rivers join to meet the mighty Mississippi and flow "unvexed to the sea."

There are railroad tracks, reminders of the men long gone who riveted them to their ties, and airports with their neat runways. Only a computer could estimate how many thousands of miles of telephone and telegraph lines crisscross the continent. What is the meaning of this great network? Does it mean that abundant food and communication made America great?

Such an oversimplification cannot be the right answer. Forget for a moment the smoke and grime of the glowing blast furnaces of the steel mills around Birmingham, Alabama; or Gary and Hammond, Indiana; or Pittsburgh, Pennsylvania. Forget the freighters moving under the Golden

Gate Bridge into San Francisco Bay. There is no industry, no stream of commerce in which America is not involved. But think instead of the men themselves, formed as they were in the crucible of the continent. Vast and varied, it had a spot where every settler could find a place of his own. Some led colorless lives in the wilderness, but others seized the

"The Brooklyn Bridge: Variation on an Old Theme" (1939), oil painting by Joseph Stella. Collection Whitney Museum of American Art, New York City.

chance it offered and succeeded brilliantly. One day a pioneer might be destitute; not many days later, he might own acres of undulating ranch land in Colorado or Wyoming, or a transcontinental railroad, or a silver mine. He might see his city devastated, as Chicago was by the Great Fire of 1871; he might go on with others to rebuild it into one of America's greatest cities. This "boom and bust" theme, the theme of man surmounting catastrophe and hardship, was a continuing factor in the special American confrontation of the achieving, expanding spirit versus the formidable territory.

"Tough" symbols, petty and great, became part of America's notion of itself: the hickory stick of the one-room schoolmaster; the rise of baseball and football, showing that Americans could play as strenuously as they worked; the "Western" saga of cowboy and bad man. There are those, patriot and radical alike, who deduce from this history that violence and freedom are inseparable partners. For proof they point to the American Revolution or the violent acts of abolitionists like John Brown in the struggle to free black men from slavery. Others argue that violence is more often the partner of insanity. For proof they point to the Mexican War, the disgraceful treatment of the Indians, the Vietnam War, and the assassination of leaders like President John F. Kennedy and Martin Luther King, Jr. Whoever is right, no one can deny that Americans have fought many wars in their history.

As one can physically view the panorama of mountains and cities, one can mentally look back across the panorama of time. Grade school history gives such a panorama. Its true charm is that it paints pictures in bright colors and makes them easy to remember. The ragged soldiers at Valley Forge, the slaves herded like cattle on slave ships, the farmer plowing his field with his wife harnessed to the plow like a horse, the fortyniner panning gold in any icy California creek—who could forget such pictures? Or who could forget the bold portraits of individual heroes: Jefferson and the Declaration of Independence, Washington with the new Constitution and government, these and others framing the Bill of Rights with its emphasis on individual conscience? Or the brooding face of Lincoln at Gettysburg, grieving for the Civil War dead? From all this comes amazement at a society where an unknown boy, born in an obscure corner of the country, could suddenly burst upon the scene as did Abraham Lincoln and Andrew Jackson; a country where Franklin D. Roosevelt, a man stricken by polio at 39, could become president.

The years of Custer's Last Stand, of the bitter Reconstruction Era following the Civil War, the invention of the automobile, the wizardry of electricity unfolding in the mind of Thomas Edison, radio and television, Lindbergh's nonstop flight across the Atlantic, the invention of nuclear bombs, the creation of the United Nations, big cold wars and little hot wars, a new type of Viking who sails to the moon—these are the developments of a new country, perhaps a "new world" in a sense Columbus could not have imagined.

It is a world full of formidable challenges. But the challenge is no greater than it was when the following advertisement appeared in a Missouri newspaper: "WANTED—Young skinny, wiry fellows not over 18. Must be expert riders, willing to face death daily. Orphans preferred. Wages $25 a week. Apply, Central Overland Pony Express."

EARL SCHENCK MIERS, Author, *Golden Book History of the United States*

NORTHEASTERN STATES

A great many of the institutions and the way of life that many people think of as typical of the United States or as typically American began in the Northeastern States. Although the United States is a relatively young country, the Northeastern States of Maine, New Hampshire, Vermont, Massachusetts, Rhode Island, Connecticut, New York, New Jersey, Pennsylvania, and Delaware have historical roots that go far into the nation's past.

It was in the Northeast that the Pilgrims landed and began a way of life and established a democratic form of government that were to be unique. It was in the Northeast that the struggle for freedom from colonial rule began. It was in this region that the young American nation's first great cities—Boston, New York, and Philadelphia—grew up. And it was from the Northeast that the country was first governed.

In modern times it has been in this region that the greatest concentration of Americans have lived. The great megalopolis, the super-city that some people feel will one day stretch solidly from Portland, Maine, to Norfolk, Virginia, is located for the most part in the Northeast. Just as the Northeast saw the beginnings of the nation, so many people feel it holds the key to the future.

The Northeastern States have much in common—and much diversity. Perhaps the most important thing they have in common is their access to the Atlantic Ocean. All of the states, except for Vermont, have direct or nearly direct access to the great waterway that has, in effect, given birth to the country and helped it grow into a modern industrial and trading power.

On the other hand, the Northeast is a vast region, and diverse cul-

---

NORTHEASTERN STATES

CONNECTICUT
CAPITAL: Hartford.
MAJOR CITIES: Hartford, Bridgeport, New Haven.
AREA: 5,009 sq. mi. (12,973 sq. km.).
POPULATION: 3,032,217 (1970 census).
PHYSICAL FEATURES: Highest point—Mount Frissell (2,380 ft.; 725 m.). **Lowest point**—sea level. **Major rivers**—Connecticut, Housatonic, Thames. **Major lake**—Candlewood.
STATE MOTTO: *Qui transtulit sustinet* ("He who transplanted still sustains").

DELAWARE
CAPITAL: Dover.
MAJOR CITY: Wilmington.
AREA: 2,057 sq. mi. (5,328 sq. km.).
POPULATION: 548,104 (1970 census).
PHYSICAL FEATURES: Highest point—442 ft. (135 m.). **Lowest point**—sea level. **Major river**—Delaware.
STATE MOTTO: Liberty and Independence.

MAINE
CAPITAL: Augusta.
MAJOR CITIES: Portland, Lewiston, Bangor.
AREA: 33,215 sq. mi. (86,027 sq. km.).
POPULATION: 993,663 (1970 census).
PHYSICAL FEATURES: Highest point—Mount Katahdin (5,268 ft.; 1,606 m.). **Lowest point**—sea level. **Major rivers**—Androscoggin, Kennebec, Penobscot, St. Croix. **Major lakes**—Moosehead, Sebago, and the Rangeley Lakes.
STATE MOTTO: *Dirigo* ("I guide").

MASSACHUSETTS
CAPITAL: Boston.
MAJOR CITIES: Boston, Worcester, Springfield.
AREA: 8,257 sq. mi. (21,386 sq. km.).
POPULATION: 5,689,170 (1970 census).
PHYSICAL FEATURES: Highest point—Mount Greylock (3,491 ft.; 1,064 m.). **Lowest point**—sea level. **Major rivers**—Connecticut, Merrimack, Charles, Housatonic. **Major lakes**—Assawompsett Pond; Quabbin and Wachusett reservoirs.
STATE MOTTO: *Ense petit placidam sub libertate quietem* ("With the sword she seeks peace under liberty").

NEW HAMPSHIRE
CAPITAL: Concord.
MAJOR CITIES: Manchester, Nashua.
AREA: 9,304 sq. mi. (24,097 sq. km.).
POPULATION: 737,681 (1970 census).
PHYSICAL FEATURES: Highest point—Mount Washington (6,288 ft.; 1,917 m.). **Lowest point**—sea level. **Major rivers**—Connecticut, Merrimack, Androscoggin. **Major lake**—Winnepesaukee.
STATE MOTTO: Live free or die.

NEW JERSEY
CAPITAL: Trenton.
MAJOR CITIES: Newark, Jersey City, Paterson.
AREA: 7,836 sq. mi. (20,295 sq. km.).
POPULATION: 7,168,164 (1970 census).
PHYSICAL FEATURES: Highest point—High Point (1,803 ft.; 550 m.). **Lowest point**—sea level. **Major rivers**—Raritan, Hudson, Passaic, Delaware. **Major lakes**—Hopatcong, Budd, Culvers.
STATE MOTTO: Liberty and Prosperity.

NEW YORK
CAPITAL: Albany.
MAJOR CITIES: New York, Buffalo, Rochester.
AREA: 49,576 sq. mi. (128,402 sq. km.).
POPULATION: 18,241,266 (1970 census).
PHYSICAL FEATURES: Highest point—Mount Marcy (5,344 ft.; 1,629 m.). **Lowest point**—sea level. **Major rivers**—St. Lawrence, Hudson, Mohawk. **Major lakes**—Finger Lakes, Champlain, Erie, Ontario.
STATE MOTTO: *Excelsior* ("Ever upward").

PENNSYLVANIA
CAPITAL: Harrisburg.
MAJOR CITIES: Philadelphia, Pittsburgh, Erie.
AREA: 45,333 sq. mi. (117,412 sq. km.).
POPULATION: 11,793,909 (1970 census).
PHYSICAL FEATURES: Highest point—Mount Davis (3,213 ft.; 979 m.). **Lowest point**—sea level. **Major rivers**—Delaware, Allegheny, Susquehanna, Ohio. **Major lakes**—Erie; Wallenpaupack, Pymatuning Reservoir (both man-made).
STATE MOTTO: Virtue, Liberty, and Independence.

RHODE ISLAND
CAPITAL: Providence.
MAJOR CITIES: Providence, Warwick.
AREA: 1,214 sq. mi. (3,144 sq. km.).
POPULATION: 949,723 (1970 census).
PHYSICAL FEATURES: Highest point—Jerimoth Hill (812 ft.; 247 m.). **Lowest point**—sea level. **Major rivers**—Blackstone, Pawtuxet, Pawcatuck.
STATE MOTTO: Hope.

VERMONT
CAPITAL: Montpelier.
MAJOR CITIES: Burlington, Rutland.
AREA: 9,609 sq. mi. (24,887 sq. km.).
POPULATION: 444,732 (1970 census).
PHYSICAL FEATURES: Highest point—Mount Mansfield (4,393 ft.; 1,339 m.). **Lowest point**—Lake Champlain (95 ft.; 29 m.). **Major rivers**—Connecticut, Winooski, Otter Creek, Lamoille. **Major lake**—Champlain.
STATE MOTTO: Freedom and Unity.

tures have developed within its boundaries because of the different peoples from all parts of the world who have lived there. The New England States of Maine, New Hampshire, Vermont, Massachusetts, Connecticut, and Rhode Island developed a unique way of life, based in part on English Common Law principles, town government, and the relationship of the people to the land and to the sea. New York, with its great port city, has had a rich heritage derived from many parts of the world. It is the largest of the Northeastern States and has formed a bridge between New England and its traditions and the Middle Atlantic States of New Jersey, Pennsylvania, and Delaware and their strikingly diverse ethnic, social, and cultural traditions.

NEW ENGLAND STATES: THE UNCHANGED YANKEES

When he turns to look at you, his sharp eyes seem to question what you're made of. As for him, his long lean face and the lift of his jaw assert that no one has done him any favors, and he's not about to do any for you. He's a Yankee and proud of it.

Whether he wears a plaid shirt and long underwear the year round and works on a fishing wharf or wears a black business suit and works in a glass-walled building, he harbors the same secret deep within him: he has learned how to exist and to support his family in a rugged and overpopulated land. It's a land of breathtaking beauty where white frame houses centered on a village green stand for a very special kind of harmony that has long been established between man and nature; but it's also a land with soil often too rocky to plow and weather that is frequently too tricky to trust.

As a result of contending with the harsh realities of his land, the Yankee has a character with a definite twist. But the twist is often misunderstood. The legend has grown up, for example, that Yankees have been so blasted by hurricanes and hardships that they never speak—except for an occasional "ayuh" or "nope." The fact is they are not at all glum or noncommunicative; it's just that each word scores a point. P. T. Barnum, the famous Yankee circus man, used to tell a story about a mailman who would ride through his native village each week to drop off the newspapers, always yelling, "News, news! The Lord reigns!" One day he rode through during a tremendous snowstorm and was heard to cry, "News, news! The Lord reigns—and also snows a little!"

The wittiness of the Yankee's speech says much about his peculiar character. For in the clipped and salty phrases, you can see the three basic elements of the New England personality and of New England society: it is independent, it is tough, and it is frugal. Though there is enormous variety within New England, all objective observers—be they geographers, economists, or historians—agree that no other region in the country is so integrated. There's no doubt where it is, what it is, who it is. And despite the great consistent pouring into New England of immigrants at many points in the region's history, the essence of that character remains unchanged.

Newcomers and old-timers alike are Yankees, sharing a common culture that is rich and made of as many different ingredients as a rum cake. The three vital parts of the Yankee character—the independence of spirit, the toughness of its thought, and the frugality of its pocketbook—all work together as parts of an unbroken circle. But, after looking at

Lobster pots are stacked on a dock in Boothbay Harbor, Maine.

The quiet beauty of a small New Hampshire town in autumn.

Narragansett Bay cuts the state of Rhode Island almost in half.

each of these links, one will have to answer another question: Is it as strong and as workable today as it was yesterday?

The Independent Man

A strange figure stands atop the capitol of Rhode Island, the smallest of New England's six states. The figure wears nothing but a tattered lion skin; in his right hand is a spear of some sort, in his left, an anchor. For years discussion raged as to who he was and what the statue represented. A prime contender was Roger Williams, the free-thinking minister who fled from Puritan-controlled Massachusetts Bay Colony to found Rhode Island in 1636. But what would a sensible, 17th-century preacher be doing in a lion skin? No, the artists must have had someone else in mind. After much research and further debate, it was decided that the statue was a representation of "the independent man," the symbol of what Rhode Islanders, and all New Englanders, honor most in mankind.

The spirit of independence in Rhode Island has, in fact, been almost excessive. Rhode Islanders were among the first colonists to commit acts of aggression against their British rulers. (They wrecked and burned two British revenue ships a couple of years before the Boston Tea Party.) Rhode Island was also the last state to give up the independence won in the American Revolution to join the other states under the new

United States Constitution. But Rhode Islanders are by no means alone in their zealous defense of each man's right to make up his own mind about where he stands. The New England historian Samuel Eliot Morison described an up-country farmer named Reuben Stebbins, who lived on the border between Massachusetts and Vermont in the late 1700's. Set in his ways, Reuben had not chosen to join his neighboring farmers in the cause of the Revolution until he heard the cannons roaring at nearby Bennington. He then saddled his horse, called for his musket, and remarked as he rode off, "We'll see who's goin' t' own this farm!"

Independence seems to bloom from the New England soil—or, more accurately, from the very rocks that crowd the soil. Each 17th- or 18th-century New England colonist who left the coast and tramped his way inland dreamed of making a self-sufficient, family-supporting farm for himself. But once he had left tilled fields behind (particularly those in the especially fertile Connecticut River valley), he found a hostile wilderness that still bore the awful scars of four great glaciers that had scoured the earth thousands of years before. The glaciers had scraped topsoil from plains, leaving in its place layers of crushed rock that had been ripped off the ridges of the mountains. So for the New England farmer—all the way from the Berkshire hills of Connecticut and Massachusetts to the "salt-water farms" of Maine's rugged glacier-carved coastline—life has been a never-ending chore of removing rocks and piling rocks and then removing rocks again the next spring. From such ceaseless, back-breaking labor toward the ideal of self-sufficiency for each man on his own cleared lot comes the attitude of Reuben Stebbins: "We'll see who's goin' t' own this farm!"

From that labor also comes one of New England's most picturesque features: the rambling stone walls that crisscross the countryside. But the pattern of the walls is not as casual as it looks. Each section was built by a man who wanted to set the limits of his land; to keep his family in and intruders (or his neighbors) out. Furthermore, each section was built not as a throw-away pile of stones from the field, but as a carefully designed structure that would endure the heavings of the winter's frost and the outpouring of the spring's freshets and would stand as a kind of memorial to his independent accomplishments. The basic formula for a well-built wall involves, first, the digging of a 3½-foot (1 meter) ditch into which the first and heaviest rocks are rolled. Then layer upon layer of rocks are stacked on top of the foundation, the layers being arranged to slant in toward the center. Small stones then may be used to fill the chinks between larger stones, knitting the whole structure together.

For those present-day Yankees who still strive for a self-sufficient, rural existence, life is usually lived in a distinctive, but by no means fancy, kind of house. It goes on and on like a square dance tune, progressing from wash house to woodshed, from woodshed to carriage house, from carriage house to hen house, until it becomes a barn. The first unit, the house itself, is often one of the handsome square structures that were built in the 18th and early 19th centuries, when Americans were designing residences that many people consider to be among the most beautiful to be built anywhere. The last unit, the barn itself, can be reached without going outside into the snow. And huge and majestic and warm it seems in comparison with the cold sheds and crowded storerooms one has walked through to get there.

But today there are fewer and fewer farmers who try to reach their barns this way or any other. Many New England farm families realized as early as 1820 that they would do better to move to the richer farmlands of the western states of those days (western New York, western Pennsylvania, and parts of the Midwest). Many others felt the influence of Yankee technical geniuses like Eli Whitney and became mill hands or factory workers. In the last 20 years the farm population of nonindustrialized New England has dropped even more sharply. Self-sufficiency of the old-time variety seems increasingly impossible to achieve in real life. But as a personality trait, the Yankee's tough and independent spirit remains as vigorous as ever.

The Tough Sentinel

In almost all New England towns there is a statue, the statue of a Civil War soldier. His jaw firmly set, his hands clasped over his rifle, he preserves peace on the village green. He seems to be a sentinel posted at the center of the town: half-way between the two churches, on the crosswalk between the library and the town hall, poised between "Main" and "Elm" streets. From Litchfield, Connecticut, to Wiscasset, Maine, and from Amherst, Massachusetts, to Peacham, Vermont, it is the same. He is the tough and conservative guardian of the proper balance of things in all the small towns of New England. Change is his enemy, especially change in government.

"What's New England?" a Yankee was recently asked. "That's easy," he replied, "It's where there's a town meeting." Thus it has always been in New England towns. Of course, in the cities of New England where the populations are in the thousands rather than the hundreds, the town meeting has had to give way to forms of government that are better suited to large populations. The basic principle of the town meeting is that each registered voter has a voice in the decisions of the government. The way it works is that each citizen speaks his mind on any and all points as frankly and pungently as civilization allows. Stomping in out of the cold to their meeting hall (often the schoolhouse, because that's the only building with room enough for all), the citizens greet each other excitedly, suspecting that there'll be fireworks tonight. And as remarkable as the wit and the friendly name-calling that goes on at the meeting may be, even more remarkable is the patience and wisdom of those town leaders who sum up the point of view of the people and get sensible legislation passed.

The Yankee insistence on minute review by the people of every governmental action extends beyond the limits of the towns. In the capitals of the New England States there is the theory that each little remote hamlet should be represented and should be able to keep tabs on the possibly high-handed maneuvers of the officials. New Hampshire, for example, has a lower house made up of some 400 town representatives—almost as many people as make up the United States House of Representatives (435 members). New Hampshiremen and Yankees from other states also want to keep a tight rein on the governor himself. There is generally a governor's council that prevents him from making many decisions without the approval of the councilors. The councilors are in some ways like the seven or eight men who sit around the stove in a country store in the village—they are often wise and "tough as nails."

The Connecticut River winds through traditional New England.

This country-store attitude—that even governors have to be kept in their place—carries through to the Yankee social scene. In the past, each social and ethnic group tended to keep its place, a fact that caused distinct strata in New England society.

In recent years the levels of New England society have been intermixed somewhat. The tough sentinels on the village greens have begun to relax their resistance to change. Such an easing has been made necessary by the swifter pace and increased mobility of all Americans, including New Englanders. It is no longer so likely that newcomers to New England will encounter provincial social attitudes or frigid reserve. Curiously, there has always been greater tolerance for new people in the small towns of upper New England, where the men share common tasks and the women are glad to have additional members of the sewing circle, than in the big cities. The fairness and impartiality of the Yankee mind, which have allowed each voice to be heard, may yet assert itself as the single most valuable aspect of the New England heritage.

The Frugal Way

New Englanders have a traditional reputation for frugality—extreme carefulness with money. Frugality in New England is more often a grim necessity, however, than a laughing matter. In the poorer parts of the region—that is, in northern Vermont, New Hampshire, and Maine as well as certain sections of Massachusetts and Rhode Island, the average income can be barely above the poverty level as determined by federal officials. Yankees therefore have had to find ways of "making do." These include everything from sewing patches on patches to refusing, absolutely refusing, to spend invested money or money in a savings account for anything (except possibly another investment).

Pinching pennies can, indeed, be an embarrassment as well as a virtue. And one of the greatest strains upon the Yankee character as

New England faces up to the challenges of today and tomorrow is how to spend money and spend it in large measure, when money is needed.

Crisis Across the Land

In recent times, New England has been forced to change its ways. It is presently going through the most severe crisis of its 3½-century history. To live in New England is to experience a desperate battle between, on the one hand, the traditional Yankee strengths and virtues and, on the other hand, old age. President John F. Kennedy made a speech some years before his election that commented on the problem, saying that in New England "... machinery is old, methods are old, and too frequently management is old." Yet he expressed the hope that the very strengths that had allowed Yankees to overcome the difficulties of their soil and their climate in the past might be reinvigorated and allow the New England way of life to move forward once again. To win this battle Yankees must make co-operation out of independence; they must make flexibility out of toughness; they must make abundance out of thrift.

If Yankees are to turn the corner and get moving, they must do so where they work—on the land, in the factory, and on the sea. But it also must be remembered that one of the variables in New England is the split between those who remained farmers and those who went into the mill towns and manufacturing centers. One part of New England, in the north, is up-country and out of touch (perhaps deliberately) with the rest of the world; the other part is industrial.

The borderline between the two ways of life in New England can be seen on a map as well as in Yankee homes and working patterns. On the map the line generally follows the border of Massachusetts, with Vermont, New Hampshire, and Maine in the poorer part and Massachusetts, Rhode Island, and Connecticut in the richer section. In the north are the lofty mountains and the incredible purple hills (blue when the morning shadows are still on them, red when they are lit by the setting sun). In the south are New England's sprawling cities and suburbs that run unbrokenly into the similar, but by no means identical, areas of New York and other states to the south and west. A wide-traveling writer from North Carolina, Jonathan Daniels, was the first to spot this physical and emotional difference. He wrote, "You cross more than the Massachusetts line on the road north into Vermont." And he recognized that agriculture in northern New England is quite different from that in southern New England; so it is also with manufacturing and with fishing.

The City

An unkind poem known by every Yankee schoolchild runs like this:

> And this is good old Boston,
>   The home of the bean and the cod,
> Where the Lowells talk to the Cabots
>   And the Cabots talk only to God.

The tough-minded exclusiveness that the poem implies has been one of the factors that has tended to hold New England back. But when the leaders of Yankee society realized after World War II that New England was dying around them, they saw that New England's leaders would have to start talking to men from every walk of life.

New England's past and future are linked in modern Boston.

What was needed most was a combination of brains and money—brains to figure out what kind of new industry could be attracted to take the place of the traditional industries (like textiles) that were disappearing from New England, and money to build the highways and industrial centers that would be required. Brains had always existed aplenty in New England—in fact, given the long list of Yankee authors and clergymen, it seems a bit difficult to tell the difference between New England's and America's intellectual accomplishments. Money, too, had always been stashed away thriftily and piled up against a rainy day. But the trouble was that the brains were locked up in the great private universities such as Yale, Harvard, and the Massachusetts Institute of Technology (M.I.T.), and the money was either handled too conservatively or invested in quick-blooming opportunities outside New England. How could New England's brains and money be brought together in the fight against old age?

The answer was supplied by a revolutionary combination of bankers, politicians, engineers, labor leaders, scientists, contractors, and businessmen. Boston College was particularly active in bringing together a diversity of talents in a series of seminars and in encouraging those who attended to take a flexible, imaginative, and bold approach to New England's critical condition.

The earliest and most important project that developed from the joint planning sessions was Route 128, a multi-lane highway that now curves completely around Boston, cutting through suburban areas and former woodlands in one wide arc several miles out from the heart of New England's largest city and spiritual capital. This tremendous expressway was New England's biggest bid to attract new industry. And though it was initially denounced by some conservatives as too expensive and too destructive of natural areas like the Blue Hills Reservation, it succeeded in helping even the most skeptical Yankees see how intergroup co-operation and daring and massive investments of talents and dollars could achieve enormous victories. One of the first pace-setting organizations to move to 128 was the Lincoln Laboratory. An offshoot of M.I.T., Lincoln Laboratory pioneered in the development of new equipment and systems to help industry keep abreast of technological progress in the defense and space fields. Even before its doors were opened many other modern industrial firms—several of which were in precision manufacturing and electronics and wanted to call upon nearby professors for guidance—began to build sprawling, streamlined plants along the highway's ample edges.

By the time of its completion, the extraordinary real estate venture was so successful that other critics began to express the fear that it would ruin downtown Boston by taking away money and working people from the city. But having started the renewal of a region, the farsighted Yankees had no idea of stopping. Still working with a tight alliance of intellectual and business leadership, they set about the building of the new Prudential Center, the highest skyscraper outside New York and Chicago; the opening up of a new research and development campus across the river from Boston, in Cambridge; and the rebuilding of some of the most depressed sections of downtown Boston, including Scollay Square. There, before the eyes of amazed but now confident citizens, a new and architecturally fascinating government center has risen, including a spectacular new city hall.

The lives of people for hundreds of miles around were intimately affected by the building of Route 128 and of similar industrial centers that soon began to spring up in its wake. Many of the best young technologists in the nation flocked to New England, men with advanced degrees in skills needed by the science-based industry. Instead of going by subway to work in the inner city these men drive from their homes in pleasant, outlying areas to their efficient plants along the bustling highways. They are, of course, subject to the ups and downs of a modern industrial economy—an out-of-work engineer is hurt even more than a farmer with a broken plow. But many wives have found that they, too, can work in technological jobs in this new Yankeeland. Children have been affected as well. In many of the towns that previously debated and argued and rejected the idea of bigger and better schools, the proposals are now approved. It has become apparent that education is an important advantage for the future. And, with incomes increasing, tax funds are available for education as well.

There are also many for whom the renewal of industrial New England is a miracle observed from a great distance—it seems to be happening in another world. In northern New England there is not much prospect that new manufacturing industries can be attracted to replace those that have disappeared. The economy must still be based, largely, on quarrying and timbering. The skillful logger who has been pitting his skill for scores of years against the stubborn brutes of trees—trying to chop them down and roll them into the river and set them on their way downstream to the mill—is still the champion of the north and is not likely to be replaced. Many of the loggers are French-Canadian in origin and remain French-speaking. Their children, too, are likely to stay in northern New England. And even within southern New England there are areas where

A typical Vermont dairy farm is nestled in a peaceful valley.

aged manufacturing workers and untrained black and Puerto Rican laborers lead poor and depressed lives.

The Farm

"There is no more Yankee than Polynesian in me," Bernard De Voto
once wrote, "but when I go to Vermont I feel that I am traveling toward
my own place." In a Vermont or New Hampshire hillside farm there is
indeed the look of home. And although the rural population is relatively
poor and depleted, there are times in the year when upper New England
seems the only proper place on earth to be—precisely because it is old-
fashioned. The upper New England climate is usually characterized as
"nine months o' winter and three months o' darn poor sleddin'." Splendid as that may be for those who flock to ride up and ski down the region's mountains, it can be grim for those who live with the reality of
frozen pipes and stalled cars. But when early spring comes, there is a
dripping from the eaves that says the ice is past. The farmer's family hear
the sound and look at one another gleefully: sugaring (the gathering of
sap for maple sugar and syrup) can begin.

Throughout the farming sections of Maine, northern New Hampshire, and Vermont, March is the time when life itself seems to revive as
the sap starts to flow in the maple trees and the horses are yoked and
the furnaces stoked to gather and boil down the rich juice. The farmer
and his team of workhorses know each section of the sugar bush (stands
of maple trees) in and out; up and down the slopes where the thick old
trees grow winds a trail wide enough for the sledge to pass with its
heavy burden—a great iron vat into which is poured the maple fluid
that has dripped through taps into the pails hung in clusters around the
trees. When the vat is filled, the horses strain to pull it down through
the snow and mud of the winding valley to the sugarhouse. There the
contents are poured into another vat, which stands on top of an im-

mense, woodburning furnace. The boiling in the vat and the smoking of the wood send billowing clouds of smoke into the cold air. It is like a festival, as vivid as the brilliant colors of autumn or the eerie "northern lights" of winter; a festival for those who choose to remember the past rather than to live in an all new world.

Another expression that characterizes rural New England is "poor as a Maine potato farmer." And though there is much sad truth in the charge and many families are literally locked in the grip of poverty, there is one happy exception—Aroostook County, Maine. Here the visitor finds not the tight valleys and taut little villages of traditional New England, but something more like Iowa—a broad horizon unbroken by hills, and communities whose street plans are spacious and mathematically regular. There, instead of rocky ridges bristling with timber, is a virtually treeless land whose soil is enormously productive. Planted and harvested by great processions of heavy agricultural equipment, Aroostook County potatoes are famous throughout the world, and their genial growers stand forth as perhaps the most surprisingly different Yankees in New England.

Almost as fortunate as his northern counterparts, but more involved in the renewal of the region, the farmer of southern New England works in the closest possible harmony with those canny food dealers who supply milk and eggs and selected vegetables to the growing populations of the industrialized communities. Using highly specialized equipment, he works his acres efficiently from both a scientific and a marketing point of view. And he does well—his freshly painted silos and his bright green fields stand out as sharp accents in the rather dreary suburban sprawl. The southern New England farmer is another indication that by entering into the economic scene as flexible and co-operative partners, men of the soil can help turn the corner to a future less restricted than the past.

The Sea

In the late 1950's a fleet appeared off the New England coast. The ships were enormous, beautifully equipped trawlers; from their sterns flew the red flags of the Soviet Union. The mission of the fleet was to capture the best of the fish harvest from Georges Bank (which lies east of Massachusetts' Nantucket Island) and from those other rich shoals that have for centuries been the private preserves of Yankee fishermen.

The special advantage of the Russian ships was that their vast size allowed them to stay at sea for months; their elaborate electronic equipment helped them pinpoint and follow the shifting fish populations. Also, their freezing equipment and their crew of technicians enabled them to process the fish they caught as they surged along. By contrast, the Yankee fleet seemed puny—almost laughable. The little, rust-streaked, undermanned ships that went coughing out into the fog seemed to have no chance whatsoever of matching the Russians. Suddenly it became clear to American statesmen and seafarers alike that unless immense and generous assistance was granted to aid the cause of developing New England's fleet, the most ancient industry of the region and an entire way of life would be destroyed.

The business of Yankee fishing had, in truth, been declining for more than a century. Since the days when valiant sailors set forth from New Bedford to find and harpoon the whales of the Antarctic Sea and when magnificent schooners like the *Bluenose* sailed from Gloucester to the Banks, fishing had become a less and less profitable or popular way for a man to make a living. The traditional life of the man of the sea—the man who lived with his family in a Cape Cod, or saltbox, house in a village on a tidal river that flowed through a buoyed channel to the Bay—had almost become a thing of the past. In the industrialized parts of New England the old houses had mostly been taken over by summer people. The villages had been taken over by those who catered to the tourists. Fishing and clam digging had become agreeable pastimes, particularly for small children and their grandfathers.

Nevertheless commercial fishermen kept at their time-honored business, bringing in huge catches to sell to the stores and food chains. Antiquated and puny though their efforts seemed alongside the Russians, they refused to yield. The New England fishermen used the seiners, whose small boats caught tuna by means of encircling nets, the trawlers, whose "otter board" scoops picked up groundfish like cod and haddock from the sea's bottom, and the scallopers, whose heavy dredges scraped over the "beds" to gather succulent shellfish.

Yet there were two other factors that prevented the commercial fishermen from winning their fight against foreign competition. After generations of industrialization, the waters close to the New England shores had become dangerously polluted. They were no longer inviting to large schools of fish. Also, the Yankee financiers, recognizing that fishing was a declining and small-change business, were seldom willing to lend money

Fishing is still big business in Gloucester, Massachusetts.

necessary to build bigger and better boats. It appeared that President Kennedy's charge was accurate in this case: "Methods are old, and too frequently management is old."

But the challenge of the ships with the red flags was just what New England fishing needed. Yankees responded with a vigor that now seems greater in many ways than the accomplishments on Route 128. Forsaking their characteristic frugality and following the lead of the concerned United States Government, the bankers of Boston and Providence released abundant supplies of capital for the construction of modern and experimental vessels. Now at work on the high seas are two giant trawlers that cost $500,000 a piece. They are to be followed by more ships that can out-fish and outperform the Russian visitors. Nor were scientists to be left behind. Perhaps the most encouraging aspect of the revitalization of the fishing business in New England is the work of marine biologists to see what can be done to reclaim the coastal waters from pollution and to increase the yield of locally caught fish. The laboratories at Woods Hole, Massachusetts, offer an exciting view of that search and of the new careers that are being opened up for Yankees.

Meanwhile, in the nonindustrialized parts of New England, the ancient struggle of a single man in a small boat against the monsters of the deep goes on. It is colorful, and it is rewarding in its own way. A much-beloved writer in New England, Louise Dickinson Rich, has said of those fishermen who continue to go down to the sea in small craft with one-cylinder engines and manual hoists: "Their minds seem to be fixed upon nature and the elements rather than upon any contrivances of man." They are as independent as the first settlers who left the known world behind them and came to these wild shores. And they are brave enough to fight a sea that is whipped by ice storms in winter and by hurricanes at summer's end. Their toughness has by no means been watered down by the temptations of the affluent society around them.

The "average" Maine lobsterman does not exist—he's too much of an individual to be averaged. But if he did and if he would talk about himself and his family, you would find that he earns about $2,400 a year from lobstering. That modest income is mostly used up in buying the lines, the traps, the pots, the gas, the paint, and the engine equipment necessary for him to remain a lobsterman. For his other needs, he picks up occasional jobs as a school bus driver or service station man or carpenter. His wife may work too: after getting up at 4:30 to see her husband off on his round of "pullin' the pots," she may catch a few minutes of sleep before going off to her job in the post office or at the grocery store.

But the doughty fishermen families who used to inhabit the myriad sparkling islands off the Maine coast are becoming fewer and fewer in number. And increasingly the younger generation of New Englanders is going off to regional high schools in distant towns where they learn about other opportunities—about the new currents that are activating industry in New England, about the careers in science that are opening up, and about the ways of living in New England that are new but still Yankee in character. By nature they will doubtless remain independent, tough, and frugal people, but they may learn to be co-operative and flexible as well and to enjoy a broader life in abundance.

RUSSELL BOURNE, Editor, *Great Ages of Man*

Upstate New York: the majestic Hudson River at Bear Mountain.

NEW YORK: UPSTATE AND DOWNSTATE

To many people the term "New Yorker" means a Madison Avenue advertising man, a Greenwich Village artist, a mink-coated Fifth Avenue shopper—a wide variety of people. But these images all concern downstate people, dwellers in New York City. A New Yorker may also be a descendant of Dutch patroons on a Hudson River estate, a winegrower whose vineyards border Cayuga Lake, a lumberjack, a Buffalo steelworker, a Dutchess county dairy farmer, or a scientist in a Rochester laboratory.

Although all these upstate New Yorkers together constitute hardly half the state's more than 18,000,000 population, they wield considerable political power—enough to start New York City people complaining furiously about the way Albany treats the metropolis. By Albany the accusers mean not just the state capital, but the entire state government, which they darkly suspect is dominated by upstate forces indifferent to their needs. Some people have even urged that New York City secede from upstate and become a separate state on its own.

But even upstate, there are many New Yorks. There is the wilderness New York and the farmer's New York of herds and vineyards. There is the old colonial-based New York of manor houses overlooking the majestic Hudson and of peaceful river towns. There is the Southern Tier, part of the Allegheny Plateau, along the Pennsylvania border, almost part of Appalachia. And there is the real industrial muscle of upstate New York, the cities of the Northern Tier, from Albany to Buffalo. These sectional differences run through the history of New York state. They arose partly because from the beginning settlement grew around two distinct centers: New York Harbor and the inland river valley systems. Although the centers needed each other in many ways, their interests were not always the same.

History

New York Harbor was probably discovered first by an Italian, Giovanni da Verrazano, in 1524. Today a bridge bearing his name connects Staten Island to Brooklyn, sweeping high above the strait where he must have sailed. The region was next visited by Henry Hudson, an Englishman working for the Dutch East India Company, who guided his bark the *Half Moon* up the Hudson River to a site near modern Albany. When Hudson reached the rapids, he concluded that the Hudson was not the stream he sought—the mythical Northwest Passage through the American continent to India. That same year the French explorer Samuel de Champlain ventured from Canada along the lake later named for him.

The Dutch based their claim to New Netherland on Hudson's discoveries. The Dutch claims included what is now New Jersey, Long Island, the Hudson Valley, and parts of southern Connecticut. Control of the fur trade and settlement was granted to the Dutch West India Company. In 1624 the company sent a boatload of French-speaking Protestants (Walloons and Dutch) to found Fort Orange (Albany). This makes Albany slightly older than New York City, which began the next year as New Amsterdam, a fort at the tip of Manhattan Island.

Settlement. Settlers did not rush to New Netherland. The Dutch preferred quick profits in beaver to wilderness farms threatened by Indians. As encouragement the company offered huge land grants to any patroon, or landowner, who would settle 50 settlers on the land. Only one, Amsterdam diamond merchant Kiliaen Van Rensselaer, established the required number of tenants. Although he never reached the New World, his sons ruled over a princely estate stretching for miles along both sides of the Hudson around Fort Orange.

By the 1660's, underpopulated, badly fortified New Netherland was the only non-English colony between Virginia and Canada. Already New England farmers were slipping onto Long Island and settling in the Connecticut River valley as well. In 1664 England's King Charles II presented his brother James with a tremendous slice of North America that included New Netherland. James, Duke of York and Albany, sent four warships under Colonel Richard Nicolls to claim his property. Though the fiery Dutch governor, Peter Stuyvesant, wanted to fight, Manhattan burghers looked down the mouths of the ship's cannon and persuaded him to surrender. Their pretty Dutch town became New York, and Fort Orange was rechristened Albany.

Governor Nicolls confirmed Dutch land grants and offered land on both sides of the Hudson to Yankee settlers. Then he found that James had given away the west side of the lower Hudson (New Jersey) to his friends Lord Berkeley and Sir George Carteret. The blow this arbitrary division inflicted on colonial town builders was nothing compared to the future complications it caused. By its geographical nature, the densely populated region now bordering New York Harbor could logically form a single metropolitan district. However, instead of having a unified government it is cut in two by the New York-New Jersey state line.

New York grew so slowly that by the eve of the Revolution it ranked 7th among the colonies. And yet 30 years after independence it was the most populous state in the Union. Initially its growth was crippled by the fact that it was the most aristocratic northern colony. There were always some small farmers—Yankee, French Huguenot, Scotch-Irish, and German—in New York. But the English governors granted huge estates to wealthy merchants, so that all along the Hudson baronial manors took in miles of the very best land. Most European immigrants, seeking freedom from Old World landholding systems, were not about to become tenants of New World landlords. They often passed New York by to go on to Pennsylvania, which had a more democratic landholding system. In 1690, less than 10 years after its founding, Philadelphia equaled New York City in population and then forged ahead, not to be overtaken again until the 1800's.

Several tenants' revolts threatened the Hudson Valley landlords. Nine years before the American Revolution, angry farmers led by William Prendergast traded shots with British Redcoats sent to restore law and order. The Revolutionary War had the enthusiastic support of upstaters seeking revenge on Tory landlords. Many manors were confiscated and their owners chased out of the country. However, some of the landowners were patriots and emerged from the Revolution stronger than ever. When New York's first governor, George Clinton, gained laws designed to weaken the manorial system, New York began attracting more settlers.

New York was also handicapped because mountain ranges blocked expansion except along the Mohawk Valley, and that great highroad to the west was held by the Iroquois. To keep the loyalty of the Iroquois, England forbade settlement west of a line near present-day Rome, New York. The Mohawk and Hudson valleys, as gateways to Canada, had critical strategic importance. This was bloody ground—fought over in four wars between England and France and their Indian allies, fought over again in the American Revolution, and even contested in the War of 1812. (There were battles at Buffalo.) While Tory New York City remained in British hands during most of the Revolutionary War, many of the Revolutionary battles took place upstate. At the pivotal battle of Saratoga, Americans won control of the Hudson. They also permanently shattered Iroquois control of the Mohawk Valley, the only northern gap in the Appalachians. Thus freed to fling a powerful arm westward to the Great Lakes, New York abruptly became the leader of the new nation.

The Move West. New Englanders poured through the Mohawk Gap to the rich lands along the Genesee River and the Great Lakes plains. Robert Fulton's steamboat began plying the Hudson in 1807, giving a great boost to river trade and to the fast-growing port of New York City. Then came the major catalyst of upstate growth: the Erie Canal, linking the Great Lakes to the Hudson at Albany, thus forming a water highway from the Midwest to the Atlantic Ocean. This, the greatest public works project of its day, was promoted by De Witt Clinton, nephew of New York's first governor, who became governor of New York himself in 1870. Another canal linked the Hudson to Lake Champlain and thus to Canada. After "De Witt's Ditch" opened in 1825, it was cheaper to ship wheat from western farms to Atlantic coastal cities than to freight it even short distances overland. New York City was now the portal of the West. Mohawk Valley farmers enjoyed boom times, and towns blossomed into cities—including Buffalo, Rochester, Syracuse, and Utica.

The combination of rich farmlands, flour mills, and cheap shipping routes made New York a leading food producer. In the 1850's Northern Tier cities were further nourished by the growth of railroad networks. Their new steam-powered industries demanded locations near water and

rail routes, providing easy shipping for the mountains of coal used in furnaces and steam engines. The burgeoning factories also demanded labor
and got it. Throughout the 19th century the tide of migration flowed past
the Statue of Liberty—the Irish escaping the famines of the 1840's; Germans fleeing political upheavals; later, East Europeans running from persecution and pogroms. Many of these people went up the river to farm
and to work in factories. By 1850 almost half of Rochester's 36,000 population was foreign born. During the Civil War, New York became a major
supplier of the Union armies. Farmers and factory workers redoubled
their efforts and turned out huge quantities of goods. In spite of tragic
human losses in the conflict, the Northern Tier cities emerged with more
muscle than ever. New York became the economic powerhouse of the
nation. In the 20th century new industries such as electronics increased
the prosperity of the cities, and new tides of migration, this time from the
American South, challenged the cities to bring Northern ingenuity to bear
upon problems of a changing urban scene.

Land

A camper climbing along a trail in Adirondack Park hikes through
land as deserted as anything in the wilds of Wyoming. Here in the far
north of this most cosmopolitan and industrialized of states lies a mountain wilderness almost as big as the state of Connecticut. Only about
100,000 people live permanently in this several thousand square miles
of forested peaks and lakes—perhaps as many as crowd within a single
square mile of some Manhattan neighborhoods. But over 500,000 people
come in summer to hunt, fish, or explore some 785 miles (1,263 km.) of
trail. They may sail on Lake George or Lake Champlain, or take a long-
boat through the deep rocky gorge of Ausable Chasm, or visit Fort Ticon-
deroga of Revolutionary War fame. To the northwest they may drive
along the St. Lawrence River with its Thousand Islands—actually a good
deal more than 1,000. In the winter they come to ski at Tupper Lake, Lake
Placid, and other resorts, braving the frigid temperatures of New York's
"Siberia."

Except as a vacationland the Adirondack region has little commercial
value, though lumber is still cut and maple sugar made from rising sap in
the spring. Over half of this region is state-owned—one of the biggest
forest preserves in the country—a refuge for when the pressures of city
living necessitate "back to nature" holidays.

In Catskill Park southern New York has a more accessible woodland
playground, west of the Hudson. Once home of the legendary Rip Van
Winkle, today the Catskills harbor many celebrated resort hotels.

Lying as it does across the Appalachian chain, New York is a mountain state, though it is seldom considered one, perhaps because its peaks
are not high. Mount Marcy, 5,344 feet (1,629 m.), in the Adirondacks is the
highest, and many are in the 4,000-foot (1,200 m.) range. But wooded uplands take up almost two thirds of the state. Beyond the Delaware and
Susquehanna river valleys, the Allegheny Plateau stretches west to Lake
Erie. This Southern Tier is a rugged, underpopulated region, with many
abandoned farms now reverting to woodland and a few cities—including
Binghamton, Elmira, Jamestown (on Chautauqua Lake), and Corning.
Binghamton is a center of shoe manufacturing, and Corning is famous for
fine glass.

To the north is the peaceful beauty of the Genesee River valley and the Finger Lakes, five long, thin lakes that curve southward like the fingers of a hand. Seneca and Cayuga are the largest. Cornell University, in Ithaca, is located as its college song suggests, "on the shores of Lake Cayuga." This rich agricultural land slopes to the Mohawk Valley and beyond to the plains of the Great Lakes. North of Buffalo, the waters from Lake Erie flowing toward Lake Ontario roar over a cliff in a cascade that is New York's greatest natural wonder—Niagara Falls.

All this natural beauty is upstate. Downstate, around the metropolis, a spreading ring of merging suburban communities engulfs the countryside for miles. But the gorge of the lower Hudson still draws holiday crowds for the boat ride up to Bear Mountain, and other sightseers drive along the river bluffs to visit West Point or Franklin D. Roosevelt's estate at Hyde Park. Far out on Long Island there are pleasant beaches and summer resort towns.

Farms.   If most people do not associate New York with mountains, still less do they think of it as a leading farm state. Yet it competes with Washington in apple production, Wisconsin in dairy products, and California in the production of wine and grapes. Vineyards stretch along the shores of Lake Erie, and the vineyards and wineries of the Finger Lakes region are famous for domestic champagne and other wines. Dairy cattle range in the Adirondack foothills and the fertile Hudson Valley pastures. Dairying produces the greatest farm income; the poultry business, centering on Long Island with its Long Island ducklings, is also important. Truck farms on Long Island and in the Hudson Valley supply the vegetable stalls that jut out every few blocks along New York City sidewalks.

Although in the past most New Yorkers farmed, today only about one in 50 is a farmer. But automation and new technology have so increased production that these few can keep less than a fifth of the state's land under cultivation and provide a respectable proportion of the insatiable food demands of the cities.

Cities

New York City, the state's—and the nation's—biggest city is discussed in the article on UNITED STATES CITIES in this volume. The Northern Tier, the area where most of New York's smaller cities are located, begins where the Erie Canal (now integrated into the New York State Barge Canal) joins the Hudson River, in the triangular metropolitan district of Albany-Schenectady-Troy. It runs west through Utica, Rome, Syracuse, and Rochester to Buffalo, on Lake Erie. Today, in addition to rail and canal connections, these cities and many smaller ones are strung along the New York State Thruway. Some experts believe that eventually they will all run together into a single megalopolis stretching the width of the state—a "city" over 300 miles (480 km.) long.

Today, however, each of the Northern Tier cities has its own distinct personality. New York's second biggest city, **Buffalo**, is the back door of the North Atlantic region. This location makes it one of America's most important inland ports and railheads. Buffalo also has the advantage of a superior power supply in Niagara Falls' hydroelectric complex nearby. Its factory smokestacks and grain elevators signal from a distance that this is a focus of heavy industry and the biggest flour-milling center in the United States. There are meat-packing plants, steel plants, and factories

Downstate New York: the bristling towers of New York City's skyline.

making heavy machinery. The steel industry probably employs the most people. Buffalo's labor market has been a magnet for immigrants. About a third of the population is Polish-American, and there are also large numbers of people of many other ethnic backgrounds.

Rochester is quite a different city. It began as a flour-milling town and later became an important shoe and clothing producer as well. However, from the 1880's on it has been famous as the home of the Eastman Kodak Company. More recently Xerox Corporation has taken a similarly important place in Rochester's economic life. The scientific experimentation and enlightened employment policies of these companies helped make Rochester an orderly, progressive city with great occupation attractions for engineers and other professionals. Its population is ethnically mixed. **Syracuse,** which began as a producer of salt and became a center of light industry and electronics, faces a dilemma that many small American cities face—the gap between required technical skills and the background of many of its job hunters.

In the **Albany-Schenectady-Troy** triangle there are distinguished research laboratories and electronics plants, as well as factories turning out textiles, plastics, paper, and many other goods. However, Albany's single greatest industry is government—its role as state capital. Several of those who lived in the governor's mansion, including the two Roosevelts, later moved to an even better address—the White House. The Albany legislature, representing as it does all the New Yorks, including the most rural areas, often finds itself at odds not only with New York City but also with Buffalo and other urban centers. The heart of the problem is that there is never enough money to take care of the escalating urban crisis of slums, poverty, job training, health needs, and racial unrest. The men who gather at Albany face the gigantic task of creating a harmony in the interests of groups as diverse as Adirondack conservationists, Hudson River factory owners, organizations fighting the pollution of the Hudson by industrial waste, dairymen and winegrowers, big-city black power groups, city mayors desperate for funds, and just plain New Yorkers.

Reviewed by IRVING WERSTEIN, Author, *New York (States of the Nation Series)*

MIDDLE ATLANTIC STATES

The southernmost division of the Northeastern States is the important industrial, agricultural, and historic area made up of three states: New Jersey, Pennsylvania, and Delaware. The life of this area is as diverse as its people are ethnically and culturally different, and as its land is varied topographically.

Many historians and geographers have debated the meaning of the term "Middle Atlantic States." New Jersey and Delaware are quite similar in most respects, and they share the Delaware Valley with eastern Pennsylvania. But the mountainous central portion of Pennsylvania is quite different from the rest of the area. And western Pennsylvania, with a Great Lakes port and a strong orientation toward the Mississippi River, has little in common with the rest of the Middle Atlantic area—or with the Northeast in general.

But the three states do have much in common historically, and they have a common interest in maintaining their region as a place where many kinds of people can live and work together happily.

Land

What kind of terrain would an astronaut see if he studied New Jersey, Delaware, and Pennsylvania from his orbiting spacecraft? Starting from the Atlantic Ocean, the shorelines of Delaware and New Jersey are flat and marshy, and most of the Jersey coast is fringed with offshore sandbar islands. Most of Delaware and more than half of New Jersey are flat, sandy coastal plain; it was an undersea area in an earlier age. Northward there are rolling hills and lakes—part of the Piedmont plateau that extends from northeastern New Jersey through southeastern Pennsylvania to the northern tip of Delaware. In the northwest corner of New Jersey are the Kittatinny Mountains. The Delaware River cuts through the ridge at Delaware Water Gap, and on the Pennsylvania side of the river the same ridge is called Blue Mountain. Pennsylvania has many other ridges of the great Appalachian Mountains, which stretch from Newfoundland to Alabama. Pennsylvania's central ridges are called the Allegheny Mountains, and westward is the Allegheny Plateau.

If the astronaut were looking at this area in the evening he would see huge concentrations of lights in the heavily populated metropolitan areas around New York City (on the fringe of the region) and Philadelphia and smaller clusters marking Atlantic City, Wilmington, Harrisburg, Scranton, Pittsburgh, and many other cities. Visible in daylight would be great river systems—the Hudson and Delaware pouring into the Atlantic, the Susquehanna emptying into Chesapeake Bay, and the Monongahela-Allegheny-Ohio system draining westward to the Mississippi.

People

The patterns of immigration into New Jersey, Delaware, and Pennsylvania in the 18th and 19th centuries were similar. The major groups, in order of their arrival, were the Dutch, English, Germans, Irish, and, after the Civil War, Italians, Poles, and people from other central and southern European countries.

In the 20th century the population has moved in mainly from other parts of the United States, settling mostly in areas adjacent to the great cities. Two thirds of the population of New Jersey now resides within 30 miles (48 km.) of New York. Much of the population of Delaware lives in the northern sector, nearest to Philadelphia. In 1790 the population of this coastal area was more than 90 percent rural, and there were very few people at all toward the west. But by 1970 the population of New Jersey was 87 percent urban, Delaware 72 percent urban, and Pennsylvania 71 percent urban. The region is thus city oriented, and yet there are vast areas of central and western Pennsylvania that are very sparsely populated, consisting mostly of forested mountains.

Language studies have exposed a well-defined linguistic region which coincides with the Delaware Valley. This is not very evident from peculiarities of pronunciation, although there are some that a keen ear can detect. The main characteristic is word usage peculiar to the region. Such words as "pavement" rather than "sidewalk," "hot cakes" rather than "griddle cakes," "bagging school" rather than "playing truant" or "playing hookey," "squares" in preference to "city blocks," and many others are peculiar to the area.

Still a distinct group, although among the earliest arrivals from Europe, are the Pennsylvania Dutch. This interesting people is actually primarily German in origin. They first came to Pennsylvania in the late 17th century, in many cases to escape religious persecution. Others came

The charming village green of New Castle, Delaware. Settlers from the Netherlands founded a colony here in 1651.

from German-speaking areas in Switzerland and in Alsace (the much-disputed province lying between France and Germany).

Some of the Pennsylvania Dutch belong to the Mennonite, Amish, and other small German Protestant sects. These groups, known as the plain people, live simple lives—primarily as farmers—and avoid modern ways as much as possible. The men are often bearded and wear round, black hats. The women wear simple, long, dark dresses and cover their heads with old-fashioned bonnets. They drive horse-drawn buggies rather than cars. However, the majority of Pennsylvania Dutch—Lutherans, Moravians, and Reformed churchgoers—have blended into the general population.

The Pennsylvania Dutch are renowned for their highly productive farms, their excellent cooking, and the colorful geometric designs they paint on their barns and their furniture. The center of the Pennsylvania Dutch community is in and around Lancaster, Pennsylvania. There is also a Mennonite colony in Delaware.

Industry

The Middle Atlantic region is a national center for manufacturing. Northern Delaware houses the great Du Pont chemical establishment. Major petroleum refineries cluster between Wilmington and Philadelphia and in the Jersey Meadows, near New York. There are huge concentrations of industry in the Philadelphia-Camden-Levittown-Trenton district, and in much of northeastern New Jersey. Other industrial centers, such as Pittsburgh, developed because they were close to iron ore and coal and grew prosperous enough to bring in raw materials from other areas when their own supplies grew scarce.

Port activity thrives in the vicinity of the eastern manufacturing districts, and Pittsburgh is a river port and rail hub. Major transportation routes—roadways, railways, and airways—follow a nearly straight line from New York City across New Jersey to Philadelphia, Wilmington, Baltimore, and Washington, D.C. Pennsylvania's "endless mountains," as the pioneers called them, are crossed from east to west by the Pennsylvania Turnpike and by the Keystone Shortway.

Agriculture

The farm population in the Middle Atlantic States keeps decreasing and farm production keeps increasing, a result of greater efficiency, more machinery, and increasing knowledge. About one third of New Jersey is farmland, and almost three fourths of Delaware. Pennsylvania's farms and the whole farming industry are vitally important to the economy of the state. The main agricultural products are poultry and eggs, milk, fruits, and vegetables. Pennsylvania's wheat growers produce more wheat per acre than do some farmers in the wheat belt of the Midwest. New Jersey's intensive farming earns almost six times as many dollars per acre as the national average. South Jersey's main crop is tomatoes.

The climate, which is quite favorable for agriculture, is nearly uniform in all the Delaware Valley. The mean temperature is about 33 degrees Fahrenheit (.6 degrees Celsius) in January and 76 degrees F. (24 degrees C.) in July. Mean annual rainfall ranges from 40 inches (100 centimeters) in the north to 48 inches (120 cm.) in the south. Nearness to the Atlantic Ocean and Delaware Bay brings high humidity to most of the

Delaware Valley and moderates the temperatures in summer and winter. In the mountains of Pennsylvania, temperatures are considerably lower, and there is heavy snowfall every winter.

Cities

Waterways were the first routes followed by explorers. After settlements were established and commerce began, travel and transportation of goods remained chiefly waterborne. Thus it was natural that inland cities developed on rivers.

The great seaport cities, New York and Philadelphia, are described in detail in the article called UNITED STATES CITIES. New Jersey shares the metropolitan areas of both of these cities. Northeastern New Jersey has several million people living in a cluster of cities grouped within the New York metropolitan area, including Newark, Jersey City, Elizabeth, and New Brunswick. Across the Delaware River from Philadephia, there are another several hundred thousand New Jersey citizens living in Camden, Trenton, and many smaller cities.

Trenton, New Jersey's capital, was settled at the head of navigation of the Delaware River about 1679. It has a number of buildings of interest from Revolutionary War days.

Wilmington, Delaware's largest city, was settled by Peter Minuit in 1638. Now known as "the chemical capital of the world," it is the headquarters of the far-flung Du Pont industrial empire. Just outside the city is the Henry Francis Du Pont Winterthur Museum, a mansion with some 100 beautifully decorated rooms of American furniture, paintings, and other objects of the period from 1640 to 1840. Delaware's capital is **Dover**, a delightful small city with the Old State House on the village green, plenty of room, and plenty of time.

Pittsburgh, Pennsylvania's Colossus of the West, began in 1754 as a fort at the strategic point where the Monongahela and Allegheny rivers join to form the Ohio. That point is now called the Golden Triangle. It is a rich downtown financial district that was developed from exploitation of the area's abundant resources of coal, gas, oil, and iron ore, and the manufacture of steel. The Cathedral of Learning, a unique 42-story skyscraper, dominates the campus of the University of Pittsburgh.

Once known as the Smoky City, Pittsburgh was one of the first American cities to attack air pollution and now claims the purest air of any major city. The towboats on Pittsburgh's rivers, which do not tow, but push strings of barges ahead of them, move an enormous amount of tonnage annually. But in summer towboats share the rivers around the Golden Triangle with water skiers.

Erie is Pennsylvania's inland port on Lake Erie. Its 7-mile (11 km.) peninsula, Presque Isle, does double duty by protecting the port and by serving as a lakeside resort, with long, white sandy beaches. A state park on the peninsula attracts over 3,000,000 visitors each year.

Scranton, Pennsylvania, used to call itself the Anthracite Capital of the World, but after a century of intensive mining, most of the hard coal has gone. It could have become a ghost town, as many mining towns have, but Scranton salvaged itself by an audacious program of building free factories to attract industries. This program was begun just after World War II. Now Scranton has many diversified industries. Many other Pennsylvania towns have followed Scranton's lead.

The city of Newark, New Jersey, lies close to Manhattan.

A street from another time: Elfreth's Alley, in Philadelphia.

Winter in Pennsylvania Dutch country: a farmer and his wagon.

The handsome campus of New Jersey's Princeton University.

Harrisburg is Pennsylvania's capital. Although its largest employers are the city, state, county, and federal governments, it also has producers of steel and other products, and is a railroading center. The city is on the east bank of the Susquehanna River. A charming park extends 4 miles (6.4 km.) along the river, which is almost 1 mile (1.6 km.) wide. The State Capitol, an interesting building in Italian Renaissance style, is open to visitors.

Interesting Places

The Middle Atlantic States are especially rich in recreation areas and in historic sites. These areas are as diverse as the people and the land of the region. There are ski slopes in northern New Jersey and in the mountains of Pennsylvania and miles of oceanfront in both New Jersey and in Delaware. There are state parks in abundance in the three states. About half the total land area of Pennsylvania, for instance, is still forest land, and much of it lies within state and national park areas. There are many historic sites, especially places connected with the American Revolution, in all three states.

The Jersey Shore.   The broad beaches of New Jersey stretch for about 127 miles (203 km.) from Sandy Hook to Cape May. Their gleaming white sands draw over 1,000,000 visitors each sunny summer day. Although New Jersey is one of the leading industrial states, its biggest single business is tourism.

Swimming and sunning on the Atlantic beaches are the main attractions. The combination of hot sun and cool sea breezes feels just right, especially when New York and Philadelphia are sweltering. Evenings on the oceanfront are usually quite cool, even in midsummer. In addition to the ocean swimming and surf-riding, protected beaches on inland waters all along the coast are perfect for all sorts of water sports. A glance at the map shows that most of the Jersey coast is fringed by offshore bars within which are great long bays and meandering rivers and tidal streams. These waters are delightful in summer for sailing, boating, water-skiing, fishing, crabbing, clam digging—and for swimming.

Resort cities are strung along the coast like beads on a string. The larger ones are Asbury Park, Ocean City, Wildwood, Cape May, and, of course, the famous Atlantic City. At Atlantic City there are amusement parks and the famous Boardwalk, with its resort hotels, shops, and restaurants.

There are still beaches in New Jersey where it is possible to be alone—on Island Beach, on Long Beach island, and at Beach Haven, but civilization is closing in fast.

Pennsylvania Dutch Country.   While Lancaster, Pennsylvania, is the heart of Pennsylvania Dutch country, there are many people of German origin in a number of Pennsylvania counties. Other Pennsylvania Dutch centers are found at Bethlehem, Kutztown, Ephrata, Bird-in-Hand, and Lebanon. There are Pennsylvania Dutch museums and working farms to visit. There are also hundreds of restaurants serving the kind of hearty farm cooking for which the region is famous. There are farmer's markets in the larger Pennsylvania Dutch towns where restaurants are also set up.

Historic Places.   There are numerous historic sites in all three states. However, New Jersey and Pennsylvania, because of their larger size, have the greatest number of interesting sites.

New Jersey has been called "the cockpit of the Revolution," and many of George Washington's crucial campaigns were waged in the state. Morristown National Historical Park preserves Washington's headquarters and a number of other sites of the Revolutionary period. Trenton also has many sites where Washington stayed or fought. North of the city is Washington Crossing State Park where the general crossed the Delaware River to take Britain's Hessian troops by surprise.

Princeton also has a number of Revolutionary period sites. The Second Continental Congress met on the campus of Princeton University. Princeton's oldest house, Morven (built in 1701), is the official residence of New Jersey's governors.

In Pennsylvania, Philadelphia has many important historic sites, which are discussed in the article on UNITED STATES CITIES. York, Pennsylvania, was briefly the capital of the infant United States, and so there are a number of historic buildings there connected with the Revolutionary period. At Brandywine Battlefield in Chadds Ford, Pennsylvania, Washington lost a battle—and almost lost the Revolution. One of the bloodiest battles of the Civil War was fought at Gettysburg, Pennsylvania. The vast battlefield area has been carefully tended, and has hundreds of markers, statues, cannon—and many facilities for guided tours. The last home of President Dwight D. Eisenhower is nearby.

Early History

It is quite likely that Giovanni da Verrazano first saw the New Jersey shore in 1524. However, there is no record of any attempt at landing or exploration. In 1609, Henry Hudson explored the New Jersey coast. He sailed into Delaware Bay, and from there proceeded to an inlet that he named Barnegat. He then anchored in Sandy Hook Bay for 10 days to trade with the Indians for supplies. Following this, he went on to explore the Hudson River, beginning in 1609. In 1618 the Dutch founded Jersey City as a trading post to obtain furs from the Lenni-Lenape Indians. They also founded Fort Nassau, south of Camden, in 1623. The Dutch settled in 1631 near Lewes, Delaware, and Swedes settled in 1638 near Wilmington. After a few more localities were settled, the Dutch drove the Swedes out, and the English, in turn, ousted the Dutch.

The whole Middle Atlantic region became part of New York for a while. Then, from 1676 to 1702, New Jersey was divided into two parts, East Jersey and West Jersey. In 1681 King Charles II granted Pennsylvania, including Delaware, to William Penn, a Quaker. Penn's policy of religious tolerance drew many settlers. Objecting to Penn's control, however, Delaware separated itself in 1704. Traders and settlers moving westward had conflicts with the French over the fur trade until after the French and Indian War of 1754–63 and a treaty with the Iroquois in 1768.

The First Continental Congress and Second Continental Congress met in Philadelphia in 1774 and 1775. In 1776 all 13 colonies declared their independence from Britain and began the Revolutionary War. George Washington fought much of the war around Philadelphia and back and forth across New Jersey. While Philadelphia was occupied by the British, York was temporary capital of the new United States. The first three states to ratify the Constitution were Delaware on December 7, Pennsylvania on December 12, and New Jersey on December 18, all in 1787.

PHILIP S. KLEIN, Pennsylvania State University

SOUTHEASTERN STATES

The Southeastern States have played a unique and vital role in the history of the United States. They were the scene of exploration and discovery, of the beginnings of representative government in the New World, of revolution, of the building of a complex plantation society and of its destruction in the disastrous Civil War. Some of America's worst problems have been faced in the Southeast. The problem of racial discrimination and segregation is a serious issue there. However, some of the best solutions to national problems have been worked out in the Southeast. For instance, many of the most treasured aspects of the unique American system of government were born in the Southeast, and many of the country's first leaders were southeasterners.

The Southeast has room for many ways of life. Despite the common history of most of the states in the region, it is by no means a unified area. It includes the Atlantic seaboard states of Maryland, Virginia, North Carolina, South Carolina, Georgia, and Florida as well as the "old west"

SOUTHEASTERN STATES

FLORIDA
CAPITAL: Tallahassee.
MAJOR CITIES: Miami, Tampa, Jacksonville, Fort Lauderdale, Tallahassee, St. Petersburg.
AREA: 58,560 sq. mi. (151,670 sq. km.).
POPULATION: 6,789,443 (1970 census).
PHYSICAL FEATURES: Highest point—345 ft. (105 m.). **Lowest point**—sea level. **Major rivers**—St. Johns, St. Marys, Suwannee, Apalachicola, Perdido, Withlacoochee, Kissimmee, Caloosahatchee. **Major lake**—Okeechobee.
STATE MOTTO: In God we trust.

GEORGIA
CAPITAL: Atlanta.
MAJOR CITIES: Atlanta, Columbus, Savannah, Macon.
AREA: 58,876 sq. mi. (152,489 sq. km.).
POPULATION: 4,589,575 (1970 census).
PHYSICAL FEATURES:: Highest point—Brasstown Bald (4,784 ft.; 1,458 m.). **Lowest point**—sea level. **Major rivers**—Savannah, Ogeechee, Altamaha, St. Marys, Chattahoochee, Flint, Alapaha, Suwannee. **Major lakes**—Sidney Lanier, Allatoona, Clark Hill Reservoir, Sinclair, Seminole (all man-made).
STATE MOTTO: Wisdom, justice, and moderation.

KENTUCKY
CAPITAL: Frankfort.
MAJOR CITIES: Louisville, Lexington, Covington.
AREA: 40,395 sq. mi. (104,623 sq. km.).
POPULATION: 3,219,311 (1970 census).
PHYSICAL FEATURES: Highest point—Black Mountain (4,145 ft.; 1,263 m.). **Lowest point**—on the Mississippi River, 257 ft. (78 m.). **Major rivers**—Mississippi, Ohio, Tennessee, Cumberland, Licking, Kentucky, Green. **Major lakes**—Cumberland, Kentucky, Barkley, Dale Hollow Reservoir (all man-made).
STATE MOTTO: United we stand, divided we fall.

MARYLAND
CAPITAL: Annapolis.
MAJOR CITIES: Baltimore, Annapolis.
AREA: 10,577 sq. mi. (27,394 sq. km.).
POPULATION: 3,922,399 (1970 census).
PHYSICAL FEATURES: Highest point—Backbone Mountain (3,360 ft.; 1,024 m.). **Lowest point**—sea level. **Major rivers**—Potomac, Patuxent, Patapsco, Susquehanna, Elk, Chester, Choptank, Nanticoke, Pocomoke. **Major lakes**—Deep Creek, Patapsco Reservoir, Triadelphia, Rocky Gorge Reservoir, Prettyboy Reservoir, Loch Raven Reservoir (all man-made).
STATE MOTTO: *Fatti maschii, parole femine* ("Manly deeds, womanly words").

NORTH CAROLINA
CAPITAL: Raleigh.
MAJOR CITIES: Charlotte, Greensboro, Winston-Salem, Raleigh, Durham.
AREA: 52,586 sq. mi (136,198 sq. km.).
POPULATION: 5,082,059 (1970 census).
PHYSICAL FEATURES: Highest point—Mount Mitchell (6,684 ft.; 2,037 m.). **Lowest point**—sea level. **Major rivers**—Roanoke, Tar, Neuse, Cape Fear, Yadkin, Catawba, Little Tennessee, French Broad. **Major lakes**—Mattamuskeet; John H. Kerr Reservoir, Fontana Reservoir, High Rock (all man-made).
STATE MOTTO: *Esse quam videri* ("To be rather than to seem").

SOUTH CAROLINA
CAPITAL: Columbia.
MAJOR CITIES: Charleston, Columbia, Greenville, Spartanburg.
AREA: 31,055 sq. mi. (80,432 sq. km.).
POPULATION: 2,590,516 (1970 census).
PHYSICAL FEATURES: Highest point—Sassafras Mountain (3,560 ft.; 1,085 m.). **Lowest point**—sea level. **Major rivers**—Pee Dee, Santee, Savannah. **Major lakes**—Marion, Moultrie, Clark Hill Reservoir, Hartwell Reservoir (all man-made).
STATE MOTTO: *Animis opibusque parati* ("Prepared in minds and resources"); and *Dum spiro, spero* ("While I breathe, I hope").

TENNESSEE
CAPITAL: Nashville.
MAJOR CITIES: Memphis, Nashville, Knoxville, Chattanooga.
AREA: 42,244 sq. mi. (109,412 sq. km.).
POPULATION: 3,924,164 (1970 census).
PHYSICAL FEATURES: Highest point—Clingmans Dome (6,643 ft.; 2,025 m.). **Lowest point**—on the Mississippi River, 182 ft. (55 m.). **Major rivers**—Tennessee, Cumberland, Mississippi. **Major lakes**—Kentucky Reservoir, Chickamauga Reservoir, Norris Reservoir, Center Hill Reservoir (all man-made).
STATE MOTTO: Agriculture and commerce.

VIRGINIA
CAPITAL: Richmond.
MAJOR CITIES: Norfolk, Richmond, Virginia Beach, Arlington.
AREA: 40,817 sq. mi. (105,716 sq. km.).
POPULATION: 4,648,494 (1970 census).
PHYSICAL FEATURES: Highest point—Mount Rogers (5,729 ft.; 1,746 m.). **Lowest point**—sea level. **Major rivers**—Potomac, Rappahannock, York, James, Shenandoah, Roanoke, Dan, New, Clinch, North Fork of the Holston. **Major lakes**—Drummond; Smith Mountain (man-made).
STATE MOTTO: *Sic semper tyrannis* ("Ever thus to tyrants").

WEST VIRGINIA
CAPITAL: Charleston.
MAJOR CITIES: Huntington, Charleston, Wheeling. Parkersburg.
AREA: 24,181 sq. mi. (62,629 sq. km.).
POPULATION: 1,744,237 (1970 census).
PHYSICAL FEATURES: Highest point—Spruce Knob (4,862 ft.; 1,482 m.). **Lowest point**—on the Potomac River, 240 ft. (73 m.). **Major rivers**—Ohio, Big Sandy, Guyandot, Kanawha, Little Kanawha, Potomac. **Major lake**—Bluestone Reservoir.
STATE MOTTO: *Montani semper liberi* ("Mountaineers are always free").

frontier of colonial times—West Virginia, Kentucky, and Tennessee, carved out of land grants originally held by Virginia, the "mother of states." With terrain varying all the way from tidewater to the highest mountains east of the Rockies, it shows striking contrasts not only between black and white populations, but also between city and country people, coast people and hill people.

THE LAND AND THE PEOPLE

From the beginning, the region's varying soil and climate dictated the kinds of farming that could be undertaken. This in turn shaped the society developed by the land-hungry colonists who came to the Southeast in search of a better life. Their first landfall was in the Virginia Tidewater, a sandy coastal plain covered with pines. Sandhills led up to the fall line, the head of navigation, where rivers tumbled down from the Piedmont Plateau. The Piedmont is a rolling foothill country of red clay soil covered with pines and hardwood trees. Although less hot and humid than the coast, it lacked the adequate water transportation vital to profitable farming in the days before good roads. Farther west are the Blue Ridge Mountains, guarding the great valley of the Appalachians, a region of fertile limestone soil, even more isolated from markets. Later the mountains proved to be rich in coal. Beyond the Appalachians is the Cumberland Plateau and then the beautiful Bluegrass country that looked like a paradise to Daniel Boone and the other early explorers of the region. Farther west, Kentucky and Tennessee touch the Mississippi. To the south is Florida with its coastal lowlands, swamps, and lakes.

The best of the Old South: the beautiful University of Virginia.

Terrain, soil, and ease or difficulty of transportation were important factors in shaping the lives of the people of the Southeast. The people who lived in the lowland areas of the region developed one way of life, and the people who lived in the mountain areas of the Southeast developed another. The people of the lowlands had plenty of good farmland and relatively easy access to water transportation. Therefore, the lowlanders developed large-scale farming (plantations) and were able to develop a distinctive cultural and social life as well. They were able to do this because of their prosperity and their easy means of communication with each other and the rest of the eastern seaboard of North America. The mountain dwellers of the Southeast lived in a land where transportation was difficult. Farming was usually limited to a single family growing enough to feed itself. Mountain people were often isolated in small communities or lived entirely within their own family circle or clan. They developed a separate way of life from the people in the lowlands of their own states. They learned to live off the land and were eventually able to profit to some extent from the minerals and other natural resources found in mountain country. Even today, a person living in the lowland (tidewater) area of Virginia has more in common with other lowlanders on the coasts of North and South Carolina than he does with a fellow Virginian living in the Appalachian or Blue Ridge mountains. And the people in these mountain areas have more in common with other mountaineers—people in the Great Smokies of Tennessee and North Carolina, for instance—than they do with fellow Virginians in Norfolk or Richmond.

However, southeasterners do have some things in common. The climate, for instance, in all of the Southeast is generally warmer than that of the Northeast and makes for a generally slower and more relaxed pace of life. And outside of Florida, southeasterners—along with the people of the South Central States—are more likely than most Americans to live near their birthplace. In 1960, 80 percent of all Georgians and South Carolinians were natives of their states. This is typical of the Southeast, and it makes for a strong sense of tradition and local pride.

Southeasterners also share a common past that includes the institution of black slavery. The problems resulting from slavery left both black and white southeasterners with an inheritance of difficult and powerful emotions about race relations. These problems and emotions are especially strong in the Southeast (and in the South Central States) because black and white people have usually lived in closer proximity to each other in these regions than they have in other parts of the United States.

The Coastal Plain

The people of the shore dwell in a sleepy, humid world of mingled water, marsh, and sand. Farther inland, the coastal plain, which was once forested and later plantation country, is now a region of farms and small towns. At the northern edge of the Southeast, Chesapeake Bay cuts Maryland in two and slices off a bit of Virginia. The isolated section is called the Eastern Shore. Summer homes dot Maryland's Eastern Shore, which is a sportsman's paradise of sailing, fishing, and duck hunting. Summer people bring a little money to the regular inhabitants, many of whom are poor oystermen, crabbers, or rock fishermen.

Chesapeake Bay.   The Chesapeake Bay region depends economically on fishing, truck gardening, and fruit growing and processing. South of Baltimore is the graceful colonial town of Annapolis, state capital and site of the United States Naval Academy. Here and there around the bay visitors can still see the great tobacco plantations that once dominated the area. In Maryland and down along Virginia's Tidewater, a few plantations, like Virginia's Berkeley Hundred on the James River, are still operating, more than 350 years after settlement.

Up the estuary of the Potomac the Virginia communities of Arlington and Alexandria provide Washington, D.C., with its "bedroom" suburbs. Across the river, Maryland's Bethesda and Chevy Chase serve the same purpose. Here the life of the people revolves around the work of keeping the great heart of the capital pumping. It is as far removed from the world of the Eastern Shore oysterman as if they lived on different planets.

Life near the mouth of the James River also tends to center around a single enterprise, in this case the armed services. Hampton, Portsmouth, Newport News, and Virginia's biggest city, Norfolk, all cluster around one of the world's greatest harbors, Hampton Roads. The Norfolk area includes not only a major naval base, but also a complex of Army and Air Force installations, shipbuilding, and maritime industries of every kind.

The Outer Banks.   Southward, the coast changes ominously. North Carolina's treacherous shore has been called the graveyard of the Atlantic. Long, thin barrier reefs run out to a point at Cape Hatteras, then turn sharply southwest to Cape Lookout. Farther south the entrance to Wilmington is marked by surf crashing on the menacing rocks of Cape Fear. On the sandy reefs, called the Outer Banks, tropical plants cling to the dunes. Occasional fishing villages or resort areas break the solitude. Hurricanes strike there with savage force. Legend has it that the people of the Outer Banks (called Bankers) are descended from pirates and shipwrecked sailors.

Swampland and Low Country.   West of the Outer Banks, the waters of Albemarle Sound, Pamlico Sound, and other sounds and bays merge with river estuaries. The waters here are too shallow for much shipping, but they are excellent for hunters and fishermen. The swamps and grassy savannas are called dismals. The Great Dismal Swamp reaches up into Virginia. Beach resorts line the coast. Inland from the bogs, pines once grew in profusion. They were the source of the tar and turpentine that gave North Carolina the nickname Tarheel State. However, the pines were cut down for plantations. Now the coast is dotted with little farms and small towns.

The lush, sultry Low Country of South Carolina begins with smooth beaches and fashionable resorts. Farther south the coast is fringed with barrier islands, called in Georgia the Sea Islands. South Carolina used to be known for rice; wild rice still grows in the state's marshes. The Low Country is a land of swamps, moss-draped cypresses, alligators, and palmetto trees. In Georgia parts of the coast are covered with pinewoods. Near the Florida border Okefenokee Swamp has become a wildlife preserve. The coast is famous for luxuriant gardens, golf courses, and the historic mansions of old colonial cities such as Charleston, South Carolina, and Savannah, Georgia. South Carolinians may still be tobacco or truck farmers, although they are more likely to work in lumber or paper mills. Pine and hardwood forests cover much of Georgia, supplying jobs in the resin industry and in the turpentine refineries. The farmers of

Georgia's broad coastal plain and the sandhills leading up to the fall line grow many crops, including pecans, peaches, and peanuts. Stock raising and poultry farming have also become a common way of life in the coastal plains and the Piedmont.

The Piedmont

Historically the rushing waters of the fall line provided waterpower for mills. This is the region, therefore, where industrialization began in the Southeast. Today, with electric power available, factories are no longer tied to the falls and have spread throughout the Piedmont. The area is highly industrialized, particularly with factories that process the forest and agricultural staples of the region.

The Piedmont begins in Maryland and Virginia as a narrow belt of hills about 40 miles (64 kilometers) wide at the Potomac, fanning out to a width of 200 miles (322 km.) in North Carolina and taking up a substantial portion of South Carolina and Georgia. It is the Southeast's most heavily populated zone. It is also the region's wealthiest and most modern area. Many of the region's famous universities are there—the University of Virginia at Charlottesville, the University of North Carolina at Chapel Hill, Duke University at Durham, North Carolina, and others.

Many people who live in Maryland's Frederick Valley in the northern Piedmont are dairy farmers, while others work in iron and steel mills. The northern Piedmont is also a land of luxurious country estates. In Virginia's Albemarle County, one of the wealthiest counties in the nation, people in traditional "pink" (really red) coats still "ride to the hounds"

Tobacco auctioneers in North Carolina take bids on a crop.

in English-style fox hunts. Farther south, North Carolina's Piedmont is the domain of the great American tobacco magnates. It is not surprising that the names of North Carolina's major cities—Winston-Salem, Durham, and Raleigh—tend to remind people of cigarette brand names. Charlotte and Greensboro are important manufacturing centers, too. However, they do not specialize in tobacco products. They have furniture and textile plants, which are also vital to the state's economy.

Textiles, chemicals, furniture, paper, and other wood products are the base of the new economic growth in the Piedmont. The two Carolinas lead the nation in the production of dress goods, yarns, toweling, and fabrics of all kinds. Textiles employ about half of South Carolina's factory workers. Textile mills are abundant, too, in the rolling red hills of Georgia. In Georgia, there is also a belt of fine white clay that led to the growth of pottery factories. Today Georgia's non-farm jobs outnumber farm jobs. In part this is because agricultural automation has brought reduced farm employment. There are still far too many poor people in Georgia, particularly displaced sharecroppers, who, lacking adequate training, have not yet made the shift to factory work.

The need of the mushrooming new industries of the Southeast for skilled, literate workers cast a glaring light on the region's educational lacks. School systems groaned under multiple demands for racial integration and better preparation of both black and white young people for new jobs. At the same time, it became increasingly difficult to get sufficient funds for the drastic changes the times required. The Southeast's factory zone is struggling with these problems. It is gradually catching up with other industrialized sections of the United States.

Appalachia

A visitor to the nuclear research laboratories of Oak Ridge, Tennessee, once asked, "How far is it from Oak Ridge to the Great Smoky Mountains?" His informant responded, "About 100 years."

Although Oak Ridge appears to be close to the Smokies on a map, there is truth to this comment. The mountaineers of Appalachia have been called "yesterday's people" because their rugged terrain has kept them relatively isolated and unchanging. They have been cruelly lampooned as shoeless hillbillies, and they have been idealized by researchers cataloging their Elizabethan folk songs, old English, and "quaint" customs. However, neither picture does justice to the Appalachian people.

The people of Appalachia are proud, clannish, individualistic, and independent. Most of them are white and native-born. They tend to intermarry with neighboring families until whole districts are interrelated. When their dominantly Scotch-Irish ancestors came to the mountains in the 18th century, they had to invent almost everything they needed. So the mountain people developed great skill at handicrafts. Now some find a market for their homespun coverlets, handmade dulcimers, rocking chairs, and other distinctive homemade articles. Far from doctors, their ancestors had to dose illnesses with herbs from the forest. Modern mountaineers collect medicinal plants for drug companies; 30 percent of the crude botanicals in America comes from western North Carolina.

Tradition still rules in many parts of Appalachia. Because the mountaineer's first loyalty is to his clan and because his idea of a "real man" requires fierce defense of honor, his quarrels sometimes have developed

A Tennessee craftsman makes a dulcimer for a folk musician.

into long-standing feuds. A natural fighting man, he has been so quick to volunteer for his country's wars that Tennessee is called the Volunteer State. His fundamentalist Protestant religion, like his whiskey and his temper, is extra-strong, sometimes galvanizing him to emotional acts. Yet a mountaineer can also be a model of rocklike endurance and strength. Often, mountain families are large. In the past the mountaineer has had little use for "book larnin'." Today, however, television brings mainstream America into his living room, decreasing his isolation and specialness. His past contacts with the outside world could hardly have made the Appalachian eager to know it better. This is particularly true in the areas where the modern world came to him in the form of coal companies that disrupted his culture and blasted his beautiful mountain country into a disaster area.

Appalachian Land. The southern Appalachian chain begins in the western panhandle of Maryland, covers most of West Virginia, takes in western Virginia and North Carolina, includes eastern Tennessee and Kentucky, and curves through western South Carolina, northern Georgia, and central Alabama. The Blue Ridge Mountains form the eastern edge of Appalachia. Behind them in North Carolina tower some of the highest peaks in the range, the Great Smokies. The land dips to the central valley and rises in the west to the Alleghenies in the north and the rugged Cumberland Plateau in the south.

There are really two Appalachias: the coal country of West Virginia and eastern Kentucky, with some counties in eastern Tennessee and western Virginia, and the rest of the mountain chain where coal is not found in so great a quantity. In both Appalachias poverty is widespread, but the non-mining areas at least have escaped devastation of the region's great natural beauty. Remnants of ancient plants are found in West Virginia's muskegs (bogs). Where it is undisturbed, Appalachia is a land of azaleas, dogwoods, wild orchids, tulip trees, and maples. Bear, deer, and other animals forage between the impenetrable laurel tangles, and spring-fed streams cascade down shaly banks and through fern-choked ravines. The wilderness is still preserved in Great Smoky Mountains National Park, in national forests, and in some backwoods valleys.

Beautiful as it is, the ravines and slopes of Appalachia never supported agriculture beyond subsistence potato or corn patches and hillside vegetable gardens. When strangers came to the region offering to buy timberland or subsoil mineral rights, the small sums offered looked huge to the mountain people, who seldom saw much ready cash. At first, the mines meant money wages to people who never had worked for wages. But the Depression, labor wars, and, finally, automation and strip mining, forced many mountain families onto relief. Strip mining also led to erosion and floods. The unemployed miner's woodsy backyard became a slag heap, and his mountain creek a sewer of chemicals and trash. Great wealth came from Kentucky, but it all flowed elsewhere. Some of the poorest counties in the nation are in Kentucky.

By the time the desperate social and economic conditions in Appalachia's coal regions were exposed by government and private agencies in the 1950's and 1960's, many people wondered if it was too late for Appalachia. Efforts to salvage the region began when President John F. Kennedy signed the Area Redevelopment Act in 1961.

Like the displaced black sharecroppers, the younger and more ambitious people of Appalachia escaped to northern cities. In the years between 1950 and 1960 there was a migration of over 1,000,000 people from Appalachia to northern and midwestern cities. Many of the migrants had trouble adjusting to city life. Their schooling had been so deficient that even the best of them often found themselves bewildered and lost, ill-trained for city jobs. But many rose to the challenge, and some even came back to teach and help their own people.

The Valleys.   The river valleys of Appalachia have had a different pattern of life and a different development from that of the mountain country. In the parts of West Virginia bordering on the Ohio and Kanawha rivers, the mountains gradually dwindle to rolling plains. One of the country's major chemical complexes is located in the Kanawha Valley. Because of industrial communities like Weirton, Charleston (the West Virginia state capital), Huntington, and Wheeling, more mountaineers now work in factories than in mining and farming combined.

Where the Tennessee River loops through Tennessee, down into Georgia and Alabama and back, a massive New Deal agency, the Tennessee Valley Authority (TVA), has installed a complex of dams and power plants that control floods and provide power. The chain of TVA reservoirs, called the Great Lakes of the South, contribute recreation areas.

Bluegrass and River Country

The Cumberland Plateau slopes west to the Bluegrass country, named for the tall blue-green grass of its sunny meadows. It centers in central Kentucky and central Tennessee. Its traditional hallmark is the

A horse-breeding farm in Kentucky's lush Bluegrass country.

"Kentucky colonel" sipping mint juleps on his white-columned veranda, while he watches his spirited horses gallop through spacious white-fenced pastures.

This whole picture is now outdated, for the breeding of Kentucky thoroughbreds and Tennessee walking horses has become a science presided over by businessmen with a keen knowledge of livestock. There are over 200 horse farms around Lexington, Kentucky, and Shelbyville, Tennessee. The Kentucky Derby, held in Louisville, Kentucky, each May is a festival rivaling New Orleans' Mardi Gras. During Derby Week, there is much feasting on hickory-cured ham and beaten biscuits and much convivial consumption of Kentucky's special bourbon whiskey, distilled at Lexington, Louisville, and the capital, Frankfort. But Lexington is more than the mecca for horse-lovers. It is also the site of a major loose-leaf tobacco market and home of the state university.

Around Louisville, Covington, and other Ohio River cities Kentuckians work in plants making metal products, machinery, and furniture. The state's western coalfields are on the Ohio River. Kentucky's oil fields and natural gas resources are also located primarily in this area. In the area between the Bluegrass and the western coalfields lies the rocky, wooded Pennyrile, named for the wild pennyroyal plant that blankets the ground. Mammoth Cave and Fort Knox are in the Pennyrile section.

West of the Tennessee Bluegrass region is a rim of hills and then the river plain sloping to the Mississippi River bluffs. Cotton plantations flourish on the rich bottomlands of the region. More black people live there, and the life style is more like that of the Deep South. Memphis, in the southwestern corner of Tennessee, is a characteristically southern river city, a place of docks, levees, and cotton markets.

Miami Beach is the center of Florida's huge resort industry.

Florida

Few places are so nearly a creation of the advertiser's art as Florida. With less than 2,000,000 inhabitants in 1940, the population had grown to over 6,000,000 by the late 1960's and had become the most populous of the Southeastern States. Millions of tourists bring in billions of dollars each year, putting tourism ahead of orange juice as Florida's main business. This is principally the triumph of real estate men and public relations experts, working on the very real base of Florida's "eternal sunshine" and warm beaches.

Unlike the other Southeastern States, Florida is all lowlands. Down its center runs a long chain of lakes, culminating in the vast Lake Okeechobee, one of the largest freshwater lakes within the boundaries of the United States. Lake Okeechobee's waters drain southward through marsh and savanna for 120 miles (193 km.) to the Gulf, forming the rich tangle of mangrove trees, ferns, and tropical swamp plants called the Everglades. A naturalist's paradise, it teems with about 600 different varieties of birds and animals. Recently, drainage schemes have changed the swamp's ecology so that conservationists fear prolonged drought might dry up Everglades National Park. Now canals are being built to insure sufficient water supply to support the park's swamp life.

From the southern tip of Florida, the Florida Keys curve southwest, about 150 miles (241 km.) from Virginia Key to Key West. The chain of little islands is formed from the exposed tops of coral reefs. Shrimp and sponge fishermen live in or near the ports. Linked by the Overseas Highway, the Keys are readily accessible to tourists bent on fishing or gathering tropical shells.

Florida's southeastern shore is called the Gold Coast. From the mansions of Palm Beach south through the college crowd's favorite city, Fort Lauderdale, to Miami and Miami Beach, the region is one continuous winter playground.

The steady tide of retired northerners seeking homes on the Gulf of Mexico shows no signs of abating. They make up about 28 percent of St. Petersburg's population and also congregate in nearby Tampa and other cities. Today they are being joined by young scientists and technicians working in the electronics and research centers that are springing up on the Gulf Coast. Florida differs from other Southeastern States in that it has a high proportion of non-natives.

Central Florida's prairie land, around Lake Okeechobee, is cowboy and Indian country. There are, in fact, many Indians there who are also cowboys. Cattle ranching is an important source of income for the Seminoles of the region. Sugarcane plantations and truck farms prosper in the fertile black soil reclaimed by drainage of lakeside swamps. To the north, the sandy, lake-dotted terrain supports Florida's billion dollar citrus fruit industry.

Northern Florida is the most "southern" part of the state—the region where the Suwannee River, immortalized in Stephen Foster's song, flows languidly under giant live oaks draped with Spanish moss, north into Georgia's Okefenokee Swamp and Wildlife Refuge. There and in the Florida panhandle are located forests, sawmills, and small farms. Government installations, such as the Navy's air base at Pensacola, help support the economy.

SOUTHEASTERN CITIES

There are wide contrasts among cities of the Southeastern States. Much of the region originally had a plantation culture that discouraged city-building. Yet some cities do have an old tradition, which they strive to maintain, while newer ones belong to a completely different world.

Both the oldest and newest aspects of America are represented on the east coast of Florida. In 1513 when Ponce de León explored the area around present-day St. Augustine (founded by the Spanish in 1565), he thought he was close to the magical Fountain of Youth. Vacationers relaxing in the sleepy Old World town today may well agree with him. But the Space Age is only about 100 miles (160 km.) down the coast. From Cape Canaveral (formerly Cape Kennedy) men are rocketed forth to walk on the moon more than 400 years after the first Europeans came to Florida.

Still farther south is Miami, one of the fastest-growing cities in the South. With over 1,000,000 people in its metropolitan district and an enormous growth in industry, Miami is becoming an increasingly vital shipping point, especially to Latin America. Across Biscayne Bay is Miami Beach, a vacationland built on what used to be a jungle-covered sandbar. About 400 hotels are crammed into its approximately 7 square miles (18 square kilometers).

There is an interesting contrast between two southeastern cities of the same name: Charleston, South Carolina, and Charleston, West Virginia. The South Carolina port is an old colonial town with houses dating back to the 18th century. Life still has a leisurely, languid pace. Charlestonians are proud of their traditions and their luxuriant gardens. They are also proud of their city's role as an international seaport.

Charleston, West Virginia, is a child of industrial America, hub of a

Charleston, South Carolina, has kept the charm of the past.

vast complex of coal, oil, natural gas, limestone, clay, lumber, and chemical production. It is one of the nation's leading sources of rayon, synthetic rubber, and nylon. In the early 19th century, salt deposits in the Kanawha Valley provided the base for the present-day chemical empire, and nearness to coal and iron did the rest. Unfortunately the backlash of successful industrialization, air pollution from hundreds of smokestacks, threatens to destroy completely the peaceful beauty of this valley.

At the falls of the James River stands Richmond, capital of Virginia, once capital of the Confederacy. Founded in colonial times, it has a capitol building designed in part by Thomas Jefferson. It pioneered in the manufacture of cigarettes. Now Richmond is diversifying its industry. Richmond has come a long way from the time when Patrick Henry proclaimed his famous "Give me liberty or give me death" in St. John's Church, or the days when Civil War battles raged nearby. However, Richmond is still a city rich in the historic traditions of the South.

Across the mountains (and south of Richmond) lies a city whose fame rests on quite a different base—in this case, on the sound of banjos and guitars. Nashville, Tennessee, is the "country and western music capital of the world." Folk singers and rock bands come from everywhere to record music with local groups. Nashville's musical rival, Memphis, is one of the biggest southeastern cities, with well over 500,000 people. Memphis has an older claim, for it was the cradle of the blues, immortalized by W. C. Handy in his earliest hit, "Memphis Blues" (1909) and later in "Beale Street Blues." Memphis is, of course, a major river port and commercial center.

Baltimore, Maryland, and Atlanta, Georgia, are (with Miami) rarities in the Southeast: both are truly big cities, with metropolitan districts numbering over 1,000,000 people. Both owe their prominence to strategic location: Baltimore is in the Chesapeake Bay area, a key coastal shipping lane; Atlanta is at the focal point of inland rail and highway transportation. While Baltimore is next door to the North, it is still half southern in tone. Atlanta, on the other hand, though deep in the South, has a hustling, energetic air usually associated with northern cities.

Baltimore, older than Atlanta by almost 2 centuries, began as a tobacco-shipping port. Its nearness to Pennsylvania's iron and steel and the South's agricultural staples, plus its superb harbor, helped Baltimore become one of the nation's leading seaports. The streets of old Baltimore present a picturesque vista of red brick row houses with white marble steps. But the city's additional importance as a railhead was not an unmixed blessing, for freight cars rumbled through the middle of town, and in time the city began to seem cramped, old-fashioned, and dingy. Many prosperous Baltimoreans moved to the suburbs. Then in the 1960's the spirit of urban renewal struck with such force that midtown Baltimore became almost a new city. Baltimore also began facing its problem of black ghettos and undertook ambitious public housing projects.

Atlanta was an "upstart" by the standards of Charleston and Savannah. These coastal cities were already centers of Old World charm at a time when the site of Atlanta was still deep forest. But in the 1840's with the spread of railroads, a town sprang up at the juncture of crisscrossing rail lines, near the spot where, allegedly, a lone peach tree grew. These two factors set Atlanta's initial mold: it became the transportation hub and economic center of the South. It became regional headquarters of many national manufacturing firms.

Atlanta is also the birthplace of Coca-Cola. Much of the resulting fortune (and other manufacturing fortunes) went back into Atlanta institutions, such as Emory University. Under the leadership of Atlanta's public-spirited businessmen, the city prospered. Initially, Atlanta's white leadership handled civil rights problems by working out an accommodation with black business leaders, ministers, or professors from Atlanta University. Negro voter registration and, in the 1960's, gradual desegregation of schools proceeded with little open conflict. But patterns of power are shifting as black voters become more nearly a majority in the central city. Black militant leaders are now challenging older black professionals. Thanks to white civil rights leaders such as Ralph McGill of the *Atlanta Constitution,* the city has escaped violent racial incidents.

HISTORY

In the 16th century the Southeast was sought by the three major trading nations of the day, England, France, and Spain. The Spanish colony at St. Augustine (1565) was the white man's first foothold north of the Rio Grande. Spanish pressure in Florida, Georgia, and South Carolina may have influenced the English to begin their settlement in Virginia. Because of this settlement, the Southeast became the oldest part of English America.

The earliest permanent settlement in the Southeast was made at Jamestown (1607), following the failure of the Lost Colony on Roanoke Island (founded in 1587). While France shifted its interest to the Mississippi Valley and the Gulf Coast, Spanish strongholds from St. Augustine to Beaufort, South Carolina, threatened English claims until 1700.

Atlanta, Georgia, has the bustling spirit of the New South.

When the Jamestown settlers looked at the sandy loam and pine-woods of the Tidewater, they wondered how to use the land. It was suggested that they produce naval stores, but the proprietors in England wanted to grow a high-priced staple, using unskilled labor.

The answer was tobacco. But although tobacco prices were high and land easy to get, white indentured servants were expensive. The obvious solution was black slave labor. So the planters bought their first boatload of African slaves in 1619 and began applying their primitive methods of cultivation so enthusiastically that at first they planted tobacco to the exclusion of food crops. Tobacco exhausted the soil quickly, and the tobacco planters grew desperate for more land. They looked westward.

So from the Tidewater "beachhead," the settlers mounted their assault on the Piedmont and the Appalachians. They were beginning the westward movement that was later celebrated by the historian Frederick Jackson Turner, who claimed it was the crucial factor in molding the American character. Turner invited his readers to stand at the Cumberland Gap and watch the progression of civilization: the buffalo, the fur trader and hunter, the Indian fighter, and finally the pioneer farmer. In the early 18th century the Germans, the English, and the Scotch-Irish left New York and Pennsylvania and poured down the Valley of Virginia, later going southward as far as Georgia. Another wave of Scots and poorer whites moved into the Piedmont, away from plantation country toward free land and open spaces. Then, in the late 18th century, Appalachia and the interior regions of Kentucky and Tennessee became the growing edge of the westward movement.

The Rural Way.   By 1700 Negro slaves had replaced white indentured servants as the chief form of labor in the Southeast. In the year of the Declaration of Independence, the slaves of Maryland and Virginia numbered around 200,000 out of a total population of 479,000. Tobacco was well-suited to plantation culture, and so were rice, indigo, and long staple (Sea Island) cotton. Then came Eli Whitney and his revolutionary invention for processing cotton, the cotton gin (1793). This invention made the cultivation of upland short staple cotton profitable. All other crops became secondary; the age of King Cotton dawned. King Cotton demanded an army of field hands, thus fastening the institution of slavery tightly around the throat of the South. By 1820 slave labor in the South was producing exportable cotton to the amount of 484,000 bales, worth $27,000,000 a year.

The first effect of the cotton revolution was an increased demand for land in the west; the second was the emergence of new planters and the growth of the planter class. Planters began moving inland, especially in the Carolinas and Georgia, where manufacturers dropped everything and turned to cotton processing. The outlook of Southern leaders became more conservative. Soil exhaustion became a great problem, since planters knew almost nothing about the terracing of farmland or the use of commercial fertilizers. For maximum profit, vast stretches of new land had to be acquired, even in Alabama, Mississippi, and Louisiana, where a great investment in slaves was necessary and would pay off. Yet by then the slave trade had been outlawed, and only the human cargo sold illegally by smugglers was available. Well before the Civil War, Virginia planters were finding it more profitable to breed slaves for sale to the Deep South (South Central States) than to continue raising cotton.

The Civil War changed large-scale farming: the labor force was no longer made up of slaves; sharecroppers farmed the land. Yet a dethroned King Cotton still held some power in the Southeast. The emancipated Negroes usually stayed where they were and, together with landless whites, provided the labor. The landowners provided land, tools, and "furnish" of necessities. Cash expenses and receipts were allegedly shared fifty-fifty. Even under this unpromising system, cotton came back economically. During World War I (1914–18) cotton again became king in the South. But the return of King Cotton was brief. The destructive Mexican boll weevil reached the United States and caused terrible damage in the cotton fields: cotton production fell from 13,000,000 bales a year in 1920 to fewer than 8,000,000 in 1921. When planters struggled back with new, purebred seeds, the Depression brought ruinously low prices for "overproduction." Thus even with plowed-under cotton and New Deal price supports in the 1930's, the economics of the situation brought about the virtual disappearance of the one-mule cotton farmer and the sharecropper. The mechanical cotton picker generally replaced hand labor (called "stoop labor" in the cotton fields because the picker had to stoop over to reach the cotton boll). To a large extent the cotton operation moved to the Southwest and to California. This left a jobless horde of field workers, black and white, in the South.

But as cotton moved west, cattle moved east, balancing the rural economy. Over-reliance on cash crops had forced the Southeast to import food and feed; now this was remedied. Where, a generation ago, the region failed to produce enough meat and dairy products to meet its needs, today there are countless cattle trucks and livestock markets. There are rural electrification co-ops that provide power for the processing plants that prepare meat and dairy products. In Georgia, where the boll weevil wiped out the marginal upland cotton farmers, the chicken-raising industry has boomed. A giant broiler industry has taken hold in the Appalachian foothills, together with feed mills and egg-producing and hatchery centers. In many other ways Piedmont and coastal farms are diversifying. Farmers are no longer dependent on fickle market prices for single crops.

The "Old" New South.   During the 1880's, Henry W. Grady of the *Atlanta Constitution* called for a New South. Industrialization, which meant attracting outside capital, played a vital role in his idea of a New South. This development was a mixed blessing. An early loss resulted from lumbermen stripping the Southeast of vast Tidewater pine forests and mountain hardwoods. Before the Depression, the lumber industry exploited a priceless natural resource with no thought for the future.

By the same token, the South's pre-Depression textile industry (almost all cotton mills) formed part of the New South's wave of industrialization. Towns would do anything to attract new payrolls and new taxpayers. However poor the pay, the hill people were glad to escape rural poverty and to cluster in bleak mill villages built to house them. Moving cotton mills to the cotton fields made sense to the millowner: he had cheap sources of fuel and waterpower, raw material nearby, and plenty of "contented Anglo-Saxon labor." That meant the 60-hour week, night work for women, child labor, and a great hatred for "outside agitators" trying to organize unions.

The idea of a New South also led men to prize education. Enlightened southerners realized that slavery had been a curse in that it had imprisoned young whites in the traditional professions, downgrading less "aristocratic" careers. So men of the Southeast established Georgia Tech, Clemson, North Carolina State, and similar institutions. In these colleges and universities they encouraged advanced training in engineering, agriculture, and forestry. Spurred by the Depression, they learned to remove resin from pine pulp, developing a new paper-making industry in those very South Carolina and Georgia counties where King Cotton had once held sway. The Civilian Conservation Corps (CCC) conducted a great test demonstration of conservation methods that made the region enthusiastic about reforestation and modern timber farming. The Tennessee Valley Authority brought abundant power, flood control, malaria control, and possibilities for tourism to the area.

THE "NEW" NEW SOUTH

Today the southern mill worker in his company shack is as rare as the sharecropper, for today's textile mill may draw its car-commuting workers from a 50-mile (80 km.) radius of the plant. Textile operations have diversified. In many parts of the region large corporations have built plants that produce man-made fibers for highly specialized manufacturing operations. There has also been a shift away from totally unskilled labor. The reservoir of presently unused labor, including women, is still largely unskilled. Therein lies the challenge for Appalachia.

Historic Harpers Ferry, West Virginia, lies in the Appalachian Mountains.

Whereas Grand Rapids was once the premier name for American furniture, that honor now goes to High Point, North Carolina, headquarters of the Southern Furniture Exposition. President John F. Kennedy's famous rocker was made in nearby Thomasville. Millions of cabinets for television sets are built. The reproducers of "antique" furniture use the region's hardwoods—including maple, cherry, and walnut.

How far the Civil War has receded into the background is typified by the twin motels, General Johnston and General Sherman, near Durham, North Carolina. This is the place where in 1865 Johnston surrendered to the Yankee Sherman, whose name could not be mentioned in polite company in an earlier South. Learning that a good motel by a popular battlefield earns more than a cotton field, the alert southerner is quick to cultivate the tourist's interest in the Southeast's historic shrines.

Once state highways only had to worry about fights with landowners. Today highway builders must consider that any relocation of state highways may bring screams of anguish from motel owners. Managing or owning roadside enterprises, mainly motels and restaurants, has become a vital occupation in the Southeast.

After many generations the Southeast has rid itself for the most part of hookworm, pellagra, typhoid fever, malaria, and infectious diarrhea. These were rural sicknesses. Some people wonder if the "new southerners" have only exchanged their old illnesses for city diseases—ulcers and heart disease. But even though growing urbanization and industrialization create new problems, they cannot be turned back by any nostalgia for a slow-paced, agrarian way of life.

To some extent machine-made products have blurred regional characteristics, making southerners more like Americans everywhere. But even TV commercials have not wiped out some of the region's unique accents found in places like North Carolina's Outer Banks or the Elizabethan-derived speech of the Appalachian mountaineer. The gain from industrialization is best reflected by an annual increase in the region's individual income.

Southeastern Places for Every Taste

If a visitor wants to see what's new about the New South, few places are more up-to-date than Tennessee's Oak Ridge atomic research center. Another spectacular evidence of modern might is the vast system of TVA dams, hydroelectric stations, recreational areas, and land development projects in the Tennessee River Valley. Glitteringly new are many of the Miami Beach hotels, Biscayne Bay mansions, and other developments on both the east and west coasts. People interested in the Space Age all want to visit Cape Canaveral, Florida.

Nature lovers who want to enjoy the highest mountains east of the Rockies might proceed from Asheville, North Carolina, west to Cherokee, North Carolina, stopping for the outdoor pageant, *Unto These Hills, A Drama of the Cherokee Indians*. They then might advance through Newfound Gap to Gatlinburg, Tennessee. A "top of the Appalachians" trip begins with the Skyline Drive atop Virginia's Blue Ridge Mountains. Great Smoky Mountains National Park, part of the Tennessee-North Carolina border, draws tourists by the hundreds of thousands.

The Civil War buff may want to seek out battlefields, such as those around Chattanooga, Tennessee, notably Lookout Mountain, or the well-known ones in Virginia, around Richmond and Petersburg. West Virginia, a state of incredible contrasts, should not be missed, if only because of the memorials to John Brown's Raid at Harpers Ferry and the wild mountain scenery of areas like Greenbrier county. The Civil War enthusiast may make a special pilgrimage to see the Battle of Atlanta by going to Atlanta's Grant Park to see the giant Cyclorama painting of the famous event. Then, to jump forward a century, he might dine at the penthouse restaurant glowing on top of Atlanta's Peachtree Center.

For years the population of the Southeast—like that of the South Central States—was made up of people who were born in the region where they lived. During the years of unrestricted European immigration to the United States, most of the immigrants bypassed the Southeast and crowded into the Northern and Midwestern cities. But recent decades have brought an important change to the Southeast. People from outside the region have begun to arrive.

Although there are some exceptions, the southeasterner has, in general, become less and less concerned about who sits where in a bus or who eats at what restaurant. Racial segregation is disappearing. In cities and towns, black and white voters are beginning to join forces to elect qualified black politicians. Many rural areas still have a way to go in this respect. However, southeasterners, like other Americans, are now more likely to argue about urban renewal plans, poverty programs, and means for curbing air and water pollution than they are to debate the old doctrine of white supremacy.

There is a growing confidence in the people of the Southeast that they can solve their region's problems. A cautious but unmistakable optimism is in the air.

JOSEPH L. MORRISON, University of North Carolina (Chapel Hill)

NORTH CENTRAL STATES

The North Central region, also known as the Middle West or Midwest, includes 12 states—Ohio, Indiana, Illinois, Michigan, Wisconsin, Missouri, Iowa, Minnesota, Kansas, Nebraska, North Dakota, and South Dakota. These 12 states occupy the northern part of the vast region drained by the Mississippi River and its tributaries, of which the Ohio and Missouri rivers are the most important. A vast, largely flat and fertile lowland stretching from the Appalachian Mountains in the east all the way to the Rocky Mountains in the west, the American Middle West constitutes perhaps the richest stretch of agricultural land of its size in the world. It is also rich in minerals and other natural resources and contains some of the country's principal industrial centers. Such major cities as Chicago, Detroit, Cleveland, and Minneapolis are located there. About 57,000,000 people, or somewhat more than one fourth the population of the United States, live in the North Central States.

This is the heartland—the geographical center of the United States and perhaps the most typically "American" region as well. Walter Havighurst, the historian, has noted that in other parts of the country a newsman would ask a foreign visitor, "What is your impression of Boston?—of New York?—of Texas?—of California?" But in the Middle West, Havighurst claims, the question is likely to be, "What do you think of America?" Perhaps the reason for this is that midwesterners are a mixture of peoples who came originally from other parts of the country or from different countries in Europe. The Middle West is the great American melting pot. This makes it very difficult to define any single life style for the region as a whole.

In fact, if anything characterizes this great middle ground of America, it is an indifference to "style." Midwesterners are likely to be more interested in how something works than in how it looks. Getting the job done, making the sale, work, production, mass production—these are the things the Middle West is known for and what midwesterners probably take greatest pride in. As a result, the region has come to be thought of as a cultural wasteland—an area with little interest in or appreciation for the arts. This sort of charge is usually made by outsiders without any real feeling for the region. But it has also been made by native midwesterners, notably Sinclair Lewis, of Minnesota, whose novels are sharply critical of middle western life.

Midwestern Culture

The Middle West is still young, having been settled to any great extent for less than 200 years. Many parts of the region have been settled for an even shorter time. For many years the people of the North Central States had to struggle to build a thriving economy. They just did not have time for the arts.

Eventually the largest midwestern cities established museums and art galleries. Many smaller communities now have museums and galleries that compare favorably with those of cities of similar size throughout the world. Theater and music are thriving today in the Middle West as never before. Chicago, Minneapolis, Detroit, Cincinnati, and Cleveland have outstanding symphony orchestras. The Tyrone Guthrie Theatre in Minneapolis is known throughout the world for its challenging theatrical productions.

The Middle West has also produced some of the country's major artists and writers. The novelists Ernest Hemingway, F. Scott Fitzgerald, James T. Farrell, Sinclair Lewis, Theodore Dreiser, and Sherwood Anderson all grew up in the Middle West, as did the poets Carl Sandburg, Edgar Lee Masters, Vachel Lindsay, and T. S. Eliot. The Middle West also gave the nation its best-known and most revolutionary architect, Frank Lloyd Wright, of Wisconsin. Much of his work was done in the Middle West and was actually inspired by the prairie. In his Prairie Houses, which had an influence on architectural styles far beyond the Middle West, Wright sought to build dwellings that would "associate with the ground and become natural to the prairie site."

BREADBASKET OF THE NATION

The North Central States are known as the breadbasket of the nation, and for good reason. The 12 states of the region provide the nation with the great bulk of such basic foodstuffs as meat and grain. They produce more than half of the wheat grown in the United States. They raise more than 40 percent of the nation's cattle and cows and about four fifths of its hogs. Not surprisingly, too, the Middle West leads in the production of livestock fodder. The grasses, grains, and other fodder of the Midwest help cattlemen to produce superior livestock and make American meat an exceptionally high-grade product.

NORTH CENTRAL STATES

ILLINOIS

CAPITAL: Springfield.

MAJOR CITIES: Chicago, Rockford, Peoria, Springfield, Decatur.

AREA: 56,400 sq. mi. (146,076 sq. km.).

POPULATION: 11,113,976 (1970 census).

PHYSICAL FEATURES: Highest point—Charles Mound, northeastern Illinois near Wisconsin border (1,241 ft.; 378 m.). **Lowest point**—at confluence of Mississippi and Ohio rivers (279 ft.; 85 m.). **Major rivers**—Mississippi, Ohio, Wabash, Illinois. **Major lakes**—Crab Orchard, Bloomington, Decatur (man-made), Springfield (man-made), Fox, Calumet.

STATE MOTTO: State sovereignty, national union.

INDIANA

CAPITAL: Indianapolis.

MAJOR CITIES: Indianapolis, Gary, Fort Wayne, Evansville, South Bend, Hammond.

AREA: 36,291 sq. mi. (93,994 sq. km.).

POPULATION: 5,193,669 (1970 census).

PHYSICAL FEATURES: Highest point—near Ohio border east of Indianapolis (1,257 ft.; 383 m.). **Lowest point**—at confluence of Wabash and Ohio rivers (320 ft.; 98 m.). **Major rivers**—Wabash, Tippecanoe, White, Kankakee, Maumee, Whitewater, Ohio. **Major lakes**—Wawasee, James, Bass, Monroe Reservoir, Geist Reservoir, Morse Reservoir.

STATE MOTTO: The Crossroads of America.

IOWA

CAPITAL: Des Moines.

MAJOR CITIES: Des Moines, Cedar Rapids, Davenport, Sioux City, Waterloo, Dubuque.

AREA: 56,290 sq. mi. (145,791 sq. km.).

POPULATION: 2,825,041 (1970 census).

PHYSICAL FEATURES: Highest point—Ocheyedan Mound, near Minnesota border (1,675 ft.; 510 m.). **Lowest point**—at confluence of Des Moines and Mississippi rivers (480 ft.; 146 m.). **Major rivers**—Mississippi River and tributaries including Wapsipinicon, Iowa, Des Moines; Missouri River and tributaries including Big Sioux, Floyd, Little Sioux, Nishnabotna. **Major lakes**—Coralville Reservoir, Spirit, West Okoboji, East Okoboji, Clear, Storm.

STATE MOTTO: Our liberties we prize and our rights we will maintain.

KANSAS

CAPITAL: Topeka.

MAJOR CITIES: Wichita, Topeka, Kansas City.

AREA: 82,264 sq. mi. (213,064 sq. km.).

POPULATION: 2,249,071 (1970 census).

PHYSICAL FEATURES: Highest point—Mount Sunflower (4,026 ft.; 1,227 m.) at western border. **Lowest point**—on Verdigris River, southeastern Kansas (700 ft.; 213 m.). **Major rivers**—Missouri, Kansas, Marais des Cygnes, Republican, Smoky Hill, Neosho, Verdigris, Arkansas, Cimarron. **Major lakes**—Tuttle Creek, Cedar Bluff; Kirwin (man-made).

STATE MOTTO: *Ad astra per aspera* ("To the stars through difficulties").

MICHIGAN

CAPITAL: Lansing.

MAJOR CITIES: Detroit, Grand Rapids, Flint, Dearborn, Lansing, Warren.

AREA: 58,216 sq. mi. (150,780 sq. km.).

POPULATION: 8,875,083 (1970 census).

PHYSICAL FEATURES: Highest point—Mount Curwood, in western part of Upper Peninsula (1,980 ft.; 604 m.). **Lowest point**—on Lake Erie (572 ft.; 174 m.). **Major rivers**—Menominee, St. Marys, Grand, Muskegon, St. Clair, Detroit. **Major lakes**—Houghton, Charlevoix, Manistique, Black. (State bordered by lakes Superior, St. Clair, Huron, Michigan, and Erie.)

STATE MOTTO: *Si quaeris peninsulam amoenam, circumspice* ("If you seek a delightful peninsula, look around you").

MINNESOTA

CAPITAL: St. Paul.

MAJOR CITIES: Minneapolis, St. Paul, Duluth.

AREA: 84,068 sq. mi. (217,736 sq. km.).

POPULATION: 3,805,069 (1970 census).

PHYSICAL FEATURES: Highest point—Eagle Mountain, near Lake Superior (2,301 ft.; 701 m.). **Lowest point**—on Lake Superior (602 ft.; 183 m.). **Major rivers**—Mississippi, Minnesota, St. Croix, Red River of the North, Rainy, Pigeon. **Major lakes**—Red, Leech, Mille Lacs, Winnibigoshish, Lake of the Woods, Rainy. (State bordered by Lake Superior.)

STATE MOTTO: *L'étoile du nord* ("Star of the North").

Over all, the North Central States account for about 43 percent of the total farm income in the United States. Iowa and Illinois are by far the nation's largest producers of corn and soybeans. Kansas and North Dakota are the two leading wheat-producing states. Wisconsin leads all states in the production of dairy products and hay. Minnesota leads in the production of oats.

The oddity about all this is that the great majority of midwesterners live not on farms but in large towns and cities. About three fourths of the people in the North Central States live in urban areas. Less than one tenth of the people live on farms. What makes it possible for this relatively small number of people to produce so much of the nation's foodstuffs is the widespread use of farm machinery. Probably nowhere in the world has mechanized and scientific farming been carried as far.

NORTH CENTRAL STATES (Continued)

MISSOURI
CAPITAL: Jefferson City.
MAJOR CITIES: St. Louis, Kansas City, Springfield, Independence, Jefferson City.
AREA: 69,686 sq. mi. (180,487 sq. km.).
POPULATION: 4,677,399 (1970 census).
PHYSICAL FEATURES: **Highest point**—Taum Sauk Mountain, southeastern Missouri (1,772 ft.; 540 m.). **Lowest point**—on the St. Francis River, extreme southeastern Missouri (230 ft.; 70 m.). **Major rivers**—Mississippi, Missouri, Osage, Gasconade, Meramec, Current, St. Francis, Grand, Chariton, Salt. **Major lakes**—Lake of the Ozarks, Wappapello, Clearwater, Table Rock (man-made).
STATE MOTTO: *Salus populi suprema lex esto* ("Let the welfare of the people be the supreme law").

NEBRASKA
CAPITAL: Lincoln.
MAJOR CITIES: Omaha, Lincoln.
AREA: 77,227 sq. mi. (200,018 sq. km.).
POPULATION: 1,483,791 (1970 census).
PHYSICAL FEATURES: **Highest point**—in western Nebraska (5,424 ft.; 1,653 m.). **Lowest point**—on the Missouri River, southeastern corner of the state (840 ft.; 256 m.). **Major rivers**—Missouri, Niobrara, Platte (and its tributaries the Loup and Elkhorn), Republican, Little Blue, Big Blue. **Major lakes**—McConaughy, Lewis and Clark, Swanson, Harlan County Reservoir, Sherman Reservoir.
STATE MOTTO: Equality before the law.

NORTH DAKOTA
CAPITAL: Bismarck.
MAJOR CITIES: Fargo, Bismarck.
AREA: 70,665 sq. mi. (183,023 sq. km.).
POPULATION: 617,761 (1970 census).
PHYSICAL FEATURES: **Highest point**—White Butte, western North Dakota (3,506 ft.; 1,069 m.). **Lowest point**—on the Red River of the North, state's eastern border (750 ft.; 229 m.). **Major rivers**—Red River of the North, Souris, Sheyenne, Missouri (and its tributaries the Little Missouri, Knife, Heart, Cannonball, and James). **Major lakes**—Sakakawea Reservoir, Oahe Reservoir, Devils.
STATE MOTTO: Liberty and union, now and forever, one and inseparable.

OHIO
CAPITAL: Columbus.
MAJOR CITIES: Cleveland, Columbus, Cincinnati, Toledo, Akron, Dayton.
AREA: 41,222 sq. mi. (106,765 sq. km.).
POPULATION: 10,652,017 (1970 census).
PHYSICAL FEATURES: **Highest point**—Campbell Hill, west-central Ohio (1,550 ft.; 472 m.). **Lowest point**—on the Ohio River (433 ft.; 132 m.). **Major rivers**—Ohio, Muskingum, Hocking, Scioto, Little Miami, Great Miami, Grand, Cuyahoga, Sandusky, Maumee. **Major lakes**—Grand (man-made), Indian, Mosquito Creek Reservoir, Berlin Reservoir. (State bordered by Lake Erie.)
STATE MOTTO: With God all things are possible.

SOUTH DAKOTA
CAPITAL: Pierre.
MAJOR CITIES: Sioux Falls, Rapid City, Pierre.
AREA: 77,047 sq. mi. (199,552 sq. km.).
POPULATION: 666,257 (1970 census).
PHYSICAL FEATURES: **Highest point**—Harney Peak, western South Dakota (7,242 ft.; 2,207 m.). **Lowest point**—Big Stone Lake, northeastern South Dakota (962 ft.; 293 m.). **Major rivers**—the Missouri and its tributaries including the Grand, Moreau, Cheyenne, Bad, White, James, Vermillion, and Big Sioux. **Major lakes**—Oahe Reservoir, Francis Case, Lewis and Clark (man-made), Traverse, Big Stone.
STATE MOTTO: Under God the people rule.

WISCONSIN
CAPITAL: Madison.
MAJOR CITIES: Milwaukee, Madison, Racine, Green Bay.
AREA: 56,154 sq. mi. (145,439 sq. km.).
POPULATION: 4,417,933 (1970 census).
PHYSICAL FEATURES: **Highest point**—Timms Hill, northern Wisconsin (1,953 ft.; 595 m.). **Lowest point**—on Lake Michigan (581 ft.; 177 m.). **Major rivers**—Mississippi, St. Croix, Wisconsin, Black, Chippewa, Rock, Fox, and Wolf. **Major lakes**—Winnebago, Pepin, Green, Poygan, Mendota, Koshkonong, Petenwell Flowage (man-made), Castle Rock Flowage (man-made). (State bordered by Lake Superior, Lake Michigan.)
STATE MOTTO: Forward.

Machines for Progress. The famous historian Frederick Jackson Turner (1861–1932) once wrote that the land of the Middle West "constituted the richest free gift that was ever spread out before civilized man." To be sure, the land was rich, but where prosperous farms and great cities have been built, the American Indian often froze and starved. The first pioneers who settled the Middle West in the 19th century subsisted at a level not much higher than the Indians'. They lived in log cabins, or if they ventured out onto the great prairies of the Middle West where there were no trees, they lived in crude houses of prairie sod. (Sod is the part of the ground that includes the grass and its roots.) The difficulties they faced included insects, disease, hostile Indians, droughts, and blizzards. The early farmer stumbled behind a horse-drawn plow, which often broke on a root or bogged down in the thick, sticky sod of

218

Antique cars in the Ford Museum's collection of American relics, Dearborn, Mich.

Tyrone Guthrie Theatre in Minneapolis, known for its repertory productions.

University of Iowa, Iowa City.

the prairie. For the most part the pioneer farmer used implements not much advanced over those used in Biblical times.

Then around the middle of the 19th century a revolution in agricultural methods began. New farm machinery was developed that in time turned American agriculture into the large-scale, mechanized commercial enterprise it is today. The revolution received its greatest impetus in the Middle West, where the uniform flatness of much of the land was particularly inviting to the use of farm machinery. A whole new spate of plows, planters, cultivators, harvesters, threshers, and other machines were developed. Improved models were turned out every year. The results were dramatic. By 1900, with the machinery available, the estimated human labor required to produce a bushel of wheat had been reduced to about 10 minutes. This was about one eighteenth the time required to produce a bushel of wheat 70 years before.

In addition to this enormous improvement in farm machinery, a number of other developments helped the farmers to increase their output. Fertilizers came to be used more widely than before. Dry farming techniques to grow crops with little rainfall were developed for the dry plains region of western Kansas, Nebraska, and the Dakotas. And the United States Department of Agriculture, established in 1862, enormously encouraged the development of scientific farming. In the 20th century, tractors and other gasoline-powered machinery, as well as electrical machinery, came into use, cutting down distances on the vast fields of the prairies. More and more was produced by fewer men, and the average farm got bigger. The midwestern farmer became the scientist and mechanic he is today.

Corn and Wheat. Running a farm in the Middle West today is likely to be a very expensive operation. This is particularly true in the Corn Belt, where the corn that fattens the bulk of the country's livestock is grown. The heart of the Corn Belt is in Iowa, Illinois, and Indiana, and it spreads into the neighboring states as well. The soil is extremely fertile, the rainfall is abundant and well-distributed among the seasons, and there is a long, warm growing season. All this makes the land extremely valuable, twice as valuable, in fact, as the average farmland in the United States. When one adds to the cost of the land, the cost of livestock, seed, buildings, machinery, fuel, and fertilizer, farming becomes a very expensive operation. Therefore, many farmers are tenants, and much of the land is owned by banks, insurance companies, or wealthy businessmen. These owners rent the land out to farmers, who generally provide machinery and labor. Some farms operate on contract to milling companies or meat-packing houses. Some large farms are actually owned by these industries. The companies buy up farms, put in managers to run them, provide the machinery to farm them, and take the produce for their own use. Machinery is often equipped with electric lighting to permit round-the-clock operation.

West of the Corn Belt—at about the 98th meridian of longitude (including the western portions of the Dakotas, Nebraska, and Kansas)—rainfall becomes too scarce for profitable cultivation of corn. Fields of tasseled corn give way to enormous flat stretches of waving wheat, for wheat requires less rainfall than corn. It can also flourish on somewhat less fertile soil. Farmers, however, generally do not like to rely on a single crop, so much of the land is not planted at all, but is retained as grazing land for cattle or sheep. Because the land is less expensive than in the Corn Belt, farmers are more likely to own their land. Farms remain very impressive operations with all kinds of machinery. Perhaps the most impressive machines of all are the huge combines, which enable a single man to harvest completely 50 acres of wheat in one day. Generally, combines are owned jointly by a number of wheat farmers who rotate them among themselves at harvesttime.

FARM AND FACTORY

Agricultural production does not end on the farm. Produce has to be processed and shipped to stores and markets all over the country and the world. Food processing had already become a major industry in the Middle West before the Civil War. In those days Cincinnati, Ohio, was known as "Porkopolis" or "Hogopolis" or "Pigopolis," and was the largest meat-packing center in the nation. Later, as settlement moved westward, Chicago, Illinois, surpassed Cincinnati as the chief hog and cattle butcher for the nation. As many as 18,000,000 animals—principally hogs and cattle—were butchered in the Chicago stockyards in a single year during the 1920's, when meat-packing operations there reached their peak. Subsequently, other centers grew up farther west in places like Omaha, Nebraska, or Sioux City, Iowa, or Kansas City, Missouri. Today

Farmers look over some new tractors at the Kansas state fair.

Combines harvest a field of rye in Nebraska.

stockyards are spread out all over the Middle West instead of being concentrated in Chicago. Packers have abandoned the enormous sheds of this city for more efficient, one-story plants nearer the farms and feed lots where the cattle and hogs are born and fattened. It is increasingly from modern packing houses like these that American meat products are shipped out to many parts of the world.

Almost as important as the meats supplied by these mechanized plants are the by-products. Everything but the squeal of the hog and the moo of the steer is utilized. There are, for example, more than 100 uses in pharmaceutical houses alone for meat by-products.

Midwesterners have developed methods for getting the most out of many kinds of farm produce. A given farm product may be put to any number of uses. Corn, for example, is used principally for animal feed. However, it is also used to make whiskey, cornmeal, hominy, and breakfast cereals. Corn oil is extracted to be used in mayonnaise, margarine, salad oil, and cooking oil. Cornstarch and corn sugar are obtained, each of which in turn goes into the making of many different food products. Another crop for which numerous uses have been found is soybeans. So many uses have been found for the soybean that it has become one of the nation's leading money crops during the last few decades. Today soybeans go into the manufacture not only of a wide variety of food products but many non-food products as well. Some kinds of paints and varnishes, floor coverings, and printing inks include soybeans or soybean oils in their composition.

Agriculture and industry are strongly dependent on each other in

Chicago's new skyline along Lake Shore Drive.

most of the Middle West. Urban areas are centers for the marketing of farm products and also serve as shopping and supply centers for the farmers. Many of the cities and towns in the Middle West are strongly identified with the farm products processed there.

Minneapolis, Minnesota, for example, is known as the "flour city" and the "flour milling capital of the world." With Buffalo, New York (on Lake Erie), it is one of the two chief flour-milling cities in the world. Milwaukee, Wisconsin, is known as the "beer city," because so much of the barley produced in the Middle West is used in making beer there. Battle Creek, Michigan, is the "breakfast food city"; Decatur, Illinois, is the "soybean capital of the world"; Sheboygan, Wisconsin, is the "wurst city of the world," because of all the sausage ("wurst" is the German word for sausage) produced there. Some towns are identified with the manufacture of farm machinery and farm implements. Moline, Illinois, for example, is called "plow city." De Kalb, Illinois, calls itself the "barbed wire capital of the world."

Heavy Industry

In addition to all this farm-related manufacturing, the Middle West has its heavy industry as well. Heavy industry is concentrated in the lower Great Lakes area, a region that has access to important sources of iron ore, coal, oil, and natural gas. Iron ore is brought by boat from the huge iron mines in northern Michigan and Minnesota. Coal needed to process iron and steel is brought by rail from Pennsylvania, West Virginia, and east central Ohio. Petroleum is piped into such lakeside cities as Detroit,

These men work at one of the world's largest steelworks, at Gary, Indiana.

Cleveland, and Toledo, Ohio, for refining all the way from the Southwest. The oil can then be shipped out by way of the Great Lakes. Natural gas is also available for industries like glassmaking. Glassmaking is especially important in Toledo.

The largest city in the lower Great Lakes region and in the entire Middle West is Chicago. It is an important service, trade, and transportation center. But it is also a center for heavy industry. Chicago has big iron and steel mills and sprawling plants where railway trains, lake steamers, and machines of all kinds are manufactured. Detroit, the second largest city in the North Central States, is the greatest center for automobile making in the world. Actually towns and cities all over the area manufacture automobile parts, car furnishings, or car accessories. These parts are finally put together in Detroit's huge assembly-line plants. Cleveland, Ohio, the third largest city in the North Central States, is known for its big factories that produce steel and steel products. In addition to these three great cities, the lower Great Lakes region has other industrial centers of national importance. These include Toledo, Ohio, a glassmaking center; Akron, Ohio, which calls itself "the rubber capital of the world"; and Youngstown, Ohio, a major steelmaking center.

TRANSPORTATION HUB OF THE NATION

All this mass production—industrial and agricultural—has been made possible by the development of a vast transportation system binding the Middle West together and connecting it with other parts of the country.

Foreign freighters are docked at Cleveland, one of the Midwest's busiest ports.

Transportation has been a preoccupation of midwesterners beginning with the first wave of settlement in the early 19th century. This was a wilderness with great potential for development, a land where a farmer could produce far more than he needed to feed his family and himself. The problem was how to get his farm produce to market, and, in particular, how to get it to the large markets that could give his produce wide distribution.

Originally the major form of transportation was by water. The 1820's and 1830's saw a flurry of canal-building activity in the three most settled North Central states, Ohio, Indiana, and Illinois. Flatboats and keelboats —and later, steamboats—plied the region's canals and rivers. These waterways connected with two general river systems. One was the Ohio-Mississippi river system that led to New Orleans, the nation's second largest port (after New York). Abe Lincoln's first long trip when he was a young man in Indiana was along this very route by flatboat all the way to New Orleans. The second major waterway system was via the Great Lakes and the Erie Canal directly to New York's Hudson River and the eastern seaboard.

Railroads.   The eastern seaboard with its big cities was the greatest potential market for the farmers of the Middle West. But at first the farmers could not ship their products to the East overland. There were no good roads across the Appalachians. Then came the railroads. They provided an immense stimulus to the economy of the Middle West. They greatly strengthened the region's economic ties with the East at the expense of its ties with New Orleans and the South. This was one of the reasons the Middle West joined with the North against the South in the Civil War.

The first railroad in the North Central region was the Erie and Kalamazoo Railroad, which, in 1836, began regular operation between Toledo, Ohio, and the town of Adrian in what was then Michigan Territory. This ushered in a great period of railroad construction in the Middle West that continued for many decades. Money to build the railroads was furnished by eastern investors, state governments, and—most important of all—the federal government.

The federal government of the United States authorized land grants to railroads. The railroads sold the land to finance the building of the lines. The railroads thereby became the biggest land brokers in the Middle West. The first land grant line was the Illinois Central Railroad, which was chartered in 1851. It was to build a line from Cairo, at the southern tip of Illinois, to Chicago and Galena at the northern end of the state. Under the terms of the Land Grant Act, which had been passed by Congress the previous year, the Illinois Central received a 200-foot (61 meters) right-of-way for track, plus alternate sections on both sides of the right-of-way, running back for 6 miles (10 km.). This act set the pattern for subsequent bonanza land grants to railroads during the next 20 years. The railroads received more than 200,000 square miles (518,000 square kilometers) of land. This area equaled the entire area of France. Most of that land was in the Middle West.

Railroad Colonization.   In the course of selling their vast lands to provide for construction costs, the railroads carried out extensive colonization. In general, settlers were good for business, for the more settlers the more commerce. Railroad colonizing was especially important in the vast treeless grasslands in the western parts of Kansas, Nebraska, and the Dakotas. The lack of wood, scarcity of water, and the harshness of the climate in that area were hardly conducive to settlement. In fact, this was part of a vast region called the Great American Desert through the better part of the 19th century.

In order to attract settlers, the railroads used all kinds of sales techniques. They arranged reduced-fare, round-trip tickets for prospective buyers, or they arranged for landviewing expeditions where prospective buyers were lavishly entertained. The railroad also had bureaus of immigration that maintained agents at the eastern seaports to greet immigrants, arrange their transportation west, and see to it they were not lured away by rival companies. Agencies were also maintained in Europe to attract immigrants. Glowing reports were published of what they would find. The Platte River valley of Nebraska, for example, where adequate rainfall has always been something of a problem, was described as "a flowery meadow of great fertility clothed in nutritious grasses and watered by numerous streams." No one knows just how many people were drawn to the North Central States by advertising of this kind. However, from 1870 to 1890, thousands of settlers, Americans and foreigners alike, streamed out to the Great Plains in the greatest wave of settlement that region has ever known.

Transportation Today.   Railroads remain a vital part of the transportation complex that draws the North Central States together. The North Central States have more miles of railroad than any other part of the United States. In fact about 40 percent of the nation's total railway mileage is located in these 12 states. The regional rail system is connected with the rest of the country principally through Chicago, the nation's greatest rail center, and also through such important railroad towns as St. Louis, Kansas City, Omaha, and Minneapolis and St. Paul.

In addition to railways, highways form an important part of the transportation complex of the North Central States. Almost all farm products, for example, are moved from the farms to their initial market by truck. Passenger service by air is available in all the larger cities. O'Hare Airport in Chicago handles more passengers than any other airport in the country. Water transportation is also still important to the region's commerce. The Great Lakes-St. Lawrence Seaway system serves as an important outlet to the Atlantic Ocean for grain, oil, and other goods. To the south, the Ohio and Mississippi rivers are used by barges carrying all sorts of cargoes. St. Louis and Cincinnati are important river ports as they have been since the 19th century.

HOW THE MIDDLE WEST WAS FIRST SETTLED

The explorers who paved the way for settlement in the North Central region were French. In 1615, the great French explorer Samuel de Champlain approached the area when he traveled from eastern Canada to the Georgian Bay area, northeast of Lake Huron. By the end of the 17th century, French explorers and missionaries, including Étienne Brulé, Jean Nicolet, Father Jacques Marquette, Louis Jolliet, and Robert Cavelier, Sieur de La Salle, had extended French exploration westward to the Mississippi River and southward all the way to the Gulf of Mexico. The French established a chain of settlements from Canada to the Gulf Coast. These settlements include key outposts in the Midwest at Detroit, at Green Bay and La Crosse in present-day Wisconsin, and at Vincennes in modern Indiana. The purpose of this chain of military and trading posts was two-fold: to conduct the fur trade with Indian tribes over a wide area, and to keep the British hemmed in in their settlements along the Atlantic Coast. In this way the French felt they could secure the heart of the North American continent for France.

This scheme was finally put to rest with France's defeat by Britain in the Seven Years War (1756–63). This was a global war, the North American phase of which was called the French and Indian War. In 1763, following its defeat in this conflict, France ceded all its land east of the Mississippi River to Britain. That land area included about half of what is known today as the Middle West. The other half, the area west of the Mississippi River, was ceded to France's ally Spain in 1762 to compensate Spain for its losses in the Seven Years War. The region was given back to France in 1800 and subsequently formed part of the immense territory bought by President Thomas Jefferson for the United States in the Louisiana Purchase of 1803.

The Northwest Ordinance.   At the end of the American Revolution in 1783, the American portion of the Middle West, the portion east of the Mississippi River, was an immense wilderness inhabited by about 2,000 French and about 45,000 Indians. With the end of hostilities, American settlers began to enter the region.

Settlement started along the upper Ohio River valley and spread westward and northward from there. Marietta, Ohio, founded in 1788, was the first American settlement in the Middle West. Cincinnati was founded later the same year. It became the governmental headquarters of the Northwest Territory, which was the administrative unit embracing all the lands north of the Ohio River and east of the Mississippi River. Five states—Ohio, Indiana, Illinois, Michigan, and Wisconsin—were eventually organized from the lands included in the original Northwest Territory.

The Northwest Territory had been created by the Congress of Confederation in 1787. The Ordinance of 1787, as this congressional act was called, guaranteed basic rights and freedoms for settlers in the Northwest Territory. It outlawed slavery. The Ordinance provided that three to five states be created eventually out of the territory. Initially government was to be by officials appointed by Congress. When the population increased to 5,000 males of voting age, a territorial legislature was to be established. When any part of this vast region contained more than 60,000 males of voting age, it could apply for statehood. By this procedure Ohio became a state in 1803; Indiana became a state in 1816; Illinois in 1818; Michigan in 1837; and Wisconsin in 1848.

THE SLAVERY ISSUE AND THE MIDDLE WEST

Meanwhile settlers were pushing beyond the Mississippi River, too. Missouri became a state in 1821, as a result of the Missouri Compromise, which had been passed by Congress in the previous year. In the Missouri Compromise, Congress sought to strike a balance between pro-slavery and anti-slavery forces in the nation. Missouri was to enter the Union as a slave state, but at the same time Maine would enter the Union as a free state (a state in which slavery was prohibited). Except in Missouri, slavery was to be prohibited in any part of the Louisiana Purchase north of latitude 36° 30′ (the southern boundary of Missouri). In accordance with

St. Louis' Gateway Arch, 630 feet (190 meters) high, celebrates the city's role as the gateway to the West in the 19th century. As settlement pushed westward across the Plains, St. Louis became a major outfitting center for migrating settlers.

the terms of the Missouri Compromise, Iowa entered the Union as a free state in 1846. The five states formed out of the Northwest Territory were free states because slavery had been prohibited in the Northwest Territory under the terms of the Northwest Ordinance of 1787.

"Bleeding Kansas."   The national conflict over slavery reached the North Central region with a vengeance, however, following the passage of the Kansas-Nebraska Act by Congress in 1854. The new law repealed the Missouri Compromise by providing that the question of slavery in Kansas and Nebraska be determined by the settlers themselves. In Nebraska slavery was never an issue. But in Kansas, the slavery question erupted into a violent struggle between pro-slavery and anti-slavery settlers. Murder and looting became the order of the day, and during the next few years the new territory came to be known throughout the nation as "Bleeding Kansas."

Actually the majority of settlers in Kansas even in those early years came for the economic opportunities that go with the opening of any new region for settlement. Of course, there were settlers from New England or the Deep South who came primarily to support (in the case of the South) or oppose (in the case of New England) the cause of slavery. But many more settlers came from Illinois, Indiana, and Ohio. Much of the violence of "Bleeding Kansas" was probably the kind of upset typical of any frontier region. In the end, the great majority of settlers proved to be opposed to slavery. When Kansas entered the Union in January, 1861, it did so as a free state.

Southern Sympathizers. At the outbreak of the Civil War all the North Central States except North Dakota and South Dakota had entered the Union. All fought on the Union side. Many settlers in the North Central region, however, had come originally from the South and had pro-Southern sympathies. Missouri, of course, was a slave state, and even though it remained officially in the Union, more than one fifth of all Missourians who fought in the war fought on the Confederate side. In other states—Illinois, Indiana, Ohio—pro-Confederate movements created difficulties for the pro-Union state governments. In Ohio, for example, there was considerable support for the Copperhead movement, which advocated a halt in fighting by the Union. A Copperhead, Clement Laird Vallandigham, came close to winning the governorship of the state in the election of 1863. Even today many people in Missouri and in southern Ohio, Indiana, and Illinois, have strong cultural ties with the South.

SETTLERS FROM MANY NATIONS

The first wave of settlers in the Midwest came mainly from Pennsylvania and southward. They made their way by road to the Ohio River and traveled down the river and up its tributaries. Then the completion of the Erie Canal in 1825 opened the way for the settlement of Cleveland, Ohio, and the lower Great Lakes region and drew increasing numbers of New Englanders to the Middle West. Pioneer farmers made rude clearings and brought the land under cultivation. As years passed they often sold their land for a profit and moved on to new frontier regions, farther west. This kind of leapfrogging from one settlement to the next happened time after time over the broad spaces of the Middle West.

In addition to this influx of native Americans, immigrants from Europe, too, settled the Midwest. Particularly important among the early immigrants were the more than 1,000,000 Germans who migrated to the United States in the 1850's. About three quarters of these Germans settled in the North Central part of the country. These were people who had left their homeland following the failure of the liberal revolution of 1848 in Germany. They brought with them a love of freedom and hatred of slavery. Their votes were an important—perhaps decisive—factor in Lincoln's victory in the presidential election of 1860. In that election, Lincoln won every North Central state then in the Union with the exception of Missouri.

The greatest period of foreign immigration to the Middle West was the last half of the 19th century and the early years of the 20th century up to World War I. Many different peoples came to the North Central States, including large numbers of Scandinavians, who settled mainly in Minnesota, Wisconsin, and the Dakotas, and Germans, who settled in many parts of the Middle West. Numerous Poles, Irish, Russians, Czechs, and Italians came as well. All these immigrant groups contributed to the development of the region. German immigrants, who settled in especially large numbers in Wisconsin, introduced new dairying techniques and also the brewing business and the educational concept of kindergarten. In Kansas, Mennonite immigrants from southern Russia introduced a drought-resistant strain of wheat called Turkey Red, which contributed to successful wheat cultivation on the Great Plains.

As a rule, the immigrants were more interested in starting a new life than in perpetuating old ways of doing things. Earlier loyalties were blunted or perhaps disappeared. This was the melting pot. People of different nations mixed together and became Americans. This was especially true in the rural areas of the Middle West where people were drawn together by common natural hardships such as floods or droughts or locusts. It was true, for example, in Galesburg, Illinois, the prairie town where the famous American poet and historian Carl Sandburg grew up. In his autobiography Sandburg recalled all the different nationalities of Galesburg and how they made him wonder. He wrote, "In Sweden all the people in a town were Swedes, in England they were all English, and in Ireland all Irish. But here in Galesburg, we had a few from everywhere and there had even been cases of Swedish Lutherans marrying Irish Catholic girls—and what was to come of it all? . . . What is this America I am part of? . . . ."

In the cities, in places like Chicago and Detroit, on the other hand, immigrant groups tended to keep to themselves and distrusted outsiders. They crowded into ethnic neighborhoods, or ghettoes—often appalling places in which to live. In time the former immigrants advanced from the ranks of unskilled labor into the middle class, but then newcomers would move in, poor people belonging to other racial or ethnic groups. And so there was always the push to move on to a better neighborhood

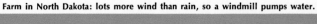

Farm in North Dakota: lots more wind than rain, so a windmill pumps water.

or eventually out to the suburbs. The slums remained for newcomers to live in.

PROBLEMS PAST AND PRESENT

The late 19th century was a hard time for farmers as well as for immigrants in the big cities. Farmers, too, often found life in the Middle West harder than expected, particularly life in the dry Great Plains region, west of the 98th meridian.

That region has always been plagued by highly unpredictable rainfall. Periods of more than adequate rainfall would attract settlers to the Plains and would encourage the farmers already there to increase their investment in land and machinery. Then there would be a series of dry years, and with them a spate of crop failures, bankruptcies, and mortgage foreclosures. What was supposed to be a land of milk and honey turned sour and bitter for many. Always there was a moving population looking for a better place and failing to find it. The sign on the wagon of one man disillusioned with the search proclaimed: "In God we trusted; in Kansas we busted." That motto could have been painted on many wagons.

What was certainly the most catastrophic of times for the Plains farmers occurred as recently as the 1930's. Thousands of farmers were uprooted by drought and financial hardship and abandoned their land, a story told eloquently in John Steinbeck's *The Grapes of Wrath*. Grasslands

The rich forage on this Wisconsin dairy farm helps produce high-quality milk.

The Badlands of southwestern South Dakota were created by wind and rain erosion.

that probably should have been left alone had instead been plowed up, and as a result the soil lacked its natural grass binding. When successive wheat crops failed because of drought, nothing at all was left to hold the dry soil, and wind whipped the soil up into black clouds that blotted out the sun. They were called "black blizzards." Today dust storms on that scale are less likely because farmers have become more sophisticated about the land and its capacities and the need for sound soil conservation practices.

The Struggle for Reform.   Farmers have also fought to improve their lot by political and social action. In the late 19th century, the farmers had good reason to be bitter against a whole array of huge corporate enterprises. These included the railroads, which the farmers felt were over-charging them to haul their freight; unscrupulous grain elevator operators, who underpaid the farmers for their grain; and monopoly companies that charged high prices for manufactured products the farmer had to buy. The farmers fought these large corporations both on local and national levels through such organizations as the National Grange of the Patrons of Husbandry (also known simply as the Grange), the Farmers' Alliance, and the People's (or Populist) Party. As a result the state and federal governments eventually put an end to the abuses the pioneer farmers had to bear.

One landmark in that struggle was the decision of the United States Supreme Court in the case of *Munn* v. *Illinois*, a decision handed down in 1876. At issue in *Munn* v. *Illinois* was a law passed by the Illinois legislature, under pressure from the farmers, setting rates for storing and handling grain. The railroads and elevator owners argued that the law violated the United States Constitution because it denied them free use of their private property. In other words, it denied them the right to set their own rates without regulation. The Supreme Court disagreed, holding that property ceased to be completely private when "used in a manner to make it of public consequence and affect the community at large." Such property, the Court ruled, "must submit to be controlled by the public for the common good."

This decision by no means brought an end to the farmers' struggle against the elevator owners and railroads and big corporations. But *Munn* v. *Illinois* and the other so-called "Granger cases" decided by the Supreme Court did lay the basis for government regulation of monopolies and large corporations, a form of regulation largely taken for granted today.

The Challenge of Conservation. Today, many of the farmer's traditional problems have disappeared. But many farmers have disappeared, too, with the growth of mechanized agriculture. Most midwesterners now live in the cities and urban areas, and in the big cities of the North Central States the problems of poverty-ridden ghettoes are perhaps more serious than ever. In addition, the pollution of streams and of the air and the creation of industrial wastelands have increased. In many ways, midwesterners have made good use of their land, but they have also abused it and exploited it. Hundreds of thousands of acres of rich farmland have been covered over by layers of asphalt and concrete, transformed into parking lots, factories, and suburban shopping centers.

Unfortunately, despoiling the natural environment is nothing new in the North Central States. In the late 19th and early 20th centuries, what were perhaps the most magnificent forests in all North America were virtually destroyed by greedy lumbermen in Michigan, Minnesota, and Wisconsin. This was the forest primeval, the home of Longfellow's Hiawatha, an immensity of pine, fir, and spruce and some hardwoods. Then along came the lumbermen. In 1870 Michigan led all the states of the Union in wood production. Twenty years later, the Michigan forests were largely depleted. Wisconsin's and Minnesota's magnificent forests were subsequently depleted as well. Farmers moved into some of the desolated forest areas, but many cut-over places remained blots on the landscape. The three states have made valiant attempts at reforestation, but the old deep forests can probably never be brought back. Hundreds of thousands of acres of bleak cut-over land remain. They stand as a constant reminder to the people of the Middle West that the bounties of even this incredibly rich land are not inexhaustible.

JOHN J. MURRAY, Coe College, Iowa; editor, *The Heritage of the Middle West*

SOUTH CENTRAL
STATES

On map:
OKLAHOMA

ARKANSAS

TENNESSEE

★ Little Rock
●Hot Springs

Mississippi River

Huntsville ●

Tennessee River

GEORGIA

Birmingham ●

MISSISSIPPI

●Shreveport   ●Monroe   Vicksburg
●
★ Jackson

Selma ●
★ Montgomery

LOUISIANA

ALABAMA

Mississippi River

Alexandria ●

TEXAS

Sabine River

★ Baton Rouge   Biloxi ●

●Mobile

FLORIDA

New Orleans ●

GULF OF MEXICO

SOUTH CENTRAL STATES

When Mississippi's famous novelist, William Faulkner, said of his homeland, "You can't understand it. You would have to be born here," he expressed an attitude typical of many people who live in the South Central States of Alabama, Mississippi, Louisiana, and Arkansas. This attitude is a mixture of pride and defensiveness. It holds that the Deep South—as this area is often called—is a special, unique world, and if an outsider criticizes it he does so because of his ignorance. Outsiders often think only in terms of the stereotyped images of the South: waxy, white magnolia blossoms, honeysuckle scenting the warm darkness of country lanes, cotton plantations, spirituals drifting over the levees, the mile-wide "Old Man River," hound dogs baying after raccoons in the moonlight. Other symbols are remnants of the cherished past of before the Civil War. On the Natchez bluff, overlooking the Mississippi River, white-columned, pre-Civil War mansions still stand beneath cedar trees draped with Spanish moss.

Outsiders sometimes see in this same lush terrain images that are close to nightmare. They see hungry children playing around broken-down sharecroppers' cottages. They remember the untimely deaths of black men who defied the white supremacy dogma that once dominated the South. But the southerner, resenting outside criticism, increasingly reminds the northerner of his own problems in urban ghettos.

It is particularly easy for the southerner to keep his feeling of "specialness" because he is far more likely than other Americans to be a native of his home region, with little experience outside it. For instance, in 1960 nearly 90 percent of Mississippi's citizens had been born in Mississippi. In the same period, Alabama's native-born population was over 80 percent, and other Southern states also had a high proportion of native-born residents.

The traditional civilization of the Deep South centers most in the Black Belt of central Alabama and Mississippi and in the Mississippi Delta. The Black Belt was named for the ebony color of its rich, loamy soil, which is ideal for growing cotton. The Delta is the vast region where the Mississippi River splits into innumerable branches, or bayous, as it fans out on its way to the Gulf of Mexico. The river's fertile floodplain runs through 400 miles (644 kilometers) of Mississippi, Arkansas, and Louisiana. The plain varies from 40 to 70 miles (64–113 km.) in width. This land of levees, swamps, and rice paddies, often stricken by crippling floods, is the last sanctuary of all that is most traditionally Southern.

In Louisiana, the Gulf of Mexico is bordered by swampy lowlands. It is an ideal region for sugarcane fields, waterfowl, and fishermen. Here in "Cajun country" (which also includes the prairies of southwest Louisiana) live the French-speaking Acadians. Their ancestors were exiled from Nova Scotia by the British and migrated to Louisiana in the 18th century. Keeping to themselves, resisting Americanization, but adopting whatever they could use of American skills, the Acadians developed rice paddies and cattle farms. They had big families, and so today they probably number more than 250,000 people.

The French left a heritage in other parts of Louisiana too. New Orleans is traditionally the city of the Creoles, the descendants of French and Spanish colonists. From the beginning the city has shown European traits in architecture, food, and social customs, although it has not been truly bilingual for more than a century. The distinctive Creole cooking is based on crayfish and other local seafood. Many streets have French names. The elegant homes of the city's French Quarter (Vieux Carré) with their walled courtyards, tropical gardens, and lacy iron grillwork are actually mementos of the still earlier Spanish occupation of the city.

Another outstanding example of French influence in the region is the prominence of the Roman Catholic Church in New Orleans and southern Louisiana. Roman Catholics are the largest single religious group. Their church is a major force in the social and religious life of the community. Except for these specific areas on the Gulf Coast, the rest of the people of Louisiana and the other South Central States are predominantly Protestant.

Northwest of Cajun country, through Louisiana and up into Arkansas, is a unique rolling woodland which is sometimes called the Piney Woods. Still farther north, in Arkansas, the land slopes up to the Ouachita Highlands and the Ozark Plateau. The world of the Ozark highlander is, again, separate and unique. His ancestors are more likely to have come from the Kentucky frontier (Daniel Boone country) than from the more sophisticated world of the plantation South. Like the Kentucky mountaineer, the Ozark highlander has preserved traces of Elizabethan (16th-century) English speech habits, customs, and folk songs. The craggy, beautiful jumble of wooded mountains made travel difficult, and so the

Ozark people managed, in their proud isolation, to hold on to traditional ways far longer than most groups could. Today, however, they are being drawn increasingly into the mainstream of American life.

Although the four South Central States are not a distinct geographical region, they share many characteristics inherited from a common past. Alabama, Mississippi, Louisiana, and Arkansas were the southern frontier of the booming cotton economy during the period between the American Revolution and the Mexican War. Together they endured grinding agricultural poverty in the years between the Civil War and World War II. More recently they have made rapid economic progress, and they are experiencing a revolutionary change in the patterns of relationship between blacks and whites. About a third of the population of the region is black. Here both blacks and whites find themselves struggling on a new kind of frontier, the frontier of racial understanding.

THE PAST

The South Central region was one of the first parts of the continental United States to be explored by Europeans. Although Hernando de Soto began his great journey from a base in Florida, much of his long and unsuccessful search for gold was in the area now occupied by the South Central States. De Soto first discovered the Mississippi River in 1541. He returned to the river to die a little more than a year later.

Another European, Robert Cavelier, Sieur de La Salle, explored the lower Mississippi and claimed it for King Louis XIV of France in 1682. It was many years before the English settlers on the Atlantic coast pushed west toward the Mississippi. The first permanent French settlements were at Biloxi, Mississippi, and Mobile, in Alabama. But New Orleans soon became the most important post, because of its strategic location

---

SOUTH CENTRAL STATES

ALABAMA
CAPITAL: Montgomery.
MAJOR CITIES: Birmingham, Mobile, Montgomery, Huntsville.
AREA: 51,609 sq. mi. (133,667 sq. km.).
POPULATION: 3,444,165 (1970 census).
PHYSICAL FEATURES: Highest point—Cheaha Mountain (2,407 ft.; 734 m.). Lowest point—sea level. Major rivers—Tennessee, Tombigbee, Coosa, Tallapoosa, Mobile. Major lakes—Wilson, Wheeler, Guntersville (all man-made).
STATE MOTTO: Audemus jura nostra defendero ("We dare defend our rights").

ARKANSAS
CAPITAL: Little Rock.
MAJOR CITY: Little Rock.
AREA: 53,104 sq. mi. (137,540 sq. km.).
POPULATION: 1,923,295 (1970 census).
PHYSICAL FEATURES: Highest point—Magazine Mountain (2,823 ft.; 860 m.). Lowest point—along the Ouachita River, 55 ft. (17 m.). Major rivers—Arkansas, Red, Ouachita, Mississippi. Major lakes—Chico, Ouachita, Bull Shoals (all man-made).
STATE MOTTO: Regnat populus ("The people reign").

LOUISIANA
CAPITAL: Baton Rouge.
MAJOR CITIES: New Orleans, Shreveport, Baton Rouge.
AREA: 48,523 sq. mi. (125,675 sq. km).
POPULATION: 3,643,180 (1970 census).
PHYSICAL FEATURES: Highest point—Driskill Mountain (535 ft.; 163 m.). Lowest point—at New Orleans, 5 ft. (2 m.) below sea level. Major rivers—Mississippi, Red, Ouachita, Sabine. Major lakes—Pontchartrain, Borgne, Maurepas, White, Calcasieu.
STATE MOTTO: Union, justice, confidence.

MISSISSIPPI
CAPITAL: Jackson.
MAJOR CITIES: Jackson, Biloxi.
AREA: 47,716 sq. mi. (123,585 sq. km.).
POPULATION: 2,216,912 (1970 census).
PHYSICAL FEATURES: Highest point—Woodhall Mountain (806 ft.; 246 m.). Lowest point—sea level. Major rivers—Yazoo, Big Black, Homochitto, Mississippi. Major lakes—Sardis, Grenada, Enid, Arkabutla (all man-made).
STATE MOTTO: Virtute et armis ("By valor and arms").

Bauxite is taken from this surface mine in the Arkansas pines.

at the mouth of the Mississippi River. The region remained mostly French, with some periods of Spanish control, until the Louisiana Purchase in 1803.

Although Louisiana was the territory farthest away from Washington, D.C., and from the centers of American life, the importance of New Orleans helped make Louisiana a state well before the other three South Central States were admitted to the Union. In those days of difficult land travel, "nearness" was calculated in terms of access by water routes, rather than in terms of miles overland. Thus, the accessibility of New Orleans by water, either through the Gulf of Mexico or down the Mississippi, made it seem closer in practical terms than frontier settlements in Alabama that were hundreds of miles nearer Washington, D.C., the nation's capital, by land.

The Mississippi River was the natural outlet to market for the produce of the new settlers throughout the Northwest Territory, the area that is now included in the North Central States (sometimes called the Midwest). It served a similar role for frontiersmen in Tennessee and Kentucky. In a time when international disputes were usually settled by war, the growing United States could not have lived in peace for long with a foreign country that would not allow Americans free navigation on the Mississippi and full access to the port of New Orleans. President Thomas Jefferson recognized the importance of New Orleans when he sent a mission to France to arrange for its purchase. James Monroe and

Cotton pickers in an Alabama field carry sacks of cotton bolls.

Robert Livingston, Jefferson's representatives, showed great statesmanship when they seized the opportunity to buy all of the Louisiana Territory, not just New Orleans and vicinity. The limits of the purchased territory were shadowy. It proved to include most of the vast American West, except for Spanish possessions. The territory that was to become Arkansas was included in the Louisiana Purchase.

King Cotton.   The rich virgin lands of the southern frontier states were far more attractive to cotton planters than the frequently worn-out acres of the eastern seaboard South. There, early overcultivation of rice, tobacco, and cotton had already eroded and exhausted the land. Indian lands on the frontier were taken over by treaties between the tribes and the federal government. The Indians were faced with the harsh reality of what amounted to forced evacuation of their traditional homeland. Louisiana became a state in 1812. The Mississippi Territory was divided into two states, Mississippi (admitted in 1817) and Alabama (admitted in 1819). Overshadowed by the river city of St. Louis to the north and the new state of Missouri, Arkansas did not reach statehood until 1836, nearly 20 years after the other South Central States had been admitted to the Union.

During this period, the South Central States were in the process of changing from part of the American frontier to the hard core of the Deep South. The change took place during the period between the end of the War of 1812 (in 1815) and the start of the Mexican War (1846–1848). Eli Whitney's invention of the cotton gin in the United States and the invention of the spinning jenny in England made cotton the most valuable raw material for a booming economy. The cotton gin so speeded the processing of cotton that it became practical to produce it in large quantities. At the same time the cloth mills of England provided the principal market for what quickly became America's chief export crop.

With the exception of those in the New Orleans area, most of the new white population of the South Central States came from the older southern states on or near the eastern seaboard. Few came directly from Europe. The opportunities of this new agricultural frontier also attracted many able, ambitious but penniless young men from the New England and the Mid-Atlantic States. Transplanted Yankees like John A. Quitman, Sergeant S. Prentiss, and Robert J. Walker in Mississippi provided an important share of political leadership on the southern frontier.

Many of the cotton planters who migrated in this period brought slaves with them to clear the land and begin cotton production. The new cotton country became America's major slave market.

The slave trade had been prohibited, but smuggled human cargo still came from Africa and the West Indies to the United States in defiance of the law. Planters also purchased slaves from the older southern states. Conditions on the frontier plantations were much harsher than in the old South. The seaboard planters could threaten slaves with the dread fate of being "sold down the river" to Mississippi or Alabama. The difficult and often harsh life on the plantations "down river" increased the growing discontent of black people, and the mounting antislavery sentiment in the North. However, although slave labor produced most of the cotton, the majority of farmers were small landowners. These men worked the fields side by side with their slaves. Many white farmers never owned slaves at all.

Although some plantations and white-columned homes resembled those of Virginia and South Carolina, Deep South cotton country was, for the most part, quite different from the eastern seaboard. Except for New Orleans, the only places where white society resembled that of Tidewater, Virginia, or Charleston, South Carolina, were the Natchez region, in Mississippi, and the cities of Mobile and Huntsville in Alabama.

Life on this new frontier was, for the most part, primitive, as it was on all frontiers. The economic life of the southern frontier was risky. A great deal of land was required to grow cotton commercially. When prices on the world cotton markets were high and looked as if they might go higher, a planter might buy more land on speculation—often on credit. If the market then fell, which it often did, he still had to pay for the land. This created a "boom or bust" economy. The southern frontier also had a law enforcement problem. Outlaw gangs were common. This situation encouraged vigilante action to suppress them. Vigilante mobs rose even more brutally to put down the threat of supposed slave rebellions. These rebellions were always a fear in the minds of white people, who were often greatly outnumbered by their black slaves.

Just as the first settlements had grown up along the rivers, economic development also followed the rivers until the Civil War. Cotton, for instance, could be shipped downriver to New Orleans much more efficiently than it could be transported overland. Railroads were slow to penetrate the Deep South. Most settlers came to northern Alabama and northeast Mississippi by way of the Tennessee River. For instance, the easiest way from New York into the Deep South was by riverboat from Cincinnati, on the Ohio River, and down the great inland river system. Railroads did not reduce the importance of river travel until just before the Civil War.

The large planters, merchants, and bankers of King Cotton's domain were usually conservative politically. Their political beliefs were similar to those of the planters, merchants, and bankers of the Old South, of

A fine, pre-Civil War plantation house in Natchez, Mississippi.

Virginia or the Carolinas, for instance. For some time they were against the idea of Southern separatism—of the independence of the slave-holding South from the Union. In the years immediately after the Mexican War, Unionists were usually equal in number to Separatists in all four South Central States. But after that the whole region became convinced that remaining in the Union meant an end to slavery. They were also convinced that their economic system could not last without slave labor. At the same time they came to believe that because cotton was so vital to Europe—especially to England and France—that European nations would support and aid an independent, cotton-producing country carved out of the southern United States.

Civil War. The conflicting economic and social beliefs of North and South reached the boiling point after the election of Abraham Lincoln as president of the United States in 1860. Lincoln had sworn to uphold the Union. In the angry days that followed the election, there was relatively little opposition to secession from the Union in the South Central States. It was fitting that Jefferson Davis, a man from Mississippi in the heart of the Deep South, was eventually inaugurated as president of the Confederate States of America.

Abraham Lincoln had rafted down the Mississippi River with a load of Illinois farm produce in his youth. He knew the vital role the river had played in the growth of midwestern agriculture. This may have influenced his wartime policy of splitting the Confederacy by taking control of all the Mississippi. New Orleans and Memphis, the two largest cities on the river system, were captured from the Confederacy early in the war. They then became important supply points for the Union Army and ports of entry into Union territory for Confederate contraband sugar and cotton. Vicksburg, the final Confederate stronghold of the region, did not fall until the brilliant siege commanded by General U. S. Grant. This victory also isolated Louisiana, Arkansas, and Texas from the rest of the Confederacy, greatly simplifying Union tactics in the final 21 months of the war.

Reconstruction.   The years immediately after the Civil War brought political and social changes which offered hope for the newly freed Negro slave in his efforts to gain a foothold in the United States as an equal citizen. Black men formed a political alliance with whites who were willing to accept change and with Union veterans who came south seeking both political and economic opportunity. These groups were called Radical Republicans. Embittered Confederate loyalists nicknamed the Southern Republicans scalawags and the Yankee outsiders carpetbaggers. The implication was that the carpetbaggers were cynical fortune hunters who came South with all their belongings in a cheap fabric carpetbag, or suitcase. Working together, the scalawags and the carpetbaggers gained control of state governments.

The Backlash.   The Reconstruction period lasted only 12 years. As soon as federal troops were withdrawn, Negroes were frightened away from the ballot boxes. All-white Democratic factions, still smarting from defeat in the war and from what they considered the outrages of Reconstruction, once again took control. Republicans were denied even the possibility of becoming a second party on the political ballot because of their connection with the blacks. Within a few years, Negroes had been virtually removed from political participation in all four states. They were removed by local custom, backed by the real threat of violence and by clauses in the new state constitutions which forbade black participation in government. These clauses, although contrary to the spirit of the 14th and 15th amendments to the United States Constitution, were, at that time, upheld by the Supreme Court of the United States.

The quick elimination of the Negro's voice in political life and government ended any chance that the black man might adjust quickly from his former status as a slave to a role as a fully equal United States citizen. No real attempt was made to improve public education for blacks for nearly 50 years. Justice in the courts was entirely in the hands of white officials, who made sure that they kept the system unchanged. Economic opportunity was restricted not only by the poverty of the region, but by the lack of education, training in advanced skills, and equal opportunity to protect any capital or property that the black man might gain. Both local custom and the law kept a rigid system of segregation and white supremacy in operation.

Many responsible white conservatives tried to soften the harshness of the system in an attempt to protect the rights of Negroes. But they had to do what they could within the established system of segregation and economic discrimination. Inevitably, however, even these white southerners were forced to yield to local pressures. Ambitious men in political life blamed the problems of the South on the Negroes. By doing this they helped to establish such a strong system of white supremacy that not even the most courageous moderates dared to attack it. Lynchings of Negroes occurred in many communities in the South Central States. The system left emotional scars on many of the people of the Deep South, black and white alike.

Economic Reconstruction. If the victorious Union government failed to carry through political reconstruction in the Deep South, it had an even worse failure in economic reconstruction. The southern farmer had been the victim of an unfair cotton-producing and marketing system even when he had slaves. After the war, he had no slaves, and the South lay economically devastated by its long, losing battle. With almost no capital left in the region, absentee-financed agriculture was the only possibility. For instance, landowners might finance their year's crop by mortgaging it to an individual or a bank in advance. If crops failed, they lost their land. The landless, both white and black, had only their unskilled labor to offer a farmer who was himself pushed to the wall and could hardly afford to pay employees. This led to the sharecropper tenant system as the chief mode of farm employment. The sharecropper system had built-in evils. It had a vicious cycle of limited returns and often endless indebtedness. This system also destroyed the soil's fertility through the repeated planting of the soil-depleting cash crops—cotton, corn, rice, and sugarcane.

In the first years after the Civil War, when the whole South suffered grinding agricultural poverty, many local leaders began to campaign for industrial development. This, they felt, would help balance and restore the economy. They were largely unsuccessful. The few cotton-spinning mills that were built paid their employees at wage levels comparable to the miserable wages paid farm laborers. In fact, the mills were often regarded as bad financial risks. The one exception was the new city of Birmingham, founded in north central Alabama after the Civil War as "the Pittsburgh of the South." Iron ore close to coal deposits in north Alabama made the new city an ideal site for major steel production. Unfortunately relatively few related industries developed over the years.

Recovery Begins

Farming or farm-related business was still the main source of employment for the majority of people in the South Central States at the time of the great Depression of the 1930's. Southern agriculture had already been in a state of depression for several years preceding the stock market crash of 1929, during a time when the rest of the nation enjoyed prosperity.

The region's richest soil, in the delta lands of the Mississippi River through Arkansas, Mississippi, and Louisiana, could not be used fully because of the constant threat of floods. Local and state efforts to provide flood protection always failed. Political pressure groups came together to push for a federal flood control program. However, they achieved no real success until after the disastrous flood of 1927. This catastrophe, coming at the height of the 1920's boom, struck the conscience of the rest of the United States. However, the resulting federal aid program for the devastated region was not put into full operation until the New Deal administration of President Franklin D. Roosevelt took over a few years later. In their desperate need for protection from floods, the people of the lower Mississippi settled for less than full development of the river's magnificent potential. Nevertheless, the benefits in flood control and navigation have paid for the federal investment many times over.

The New Deal programs of President Franklin D. Roosevelt were the first direct attack on the poverty of the region. They were enormously popular. For many years the people of northern Alabama, in the Tennessee Valley region, had asked for a federal development program. They did not get it until President Roosevelt sponsored the Tennessee Valley Authority. The development that followed has helped to give northern Alabama the highest level of income of any part of the South Central States. At the same time, elsewhere in the region, stabilization of farm prices ended the relentless chain of farm bankruptcies and foreclosures.

By the time World War II was over, agriculture in the South Central States had become a relatively prosperous and satisfactory way of life for farmers with large landholdings. For the unskilled farm laborer, however, conditions became worse instead of better. The development of new and efficient farm machinery reduced the opportunities for employment. Many families of unskilled farm workers were left in abject poverty. They were forced to live on restricted, unbalanced diets and many people developed severe malnutrition. In the prosperous 1960's, Americans were forced to realize that some of their countrymen were literally starving to death.

Black people, victims of educational and economic discrimination, inevitably suffered the most severe hardship. Nevertheless, rural poverty was widespread among white people as well. Southern agriculture simply did not offer enough opportunity for the traditional farming community to earn a decent living. The natural result was migration northward.

The flight of black people brought significant changes in the population ratios of the South Central States. Before World War I, Negroes outnumbered whites in Mississippi and accounted for over a third of the population in the other three states of the area. Black workers first began moving north in large numbers during World War I, when industrial jobs opened up in northern cities. Most of the migration was along the railroad lines due north to places like St. Louis, Chicago, and Detroit. The Depression reversed the migration, bringing thousands who lost their jobs back to the countryside, which seemed better than the breadlines of the big cities. But the northward movement increased again during and after World War II.

Migration northward from the Deep South was not confined to Negroes. During World War I and World War II whites also moved out at about the same rate as blacks in search of economic opportunity. Part of the North's attraction for Negro migrants, however, was a hope of freedom from some of the racial problems of the South. This movement of black people became even greater in the 1950's and 1960's. The movement of Negroes to northern industrial areas took place in numbers large enough to rank as one of the great mass migrations of world history. Only in the late 1960's, as job opportunities began to open up for blacks in new local industries in the South, did the movement begin to slow down. One result of the migration was the overcrowding of black residential areas in the North. These neighborhoods became known as ghettos and quickly became trouble spots. All too often the southern newcomers, black or white, were not trained in skills needed by northern employers. They found it very hard to get good jobs.

The South had transportation problems in addition to other difficulties. Like all of the South, the South Central area suffered from discriminatory freight rates and lack of local capital to finance local industry. The freight rate handicap was removed by law and executive action in the period following World War II.

All four state governments of the region set up systems to finance industry. Various government programs, started during the New Deal in the 1930's and expanded under presidents Truman, Kennedy, and Johnson, made up for the region's lack of capital by giving grants to local development and planning groups. Government loans—direct or indirect—were made to industries in the region. Another advance was made when national industries began to build branch plants in the southern countryside. National industry had realized that in this way they could bring their production closer both to raw materials and to markets. And there were many people in the South who needed work.

SOUTH CENTRAL STATES TODAY

Today the South Central States, like their neighbors in the rest of the South, have caught up with the rest of the United States in their rate of industrialization. There is hardly a town of two or three hundred people that lacks an industrial plant of some kind, often a branch of a national manufacturing concern. The pattern of the 1930's, when four out of five people were employed in agriculture, has been reversed. Today the proportion of farm workers in the South Central States is less than one in five.

The development of oil and gas resources has been an important factor in the economic growth of all four states, although it is still a relatively minor industry in Alabama. Oil is now the largest industry in Louisiana, spilling over into the petrochemical industry which spreads

Steel is produced at this busy mill near Birmingham, Alabama.

along the Intracoastal Waterway and the length of the Mississippi River as far north as Baton Rouge. Important chemical industries are also found along the waterways of the other three states.

In spite of heavy industrial employment, average wage scales in the South Central States are among the lowest in the country. Average per capita income also finds all four states at the bottom of the ladder.

Service industries, which often reflect the general level of economic life in any region, also lag behind in the South Central States. They have made less progress in this area than in any other part of their economy. Employment in communications and the cultural arts is well below average. This is another sign of the difficulty the local economic system has in meeting the challenge of improving the quality of life in the region. A related problem is the lag in educational levels. This stems both from regional poverty and from conflicts over the changing status of black citizens and their right to equal educational opportunity.

Cities. Aside from the great port city of New Orleans, the South Central States did not begin to develop large urban centers until after the Civil War. The cities of the area, before that time, were usually market centers or river ports where the products of the region's farms and plantations were brought to be sold and shipped. With the movement toward industrialization that began after the Civil War and has continued to the present day, cities of the region began to take on more of the look of the cities of the Midwest and Northeast. However, despite many changes, the South Central region is by no means an area of crowded cities and endless industrial complexes. Much of the region—and many of its cities—are still geared to the needs of agriculture, to the marketing and shipping of farm products.

In Alabama, the state capital, **Montgomery**, is a city with a diverse economic life. It still fills its traditional role as an agricultural market center and is the regional center for the marketing of cattle. However, it has also developed a modern industrial life with meat-packing plants, textile mills, and a number of other manufactures. **Birmingham** has a phenomenal history. In less than a century it has become a major industrial city. It is the South's only major steel producer, and it has a great variety of other industries as well. **Mobile**, the state's second largest city, is Alabama's only seaport and one of the major Gulf Coast ports. It has also become a center for industry, in part because of its shipping facilities.

Much of Arkansas is still farmland and mountain country. **Little Rock**, the state's capital and major city, is the marketing center for the agricultural production of the state—especially cotton and rice. It also is one of the state's major industrial centers. Little Rock is located in the heart of Arkansas and is the focal point of all aspects of the state's life. **Hot Springs** and **Hot Springs National Park** are located in the state's most beautiful lake and mountain country. The city of Hot Springs is a popular vacation spot, and its thermal springs are visited by people from all over the United States.

Louisiana's major cities have always been linked to transportation—to the rivers of the South and to the Gulf of Mexico. **New Orleans**, which is the largest city in Louisiana and one of the most fascinating of American cities, is a major Mississippi River port and one of the most important merchant shipping centers in the United States because of its access to the

A street in the famous French Quarter of New Orleans, Louisiana.

Gulf. A booming modern city, with its famous French Quarter and its harbor filled with ships from all over the world, New Orleans has always been a fascinating place. It has also played a key role in American history and in the development of the nation.

Baton Rouge, the state capital, lies northwest of New Orleans. It is a major deepwater port and a center of Louisiana's vital oil industry. **Shreveport**, the second largest city in the state, is Louisiana's major Red River port. It is the most important city in northern Louisiana. It is a major cotton market and a center for the oil and gas industry.

Mississippi, like Arkansas, is still deeply involved in agriculture. As a result of this, there are no very large cities in the state. **Jackson**, the state capital, is the largest city. It has developed a chemical and a furniture industry. **Biloxi**, Mississippi's major Gulf port, is a resort center. It is also an important fishing port.

Civil Rights. The South Central States have been the scene of the most concentrated official and public resistance to the civil rights movement in the United States. Although the forces of change have been slowed down here in many cases, this same region shows signs of having changed its attitudes toward the recognition of equal rights for all American citizens enormously.

Little Rock, the capital of Arkansas, was the scene of the first great confrontation of the civil rights movement. The United States Supreme Court had outlawed racially segregated schools in 1954. In 1957 President Dwight D. Eisenhower had to send in federal troops to secure compliance with a court order for the admittance of Negro children into Little Rock's Central High School. The Montgomery (Alabama) bus boycott; the freedom rides on buses to places like Birmingham, Alabama, and Jackson, Mississippi; the confrontation at Selma, Alabama; and the riot that followed the enrollment of a black student, James Meredith, at the University of Mississippi were some of the dramatic events in the struggle to overturn the traditional system of segregation.

The fervent resistance to elimination of segregation barriers in the Deep South merely contributed to national support of efforts to break down these barriers. Drives to register black voters have begun to change patterns of political participation. Occasional towns in the Deep South elect black mayors or sheriffs. Resistance still continues, but the changes that have already taken place amount to a major social revolution in less than a generation.

Most of the changes in education, employment, government, and politics have come in compliance with federal law. However, a significant number of changes have come through local acceptance of reality and a new willingness to change. Black initiative, first demonstrated in the Montgomery bus boycott and repeated with each new voter registration drive, is playing an important part in every change. It is obvious that black leadership will have an important part in the future of all four of the South Central States.

THE FUTURE

Even though the South Central States still rank at the low end of the economic scale in the United States, overall economic improvement has in recent years come more rapidly to the South Central States than to the United States as a whole. As the whole economy of the United States becomes more centralized, there is a good chance that even more benefits of American society and the American economy will reach the Deep South and other formerly depressed areas. One important reason for this is the increasing belief among people that they must use the full resources of their state and local governments, as well as private business, in planning for their own economic development.

In education, too, although federal government has done much to improve the situation, progress has come when people in the region have realized that they can no longer afford poor schools. Only through a greatly improved educational system can the demands for skilled labor and professional know-how be met. Without such highly trained people the economy of the region cannot grow. In the past, opportunities for talented young people without family resources were very limited. Today the outlook is changing radically. Many imaginative young people, seeing the new opportunities in the Deep South, may help to stop the talent and leadership drain from which the region has suffered for a century. Dedicated black professionals return in increasing numbers from training in the North to help lift standards in the South.

These changing racial patterns and rapid economic advances make it clear that the Deep South will increasingly lose its isolation, its "specialness," and its differences from the rest of the United States. More and more it is moving into the mainstream of American life.

FRANK E. SMITH, Director, Tennessee Valley Authority

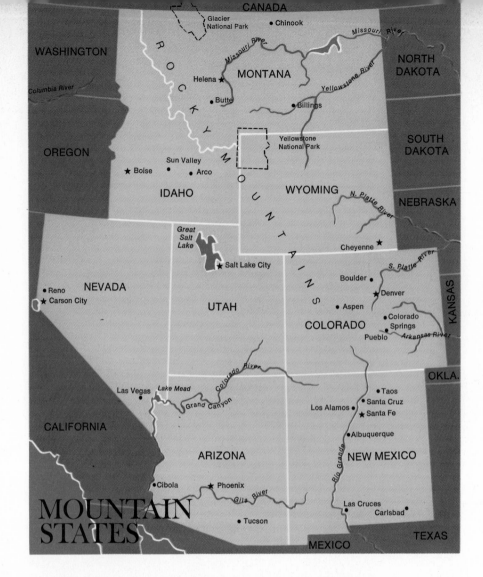

MOUNTAIN
STATES

MOUNTAIN STATES

Of all the major geographical regions of the world, only equatorial Africa near the headwaters of the Nile remained a blank on the map as late as did the region that is now divided into the eight Rocky Mountain states. Although the Spaniards were already skirting the California coast 50 years after Columbus' voyages to the New World, the immense area between the northward bend of the Missouri River and the central valley of California remained a mystery for another 3 centuries.

But once the pall of ignorance started to lift early in the 19th century, knowledge of the American Far West spread like light after sunrise. Before the century ended, the magnificent region had become better-known than any comparable area on any continent. The names of its monumental natural features—the Grand Canyon, Great Salt Lake, Yellowstone Park, Pikes Peak, Monument Valley, Grand Teton, the Garden of the Gods—had become household words in almost every corner of the globe. The startling contrasts between glacier-cooled mountain meadows and sun-scorched sand dunes, between blue alpine lakes and blackened lava beds, between rushing rivers and vast burning deserts, and between mountain ranges extending east and west and adjacent ranges extending north and south had made the solution of the mystery of the Rockies extremely difficult. These very contrasts and differences led to a fascination with the heartland of the Rockies that captured and held the world's interest.

What added extra zest was the romance and legends that grew up around the struggles of the men who first conquered the region. The natural wonderland of towering mountains, plains, and deserts assumed attributes as entrancing as those of King Arthur's enchanted realm. Song and story, and later motion pictures and television, peopled the "Wild West" with semimythological figures—the cowboy, the Indian, the cavalryman, the sheriff, the stagecoach driver, the badman, the gunfighter, the dance-hall girl, the schoolteacher, the gambler, the miner, the cattleman, and the homesteader. These moving shadows all became familiar throughout the world. Fact and fiction mingled to create the most famous storybook country of all time. Although the Rocky Mountain West now shelters today's industry and tomorrow's science, its history and its legends are still a bone-deep part of its modern cities and sturdy people.

ACROSS THE SHINING MOUNTAINS

For more than a century before the first white man sighted the Rockies, the legend had been growing, fed by hints from Indians, that somewhere far to the west lay a gigantic mountain range, the "Shining Mountains." The first white men of record to sight and cross the American part of this range were the men of the memorable Lewis and Clark expedition of 1804–6.

After Thomas Jefferson bought the Louisiana Territory from the French leader Napoleon Bonaparte in 1803, he sent a band of explorers led by Meriwether Lewis and William Clark to find out not only what lay within the Louisiana Purchase but also what lay beyond. The southern reaches of the territory, including what is now Texas, New Mexico, Arizona, and other states, belonged to Spain. Many Americans believed that north of that area their newly bought domain must extend west indefinitely. In one of the most skillful explorations ever conducted, the Lewis and Clark expedition ascended the Missouri River, crossed the Rockies, wintered at the mouth of the Columbia River, and returned in triumph to St. Louis on September 23, 1806. During more than 2 years of fierce hardships, these supreme explorers lost only one man, and he died of appendicitis as the journey began.

Yet the expedition's report was disappointing. The party had assailed the Rockies through the north, where the crossing was exceptionally difficult. They had to report that they found no navigable water link between the Missouri and the Columbia rivers, which destroyed Thomas Jefferson's dream of a transcontinental trade route. However, another report given by the expedition was to be far more important: the explorers told of the astounding number of beaver swarming in Rocky Mountain streams. The very next summer hundreds of American trappers from St. Louis were toiling up the Missouri and the Yellowstone rivers to gather these riches.

The length of the journey and the violence of Indian opposition to

MOUNTAIN STATES

ARIZONA
CAPITAL: Phoenix.
MAJOR CITIES: Phoenix, Tuscon.
AREA: 113,909 sq. mi. (295,025 sq. km.).
POPULATION: 1,772,482 (1970 census).
PHYSICAL FEATURES: Highest point—Humphreys Peak (12,670 ft.; 3,862 m.). **Lowest point**—100 ft. (30 m.). **Major river**—Colorado. **Major lakes**—Mormon Lake, Lake Mead (man-made).
STATE MOTTO: *Ditat Deus* ("God enriches").

COLORADO
CAPITAL: Denver.
MAJOR CITIES: Denver, Colorado Springs, Pueblo.
AREA: 104,247 sq. mi. (270,000 sq. km.).
POPULATION: 2,207,259 (1970 census).
PHYSICAL FEATURES: Highest point—Mount Elbert (14,423 ft.; 4,396 m.). **Lowest point**—3,350 ft. (1,021 m.). **Major river**—Colorado. **Major lake**—Lake Granby.
STATE MOTTO: *Nil sine numine* ("Nothing without the divine will").

IDAHO
CAPITAL: Boise.
MAJOR CITY: Boise.
AREA: 83,557 sq. mi. (216,413 sq. km.).
POPULATION: 713,008 (1970 census).
PHYSICAL FEATURES: Highest point—Borah Peak (12,662 ft.; 3,859 m.). **Lowest point**—720 ft. (219 m.). **Major river**—Snake. **Major lakes**—Lake Pend Oreille, American Falls Reservoir (man-made).
STATE MOTTO: *Esto perpetua* ("May she endure forever").

MONTANA
CAPITAL: Helena.
MAJOR CITIES: Billings, Great Falls, Helena.
AREA: 147,138 sq. mi. (381,088 sq. km.).
POPULATION: 694,409 (1970 census).
PHYSICAL FEATURES: Highest point—Granite Peak (12,662 ft.; 3,859 m.). **Lowest point**—1,800 ft. (549 m.). **Major rivers**—Clark Fork, Missouri, Yellowstone. **Major lakes**—Flathead Lake, Fort Peck Dam (man-made).
STATE MOTTO: *Oro y plata* ("Gold and silver").

NEVADA
CAPITAL: Carson City.
MAJOR CITIES: Carson City, Las Vegas, Reno.
AREA: 110,540 sq. mi. (286,299 sq. km.).
POPULATION: 488,738 (1970 census).
PHYSICAL FEATURES: Highest point—Boundary Peak (13,145 ft.; 4,007 m.). **Lowest point**—470 ft. (143 m.). **Major river**—Humboldt. **Major lakes**—Pyramid Lake, Lake Mead (man-made).
STATE MOTTO: All for our country.

NEW MEXICO
CAPITAL: Santa Fe.
MAJOR CITIES: Albuquerque, Santa Fe.
AREA: 121,666 sq. mi. (315,115 sq. km.).
POPULATION: 1,016,000 (1970 census).
PHYSICAL FEATURES: Highest point—Wheeler Peak (13,151 ft.; 4,008 m.). **Lowest point**—2,817 ft. (859 m.). **Major rivers**—Rio Grande, Pecos. **Major lake**—Elephant Butte Reservoir (man-made).
STATE MOTTO: *Crescit eundo* ("It grows as it goes").

UTAH
CAPITAL: Salt Lake City.
MAJOR CITIES: Salt Lake City, Ogden.
AREA: 84,916 sq. mi. (219,933 sq. km.).
POPULATION: 1,059,273 (1970 census).
PHYSICAL FEATURES: Highest point—Kings Peak (13,227 ft.; 4,032 m.). **Lowest point**—2,000 ft. (610 m.). **Major river**—Colorado. **Major lakes**—Great Salt Lake, Lake Powell (man-made).
STATE MOTTO: Industry.

WYOMING
CAPITAL: Cheyenne.
MAJOR CITY: Cheyenne.
AREA: 97,914 sq. mi. (253,598 sq. km.).
POPULATION: 322,416 (1970 census).
PHYSICAL FEATURES: Highest point—Gannett Peak (13,785 ft.; 4,202 m.). **Lowest point**—3,100 ft. (945 m.). **Major rivers**—Green, Sweetwater, Yellowstone. **Major lakes**—Yellowstone Lake, Flaming Gorge Reservoir (man-made).
STATE MOTTO: Equal rights.

intruders on their land made trapping in the Rockies so hazardous that after 3 years of death and disaster, it was abandoned by most of the men who had hoped to make their fortunes there. In the meantime a New York merchant, John Jacob Astor, dreaming of commercial empire, sent a seaborne expedition around Cape Horn to found Astoria, a trading post at the Columbia's mouth. He hoped to link the northwest sea otter trade to the great markets of China. He also sent a supporting overland expedition, which struggled west under Wilson Hunt. The party that went by sea arrived at the mouth of the Columbia in 1811, and the overland expedition arrived in 1812. A smaller return party under Robert Stuart found another route, crossing eastward through South Pass. This route would later become the key to transcontinental travel.

The War of 1812 blasted Astor's plans. Not until 1820 did the Americans take another major step in their conquest of the Rockies. In that year Major Stephen Long led a small party up the Platte River to the eastern face of the Rockies, climbed Pikes Peak, and returned down the

Arkansas River. He reported that the whole area was too barren and arid ever to be truly habitable. The term "Great American Desert" had been coined as a label for the entire region from Missouri to California, and it was to haunt every American schoolbook for the next two generations.

But the curtain was going up on a titanic battle between two antagonists who would struggle for 25 years to determine permanent possession of the Rockies. The British champion was the Hudson's Bay Company. The company sent trapper brigades from its Columbia River bases deep into the mountains and as far south as the lower Colorado River. The British maintained that United States territory did not reach west of the Great Divide, and the trappers were their advance guard in their effort to make good that claim.

The champions of United States interests, the mountain men, were to prove even more formidable. Loosely allied to various American fur companies, the mountain men began to swarm through the Rockies. They were sons of fathers who had been born in Kentucky stockades, of grandfathers who had been first across the Alleghenies. They were members of frontier families who had been storming barriers on their way west for over half a century. As families, they stopped at the Missouri, awed by the treeless expanse of the Great Plains. How could they live without wood and water? But their sons cut loose and struck out for adventure. These were the mountain men. Some made for Santa Fe to trade American goods for Mexican silver, or ventured farther, trapping westward out of Taos. Others headed up the Missouri or directly overland in pursuit of mountain beaver. During the 1820's and 1830's, these free trappers were roving through the Rockies from the Gila River in the south to the Flathead River in the north. Thus the Anglo-American struggle for empire was settled not by armed conflict, but by trade competition. The weapons were initiative, daring, and the capacity to endure hardships and danger. Eventually the Hudson's Bay Company withdrew behind the boundary of the Columbia River.

The mountain men roamed the loneliest stretches of the mountains for years at a time. They got together with other mountain men only once a year, for the gargantuan frolics of the summer rendezvous, when they all met with their year's catch at an appointed spot in the mountains. Every winter they struggled for months through the icy waters of mountain streams. They were subject to starvation, thirst, freezing, and the attacks of Indians and grizzly bears. Hundreds of them died violent deaths. But they had the supreme satisfaction of knowing themselves to be bolder, hardier, and freer than other men. They postured and struggled and boasted and gambled and drank themselves into a stupor. They bedecked their horses, their Indian brides, and themselves in the most expensive finery. They were complete barbarians, and they took and held the Rockies by turning its most remote canyons into their own backyard.

The greatest, although not the most typical, mountain man was Jedediah Smith. Smith was one of mankind's most impetuous travelers. By 1830 Smith had traveled into mountains and deserts totally unknown until his coming and into hostile regions where the way was frequently barred by Indian assaults. Merely to trace his travels on a map is a breathtaking experience. As a result of his roamings, the last great blank space on the map of North America was filled in. He was first to make westbound use of the Sweetwater-South Pass mountain gateway, first to cross from the banks of the Missouri River to the Pacific shores of California, first to identify and cross the forbidding Sierra Nevada range, and first to cross Utah's man-killing Great Basin. His last journey ended near Santa Fe, where he was murdered by Indians.

The day of the mountain man was brief. Men's hat styles changed—the beaver hat was out—and the price of beaver went down. Beavers were becoming scarce in any case. The 1840 rendezvous of the mountain men was the last. But they had fulfilled their mission. They knew the Rockies, and they were ready to guide the wagon trains of the great westward migration. For in the 1840's, frontier families again began marching west.

The first organized emigrant train, the Bidwell Party, set out in the spring of 1841, guided by mountain man Thomas Fitzpatrick, a companion of Jedediah Smith. Though the party had to abandon its wagons at Fort Hall and in the Humboldt Sink, they eventually made it, some to California and some to Oregon. Each year they were followed by larger wagon trains, until sometimes the Oregon and California trails were almost crowded. The landmarks on these historic routes became landmarks in the nation's history: Scott's Bluff, Chimney Rock, Fort Laramie, Independence Rock, Devil's Gate, the Wind River Range, South Pass, Fort Bridger, Fort Hall, the Tetons, the Humboldt, the Dalles, Emigrant Gap, Sutter's Fort, Fort Vancouver. By force of numbers they made it inevitable that the territory would become American. The Mexican War (1846–48)

This traditional Indian pueblo is located at Taos, New Mexico.

hastened the process. With victory the United States annexed the present states of Texas, Colorado, New Mexico, Utah, Arizona, Nevada, and California. The border between the present-day state of Washington and Canada was settled by treaty with England.

SETTLEMENT BEGINS

Until 1847 the region that became the Mountain States had been regarded as a fine place to trap beaver and a challenge for hardy souls to cross, but few American families dreamed of living there. The sleepy Mexican towns of Taos and Santa Fe in the south were the only important settlements. Then, in the spring of 1847, Brigham Young led the advance party of Mormon pioneers to a desolate waste of sand near the Great Salt Lake and, according to legend, proclaimed: "This is the place." It was apparently a place fit only for lizards and tarantulas, and the Mormons hoped others would find it too harsh and would let them live there in peace. "The place" became green and lovely Salt Lake City, a monument to faith, grinding toil, and excellent irrigation engineering. It was home base for a realm that Young and his followers called the State of Deseret ("honeybee"). Originally Deseret included portions of several Mountain States, but it was whittled back to the present state of Utah and accepted into the Union in 1896.

From mid-century on, the course of events in the mountains became ever more kaleidoscopic. In 1859 gold strikes near modern Denver, Colorado, and silver strikes in Nevada's Comstock Lode brought prospectors swarming through the region. Wagons labeled "Pikes Peak or Bust" carried treasure hunters into Colorado canyons, and within a few years the prospectors were exploring Last Chance Gulch, Montana, and other spots. Mining has been a principal occupation of the inhabitants of the Mountain States from that time to the present day of uranium.

Completion of the first continental railroad in 1869 tied the United States together. It was soon followed by other rail lines. The frontier ceased to be a line moving westward and became a ring contracting inward upon the mountains and the southwestern desert. The narrowing of this ring was marked by the dates of admission into the union of the Mountain States: Nevada, 1864; Colorado, 1876; Montana, 1889; Wyoming, 1890; Idaho, 1890; Utah, 1896; New Mexico, 1912; Arizona, 1912. Settlers were no longer only explorers, trappers, and prospectors. They were also ranchers, farmers, and builders who had come to stay. Towns were sprouting up and speedily growing into cities.

In this period the country took on the fabulous aspects now so familiar to moviegoers and television viewers the world over. The newcomers were arriving in advance of the law, and white men were competing with each other with more vigor than restraint. The Indians, who had formerly let many wagon trains pass untroubled because the white man was only passing through, were now resisting the invasion of their living space and the killing of the animals that furnished their food and clothing. Their resistance became utterly hopeless with the near extermination of the buffalo in the early 1880's. The Indians had depended on the buffalo for food, clothing, and trade. At the same time, cattlemen were driving their herds of longhorn cattle north from Texas to occupy huge ranches in Colorado, Wyoming, and Montana. For a brief decade or so, each new white community was a primitive society in which personal

Virginia City, Nevada, has kept the spirit of the Old West.

initiative was the primary rule of behavior, and "high noon" shoot-outs led to burial on Boot Hill. But the steady increase in population and improvement in communications was steadily taming the Wild West.

THE FRONTIER COMES OF AGE

The pitfalls and glories of the Rocky Mountains remain today. The Mountain States area is still poor in water but rich in beauty, in space, in challenges, and in precious metals. Much else has changed. Irrigation projects have transformed forbidding deserts into thousands of square miles of gardens and orchards. Snowfields across which frostbitten explorers crawled are now crisscrossed by festive swarms of skiers. Where once the dance-hall girl cavorted, nationally famous theaters now stand. Distances that cost the wagon train months of toil are passed in a day by train or car and flown over by jet planes in an hour. The grandeurs of peak and canyon that once awed a lone mountain man now attract millions of visitors a year.

The present inhabitants of the Mountain States enjoy a unique advantage over people who live elsewhere. Much of their land is still as spectacular and majestic as when it enthralled the first white man to see it. But to many residents this advantage seems a mixed blessing. The appeal of their marvelous land is luring so many people from other places that they fear even so spacious a country may become crowded. Just as the advertised "wilderness" of the great national parks attracts hoards of campers, so the very sparseness of settlement attracts new settlers escaping the people-choked cities. Yet there are still wide-open spaces to spare in spite of this trend. Though the population has doubled (approximately 4,000,000 to about 8,000,000) since 1940, Colorado, the most thickly populated state, has only 17 people per square mile, and Nevada has less than three.

The original economic bases of the region, ranching and mining, persist. Tourism, which began in the late 19th century, has expanded mightily. Improved roads not only bring herds of cars and house trailers in summer to Yellowstone, Grand Teton, Rocky Mountain National Park, the Grand Canyon, and other spots, but they also carry the winter tide of vacationers to the ski runs of Sun Valley, Aspen, and other centers for winter sports. To these economic mainstays the Space Age has added new ones—missile ranges, tracking stations, space and military industries, and manufacturing.

THE STATES

Although to an outsider the Rockies may seem a single region, to their inhabitants each of the eight mountain states has its distinct individual flavor. The northern tier of states—Idaho, Montana, and Wyoming—slopes up from the Dakota prairies on the east to the wild peaks and gorges of the Hell's Canyon region, where Idaho meets Oregon. Much of Idaho and northwestern Montana is still untamed wilderness, accessible only to hardy souls exploring trails on foot, riding on sturdy packhorses, or daring the Salmon River rapids in rubber rafts. But **Idaho** is also the land of potato farmers, lumbermen, and Basque sheepherders. The Atomic Energy Commission's National Reactor Testing Station—a touch of the future in a land whose remotest canyons have not changed much since the days of Lewis and Clark—is located near Arco, Idaho.

Most of heavily wooded northwestern **Montana** is devoted to na-

Cowboys still ride the range on this Montana ranch.

256

A lone Navajo sheepherder at work in Monument Valley, Arizona.

A lead smelter operates in the mountains of northern Idaho.

Denver, Colorado, is the biggest city of the Mountain States.

A lush crop of winter wheat flourishes beneath
snowcapped mountains near Salt Lake City, Utah.

tional forests, Indian reservations, Glacier National Park, and lumber camps. Montana is the largest of the mountain states. Montana Power and Anaconda Copper, near Butte, are the state's industrial titans. There are also Air Force installations. Montana's baronial cattle ranches claim 3,000,000 head of cattle, and its sparkling modern dude ranches lure an increasingly large number of tourists.

In the northwest corner of **Wyoming**, spreading over into Montana and Idaho, is the great grandfather of all the American national parks—Yellowstone, with its geysers and sulfur springs. To the south the perennially snowcapped Teton range soars with shocking abruptness over a mile (1.6 kilometers) straight up from the Wyoming plains. The legendary Buffalo Bill country rolls eastward from these majestic cliffs. Today it is populated mostly by working cowboys, eastern dudes, mining engineers, and businessmen who have wrested a fortune in black gold from the Wyoming oil fields.

In the center tier, the Rocky Mountain states reach across a third of a continent—1,000 miles (1,600 km.) from the Colorado border to the Nevada-California state line at the edge of the Sierra Nevadas. The westbound traveler knows he is really in the West when he gets to Denver, a modern cosmopolitan city that still has the feel of gold strikes and cowboy adventures. **Colorado**, "the roof of the Rockies," averages 6,800 feet (2,100 meters) in altitude, and even the low spots are often a mile high. This is the richest of the Rockies states, with the most varied economic base—busy United States Government establishments, mining, resorts, manufacturing, farming, and a large cattle industry. The United States

The Teton range towers above the Snake River in Wyoming.

Air Force Academy at Colorado Springs and the University of Colorado at Boulder are nationally known educational institutions.

West of Colorado is **Utah**, still the land of the Mormons. Seventy percent of the residents of the state are Mormons. The state capital and the center of the Mormon religion, Salt Lake City, is one of the neatest and most orderly of American cities. It is the site of the famous Mormon Temple and of the Mormon Tabernacle, with its superb choir. Nearby, the Great Salt Lake covers almost 1,500 square miles (4,000 square kilometers) with water so salty that it is impossible to sink in it. On the Bonneville Salt Flats, motorcyclists race, and skiers in bathing suits flash down the solid salt dunes of the desert. Utah boasts the largest man-made hole in the world—the rich Bingham Canyon open-pit copper mine.

From Utah's Wasatch Range the desolate Great Basin stretches west through **Nevada**—a moonscape wasteland fit only for missile tests and desert rats. But get-rich-quick dreamers still head for Nevada today as they did in the time of the Comstock Lode. However, their mecca is now Las Vegas, where another historical Wild West occupation, gambling, has been raised to the status of big business. The pleasant town of Reno, far to the north near the Sierra Nevada's Donner Pass and Lake Tahoe, has its share of the entertainment industry, but it is home also to the University of Nevada.

In the southern Mountain States, the low deserts of **Arizona** and the high deserts of New Mexico are dotted with prehistoric pueblos and ultra-modern oases in the form of winter resorts and atomic or missile installations. Northern Arizona's Grand Canyon awes visitors from all over the world. The state's northeast corner is taken up by vast Indian reservations, especially the preserve of the Navajo, the biggest tribe. To the south the sophisticated suburbs and retirement colonies of Phoenix lure the lovers of sun and cactus and red buttes. Near Tucson is the Kitt Peak National Observatory. Arizona is the richest mining state. In 100 years its mines have yielded about $11,000,000,000 worth of metals.

Unlike most Rocky Mountain states, **New Mexico** has a colonial heritage. Some of its old Spanish buildings date back to the 17th century. Today the sleepy Mexican charm of the past and the ancient pueblos of a dimmer Indian past contrast with the brisk futuristic challenge of atom smashing and missile testing. Albuquerque, with its Atomic Energy Commission operations center, calls itself the heart of the Nuclear-Space Age. White Sands Proving Grounds is the Western Hemisphere's largest land-missile testing center. And it was at Los Alamos, near Santa Fe, that the first atom bomb was developed. But around the dreamy town of Taos, still a congenial place for artists, the traveler can sometimes witness the descendants of the Pueblo Indians performing their ritual dances.

Throughout the Rocky Mountain states, one is never very far from a bit of the pure past, whether it be a mining ghost town, a Spanish mission, or a waterfall in a gorge so wild that it is hard to believe man has ever set foot there before. The old conquered frontier lies preserved here like the prehistoric trees turned to stone in the Petrified Forest of Arizona. But for physicists, astronomers, and other scientists testing the limits of the latest technologies, the Rocky Mountains still offer a frontier to conquer—perhaps this time one that will lead to the planets.

DALE VAN EVERY, Author, *The American Frontier*

SOUTHWESTERN STATES

The Southwest is a region of great semi-arid plains, of old Spanish forts and churches and missions, of Mexican-Americans, of cowboys and Indians, of oil and cattle, and of big money and mushrooming cities. But the Southwest—which includes Texas, Oklahoma, Arizona, and New Mexico—is also an immense region. What is generally true for the region as a whole is not necessarily true for every part of it.

The eastern, woodland regions of Texas and Oklahoma, for example, are not dry and may get more rain than parts of the eastern seaboard of the United States. Arizona and New Mexico are quite dry, but they are also fairly mountainous, particularly in their northern reaches. In fact, topographically Arizona and New Mexico are more like the Mountain States to the north than they are like Texas and Oklahoma. Therefore they are also discussed in the article on the MOUNTAIN STATES in this volume.

But culturally Arizona and New Mexico belong to the Southwest. They share a common Spanish heritage with Texas and have a large Indian population like Oklahoma. Texas, Arizona, and New Mexico were all settled by Spaniards before the end of the 17th century. All three states border on Mexico, and all three have large Mexican-American populations. Oklahoma has few Mexican-Americans, but it does have a large population of American Indians. In fact, close to half the Indians surviving in the United States today live in Oklahoma, New Mexico, and Arizona.

THE PEOPLE

The Southwest, too, may very well be the fastest changing part of the country. Today the population of the four Southwestern States is over 16,000,000 and growing fast. Before World War II, Indians and Mexican-Americans constituted about two thirds of the population of New Mexico. Today in New Mexico's largest cities—and in Arizona's largest cities—those two groups together have become a distinct minority. Tourists, prospectors, artists, scientists, government employees, factory workers, and retired people have swarmed in from every direction. Taos, Santa Fe, and Albuquerque in New Mexico and Phoenix and Tucson in Arizona have become modern cities with mixed populations. On a larger scale, to the east, Houston, Dallas, and San Antonio in Texas and Oklahoma City in Oklahoma have been growing and spreading rapidly and are now taking their place among major American cities.

Relative to the rest of the country, the Southwest has experienced its major economic growth rather recently. The region's giant aerospace, defense, and chemical industries have developed since World War II. The massive exploitation of the Southwest's vast oil, gas, and mineral reserves has only occurred within the last generation or two. Arizona, Oklahoma, and New Mexico, in fact, were among the last states to be admitted to the Union, all three achieving statehood after the start of the 20th century. The days of the frontier are still a fairly recent memory in the Southwest. And all the newness, all the change, have kept the people's brash frontier spirit alive. Stereotypes of southwesterners have emerged—the boastful Texan, the extravagant oil tycoon. All this is part of frontier exuberance, the spirit of a people who still see no limit to what they can do. The relentless hand of nature has fashioned southwesterners into a special breed. In spite of droughts, floods, dust storms, tornadoes, and crop-killing freezes, they have retained their optimism and their enterprise.

Present and Past.   These dynamic people also have roots that go deep into the past. The Southwest, in fact, can lay claim to some of the oldest settlements in North America. Centuries before Columbus discovered America, the Pueblo Indians of the upper Rio Grande Valley were settled in villages and were irrigating fields of corn, beans, and squash. The Spaniards had established settlements in the Southwest before the English made their first permanent settlements along the Atlantic seaboard. And, of course, the Indians and Spanish-Americans still live in the Southwest in substantial numbers.

Architecturally, the Southwest retains a Spanish look, with certain Indian influences apparent as well. These old styles are not found just in the region's old forts, missions, and churches. They have been incorporated into relatively recent buildings as well. The now-traditional American ranch-style house was born in the Southwest. The modern government buildings and the buildings of some of the region's university and college campuses also show the influence of Spanish colonial styles of architecture.

In general, it is a combination of exuberance and age that sets the region apart. Southwesterners are something of a contradiction—a fast-

SOUTHWESTERN STATES

OKLAHOMA
CAPITAL: Oklahoma City.
MAJOR CITIES: Oklahoma City, Tulsa.
AREA: 69,919 sq. mi. (181,090 sq. km.).
POPULATION: 2,559,253 (1970 census).
PHYSICAL FEATURES: **Highest point**—Black Mesa (4,978 ft.; 1,517 m.). **Lowest point**—300 ft. (91 m.). **Major rivers**—Arkansas, Red. **Major lakes**—Lake Texoma (man-made—shared with Texas), Lake of the Cherokees (man-made).
STATE MOTTO: *Labor omnia vincit* ("Labor conquers all things").

TEXAS
CAPITAL: Austin.
MAJOR CITIES: Houston, Dallas, San Antonio, Fort Worth, El Paso, Austin.
AREA: 267,338 sq. mi. (692,406 sq. km.).
POPULATION: 11,196,730 (1970 census).
PHYSICAL FEATURES: **Highest point**—Guadalupe Peak (8,751 ft.; 2,667 m.). **Lowest point**—sea level. **Major rivers**—Canadian, Red, Colorado, Brazos, Trinity, Sabine, Rio Grande, Pecos. **Major lakes**—Lake Texoma (man-made), Sabine, Caddo.
STATE MOTTO: Friendship.

changing people who are also much taken up with their own past, its traditions, and its many colorful frontier figures.

East and West

What is happening today in the Southwest is that the frontier itself is becoming more of a tradition than a reality. Southwesterners still like to think of themselves as close to the land. But the fact is that about three fourths of the people in Texas, Oklahoma, New Mexico, and Arizona now live in urban areas. In Texas and Oklahoma, more than 80 percent of the people live in the section east of the 98th meridian, which is the most heavily urbanized region in the Southwest.

The 98th meridian runs approximately through San Antonio, Dallas-Fort Worth, and Oklahoma City, and it is the vast region that lies to the west of that line that remains the most typically southwestern. In fact, there is a saying in Texas—"Dallas is where the East ends, Forth Worth is where the West begins." West of the 98th meridian the land lies open and the horizons are far in the distance. Cowboys still ride the range. Sheep and goats are herded by lonely shepherds. The Edwards Plateau and the trans-Pecos country (the region south of the Texas Panhandle and north and west of San Antonio) has probably changed less than any other sizable part of the Southwest. Here the land is frequently broken by canyons, hills, and mesas. There are still cedar, cactus, and sotol as far as the eye can see. Cattle, sheep, goats, oil derricks, and water-pumping windmills have much of the landscape to themselves. Now and then a city such as Odessa or Midland rises on the distant horizon.

But even in the country west of the 98th meridian, things are changing. Farms and ranches tend to be large and highly mechanized, and helicopters and airplanes are frequently part of a ranch's equipment. Long ribbons of concrete highway connect the far-flung cities and towns. Driving their big cars at very high speeds, the people cover great distances in relatively little time.

HISTORY

In the Southwest, a region rich in lore, recorded history begins with an Indian legend that fascinated adventurers coming to the New World. It was the legend of the Seven Cities of Cibola, fabulous places where the houses were said to be built of gold and the streets paved with gold.

The legend reached Spain in an odd way. In 1528—36 years after Columbus discovered the New World—survivors of a Spanish expedition landed at Galveston Island, on the Gulf of Mexico in present-day Texas.

All but four of the survivors soon died of starvation or were killed by the Indians. The names of two of the remaining men are well remembered—Álvar Núñez Cabeza de Vaca and Estevanico (who was a former slave of Moorish descent). Cabeza de Vaca and his three surviving companions wandered for 8 years through the Southwest. In 1536 they finally arrived in Mexico City. When Cabeza de Vaca was able to return to Spain, he told the fascinated Spaniards the legend of the Seven Cities of Cibola, which Indians he had met in his wanderings had told to him.

In 1540 an expedition to find the Seven Cities of Cibola left the west coast of Mexico. It was led by Francisco Vásquez de Coronado and included soldiers and Indians. Coronado had with him as guide Brother Marcos de Niza, a Franciscan friar who had previously seen the cities of Cibola, though only from a distance. Between 1540 and 1542 Coronado made a 4,000-mile (6,400 kilometers) journey across Arizona, New Mexico, and the Texas and Oklahoma panhandles. He also explored that part of the North Central States that includes Kansas. Virtually all of his travels occurred west of the 98th meridian. He found the "cities" of Cibola near the present Arizona-New Mexico border, but they proved to be ungilded, mud-covered, and poverty-stricken Indian villages.

Coronado's expedition did discover the Grand Canyon. They also found great herds of "humpback oxen," or buffalo, and the open, trackless plains of Texas, Oklahoma, and western Kansas. In Coronado's days these vast stretches were covered with cedar, cactus, sotol, and seas of grass stirrup-deep. Today the Panhandle plains have been sown with newer, richer strains of grass that are better for grazing. Other riches flow from the land as well. Gigantic underground reservoirs of water have transformed much of the area into cropland. Wheat, cotton, small grain, and vegetables are produced in quantities that stagger the imagination. And, of course, oil is brought from underground. But Coronado was seeking gold and silver, and not a trace of either was found.

Houston, Texas, is one of the great cities of the new Southwest.

Cattle ranching is still an important industry in the region.

Spanish Settlements

Although missionaries occasionally ventured north of the Rio Grande to work among the Indians, the Spaniards generally showed little interest in the Southwest for more than half a century after Coronado. Not until 1598 did they plant their first colony in what is present-day New Mexico. They named the site San Juan de los Caballeros. It preceded the founding of Jamestown, which was the first permanent settlement in British North America, by 9 years. Other settlements followed, mostly in the vicinity of well-established Indian villages. The Indians were far from happy with the intruders. When they tried to rebel, the Spaniards punished them ruthlessly. In the early 18th century there were perhaps 10,000 people of Spanish descent living in the Southwest and a considerably larger number of Indians, many of whom were members of nomadic tribes continually moving about. The main centers of Spanish settlement were Santa Fe, Santa Cruz, Albuquerque, and El Paso. Officials in Mexico also showed interest in the vast regions to New Mexico's east and west. In the east Spanish claims extended for more than 1,000 miles (1,600 km.) from their New Mexico settlements. This vast province came to be known as Texas, after the Indians of the region whom the Spaniards called Tejas.

When the French explorer Robert Cavelier, Sieur de La Salle, landed on the Texas coast in 1685, the Spaniards were galvanized into consolidating their far-flung holdings north of Mexico. They built a series of log forts in eastern Texas, only to abandon them as unnecessary a short time later, after learning that La Salle's own men had assassinated him. Subsequently, when French fur traders from Louisiana became active in the vicinity of eastern Texas and eastern Oklahoma, the Spaniards became alarmed once again. By 1721 the Spaniards had opened a trail from

A reminder of the Spanish past: San Jose Mission in New Mexico.

present-day Del Rio, Texas, on the Rio Grande, to the vicinity of the Sabine River. They also had planted three outposts of civilization—at San Antonio, Nacogdoches, and La Bahía (later Goliad).

Spain continued to keep a watchful eye on the French in Louisiana until 1762, when Spain signed a treaty with France that granted to Spain undisputed possession of all the territory west of the Mississippi River. But Spain's problems were far from over. For one thing, the warlike and nomadic Comanche and Apache of Texas, New Mexico, and Arizona remained far less manageable than had the Aztecs of Mexico or the Incas of Peru. For another, the hostile environment of the Southwest made settlement difficult for Europeans.

The Anglo-Americans Arrive

In 1800, under the terms of the then-secret Treaty of San Ildefonso, Spain returned the vast Louisiana territory to France. Then the young republic of the United States purchased Louisiana in 1803. The United States became Spain's new neighbor in the Southwest. Subsequently a controversy arose between Spain and the United States as to the exact boundaries of Louisiana. The United States contended that the territory extended all the way to the Rio Grande. War threatened before the matter was finally settled by the Adams-Onís treaty of 1819. Under the terms of the treaty, the southwestern boundary of the United States was set at the Sabine River (which today separates Texas and Louisiana), the 100th meridian, and the Red River, which today is part of the boundary between Texas and Oklahoma. Before this time Spain had denied foreigners the right to enter its northern provinces in North America. After the treaty was signed, Spain, and later Mexico, relaxed the restrictions on immigration into the Southwest.

The Settling of Texas

Into Texas poured thousands of land-hungry citizens of the United States, led by Stephen F. Austin and other *empresarios* (as the colonizers in Spanish territory were still called). The newcomers settled mainly in eastern and central Texas, as well as along the Gulf Coast.

Texas Fights For Independence. By 1835 the Texans had grown dissatisfied with Mexican rule, and they clamored for complete independence. In response, the president of Mexico, General Antonio López de Santa Anna, marched northward across the Rio Grande with more than 5,000 troops to put down the growing insurrection. Santa Anna quickly surrounded a group of rebels at San Antonio. The rebels had taken refuge in the old fortified mission called the Alamo. The Alamo's defenders, about 150 strong, were led by James Bowie (after whom the famous bowie knife is named) and by a young hothead named William B. Travis. During a 13-day siege in February and March, 1836, the garrison inside the Alamo received additional recruits until it numbered about 185 men. Included among the defenders was Davy Crockett, a famous bear hunter and former congressman from Tennessee. The Alamo fell on March 6, and all the defenders perished.

Meanwhile, the Texans held a series of conventions and declared their independence from Mexico. Sam Houston, former governor of Tennessee, became commander in chief of the Texas Army. Houston led a demoralized collection of volunteers in retreat eastward before the advancing Mexican Army. Only a man of Houston's extraordinary personality and character could have held his ragtag forces together. Finally, in one of the most surprising reverses in military history, the small Texas Army of 800 men caught Santa Anna's main column near the San Jacinto River just east of Houston during siesta time on the afternoon of April 21, 1836. Within 20 minutes the Texans killed or captured approximately 1,200 enemy soldiers. General Santa Anna himself was taken prisoner the next day. By this overwhelming victory, the Texans effectively won their independence. In October, 1836, Sam Houston took the oath of office as first president of the Republic of Texas.

Texas Statehood. The republic lasted until December 29, 1845, when Texas was finally admitted to the Union as the 28th state of the United States. Houston served for 5 years as president of the Republic of Texas. He battled constantly with his political enemies, faced threats of renewed invasion by Mexico, and struggled with many other problems. More than any other individual he was responsible for eventual statehood. Statehood saved the young republic from a rapid decline into bankruptcy and anarchy. Texas fared well as a state, and by 1860 the population had surpassed 600,000. The great majority of the population came from the southern United States.

In 1861 Texas cast its lot with the Confederacy. At the end of the Civil War the state was poverty-stricken. But the Old South was even worse off. Thousands of poor people left Mississippi, Georgia, Alabama, and Louisiana to settle on the unoccupied lands of the Texas river bottoms and prairies. The 1870 population of 800,000 doubled by 1880. Some Texans already were making fortunes in the cattle business. Cattlemen also led the way in settling western Texas. Each year millions of longhorns from all over Texas were driven up the Shawnee, Chisholm, Western, or Goodnight-Loving trails to the railroads and cow towns of

These huge grain elevators are on the vast plains of Oklahoma.

Kansas or to the grazing lands beyond. The cattle were then shipped to the slaughterhouses of Chicago and other midwestern cities.

The Opening of Oklahoma

Most of the cow trails ran through Oklahoma. It was inevitable that the culture of this important part of the Southwest would be greatly affected by the cattle industry.

The name Oklahoma is a combination of two Choctaw words: *okla,* which means "people," and *humma,* which means "red." Although the Oklahoma territory became a part of the United States legally in 1803 as part of the Louisiana Purchase, it did not take its present shape until 1819, with the signing of the Adams-Onís treaty, so important in Texas' history. The early explorers of North America included Oklahoma in the vast, almost unknown stretches of the region they called the Great American Desert. Much of what was considered desert lay within the area now called the Great Plains, a region that has proved to be one of the most productive in the world and anything but a desert. Nevertheless, Oklahoma was thought as unsuitable as the rest of the Great American Desert for white settlement. However, Oklahoma was considered quite suitable for Indians displaced by white settlers east of the Mississippi.

Between 1828 and 1846 approximately 50,000 members of the Five Civilized Tribes—Cherokee, Choctaw, Creek, Chickasaw, and Seminole —were moved from their traditional homes in the Old South into the eastern woodlands of present-day Oklahoma. The Civilized Tribes were also known as Nation Indians. They were not, theoretically, under full control of the federal government of the United States but were said to constitute a nation in themselves. The term "civilized" applied to these tribes was not an exaggeration, for many tribes were made up of intelligent farmers and tradesmen, no less trained or educated in democratic processes than many whites of the time. By contrast, the western half of

Oklahoma was occupied by nomadic and often fierce tribes such as the Comanche, the Apache, the Kiowa, and later the Cheyenne. After the Civil War even the nomadic tribes were established on reservations.

Eventually the federal government broke up the reservations and distributed the lands on a severalty basis. This meant that each Indian family received an individual tract of land. This kind of individual land-holding system was completely different from the traditional policy of tribal ownership of land, in which land was held in common by all members of a tribe. This old landholding system was changed in tribe after tribe. Reservation land in excess of that distributed to the individual members of a tribe was soon thrown open to settlement by whites. The first Oklahoma land rush—or land run, as it was called at the time—took place in April, 1889, under the supervision of the United States Army. It turned into a wild stampede in which probably about 50,000 homeseekers literally ran in to stake claims. Those who violated the rules and entered the reserve before the official opening became known as Sooners, a nickname that Oklahomans use today with pride.

As other runs followed the first, all of the surplus lands in the Oklahoma region were occupied. In July, 1907, a special census was taken in Oklahoma Territory and in the Indian lands collectively called Indian Territory. Pressure for statehood had been growing, but the Five Civilized Nations had been holding out for a separate Indian state. But Congress decided upon one government for all Oklahomans and in November, 1907, Oklahoma was admitted to the Union as the 46th state.

A symbol of the modern Southwest: an oil rig against the sky.

ECONOMY

Following the admission of Oklahoma, only two territories in the conterminous United States remained out of the Union—Arizona and New Mexico. Arizona and New Mexico became states in 1912, but the major changes for them did not begin until World War II.

In Texas and Oklahoma, most recent development has been in the populous section, east of the 98th meridian. Since World War II millions of new residents have been attracted to cities along the Gulf Coast. This "chemical crescent" extends from Brownsville to Beaumont and has been especially favored because of the concentration nearby of oil and gas fields and generous supplies of sulfur, salt, and other raw materials. The largest city in the area is Houston, one of the fastest-growing metropolitan centers in the United States. Its rapid expansion rests upon many factors, not the least of which is the man-made ship canal that connects it to the Gulf of Mexico 50 miles (80 km.) to the south. Houston is the heart of a great concentration of oil refineries, petrochemical plants, cattle ranches, and rice plantations. Houston is the third-ranking port in the United States. With its rail connections to the nation's wheat-growing regions, it is perhaps the greatest wheat exporter in the world.

The most recent boost to Houston's economy is the $240,000,000 Lyndon B. Johnson Space Center for the National Aeronautics and Space Administration. Sprawled across the nearby coastal prairies is a multi-million dollar complex of office buildings, shops, and testing facilities associated with the new Space Age.

Extending north from the Gulf of Mexico to the Kansas border, the terrain of Texas and Oklahoma becomes more hilly and wooded. The largest cities are in this subregion. Houston is the most populous of these. Dallas is a major manufacturing, distributing, banking, and insurance center. Nearby Fort Worth has aircraft manufacturing, grain milling, meat-packing, and oil refining. San Antonio is a commercial city and a center of military installations. Oklahoma City and Tulsa are important for oil production and meat processing.

This eastern section also has the Southwest's best cropland. There are great oil and gas fields, pine forests, steel and glass plants, and dairy farms. In Oklahoma, the recently constructed Arkansas River Project is already showing promise of bringing about a great increase in commercial navigation and industry. The Arkansas River was once a shallow river and a great problem for navigation. Today a deepwater channel has been created all the way from the Mississippi River to the vicinity of Tulsa, Oklahoma.

Both Oklahoma and Texas are blessed with vast reserves of metallic and nonmetallic minerals. The principal ones are gas and oil (nonmetallic minerals). Texas ranks first in United States production of crude oil and Oklahoma ranks fourth. Oil has brought untold material wealth to the Southwest. Oil has also brought another kind of wealth to the region. It has played a major role in supporting universities, symphony orchestras, museums, and other cultural, scientific, and business institutions. Thus it is that the grit and sweat of the frontier are today producing a new southwesterner, better educated, more cultivated, more sophisticated than his hardworking forebears. A new generation emerging from the universities of the Southwest is bringing a new style to the region.

W. EUGENE HOLLON, Author, *The Southwest Old and New; The Great American Desert*

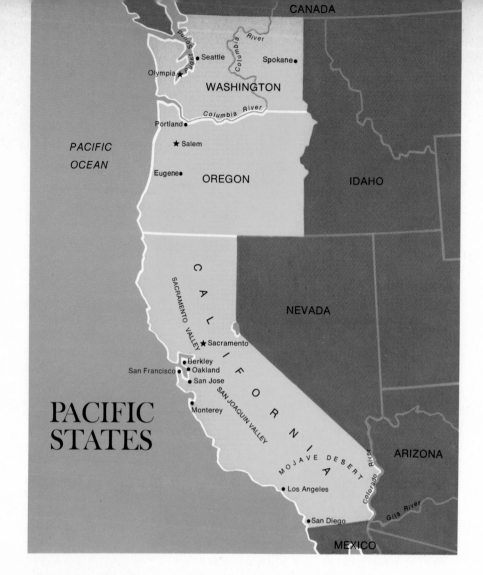

PACIFIC STATES

To many people, everything seems "more so" in the Pacific States of Washington, Oregon, and California. There is more money, more outdoor living, more sports and leisure in the sun. People in the Pacific States move more often than people in other parts of the United States. They drive faster and farther along some of the nation's most modern super-highways. Although the Pacific Coast is still a region with large areas of unique wilderness beauty, most of the people choose to settle in cities.

Westerners are traditionally very enthusiastic about their home states. The people of Washington, Oregon, and California are no exception. Their attitude can be summed up in the old cowboy expression "gone West." To the cowboys this meant "gone to heaven." However, there are problems in the Pacific States. California, for instance, is beginning to have a problem of overpopulation. All of the reports of how fine life is in the West have brought floods of new residents to California from other parts of the United States. All of the Pacific States are coping with problems of urban unrest, air and water pollution, destruction of nature, and the now rapidly expanding use of farmland for housing developments. But westerners are determined to find ways to overcome these problems.

Each of the Pacific States took its name from a different American tradition. Washington is the only state in the United States named for an American president. "Oregon" was the American Indian word for the legendary Great River of the West. (The Indians were probably referring to the Columbia River.) The name "California" may well have come from the pages of a Spanish romance. It was originally the name of a magical island inhabited by fierce griffins and warrior women. As the names of the Pacific States come from different cultures, so the present cultures of the states are different.

California has the reputation of being flamboyant and uninhibited, Oregon of being friendly and stable (some people would say conservative). Washington is known for the vitality of its people and for the pride they take in their state's exceptional mountain wilderness. Even within the states there are regional differences. For instance, cosmopolitan San Francisco has a different style from restless, sprawling Greater Los Angeles. Still, all Pacific Coast dwellers have things in common that make them a different breed of people from those "back East."

THE LAND

One of the things the people of the Pacific Coast share is pride in the scenic beauty and astounding physical variety of their land. For example, imagine yourself flying in an airplane due east from the picturesque seaport of Monterey, once capital of Spanish California. Leaving behind the crashing surf, Monterey cypresses, and artichoke fields, you cross the Salinas Valley, "lettuce capital of the world." Then you fly past the Gabilan Range, a small valley, and then the Diablo Range, until you reach the broad expanse of the San Joaquin Valley, stretching eastward like a patchwork quilt of green and tan. Irrigation has made the San Joaquin Valley one of the world's richest farming areas. Ahead rise the mighty peaks of the Sierra Nevada, and the green spikes below are the giant redwood trees of Sequoia National Park, some of them older than the Christian Era. Next the plane skims over Mount Whitney, 14,495 feet (4,418 meters) high, the highest point in the United States outside of Alaska. But after crossing the Owens Valley and the Panamint Range, you suddenly stare down upon the lowest spot in the Western Hemisphere, the forbidding desert appropriately named Death Valley. It is as much as 282 feet (86 m.) below sea level and one of the hottest places on earth in summer. Beyond it, the ominous Funeral Mountains mark California's eastern boundary. All of this great geographical variety can be seen in a flight of only 300 miles (430 kilometers) on a straight east–west course.

As a physical unit, the Pacific States resemble a slender, slanting letter H. Along the ocean extends the Coast Range, geologically very young and still undergoing movement. Its most famous fault line, the San Andreas Fault, can produce earthquakes like the San Francisco disaster of 1906. Farther east, paralleling the Coast Range, are the higher Cascades (in the north) and the Sierra Nevada (in the south). The Klamath Mountains of northern California and southern Oregon, connecting the systems, form the crossbar of the H. Between the ranges lie the valleys of

Puget Sound (in Washington) and of the Willamette River (in Oregon), and farther south of the Sacramento and San Joaquin rivers, the last two forming California's great Central Valley. Another cross range, the Tehachapi, curves around the southern end of the Central Valley, cutting it off from Southern California, which is a world to itself.

Although the notion that "it never rains in California" is not true, it may seem that way to summer visitors because most Californians rarely see rain from April to October. On the West Coast precipitation is generally heavier in the north than in the south and heavier in winter than summer. Mountains are wetter than valleys, and western slopes wetter than eastern slopes. Low clouds and fog blowing east from the ocean often turn to rain along the Coast Range. However, higher, moisture-laden currents tend to skip the valleys and precipitate as rain (or snow in winter) when they strike the higher peaks of the Cascades and Sierra Nevada. Thus some of the most fertile valley farmland with excellent soil and long growing seasons has inadequate rainfall, or gets a year's supply in one winter flood and hardly a drop for the next 9 months. Therefore, irrigation and flood control are necessary to bring out the full potential of even the best farmland.

Indeed water is king, and a capricious despot at that. To curb its despotism there are gigantic irrigation schemes, dams, and aqueducts. The Los Angeles area, with 60 percent of California's people and 2 percent of its water, gets some of its water supply from the Owens Valley, over 200 miles (322 km.) north. New water systems are constantly being developed. Water is vital for the region's vast commercial agriculture and for home gardens as well.

One reason for the fame of the Pacific Coast climate is that the sea moderates the temperature of the coastal strip, where much of the population is concentrated. For instance, Seattle, Washington, though farther north than Minneapolis, Minnesota, averages 26 degrees warmer in January and more than 7 degrees cooler in July. But away from the coast the thermometer may hit extremes hardly rivaled anywhere else in the United States.

FACTS AND FIGURES

CALIFORNIA

CAPITAL: Sacramento.

MAJOR CITIES: Los Angeles, San Francisco, San Diego, San Jose, Long Beach, Oakland, Sacramento, Fresno.

AREA: 158,693 sq. mi. (411,015 sq. km.).

POPULATION: 19,953,134 (1970 census).

PHYSICAL FEATURES: **Highest point**—Mount Whitney (14,495 ft.; 4,418 m.). **Lowest point**—Death Valley, 282 ft. (86 m.) below sea level. **Major rivers**—Sacramento. Klamath, Eel, San Joaquin, Colorado. **Major lakes**—Clear, Tahoe; Shasta, Salton Sea (both man-made).

STATE MOTTO: Eureka ("I have found it"). Refers to the discovery of gold in California.

OREGON

CAPITAL: Salem.

MAJOR CITIES: Portland, Eugene, Salem.

AREA: 96,981 sq. mi. (251,181 sq. km.).

POPULATION: 2,091,385 (1970 census).

PHYSICAL FEATURES: **Highest point**—Mount Hood (11,245 ft.; 3,427 m.). **Lowest point**—sea level. **Major rivers**—Columbia, Willamette, Deschutes, John Day, Snake, Umpqua, Rogue. **Major lakes**—Upper Klamath, Crater; McNary Reservoir (man-made).

STATE MOTTO: The Union.

WASHINGTON

CAPITAL: Olympia.

MAJOR CITIES: Seattle, Spokane, Tacoma.

AREA: 68,192 sq. mi. (176,617 sq. km.).

POPULATION: 3,409,169 (1970 census).

PHYSICAL FEATURES: **Highest point**—Mount Rainier (14,408 ft.; 4,392 m.). **Lowest point**—sea level. **Major rivers**—Columbia, Spokane, Yakima, Snake, Skagit. **Major lakes**—Chelan; Franklin D. Roosevelt (man-made).

STATE MOTTO: Alki (from Chinook Indian words meaning "by and by").

Mount Rainier looms above Tacoma, Washington, and Puget Sound.

HISTORY

Climate and natural resources shaped the life style of the original inhabitants of the Pacific States as well as that of later ones. For the most part, Pacific Indians, unlike movie Indians, were not great hunters or horsemen. Few of them wore feathered headgear, and few took scalps. Nor did many plant crops. For the most part, the Pacific Indians gathered nature's bounty—acorns, grass seeds, berries, fish, and small game. California tribes lived in small villages, many speaking their own languages.

On the northwest coast, the Indians lived primarily on the abundant salmon and other fish. They were fiercer warriors than the Californians and were expert woodworkers, creating elaborately carved totem poles. They emphasized accumulation and lavish display of wealth. At a feast, or potlatch, the host might destroy a canoe or a pile of blankets or even burn down his house in order to demonstrate his affluence. On the Columbia Plateau east of the Cascades, Indian life combined some features of coastal culture with customs of the neighboring Plains Indians.

California Indians were no match for the white men who invaded their land in the 18th and 19th centuries. In the Northwest the Indians put up a stronger fight. Most amazing were the exploits of young Chief Joseph and a few hundred Nez Percé warriors in the summer of 1877. After a vain effort to defend their east Oregon home against white settlers, the tribe set out on a heroic trek toward Canada. Again and again, for more than 1,000 miles (1,600 km.) the warriors outfought pursuing United States Army troops (who were far superior in number). They fled through Washington, Idaho, and Montana. They were finally forced to surrender in Montana, just 30 miles (48 km.) below the Canadian border.

Military conquest and white men's diseases took a heavy toll among the Pacific tribes. Ancient Indian ways of life were destroyed, except for remnants preserved on isolated reservations. Today, in the Pacific States, only about 60,000 Indians live where perhaps four times as many lived in the 18th century. Most of them are very poor. Some of them live by farming on the reservations while others migrate to cities to take factory jobs. In recent years, like other minorities, they have become more outspoken in their demands for justice at the hands of the white majority. In the Northwest they struggle against the government to maintain their tribal salmon fishing rights.

European Exploration. Beginning with the voyages of Juan Rodríguez Cabrillo, a Portuguese navigator sailing for Spain, and the Englishman Sir Francis Drake in the 16th century, European powers explored the Pacific Coast for over 200 years before colonizing. Some crucial discoveries came surprisingly late. San Francisco Bay was not discovered until 1769; the Juan de Fuca Strait in 1787; and the mouth of the Columbia River in 1792. By the late 18th century, Spanish colonization had begun from Mexican bases. Farther north, Russian, British, and American ships carried on trade with the Indians for furs, which they, in turn, traded in China for tea, silk, and spices. Overland exploration began with the Lewis and Clark expedition (1804–06) and continued with the adventures of mountain men like Jedediah Smith. In the early 19th century the Russians, too, had a trading post, Fort Ross, in northern California.

California was first a Spanish province (1769–1822) and then a Mexican one (1822–47). Settlement was spearheaded by Franciscan friars like Father Junípero Serra, who established a chain of missions extending along the coast from San Diego to an area north of San Francisco Bay. The mission priests converted thousands of Indians to Christianity and taught them agriculture and simple industrial arts. They introduced crops that later became California specialties, such as orange trees and grapevines. While they were at it, they reduced the natives to a state close to slavery. With Indian labor, the missions flourished as proprietors of vast lands and huge herds of sheep and cattle.

In the 1830's, the Mexican Government abolished the extensive landholding system of the missions. The Indians who had worked on mission lands scattered, the buildings fell into ruin, and the lands and herds passed into the hands of private ranchers. Only much later were some of the missions restored as historical sites and tourist attractions.

By the time the missions were abandoned, several hundred Americans had settled in the region, many of them among the leading merchants and landholders. Cattle raising and the "hide and tallow trade," so called because of the use of hides for leather and fat for tallow candles, were the economic mainstays. Yankee ships, for instance, traded manufactured goods for the stiff cattle hides that were called "California bank notes."

American Claims. Meanwhile rival nations claimed the Northwest. In 1819 Spain gave up claims to the region north of California, and soon Russia accepted the latitude 54° 40′ as the southern limit of its Alaskan colony. The United States and Britain continued to claim the Oregon territory. They settled, theoretically, for joint occupation, but in practice the British Hudson's Bay Company controlled Oregon until the 1840's.

No military conflict developed. America's strongest claims in the area were established by the free fur trappers and, later, by American settlers. The first overland wagon train, the Bidwell party, were farmers, ready to travel for 3 or 4 months over 2,000 miles (3,200 km.) of unsettled country in the hope of making a new start on virgin land. They followed a route that would soon become famous as the Oregon Trail. At Fort Hall the party divided, half going to Oregon and half to California. Marcus Whitman and other famous missionaries also headed for Oregon and sent back glowing reports. By 1843 the trickle of people traveling the Oregon Trail had become a flood: it was called the Great Migration. More than 1,000 settlers crowded the route, most of them heading for the meadows of Oregon's idyllic Willamette Valley.

The question of who owned Oregon was finally settled by a treaty between Britain and the United States, signed in 1846. Although each side had previously claimed much more, the compromise divided the Oregon country at the 49th parallel, which was already the international boundary farther east. The American share, the Territory of Oregon, included what became Washington, Oregon, Idaho, and part of Montana. Oregon became a state in 1859 and Washington in 1889.

California, on the other hand, was the prize of military conquest. In June of 1846 settlers in the Sacramento Valley rebelled against Mexican authority. With the support of explorer John C. Frémont they proclaimed the Bear Flag Republic. Soon their little revolution was engulfed in the larger conflict of the Mexican War. Through war the United States took California and the whole Southwest, ceded by Mexico in the peace treaty of 1848.

Gold. Thus, the United States acquired all its Far West within a 2-year period. Although settlement of such a vast, remote land would normally not be rapid, a stroke of luck was to make the settlement of California unique. On January 24, 1848, James Marshall noticed glittering particles in the tailrace of a sawmill near Sacramento, and soon the cry, "Gold in California!" echoed around the world. It was the signal for one of the most hectic mass migrations in history. Beginning in 1849, thousands of forty-niners arrived by land and sea. Within a few months New York bank clerks, Illinois farmers, Germans, Frenchmen, Mexicans, South Americans, Chinese, and Australians were all digging away frantically in the foothills and streams of the Sierra Nevada. California's population rose from about 15,000 in 1847 to nearly 250,000 in 1852.

Digging out ore and washing it for gold was hard work, whether done with pick, shovel, and pan, or with the more complex technology that soon developed. The grubby mining camps were colorful, but they were also uncomfortable. Few miners realized their dreams of striking it rich. Many endured aching muscles and bad food, illness and homesickness, only to meet repeated disappointment. Yet looking back later, the forty-niners remembered mostly the rowdy good times, the comradeship, and the excitement of their great adventure.

Because of the sudden population increase, California was able to skip the territorial stage and gain statehood as part of the famous Compromise of 1850.

Settlement of the Pacific Northwest proceeded more slowly. There were modest gold rushes to Oregon and northeastern Washington in the 1850's. But only east of the Cascades, in what became Idaho and Montana, did mining develop on the grand scale. Agriculture, lumbering, fisheries, and commerce were the less flamboyant but more stable foundations of economic growth in Oregon and Washington.

Transportation

By wagon train from the Missouri Valley, or by the swiftest clipper ship around the Horn from Boston, it took 3 or 4 months to reach the Pacific Coast. This remoteness had profound effects upon the character of the region. It isolated the far westerners from the affairs of the rest of the nation and made them more dependent upon their own resources. Only gradually did a variety of technological changes draw the Pacific States into closer union with older regions. In 1858 the Butterfield Overland Mail cut the St. Louis–San Francisco time to 24 days. The famous Pony Express speeded communication still more but required at least 10 days to deliver a letter from Missouri to California. The ponies gave way to the transcontinental telegraph in 1861. Not until 1915, however, could a New Yorker reach for his telephone and talk to someone in San Francisco. Network radio broadcasting further reduced western isolation in the 1920's. After World War II network television tied the Pacific States even more closely to the rest of the country.

In the history of western transportation, no date is more important than May 10, 1869, when officials ceremoniously drove the Golden Spike to join the tracks of the Union Pacific and Central Pacific Railroads near Ogden, Utah. Among other transcontinental lines were the Northern Pacific, which reached Portland in 1883, and the Santa Fe, which entered Los Angeles in 1883. The coming of the railroads caused an influx of new settlers and an economic boom. Another major event, the opening of the Panama Canal in 1914, greatly reduced the distance by sea to the Atlantic Coast and to Europe. Then came the automobile and the airplane to complete the transportation revolution. Today's jet planes are able to fly as far in an hour as the covered wagons of the pioneers could travel in a month.

Freshly cut Oregon timber is sent on its way to a plywood mill.

ECONOMY

By the 1890's about 2,000,000 people were living in the Pacific States, two thirds of them in California. Washington, still a frontier state, grew the most rapidly during the next 20 years. By 1910 its population was almost half that of California. But after World War I, migration to California became a flood that has never ceased. Today almost half of the population of the Pacific States lives in Southern California.

Agriculture. Until recently, the economy of the Pacific States rested primarily upon agriculture and the extractive industries. The list of major products include oranges and petroleum from Southern California; beef cattle, cotton, fruits, and vegetables from the San Joaquin Valley; lumber from the Northwest; salmon from the Columbia River; apples from the Hood River district in Oregon; and wheat from Washington's Inland Empire region. California leads all the states of the nation in the value and variety of its agricultural production.

It was irrigation that enabled California to overcome the handicap of inadequate rainfall and take advantage of the long growing season—a record 300 days in the Imperial Valley, sufficient for six harvests of the alfalfa crop. Water diverted from the nearby Colorado River has converted this former desert in southeastern California into a garden of astonishing productivity. In the Pacific Northwest, too, large areas of the drier interior have been brought under irrigation. There, the biggest undertaking is the Columbia Basin development in eastern Washington. Oregon's projects are scattered and on a smaller scale. However, Oregon does have more irrigated acreage per capita than either of the other two Pacific States.

Water development in the modern Far West has been heavily subsidized by the federal government. Irrigation is only one of several objectives. Great regional projects like those in the Columbia Basin and the Central Valley are also designed to provide hydroelectric power, flood control, and recreational facilities. About a third of the potential hydroelectric power in the nation is available in the Columbia system, though only a portion is now being tapped. For power production high dams are desirable. That is the reason for such spectacular structures as Grand Coulee Dam in Washington, Shasta Dam in northern California, and Hoover Dam on the Colorado River (on the border between Nevada and Arizona), which supplies power and water to Southern California.

Industry. Despite the importance of agriculture, the Pacific Coast has predominantly an urban society. Even as early as 1910, about half the population of Washington and Oregon lived in cities and towns. Maritime commerce and mining industries drew people together in seaports, mining towns, logging towns, and fishing villages.

Manufacturing got an early start in the Pacific States, in part because of the remoteness of the Far West. It was cheaper to buy locally manufactured products. Products brought all the way from the East could not help but be more expensive.

In earlier times, the typical industry in the Pacific States was a cannery, winery, or sawmill, engaged in processing one of the region's natural resources. Such plants produced the famous California wines, or processed the lumber of Oregon. Recently, manufacturing has become more diversified. Seattle's lumbering and salmon fishing are almost overshadowed by its biggest manufacturer, Boeing Aircraft. The shift is particularly true in California, where aerospace, electronics, and film industries are among the leading enterprises. Californians—about 20,000,000 of them—constitute not only a huge market but a great reservoir of labor and technical skill. The people themselves are now the state's leading resource. Though the favorable climate may have been the original factor attracting industries like motion pictures and aircraft manufacture, the fame of the companies themselves now acts as an additional magnet for new talent.

WAY OF LIFE

Thus the Pacific States present the paradox of wide-open spaces with most of the people concentrated in urban masses. Surrounded by mountains, forests, and sea, the typical far westerner spends more time fighting traffic than enjoying nature, and he breathes more bad air than good. On a sunny weekend or holiday, he may join the urban pilgrimage to the wilderness, but he usually finds a crowd when he gets there.

Cities.   Each of the major urban centers has its own distinctive personality. **San Diego** is the southernmost and sunniest, stretching from the Mexican border along many miles of Pacific shoreline. The oldest community in California, it has only recently become a big city. Carefully planned, it blends its Spanish past with the new technologies.

Farther north, **Los Angeles**, third largest American city after New York and Chicago, sprawls over a huge area. Never before has so large a city grown so fast or so shapelessly. It merges with many other nearby communities to form an enormous urban complex.

Laguna Beach is typical of California's seaside communities.

San Francisco, with its cable cars and views, is a unique city.

In some ways, **San Francisco** seems more like a big city than Los Angeles, and for a good reason. Although only a tenth as large in area, it has three times as many people per square mile. Kept from expanding by its location on a peninsula surrounded on three sides by water, it has a greater population density than any of the nation's 10 largest cities except New York. Nearly every visitor falls in love with San Francisco, with its steep hills and magnificent vistas of ocean and bay, with its cosmopolitan atmosphere and the clang of its antique cable cars. But behind the charm there is also much misery, manifested in the high level of alcoholism and suicide. Today San Francisco is only part of an urban complex that extends all around the San Francisco Bay and includes other large cities like **Oakland** and **San José**.

Portland, Oregon, is a seaport about 100 miles (161 km.) from the ocean. It straddles the Willamette River, near the point where that stream empties into the Columbia River. It is renowned for its roses and its backdrop of snowy mountain peaks.

Like Portland, **Seattle** is a seaport far from the sea. Like San Francisco, it has a dramatic setting of steep hills and expanses of water, but unlike that city it has a backdrop of snowcapped peaks. Mount Rainier can be seen on a clear day. But Seattle is a young giant commanding a unique region, Puget Sound, and may have more untapped potential than any other western city.

Developments and Problems.   World War II spurred urban industrial growth and introduced a new era on the Pacific Coast. For the first time, the region became a major focus of war production and a military center. Because the United States has been deeply involved in Asia ever since, the Pacific States no longer seem to be on the far outer edge of national affairs.

The war also started the first mass movement of black Americans to the Pacific Coast. The black population of California rose from 124,000 in 1940 to 462,000 in 1950, and passed the 1,000,000 mark by the early 1960's. Previously in the Pacific States clashes between dominant white society and minorities had mainly involved Orientals. When Japanese residents, many of them American citizens (called Nisei), were removed from communities on the Pacific Coast in 1942 and confined in "relocation camps," authorities attempted to justify the move as a defense measure. However, many people suspected it was inspired by racial prejudice. Today, however, California has become a major scene of the black revolution that began in the 1950's. More recently the chorus of protest has been swelled by the voices of Mexican Americans, who are even more numerous than blacks in the region but have long suffered in silence the indignities of second-class citizenship.

On the Pacific Coast, as in other parts of the country, college campuses have become storm centers of social activism. Indeed the University of California at Berkeley is widely recognized as the symbolic world capital of student rebellion, although in the later 60's clashes at San Francisco State College drew more headlines. In the West, as elsewhere, the chief trouble spots are the cities. For many years urban, middle-class whites have been moving out to the suburbs and to newer communities beyond the suburbs. The core cities have been left to fight endless battles against poverty, crime, racial strife, and physical decay.

The effects of urban concentration and suburban sprawl are most visible on the streets and highways. In the Pacific States there are about six registered motor vehicles for every 10 residents, and the ratio is increasing. Much of the region grew to maturity during the age of the automobile. The good and the bad results of the automobile age are apparent everywhere in the Pacific States. They are apparent in freedom of movement and easy access to wilderness areas; in suburban shopping centers and drive-in movies; in roadside litter, smoggy skies, and hills slashed with concrete. Many westerners think nothing of driving a 200-mile (322 km.) round trip to go to a picnic or dinner date. In Southern California, some people commute huge distances daily to work.

Tourism

The automobile revolutionized American vacation habits and made the tourist industry big business in the Pacific States. Millions of visitors arrive annually from other parts of the nation and from foreign countries. But a majority of the tourists crowding the roads are themselves westerners. All the vacations of a lifetime cannot exhaust the variety of interesting places and natural wonders.

The scenic splendor of the Pacific Coast probably ranks first among its tourist attractions. Washington's most famous landmark is Mount Rainier, rising magnificently to 14,408 feet (4,392 m.) and covered with some 26 glaciers. Seasoned hikers can circle the whole mountain by the 100-mile (161 km.) Wonderland Trail. Puget Sound is a paradise for sailing enthusiasts, and boatless visitors may sample its delights by taking a ferry-boat ride through the lovely San Juan Islands. Farther west, a drive through the rain forests of Olympic National Park reveals what the coast once was like from Alaska to Northern California.

Oregon, too, has its special mountain, Mount Hood, which can be viewed from all sides on the 170-mile (274 km.) Mount Hood Loop Highway. Another favorite drive goes through the Columbia Gorge east of Portland. But for the state's most dazzling beauty one must travel high up into the Cascades of southern Oregon, to Crater Lake. The lake is set in an extinct volcano—a circle of incredibly blue water 6 miles (10 km.) wide and 2,000 ft. (610 m.) deep.

California, with its larger area and greater climate range, offers the widest variety of scenery: the silent majesty of the giant redwoods seen from the Redwood Highway north of San Francisco or in Sequoia National Park; the Mojave Desert in flamboyant springtime bloom; the breathtaking beauty of the Big Sur on the coast below Monterey. But if California has an incomparable spectacle, it must be the Yosemite Valley. The meadowlike floor is almost completely encircled by perpendicular walls and dramatic pinnacles rising straight up for thousands of feet. Waterfalls tumble down on all sides.

Man also has provided diversions for the Pacific tourist. He can inspect one of the huge dams like Grand Coulee, view Seattle from the top of its 600-foot (183 m.) Space Needle, stroll through San Francisco's picturesque Chinatown, or visit the world's largest telescope on Mount Palomar, near San Diego. If he likes history, he will be drawn to California's missions and gold towns, to the restoration of Russian Fort Ross, or to Sutter's Fort in the center of Sacramento. There are seasonal events— Pasadena's Tournament of the Roses and the annual Shakespeare Festival at Ashland, Oregon. A generation ago, no California visit was complete without a "seeing-stars" tour of Hollywood. However, Disneyland is now Southern California's supreme tourist attraction.

Two Worlds.   The discerning visitor will note that the Pacific Coast is in many ways two different societies, divided a little north of San Francisco. The southern section contains the larger, more restless, faster-growing population. One of the great centers of modern civilization, it would rank among the leading industrial countries of the world if it were an independent nation. Its leading universities are internationally famous, and its political influence weighs ever more heavily in national affairs.

The Pacific Northwest, including the northern third of California, Oregon, and Washington, is a younger, greener, less hectic world than the area to the south, somehow closer in style to the West of the pioneers. Its population is increasing at a more moderate rate, and its people are more rooted and less mercurial. By the 1980's, California will probably have about five times as many people as Washington and Oregon together. It remains to be seen which region will be better off as a consequence.

DON E. FEHRENBACHER, Stanford University

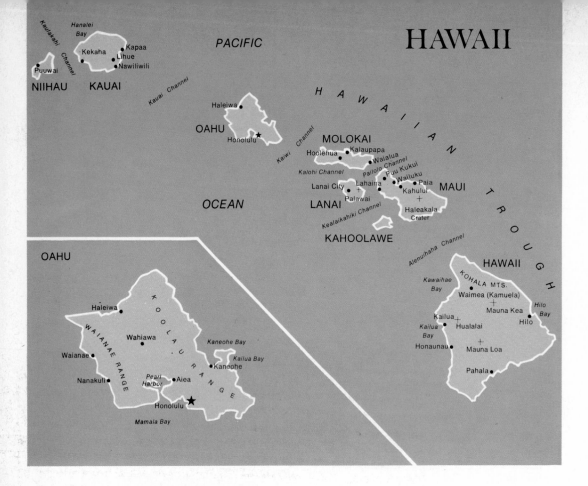

HAWAII

Hawaii is the only one of the 50 states of the United States not located on the North American continent. It is the southernmost and westernmost state, the only island state, and the latest state to enter the Union. Uniqueness is Hawaii's very essence. It is the only state in which white people are a minority. Its large population of Oriental descent and its colorful Polynesian heritage set it off from the rest of the United States. At the same time, Hawaii is thought of as one of the most "American" of states, a melting pot of different peoples in the best tradition of American democracy.

Hawaii is also the only state created by volcanoes. More than 1,000,000 years ago a great volcanic eruption split the floor of the Pacific Ocean. For centuries lava flowed from the great fissures, or cracks, in the ocean floor caused by the eruption. This flow of lăva created a huge underwater mountain chain, some of whose peaks rose thousands of feet above the surface of the water. These peaks form the 1,500-mile-long (2,500 kilometers) island chain that came to be called the Hawaiian Islands.

Although the Hawaiian island chain does cover a vast area of the Pacific, the islands of greatest size and greatest importance to the state are located within a few hundred miles of each other at the southeastern end of the Hawaiian island group. These eight key islands are called the main islands. For all practical purposes, the main islands are what is meant when one speaks of the state of Hawaii.

THE PEOPLE

Located as it is in the middle of the Pacific Ocean, about equidistant from North America and Asia, Hawaii has become a meeting ground for Western and Oriental peoples. In Hawaii marriages between people of different races and nationalities have been commonplace. Today about one third of all Hawaiian marriages are mixed marriages.

It is hard to state exactly the ethnic composition of Hawaiians. The census bureau bases its statistics largely on how the people describe themselves. According to the census, about one third of Hawaii's population is white. This includes many members of the United States armed forces stationed in Hawaii and their families. Another third of the population is of predominantly Japanese ancestry. About one sixth of the people are described as Hawaiian or part Hawaiian. This means that they are descended from the original Polynesian inhabitants of the Hawaiian Islands. Most of the remaining people are of Filipino descent. There is also a fairly large number of people of Chinese ancestry. All told, Hawaii's multiracial population now exceeds 750,000.

In addition to Hawaii's resident, or permanent population, well over 1,000,000 tourists from the United States mainland visit every year. "The loveliest fleet of islands that lies anchored in any ocean," is how Mark Twain once described Hawaii. With its year-round balmy climate, its fine beaches, and its beautiful scenic vistas, Hawaii has become one of the most popular vacation playgrounds in the United States.

In fact, with the growth of jet travel in the 1960's, mainland tourists began arriving in such droves that Hawaiians began to fear that their lovely islands would become too commercialized. This is particularly true in Oahu, by far the busiest of the islands. Hawaiians have other problems as well. The cost of living tends to be high because many goods have to be transported from the continental United States over 2,000 miles (3,200 km.) away. Young Hawaiians often find island life too confining. In recent years, many young people have left Hawaii.

THE LAND

Whatever the disadvantages of living on an island in the mid-Pacific may be, there is no question that Hawaii is a very beautiful state to visit. Actually, Hawaii is not large, even though it is spread out over hundreds of miles of ocean. There are only 6,424 square miles (16,638 square kilometers) of actual land area. This means that Hawaii is the fourth smallest of the 50 states. Within its relatively small area, however, there are striking variations and contrasts. Hawaii is possibly the only place in the United States where a man lying under a palm tree on a tropical beach can look up at the snowy peak of a mountain.

FACTS AND FIGURES

HAWAII is the name of the state.
CAPITAL: Honolulu, on the island of Oahu.
MAJOR CITY: Honolulu.
AREA: 6,450 sq. mi. (16,706 sq. km.).
POPULATION: 769,913 (1970 census).

PHYSICAL FEATURES: Highest point—Mauna Kea, on the island of Hawaii (13,796 ft.; 4,205 m.). **Lowest point**—sea level.
STATE MOTTO: *Ua mau ke ea o ka aina i ka pono* ("The life of the land is preserved in righteousness").

Sugar workers lay narrow-gage track in a canefield on Kauai.
A small train will be run in to carry out the sugar harvest.

The landscape is dominated by steep, emerald-green mountains, some of which rise out of the surf itself. The windward sides of the mountains—that is, the sides that face the prevailing winds—receive large amounts of rain, some slopes getting as much rain as any place on earth. The clouds rain themselves out on the windward side, leaving very little rain for the leeward side of the islands—which often have a semi-arid climate. Thus, a rainy area may have forests of tree ferns 20 feet (6 m.) high or lush gardens bright with hibiscus (the state flower), bougainvillea, or orchids. No more than 15 or 20 miles (24–32 km.) away there may be very little rain, and vacationers can depend on being able to go to the beach almost every day.

Most of Hawaii's coastline is rocky, but nevertheless, Hawaii is

Pineapple workers on Oahu load a conveyor belt with fruit.

A young surfer rides in on one of Hawaii's legendary big waves.

famous for its beaches. There are glistening pink-tinted or white beaches of coral sand, black beaches of eroded lava, and even beaches with greenish sand produced by olivine, a mineral found in some quantity in Hawaii. The great Pacific rollers that come crashing in upon the beaches have made the island a mecca for surfboard riders from all over the world. Waikiki Beach on Oahu is especially popular with surfers. In fact, the sport of surfboarding, now internationally popular, originated among the Polynesian people native to the Hawaiian Islands.

Island Hopping

Flying in a zigzag pattern from southeast to northwest, one would reach the main islands in this order:

A fisherman on Maui casts his net with both skill and grace.

Hawaii, nicknamed Big Island, is by far the largest of the islands, with a greater land area than all the other islands combined. It is also the only island with active volcanoes. They are Mauna Loa, 13,675 feet (4,176 m.) high, which erupts on an average of once every 3½ years; and Kilauea, which is smaller but which erupts more frequently. Both volcanoes are located in Hawaii Volcanoes National Park, in the southern part of the island. Although small villages have been destroyed by lava flows on occasion, eruptions are not dangerous if observed from a safe distance. Many people visit the park precisely for that purpose. Visitors who come at other times can tour all around the volcanoes' huge craters or explore such oddities as black rivers of hardened lava or hissing steam banks caused by the seepage of rainwater to hot areas below the ground.

Hawaii island boasts the highest peak in the state, Mauna Kea (13,796 ft.; 4,205 m.), an extinct volcano. On the western side of the island is the famous Kona Coast, with its ancient historical relics and excellent sport fishing. Of less interest, perhaps, to tourists are the vast waving fields of sugarcane. Hawaii island produces one third of the state's total harvest of sugarcane. Orchid growing and ranching are also important pursuits on Hawaii. The Parker Ranch, one of the largest cattle ranches in the United States, is located on Hawaii island.

Maui, north of Hawaii island, is the second largest island. It is dominated by the huge dormant volcano Haleakala. The slopes of the volcano are now used for grazing cattle.

Kahoolawe, off the southwestern tip of Maui, is the smallest of the main islands. It is a dry, desolate, uninhabited piece of land and is used as a target range by the United States armed forces.

Lanai is called the Pineapple Island. Practically all the island is owned by the Dole Pineapple Company, and the most common sight there is row upon row of green, swordlike pineapple plants.

Molokai is probably best-known for the Kalaupapa leper settlement, which is located on the island's northern coast. The famous Belgian priest Father Damien worked here among the lepers until he succumbed to the disease himself in 1889. Today, advances in the treatment of Hansen's disease, or leprosy, have substantially reduced the number of cases confined to the colony. The rest of the island consists of small rural communities, dependent on beef raising and pineapple growing.

Oahu is by far the busiest and most populous of the islands—largely because the city of Honolulu is located there. More than three fourths of the state's population live on Oahu. The majority—more than 300,000 people—live in Honolulu itself.

Honolulu is the state's capital city and its major commercial and tourist center. It is a crowded, bustling place, with some of the same problems that the large mainland cities have, including traffic congestion. However, it does not have the high crime rate of many large mainland cities. Among places of interest in Honolulu are the Iolani Palace, former palace of Hawaiian kings and the only royal palace in the United States; Ala Moana Park, which contains a replica of an ancient Hawaiian village; the University of Hawaii, the state university; and the Bishop Museum, famous for its extensive collections relating to the ancient cultures of the Pacific peoples. Probably the city's greatest attraction is Waikiki Beach, which draws surfboarders and beach lovers from all over the world.

Honolulu, the island-state's capital, is a beautiful modern city.
Its famous landmark, Diamond Head, lies in the background.

The capital is also a resort: bathers relax at Waikiki Beach.

Just outside Honolulu is Pearl Harbor, the site of one of the United States Navy's major Pacific bases. It was the Japanese surprise attack on military facilities at Pearl Harbor on December 7, 1941, that finally brought the United States into World War II. Today the men who lost their lives in that attack are commemorated by the U.S.S. *Arizona* National Memorial, a white concrete-and-steel structure that spans the actual hull of the U.S.S. *Arizona*. The *Arizona* was one of the ships that sank in the Pearl Harbor attack.

The area around Pearl Harbor still has a number of important Army, Navy, and Air Force installations, which provide employment for thousands of islanders. In fact, military expenditures of one sort or another form the most important part of the island's—and the state's—economy, ahead of tourism and agriculture.

Kauai, the Garden Isle, about 100 miles (160 km.) northwest of Oahu, is known for the rich growth of tropical vines and plants that hangs like a tapestry over the walls of its deep canyons. Waimea Canyon at the western end of the island is a particularly beautiful scenic attraction. The upper part of the windward slope of Mount Waialeale, in central Kauai, is reputed to be the wettest spot on earth, with the highest average rainfall per year to be found anywhere.

Niihau, westernmost of the main islands, is owned by a single family. Uninvited visitors are not permitted. Most of the island is low and dry and is used for grazing livestock.

HISTORY

Originally the islands were inhabited by a tall, brown-skinned people, who first migrated there 1,000 or more years ago from other islands in the Polynesian group of Pacific islands. Today their descendants live much the same way as other Hawaiians—and mainland Americans—live. As long ago as 1939 an anthropologist maintained that there was not a native Hawaiian left who could build a traditional thatched hut or carve a real dugout canoe. However, many ancient customs are still followed and many ancient ceremonies are still performed—even if primarily for the tourists.

The people of ancient Hawaii lived in villages near the sea. Fish, a staple of their diet, came from the sea. They did almost all of their traveling—both around their home islands and from island to island—in their outrigger canoes. Each canoe had attached to it a long pole running parallel to one side. The pole provided balance and kept the small, light craft from capsizing in rough seas. The Hawaiians of today travel around their home islands by car and travel from island to island by plane whenever possible. The most common food of the ancient Hawaiians was fish eaten with poi, a gritty, pastelike substance made from the root of the taro plant. The taro plant is still cultivated in Hawaii, but today sandwiches are easily as popular with Hawaiians as fish and poi. Japanese dishes such as sukiyaki and tempura shrimp, as well as a whole range of Chinese dishes, are very popular in the islands, too.

The people of ancient Hawaii also raised pigs, chickens, and dogs for food (dogs were considered a great delicacy). They gave great feasts called luaus, at which meat was roasted over open pits. Imitations of the ancient luau feasts are prepared for visitors to Hawaii today. At the ancient feasts poems were recited and the hula was danced. "Hula" actu-

The sheer cliffs of Nuuanu Pali rise from a tropical valley.

ally means "dance" in the language of the Hawaiians. The hula was originally a sacred dance with highly stylized gestures, and it resembled only superficially the hula danced in Hawaii today. It was also performed without the now familiar ukulele accompaniment. The ukulele was first brought to the island by Portuguese laborers in the 19th century.

The society of the ancient Hawaiians was similar in some ways to the feudal society of medieval Europe. A class of aristocrats owned all the land, and the farming was done by landless commoners. The people wore little clothing, but the aristocrats were outfitted with magnificent helmets and cloaks made of as many as 80,000 feathers. Some of these extraordinary feather garments may be seen today in museums. The Bishop Museum in Honolulu has a fine collection of them. The Hawaiians had no woven cloth. The muumuu, the loose, sacklike garment associated with Hawaii today, was first brought to the islands by American missionaries intent on covering the partial nakedness of the Hawaiian women.

The Coming of the Haole

For a long time many of the islands had their own kings. Then in the late 18th and early 19th centuries a great king from the island of Hawaii, Kamehameha, unified the islands into a single kingdom. But by that time the ancient culture of the Hawaiians was disappearing rapidly.

The main reason for the disappearance of the old culture was the presence of the white foreigner, or haole, as he was called on the islands. The first haole to arrive was the famous British explorer James Cook, who discovered the islands in 1778. The next year Cook was killed in a skirmish with the natives, but in subsequent decades haoles kept coming to the islands. They were explorers, sailors, and traders—Americans as well as Europeans. The haoles introduced sheep and cattle to the islands, as well as manufactured products, such as mirrors, guns and ammunition, woven cloth, and furniture. But they also exposed the Hawaiians to various infectious diseases unknown in the islands before, which took an enormous toll of lives among the natives. The haoles also introduced alcoholic beverages, with disastrous effects on the health of the Hawaiians. About 300,000 people are believed to have inhabited the islands at the time of Cook's discovery. Fifty years later, the population had fallen to about 130,000. By 1850 the population of native Hawaiians was down to about 75,000.

Missionaries.   The American missionaries who began arriving in Hawaii in 1820 attempted to help the Hawaiian people. The Reverend Hiram Bingham, who arrived with the first groups of American missionaries, tried to put through laws forbidding the sale of liquor in the islands. His conflicts with American seamen in Hawaii over this issue reached such a crisis that he barely escaped lynching.

If less than successful in curbing the sale of liquor, Bingham and other Protestant missionaries did gain enormous influence in Hawaiian affairs. Originally the Hawaiians had practiced a form of nature worship, one aspect of which involved human sacrifice. Through the work of the missionaries, Christianity was accepted by the people. Missionaries also made Hawaiian—previously only a spoken language—a written language. They created a modern constitution, redistributed some of the land to the previously landless common people, and set up a system of voting as a first step toward democratic government in Hawaii.

American Possession

In the second half of the 19th century descendants of the early missionaries began to take a business interest in the islands, as did various other American financiers. Hawaii proved to be an excellent place to grow sugarcane. American companies obtained large tracts of land for that purpose, particularly after 1875. In 1875 a Hawaiian-American treaty was signed, effective the next year, providing for duty-free entry of Hawaiian raw sugar into the United States.

A new aristocracy of white planters began to supplant the Hawaiian nobles in importance. In addition to controlling most of the islands' business, the Americans were determined to gain firm control of the kingdom as well. The fact that several Hawaiian monarchs had been incompetent played into their hands. Finally, in 1893, the last of the monarchs, Queen Liliuokalani, tried to strengthen the monarchy at the expense of the American-dominated legislature. At that point, and with the help of United States Marines who landed at the order of the American ministry, the business interests in Hawaii deposed the queen.

For a few years after the fall of the monarchy, Hawaii was an independent republic under the presidency of Sanford Dole, the Honolulu-born son of an American Protestant missionary. (Dole was also the distant cousin of James D. Dole, who pioneered in Hawaii's pineapple industry in the 20th century.) But basically the American-Hawaiians like Dole wanted the islands to be annexed by the United States. This was accomplished in 1898. Hawaii became a territory of the United States on April 30, 1900, and Sanford Dole became territorial governor.

The New Peoples

For the sugar industry to grow, laborers were needed to do the hard work in the canefields. Around 1900 pineapple cultivation was also begun, creating an additional need for agricultural labor.

Initially, Hawaii's labor need was met by Chinese, about 25,000 of whom were imported as contract laborers by 1885. The Chinese had a tendency to set up businesses of their own once their work contracts expired, and so recruitment was shifted to Japan. About 180,000 Japanese were brought to the islands between 1886 and 1908, when a United States-Japanese agreement ended the recruitment. Later, Filipinos were brought over in large numbers. Other people, too, came to the islands as contract laborers, including Koreans, Puerto Ricans, Spaniards, and Portuguese.

People of many races and nationalities toiled in the fields for low wages, while a few white families came to control virtually all the business of any size on the islands. This economic control was exercised by the "Big Five," five large, highly diversified companies owned by the leading American families. The Big Five controlled not only most of the sugar and pineapple production, but the major banks, department stores, insurance companies, radio stations, transportation companies, utilities, and various other enterprises as well. This monopolistic situation continued more or less undisturbed until the outbreak of World War II, but since that time it has changed very substantially. Labor unions have become active in the islands. They have raised the standard of living of the workers enormously. Outside enterprises have moved in and have provided competition for the Big Five in many fields. The rapid growth of defense industries during World War II drew many workers out of sugar and pineapple cultivation. Agricultural machinery made fewer farm workers necessary. That was just as well, for the fact was that the children of the field laborers, having reaped the benefits of American-style education, did not want to do the backbreaking work their fathers did, even at higher wages.

War and Statehood

World War II was a difficult time for Hawaii because such a large number of its people were of Japanese ancestry. But an overwhelming number of Japanese-Americans proved loyal to their homeland and had heroic combat records in the United States armed forces. In fact, the war record of Japanese-Americans greatly improved Hawaii's chance for statehood.

Efforts to achieve statehood, begun as far back as 1903, were intensified after World War II. After a long political struggle, Hawaii officially became the 50th state of the United States on August 21, 1959.

An economic boom followed statehood and has opened up new economic opportunities for all Hawaiians. The pattern of the concentration of wealth and power in a still largely white minority remains. But, more and more, Hawaii has come to live up to the description of it given by Dwight D. Eisenhower, the President of the United States who signed the act that made Hawaii a state. He called Hawaii "a unique example of a community that is a successful laboratory in human brotherhood."

H. R. HAYS, Author, *Kingdom of Hawaii*

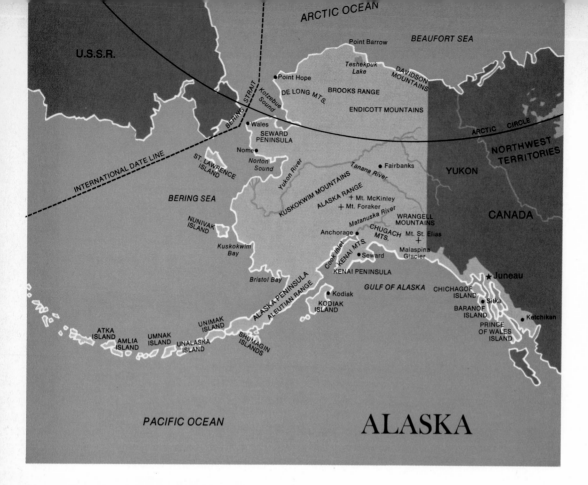

ARCTIC OCEAN

BEAUFORT SEA

U.S.S.R.

Point Barrow

Teshekpuk
Lake

DAVIDSON
MOUNTAINS

Point Hope

DE LONG MTS.

BROOKS RANGE

ENDICOTT MOUNTAINS

ARCTIC CIRCLE

Kotzebue
Sound

NORTHWEST
TERRITORIES

Wales

SEWARD
PENINSULA

YUKON

INTERNATIONAL DATE LINE

Nome

Norton
Sound

Tanana River

Fairbanks

ST. LAWRENCE
ISLAND

Yukon River

KUSKOKWIM MOUNTAINS

ALASKA RANGE

Mt. McKinley

Mt. Foraker

WRANGELL
MOUNTAINS

CANADA

BERING SEA

Matanuska River

CHUGACH
MTS.

Mt. St. Elias

NUNIVAK
ISLAND

Anchorage

Kuskokwim
Bay

Cook Inlet

KENAI MTS.

Seward

Malaspina
Glacier

KENAI PENINSULA

Juneau

Bristol Bay

ALASKA PENINSULA

ALEUTIAN RANGE

GULF OF ALASKA

CHICHAGOF
ISLAND

Kodiak

Sitka

KODIAK
ISLAND

BARANOF
ISLAND

Ketchikan

ATKA
ISLAND

AMLIA
ISLAND

UMNAK
ISLAND

UNIMAK
ISLAND

UNALASKA
ISLAND

SHUMAGIN
ISLANDS

PRINCE
OF WALES
ISLAND

PACIFIC OCEAN

ALASKA

ALASKA

In 1959, a young giant joined the Union: Alaska, the 49th state, nearly one-fifth the size of all the other states put together. Much that is typically Alaskan is on this same grand scale. The Malaspina Glacier— 1,248 square miles (3,232 square kilometers)—is larger than the whole state of Rhode Island. Mount McKinley, north of Anchorage, is the highest mountain in North America. It is 20,320 feet (6,194 meters) high. The Indians call Mount McKinley Denali ("home of the sun"), and they call a nearby 17,000-foot (5,100 m.) peak "Denali's wife." Even the "children," as the surrounding peaks are called, are over 10,000 feet (3,000 m.) high.

Alaskan farmers grow cabbages bigger than basketballs and delphiniums 9 feet (3 m.) tall. Alaskan sportsmen boast of the world's largest salmon, which may weigh as much as 100 pounds (45 kilograms); an Alaskan king crab may measure 6 feet (2 m.) from claw tip to claw tip. The world's biggest bears—brown, grizzly, and polar—reach weights of 1,600 pounds (725 kg.) and grow tall enough to peek into second-story windows, at least of small houses.

Tales about the new state also grow tall. Some people think of it as a vast refrigerator, with isolated prospectors and Eskimo shivering in igloos through eternal nights. Others regard it as a place to get rich quickly and easily. Alaska is not that simple. It is a place of variety and contrast, a state with four time zones and many different kinds of weather. Only about a quarter of the state lies above the Arctic Circle, and the Panhandle (the southeast) is no colder than most of the continental United States. As for getting rich, Alaska offers many opportunities, but exploiting them takes hard work, endurance, and imagination.

THE PEOPLE

Alaska is not only the biggest state of the United States, it is also the state with the fewest people. There are 300,000 residents; about 60,000 of them are Eskimo, Indian, and Aleut. The Eskimo and Aleuts live mostly in western Alaska, the Aleutian Islands, the western interior, and the coastal areas along the Arctic Ocean, the Bering Sea, and Bristol Bay. The Tlingit and Haida Indians live in villages scattered along the Panhandle.

Many of Alaska's Indian and Eskimo citizens now live in frame dwellings lit by electricity and equipped with indoor plumbing. Eskimo wear fur-lined parkas with a bright cotton print covering the outsides. On their feet they wear mukluks, with soles of *oogruk,* or sealskin, and uppers of hair-seal fur.

Most Alaskans are less isolated than the legends assume. Close to a third of the population of the state lives on the southern coast, within a 10-mile (16 kilometers) radius of Anchorage, the largest city. Many live in other coastal towns or around Fairbanks, the next biggest city. Alaska has more young people than other states, and many are newcomers, having arrived within the last 10 years. Alaskans tend to be vigorous, rugged, independent, and friendly people. They are people who love the outdoors and wilderness sports and who enjoy working hard to build free and spacious lives.

THE CLIMATE

The people of Alaska have good reason to live mostly on the state's southern coastal rim. Warmed by Pacific currents, this region has a climate not much different from Idaho's, except for the shortness of winter days and the great length of summer days.

From the central coast two long thin arms stretch out—the Panhandle to the southeast and the Alaska Peninsula and Aleutian Islands running far southwest. The Panhandle is a narrow strip of coast broken into islands and peninsulas, most of its communities having no direct transportation link with the rest of the state except by boat or plane. The main city of the Panhandle, Juneau, the state capital, is tucked into a tiny valley between mountains and sea. Juneau's climate is mild and extremely wet and foggy, with winter temperatures of about 20 degrees Fahrenheit (–7 degrees Celsius), summer temperatures in the 50's F. (10–15 degrees C.), and as much as 30 inches (76 centimeters) of rain in

FACTS AND FIGURES

ALASKA is the name of the state.

CAPITAL: Juneau.

MAJOR CITIES: Anchorage, Fairbanks, Juneau.

AREA: 586,412 sq. mi. (1,518,807 sq. km.).

POPULATION: 302,173, (1970 census).

PHYSICAL FEATURES: Highest point—Mount McKinley (20,320 ft.; 6,194 m.). Lowest point—sea level. Major rivers—Yukon, Kuskokwim. Major lakes—Iliamna, Becharof, Teshekpuk.

STATE MOTTO: none official.

Lush meadows and snowy mountain peaks are not unusual in Alaska.

a month. The southwestern arm, which consists of the Alaska Peninsula and the long Aleutian chain, is quite different. It is a wild, treeless land of volcanoes, glaciers, and fierce wildlife (including the Kodiak bears of Kodiak Island). In the Valley of Ten Thousand Smokes, on the peninsula, live volcanoes smolder and sometimes erupt. Alaska's giant wind, the williwaw, blows in gusts that may reach 90 miles (145 km.) an hour.

North of the coast in the interior is Alaska's heartland, a place of little rainfall and extreme temperatures—as low as –70 degrees F. (–57 degrees C.) in winter and as high as 100 degrees F. (38 degrees C.) in summer. The great Yukon River flows through the interior to the Bering Sea. In Fairbanks, the main city of the heartland, the midwinter sun appears only from 9:58 A.M. to 1:40 P.M. In summer, on the other hand, a major sports event is a midnight baseball game played without artificial lights.

North of the interior basin the Brooks Range extends across the state entirely above the Arctic Circle. The northernmost region, the Arctic Slope, stretches to the Arctic Ocean. This is the frozen north of storybook Alaska, where summer seldom brings more than 60 days between killing frosts, and the permafrost (permanently frozen grounds) has never been penetrated.

HISTORY

Although Alaska is new as a state, it has a fairly old history as a region. A map drawn in 1597, now in the National Museum in the Netherlands, has inspired various theories. One theory holds that Marco Polo, the famous Italian adventurer, heard of the land on his travels to China in the 13th century. Chinese coins found near Wrangell suggest that there may have been an Oriental colony in Alaska. But the first people to establish permanent Alaskan settlements were Russian traders about 1741. They explored the coast from the Aleutians to California, seeking furs. In the region the Indians called Alakshak ("great land") they did find a treasure of sea otter, which they could buy cheaply from the natives and sell to fur merchants in Peking. In this area, which they re-named Russian America, they founded their capital, New Archangel (later Sitka). It was a city of 1,000 people before there were 100 residents in San Francisco.

Alaska was a fierce frontier at that time, a place where many died of starvation, disease, and Indian raids. Many brave men struggled to acquire the new colony for Russia, including Vitus Bering (a Dane in the service of the Czar), Aleksandr Baranov, and Grigori Shelikhov. But Russians could not keep traders of other nations from poaching on their fur preserves, and the Russian Czar found his distant colony expensive to maintain. He wanted to dispose of it, and he preferred to have it belong to the United States rather than to one of his European rivals. Since the Secretary of State of the United States, William H. Seward, had visions of his country acquiring all of North America, he was delighted to learn of the Czar's intentions.

Negotiations began, at first in secret. When Seward's plan came to light, it raised a storm of disapproval from Congress and the press, who called Alaska Seward's Folly, Seward's Icebox, and Seward's Frog Pond. Seward persevered, and on October 18, 1867, officials ran the Stars and Stripes up the flagpole at Sitka. Congress delayed for a year before reluctantly appropriating the purchase price—$7,200,000, or about 2 cents an acre—an almost unbelievable real estate bargain. By 1906 more than $7,000,000 in gold alone had been sifted from the beach at Nome.

At the time of the purchase a century ago, fewer than 1,000 white men lived in Alaska. For 17 years Congress refused to provide Alaska with any government. However, in 1884 they made Alaska a district, with a governor, a judge, and a customs collector. The Alaskan gold rush, around the turn of the century, brought additional government services to the territory. A voteless delegate to Congress was provided in 1906. Six years later Alaskans were allowed to elect their own legislature, although Congress retained the right to veto its acts.

During World War II, when the Japanese occupied some of the Aleutian Islands, Americans woke up to the strategic importance of Alaska. The United States Government established a network of military installations in the territory. Wartime pressures also sped the completion in 1942 of the Alaska Highway, an overland route from the United States proper to Fairbanks. After the war, pioneers began to head for Alaska. In response to the demands of Alaskans for self-government, Alaska finally achieved statehood in 1959.

THE PRESENT AND THE FUTURE

Statehood heralded a new day for Alaska. Another influx of settlers trooped north to seek their fortunes, to homestead, to hunt, and to fish, as Americans discovered Alaska all over again.

Statehood meant that Alaskans were free to determine how their own natural resources would be developed. Oil, fish, timber, and tourism are Alaska's principal industries. Alaska is rising rapidly among

An oil well in northern Alaska brings new wealth to the state.

oil-producing states and could very well jump to first place when the new discoveries of oil on the Arctic Slope are put into production. The oil of the Arctic Slope has been described as the biggest single petroleum reservoir in the world.

Military and industrial installations in Alaska bring hoards of young men with husky appetites to the state, and it is expensive to transport food long distances. Many Alaskans have freezers, which they stock with the game they shoot. Alaska's waters provide gourmet delicacies, including salmon, halibut, crab, shrimp, and scallops. Hard-working pioneers have homesteaded farms in the Matanuska Valley near

A wood pulp mill in operation near Ketchikan in southern Alaska.
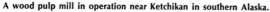

Part of Alaska's salmon fishing fleet at anchor in Juneau harbor.

Anchorage and the Tanana region around Fairbanks, where they produce milk, potatoes, eggs, cereals, and some oversized vegetables that
grow with amazing speed in the nearly continuous summer sunlight.
But high transportation costs also mean that Alaskan crops are usually
sold locally; therefore a boom harvest in Alaska could produce almost
useless surpluses.

One of Alaska's greatest attractions is its rugged unspoiled wilderness. Trophy hunters come from all over the world to stalk the great
bear, Dall sheep, goats, and bull moose, which may weigh 1,400 pounds
(634 kg). Tourists camp back into the mountains, take scenic boat trips
through the Inside Passage of the Panhandle, explore the fiords, fly over
the volcanoes, and marvel at the glaciers and peaks of the state. Some
find the escape from crowded, noisy urban life so appealing that they
never go home. Week-long sports carnivals are held in all major communities in both winter and summer.

The airplane has revolutionized Alaskan transportation. Alaskans fly
more than most other people. Many have private planes and have mastered bush-pilot skills necessary for flying in rough weather and landing
and taking off in rugged terrain.

Today Alaska is coming of age culturally as well as economically.
The state university, located at College, near Fairbanks, has community
college branches in each of the major towns. There are also two private
colleges: Alaska Methodist University, a 4-year liberal arts college in
Anchorage, and Sheldon Jackson Junior College in Sitka.

To Alaskans the future offers an exciting challenge and the opportunity to play an imaginative role in making this great northern empire
the brightest star in the Union. One and all, Alaskans are aware that it
is their special destiny to live on America's last frontier.

EVANGELINE ATWOOD, *Anchorage Daily Times*

CANADA

UNITED STATES

GREAT LAKES

Boston ★

Detroit • New York •
Chicago • Philadelphia •

Washington, D.C. ★

San Francisco-Oakland •

Los Angeles •

ATLANTIC
OCEAN

PACIFIC
OCEAN

Houston •

MEXICO

GULF OF MEXICO

UNITED STATES CITIES

When the American colonists came to the New World, they built towns in the wilderness. New England towns grew up around village greens lined by church, town hall, shops, and homes. Larger towns containing a few thousand people—such as Philadelphia, Newport, Boston, New York, and Charleston—developed as seaports on protected bays at the mouths of rivers. In a time when land transportation was difficult, these port cities became natural trade centers and hence focal points for social and cultural life.

Americans have always wanted elbowroom, escape from the restraints crowded living imposes. As the eastern seaboard became built-up, Americans migrated westward. Where fur trade was the main business, they built trading posts, usually at the junctions of rivers. Sometimes they took over posts and settlements, such as St. Louis, Detroit, Mobile, or New Orleans, that had been established earlier by the British and French. In the vast Middle West they laid out towns where few people lived but to which farmers from miles around came to buy and sell. In gold rush times they built mining villages and turned a sleepy Mexican town into the brawling port of San Francisco.

Industrialization and booming commerce in the late 19th century concentrated job opportunities in cities, with the result that the cities rapidly doubled and tripled in size. Big ports such as New York, Boston, and San Francisco served as portals for floods of immigrants from overseas.

The Expanding City. Unlike Europeans, most Americans have never considered the heart of the city a good place to live, even though it has been the choice of some of the wealthy, the sophisticated, and the artistic. Many people do not consider a dwelling to be a real home unless it is a separate house with a garden. This feeling has combined with affluence and mobility to help shape the exploding metropolis into a vast urban sprawl.

Today the population of the nation's suburbs actually exceeds that of its cities. Metropolitan regions have mushroomed, often merging with suburbs of neighboring cities. The largest "strip city," or megalopolis, runs from Boston to Washington, an area almost continuously built-up, with an average of 700 people per square mile (270 people per square kilometer). Along the Great Lakes and around San Francisco and Los Angeles, similar strip cities are forming. Los Angeles has a metropolitan region covering 4,069 square miles (10,539 square kilometers), with the city of Los Angeles itself occupying about one tenth of this.

Such "scatterization" results partly from the rapid increase of automobiles and also from the dispersal of factories and employment opportunities to outlying areas. People who still work downtown can live far from their jobs and drive into the city. This leads to hours of bumper-to-bumper freeway commuting and monumental downtown traffic jams.

Hardening of the urban arteries is only part of the trouble facing cities today. Many cities have critical water and air pollution problems. Population shifts also create difficulties, as poor people from rural areas

Independence Hall, Philadelphia, where the nation was born.

POPULATIONS* (based on 1970 census)			
Boston	641,071	New York	7,895,563
Chicago	3,366,957	Philadelphia	1,948,609
Detroit	1,511,482	San Francisco	715,674
Houston	1,232,802	Washington, D.C.	756,510
Los Angeles	2,816,061	* For areas within city limits.	

migrate to the central cities. Many of the newcomers are American Negroes or migrants from Latin America or the Caribbean. As whites move out to the suburbs, the population of some major cities has become more than 50 percent non-white, many of them poor and unemployed. Often they are badly in need of health and welfare services, and with so many middle-class taxpayers leaving for the suburbs, a number of cities have found themselves in severe financial straits.

The crisis of the cities has brought forth a flood of suggestions and governmental actions. Some urban planners question whether the heart failure of the cities can be cured by revitalizing the city core. Possibly the future will bring more decentralization. On the other hand, urban sprawl has its disadvantages too, for it uses up good farmland or forests or countryside.

Boston

Boston, one of the nation's oldest cities, has many buildings associated with the American Revolution. It is fairly easy to find these buildings and monuments by following the Freedom Trail pointers through Boston's downtown streets. The Old North Church, also called Christ Church, was used to signal Paul Revere that the British were coming, the signal being the glimmer of a lamp swinging in the church belfry. Old South Meetinghouse was the scene of many fiery pre-Revolutionary meetings, as was the somewhat smaller Faneuil Hall. The Old Statehouse served as British governmental headquarters in colonial days and later as the first statehouse of the Commonwealth of Massachusetts. Also, the house in which Paul Revere lived is still standing and is probably the oldest structure in the city, dating back all the way to about 1670.

These historical landmarks are only part of the rich architectural heritage of this historic city. The Beacon Hill section, in particular, is known for its fine residences. The gold-domed State House located in Beacon Hill was designed by the famous architect Charles Bulfinch in 1795. Beacon Street fronts on the Public Gardens, where visitors cruise lazily around a small, artificial lake in swan boats, and it also fronts on the Boston Common, which was the common pasture for livestock in colonial days. Handsome Copley Square, nearby, has two famous 19th-century structures, the Boston Public Library and Trinity Church.

For a long time a city ordinance restricted the height of any building in Boston to 125 feet (38 meters) or less. As a result, skyscrapers have been a fairly recent development in Boston. They now include the 52-story Prudential Tower. A huge new city hall, part of the new Government Center, lies in back of the Old Statehouse.

Boston has long been a noted medical center and the home base of many leading educational institutions, including Boston University, Northeastern University, the New England Conservatory, and Tufts University. Harvard University and Massachusetts Institute of Technology are located across the Charles River in the separate suburban city of Cambridge and have played a major role in the cultural life of Boston.

Chicago

Chicago is the largest city in the American Middle West and one of the leading industrial and commercial cities of the United States. Chicago was once a great center for stockyards and slaughterhouses, a pre-eminence the city no longer retains.

Chicago has been very much in the vanguard of creative urban architecture. It boasted the world's first skyscraper, the 10-story Home Insurance Building (1885–1931), designed by William Le Baron Jenney. Two of America's greatest architects, Louis Sullivan and Frank Lloyd Wright, did much of their best work in and around Chicago. Several of Sullivan's buildings still survive, including the famous Carson Pirie Scott department store in the Loop section of the city. Frank Lloyd Wright's Robie House (1909), one of his masterpieces of domestic design, has recently been spared from destruction. Since World War II several tall buildings of architectural distinction have been erected in Chicago, no-

Chicago's Sears Tower. At 1,454 feet (443 m.) it is the world's tallest building.

tably the Prudential Building, Marina Towers, and the John Hancock Center. In 1973 the Sears Tower was topped out at 1,454 feet (443 meters), making it the tallest building in the world.

Parts of the City. "Downtown" in Chicago means a relatively small area near the point where the Chicago River flows westward out of Lake Michigan. The heart of the downtown area is the Loop, so called because of the elevated railway that makes a loop, or circuit, around the area.

At the western edge of downtown Chicago, the Chicago River divides into a north and south branch, which separate at a wide angle. The area between the north branch and Lake Michigan is called the North Side; the area between the south branch and Lake Michigan is called the South Side; and the area between the two branches is called the West Side. The North Side is known for its private mansions, grand hotels, and luxury apartment houses. On the North Side are also located De Paul University, the Chicago Historical Society, and Wrigley Field, the baseball park of the Chicago Cubs. The West Side is largely an industrial and commercial section. The South Side, also an industrial section, is the home of most of Chicago's Negro population and also of large Polish, Lithuanian, and Czechoslovakian communities. The University of Chicago is also located on the South Side.

History.   The French explorers Jacques Marquette and Louis Jolliet visited the Chicago area in 1673. The first settler was Jean Baptiste Pointe Du Sable, a Negro, who established a fur-trading post on the Chicago River, then abandoned it in 1800. In 1803 Fort Dearborn was built by the United States Army on the south bank of the Chicago River, and a little settlement grew up around the fort.

Chicago (the name was based on the Indian name for the site) was incorporated as a town in 1833 and as a city in 1837. The city's early growth was spurred by the opening in 1848 of the Illinois and Michigan Canal linking Lake Michigan to the Mississippi River system. Beginning about 1850 railroads came to Chicago, providing an even greater impetus to growth. Chicago quickly became the biggest railroad junction in the nation, a pre-eminence it still retains today.

On October 8 and 9, 1871, the city was swept by a raging, wind-blown fire that destroyed almost all the downtown area. People from all over the world contributed toward the city's rebirth.

Detroit

Detroit, Michigan, is best-known as the headquarters of the American automobile industry. The country's three largest automobile manufacturers, General Motors, Ford, and Chrysler, all have big plants within the city limits or in its suburbs.

The city is situated on the west bank of the Detroit River, which actually is a connecting passage, or strait, between Lake St. Clair on the north and Lake Erie on the south. The city of Windsor is directly across the river, in Canada, and is connected to Detroit by bridge and tunnel. Aside from the various auto plants, Detroit has two main centers of activity. The 72-acre (29 hectares) Detroit Civic Center, located by the river, includes the City-County Building, housing local government offices; Cobo Hall and Convention Arena; and various other buildings and meeting places. The downtown section near the Civic Center is the city's central business, financial, and shopping area.

One of metropolitan Detroit's popular tourist attractions is located in suburban Dearborn, south of the city. It is the Henry Ford Museum and Greenfield Village State Historic Site. The Ford Museum has exhibits illustrating the history of the automotive industry. Greenfield Village includes early American buildings acquired and moved there through the efforts of Henry Ford.

History. A fort called Fort Ponchartrain du Détroit (*détroit* is the French word for "strait") was built on the river in 1701 by French soldiers and fur traders. The settlement was ceded to Great Britain in 1763, and the town was formally possessed by the United States in 1796. Detroit was incorporated as a city in 1806.

In the last half of the 19th century Detroit was noted for the manufacture of carriages and of machinery. The auto industry arrived with the opening of the first automobile factory in 1899. In 1900 the city's population was 285,000. By 1930 it had risen to more than 1,500,000.

Houston

Space City, U.S.A., is what the brash young city of Houston calls itself, and anyone who has seen men on the moon via television knows that the astronauts are directed from the Lyndon B. Johnson Space Center near Houston, Texas. Space flight is only the latest of many enterprises that have brought great prosperity and 1,000 new people each week to Houston, a prairie city that almost seems to be sprouting new skyscrapers each month.

Although it is 50 miles (80 km.) from the Gulf of Mexico, Houston is also one of the nation's largest seaports. The Houston Ship Channel makes the existence of this port possible at the center of an area bountiful in petroleum, gas, sulfur, salt, lime, cotton, rice, and cattle. Houston is the largest United States exporter of wheat, which is brought there by rail from the north. In the city and its surrounding area are one third of the nation's oil refineries; chemical plants producing half the nation's synthetic rubber and two thirds of its sulfur; as well as paper and cement factories, grain elevators, and shipyards.

Rice University and the University of Houston are the most noted of Houston's senior colleges. There are several museums, a symphony orchestra, and opera, ballet, and theatrical companies. Medical schools, hospitals, and research institutes make Houston a major medical research center.

Los Angeles

Roughly 50 miles (80 km.) long by 30 miles (54 km.) wide, Los Angeles seems to be the typical American small town spreading in all directions and then gashed with freeways to accommodate its awesome load of automobile traffic.

Los Angeles County contains more than 60 incorporated cities, some of which are completely surrounded by the City of Los Angeles. The perimeter of the city is therefore extremely irregular. A long, very narrow strip, for example, connects the rest of the city to Los Angeles Harbor. Without a map it is difficult to know where one municipality ends and another begins, for city and suburbs alike consist of street after street of one-family houses. Los Angeles County, too, blends into adjacent counties north and south—a huge metropolitan area that keeps expanding.

Downtown. But there are many centers of interest. One is the old downtown area, long dominated by the 32-story City Hall and partially decayed to slums. Rebuilding began in the early 1960's. By the 1970's 50- and 60-story skyscrapers were going up, and there were plans to revitalize the downtown area and provide a long-needed rapid transit system for the whole city. The business district, with large hotels, office buildings, and department stores, centers on Pershing Square, which has a large parking garage beneath it. The Music Center is the home of the Los Angeles Philharmonic Orchestra and has several stages for concerts, ballet, and musical comedies. New Chinatown and Little Tokyo have Oriental restaurants and curio shops. Olvera Street is a showcase for the city's Mexican-Spanish heritage, with colorful tile pavings, adobe buildings, Mexican restaurants, shops, and nightclubs. West of downtown on Wilshire Boulevard are the exclusive shops of the Miracle Mile.

Movies and Tourism. Los Angeles historically was a great producer of cattle and fruit. Today, ranches and orchards have been converted to housing developments, and Los Angeles' 17,000 factories make it the third greatest manufacturing area in the country. But the best-known product of the Los Angeles area is entertainment, especially movies. The first film was made in 1908, and Hollywood soon became the world capital of cinema. After World War II, when the motion picture industry was hard hit by television, the studios began producing films for television. Universal Studios in the San Fernando Valley is one of the city's most popular tourist attractions. Live television shows also originate in Hollywood and Burbank.

Tourism, inspired by the excellent climate, the lure of Hollywood, and the fine roads and other transportation facilities, is also a major industry. America's favorite entertainment complex is Disneyland, in suburban Anaheim. Marineland of the Pacific is an outstanding oceanarium. Hollywood Bowl is a natural amphitheater that has long attracted music

The Dorothy Chandler Pavilion, part of the Los Angeles Music Center.

lovers. The San Gabriel and San Bernardino mountains east of Los Angeles are used for skiing, hiking, camping, fishing; the many miles of Pacific Ocean beaches and bays for swimming, surfing, fishing, and boating.

New York City

Fun City is a nickname that was applied to New York City during a campaign for the mayoralty in the 1960's. New Yorkers, plagued by their city's many problems, may speak with sarcasm of "Fun City," but the fact is that over half of New York's 16,000,000 visitors each year come to the city "just for fun."

As a world capital of entertainment and culture, New York City is where American stage plays earn either fame or oblivion; where opera, ballet, symphony, painting, movies, and sculpture have their most appreciative, and most critical, audience. New York is also a center for television and radio and publishing. New York is the capital of American advertising, retailing, and wholesaling, as well as of stock trading and international finance. In thousands of small factories it manufactures clothing, machinery, electronics equipment, books, and food.

When the United Nations was established in New York after World War II, New York became also the capital of world diplomacy.

All Kinds of People.   Of the many kinds of people attracted to New York City, most have been the very poor, escaping harsh conditions elsewhere. To these the city has given hard work, a meager living, and a chance to improve their lot.

People with talent and ambition also flock to New York, for this is where they must make their mark to achieve national recognition. Many seek fame as writers, composers, painters, conductors, singers, or dancers. But while a few reach their goals, the majority work out their lives in secondary jobs.

Among the refugees from wars in Europe, especially during and after World War II, New York City gained many people with brilliant achievements in all the arts and sciences. They give New York an international outlook unique in America.

Ever since 1790, many of the constant stream of migrants to America have remained in New York, where they landed. About two thirds of the population, at most times, have been foreign-born or the children of immigrants.

When poor migrants arrived in large numbers from any single country, especially if they spoke a foreign language, they tended to settle together in areas where rents were low. Often they formed neighborhoods where most speech was in their native language. Some areas have been inhabited by successive nationalities. One example is Harlem, in upper Manhattan. Between 1889 and 1909, the majority of Harlem residents were German immigrants who were, in turn, followed by immigrant Irish. Around 1905, there was a drop in rents caused by overbuilding, and Negroes began moving in. By 1915 the Negroes constituted a sizable community. A section called Italian Harlem had developed by 1915, and after World War I there was Spanish Harlem. Negroes subsequently became the largest group in Harlem. By 1960 most of the Italians had left, and Spanish Harlem was much enlarged by Puerto Ricans.

City of Islands.   Three islands and a peninsula hold the five boroughs of New York City. Manhattan Island, which is also the Borough

New York's magnificent skyline as seen from Brooklyn across the East River.

of Manhattan, has the broad Hudson River on the west and the narrow Harlem River to the north. On the east is the swift-flowing East River. New York Harbor, one of the largest and busiest in the world, has been the main reason for the city's phenomenal growth.

Brooklyn and Queens, the two largest boroughs, share the western end of Long Island. Brooklyn was named for the town of Breukelen in the Netherlands. Queens was named for Catherine of Braganza, wife of King Charles II of England.

The Bronx is bounded by Westchester County, Long Island Sound, and the Hudson, Harlem, and East rivers. It was named for a Dane, Jonas Bronck, who obtained a land patent and started a farm there in 1639.

Staten Island was formerly known as the Borough of Richmond. Henry Hudson is said to have named it Staaten Eylandt in 1609, in honor of the Staaten, the governing body of the Netherlands. The former name, Richmond, comes from the Duke of Richmond, a son of Charles II.

Many Cities in One.   The typical visitor's New York is actually a very small part of the city—midtown Manhattan. Here are found the theater district, the great department stores, luxury shops, hotels, the United Nations, Lincoln Center for the Performing Arts, and Rockefeller Center, the Empire State Building, and other skyscrapers.

The casual visitor might leave midtown to visit various museums or Greenwich Village or Chinatown or the New York Stock Exchange on Wall Street or the twin towers of the World Trade Center or the Statue of Liberty on its island in New York Harbor. Greenwich Village, since about 1920 a haven for bohemian writers and artists, is now principally a tourist attraction with many restaurants, small shops, and off-Broadway theaters. Apartments there became increasingly expensive by about 1955, and the regularly renewed crop of bohemians drifted east toward Tompkins Square, an area that came to be known as the East Village. Chinatown centers around an 8-block district, where several thousand Chinese still live. The district has Chinese restaurants, stores, banks, cinema houses, and even pagoda-style telephone booths.

Except on his way to or from Manhattan, the average tourist gets to see little of the other boroughs. Aside from industrialized waterfront sections, most parts of Brooklyn, Queens, Staten Island, and the Bronx are residential, as is more than half of Manhattan.

Exploration and Settlement. The New York area was lightly populated by the Manhattan, Canarsie, and other Indian tribes before Europeans came. Giovanni da Verrazano, an Italian in the service of France, was the first European known to have seen Manhattan, in 1524. Henry Hudson, an Englishman sailing for the Dutch East India Company, explored the Hudson River in 1609 and returned with valuable furs.

In 1625 a tiny settlement of Netherlanders, called New Amsterdam, was founded on the southern tip of Manhattan. The next year the governor, Peter Minuit, bought Manhattan from the Canarsie Indians of Long Island for $24 worth of trade goods. The English seized the colony in 1664 and named it New York.

Philadelphia

Philadelphia, Pennsylvania, a major port city on the Delaware River, is perhaps best-known as the site of important buildings associated with the American Revolution and the founding of the United States. In the oldest section of the city, a few blocks from the Delaware River, stands Independence Hall, where the Declaration of Independence was signed in 1776. That document is now housed in the National Archives in Washington, but the Liberty Bell, which rang out the news of the signing of the Declaration of Independence, is still on view in Independence Hall. Nearby is Congress Hall, completed in 1789, where the Continental Congress met from 1790 to 1800, when Philadelphia was the capital of the United States. Two blocks away is Carpenter's Hall, where the First Continental Congress first met in 1774. And various other places of historic interest are right at hand, including the American Philosophical Society Building, one of whose founders was Benjamin Franklin; the Betsy Ross House; and the graveyard where Franklin and several other signers of the Declaration of Independence are buried. The restoration of the area around these historic buildings has been part of the city's urban renewal program.

About eight blocks west of Independence Hall, in the heart of downtown Philadelphia, is City Hall, topped by a statue of the city's founder, William Penn. At 548 feet (178 m.), City Hall is the tallest building in Philadelphia, and a city law decrees that it must remain so. Other points of interest in downtown Philadelphia are the Academy of Music, where the Philadelphia Orchestra performs; the Pennsylvania Academy of Fine Arts; and the Franklin Institute. The downtown area is notable for its handsome squares that date from the early days of the city.

At the western edge of the downtown section flows the Schuylkill River, which eventually enters the Delaware River in south Philadelphia. The University of Pennsylvania is across the Schuylkill River from the downtown section of the city. To the north is Fairmount Park, a natural wilderness of about 4,000 acres (1,625 hectares) that straddles the Schuylkill River. West of the park, and across the city line, is the "Main Line," a series of residential suburbs, known for its old, wealthy families.

History. The Philadelphia area was settled by a group of Swedes from New Sweden in Delaware in the 1640's. But the actual founding of the city and laying out of the streets dates from the arrival of William Penn and his fellow Quakers in 1682. The name Philadelphia, bestowed on the settlement by Penn, was a literal translation into Greek of "brotherly love." Philadelphia quickly became a haven for persecuted sects, including German Mennonites and Welsh Quakers.

By the time of the American Revolution, Philadelphia had become the largest city in the colonies. Although later surpassed in size by other cities, Philadelphia has always benefited from its strategic location, first as a port and later as a railroad and highway junction.

San Francisco

One of San Francisco's proudest traditions is its role as a haven for tradition-breakers. This means turbulence, which San Franciscans have a way of transforming into a city attraction. Early San Francisco flaunted its notorious Barbary Coast section, and today San Francisco remains a city of daring shows and glittering night life. In the 1950's rebels, artists, and writers of the Beat Generation staked out the North Beach section as their capital. Later the hippies took over the Haight-Ashbury section. While sober citizens protest, the city mostly treats its current "freaks" as it always has treated its tradition-breakers: it humors them and turns them into tourist attractions.

San Francisco is a mecca for people of many nations and backgrounds. The city is known for its Chinatown. On the Embarcadero, a broad street overlooking the waterfront, Italian fishermen mend their nets while their rich brothers run Fisherman's Wharf restaurants. The city also has sizable Irish, Jewish, Negro, and Latin American populations.

San Francisco is the taste of salt fog and wind, the sun glinting through eucalyptus in Golden Gate Park, the creaking of fishing boats lashed to the wharves. It is the majestic Golden Gate Bridge. San Francisco is cable cars crawling up incredibly steep slopes and homes seemingly stacked one on top of another. San Francisco is landmarks: the Mission Dolores and the Presidio, dating from Spanish colonial days; Portsmouth Square, the heart of town during the gold rush of 1849; Nob Hill, once the neighborhood of millionaires' mansions.

Above all, perhaps, San Francisco is a state of mind, a personality, a way of looking for the bright side of things. To San Franciscans the fog coiling over the hilltops is not bad weather, but a thing of ethereal beauty. San Franciscans are people who could look upon miles of city laid waste by the earthquake and fire of 1906, proclaim it the finest ruins ever, and set about at once rebuilding a lovelier city.

Washington

Washington, D.C., the nation's capital since 1800, is a spacious city with wide thoroughfares and famous buildings and monuments. It is bordered on three sides by the state of Maryland and on the fourth side is separated from Virginia by the Potomac River. Most government employees commute to Washington from Maryland and Virginia suburbs.

Washington was chosen as the site of the nation's capital in 1791, 9 years before the capital was actually moved there from Philadelphia. A French military engineer, Major Pierre Charles L'Enfant, who had served

The governmental heart of the nation: the Capitol in Washington.

the American cause in the Revolutionary War, was chosen by George Washington to plan the layout for the new city. L'Enfant made the Capitol, where Congress meets, the focal point of the city. Streets and avenues radiated from the Capitol to other focal points, where intersections formed squares or circles. That basic design prevails in Washington today.

Places of Interest. In back of the Capitol are the Supreme Court building and the Library of Congress. From the front of the Capitol a huge mall leads to the Washington Monument, beyond which lies the Lincoln Memorial with its reflecting pool. The tidal basin adjacent to the Washington Monument is known for the gorgeous flowering of its Japanese cherry trees in early spring. Across the basin from the monument is the Jefferson Memorial. The White House is about a mile up Pennsylvania Avenue from the Capitol.

Washington is also known for its outstanding museums. The Smithsonian Institution, a semi-private organization under the guardianship of the federal government, administers a number of museums of great renown. They include the Museum of Natural History, the Museum of History and Technology, the Freer Gallery of Art, and the National Gallery of Art. All these museums are located on the Mall. Not too far away is the Corcoran Gallery, with its great collection of American art.

Farther from the Mall, in northwest Washington, is the city's most picturesque residential area, Georgetown, a section of neat, bright-colored, three- and four-story houses. Georgetown is also the home of Georgetown University.

A number of points of interest are located outside the city. Mount Vernon, George Washington's home, is in nearby Virginia. So are the Pentagon, home of the nation's military establishment, and the Arlington National Cemetery, containing the graves of many American statesmen and of thousands of war veterans.

Reviewed by ROBERT SCOTT MILNE, Society of American Travel Writers

The gently rolling Green Mountains, part of the northern Appalachian range, rise above a peaceful Vermont farm.

APPALACHIAN MOUNTAINS

The dark, wooded ridges of the Appalachian Mountains, North America's oldest mountain range, have meant many things to Americans —challenge and fear, freedom and violence, great wealth and abject poverty. The Appalachians, North America's eastern mountain system, extend about 1,600 miles (2,600 kilometers) from the Gulf of St. Lawrence to central Alabama. They are not exceptionally high mountains. The highest mountain in the system, Mount Mitchell in North Carolina, is 6,684 feet (2,037 meters).

The Appalachians form a divide between streams destined for the Atlantic and those destined ultimately for the Gulf of Mexico. Rivers cutting through the range make natural gateways (water gaps) into the central valleys, which run from the Hudson Valley in New York south through Pennsylvania and Virginia. The northern Appalachians include New England's White Mountains, Green Mountains, and Berkshire Hills—noted for their summer homes, ski resorts, artists' colonies, and music festivals. New York's Adirondack and Catskill mountains— beautiful and popular resort areas—lie, for the most part, in the Appalachian range, too. Much of Pennsylvania lies within the Appalachians, and almost all of West Virginia. Farther south the Great Appalachian Valley separates the Blue Ridge Mountains on the east from the Allegheny Plateau on the west, which slopes into the Cumberland Plateau of Kentucky. To the southwest rise North Carolina's evergreen-covered Black Mountains, the highest portion of the Appalachians, and the Great Smokies of Tennessee and North Carolina.

The Frontier. By 1750 the hunger for land lured settlers and land speculators through the water gaps of the Appalachians into the fertile interior valleys, where only hunters and trappers had ventured before. New Englanders built cabins in the White and Green mountains. German immigrants, in many cases refugees from European wars, settled along the Mohawk and the Susquehanna and in other river valleys. American-born colonists, often of Scotch-Irish descent, spread into the Shenandoah Valley of Virginia and beyond. These were hardy people, usually poor, who were driven west by a fierce desire for farmland, open space, and freedom. In the south they were stopped by the forbidding Allegheny Front, and throughout the Alleghenies warring Indians and unfriendly French traders discouraged further expansion. However, in 1750 Thomas Walker, an American physician, soldier, and explorer, discovered the Cumberland Gap, a passageway through the mountains. In 1763 a British colonial victory in the French and Indian War removed another stumbling block to American expansion. Settlements spread rapidly in the Mohawk Valley and in Pennsylvania. In 1775 Daniel Boone blazed the Wilderness Road through the Cumberland Gap and into the game-rich wilderness that was to be known as Kentucky. By 1800 an estimated 300,000 had followed Boone's trail. During the 19th century most settlers who passed through the great barrier of the Appalachians chose to move on to the gentle farmlands of Ohio and the Midwest. However, the southern Appalachians, stretching from Pennsylvania to Alabama and forming the region sometimes called Appalachia, held a unique charm for those clannish and fiercely independent people who wished to stay, the true mountaineers.

Appalachia. In the 19th and early 20th centuries, railroads and industry reached Appalachia. Industrialists bought up mineral and timber rights in the area for tiny sums, since mountaineers knew little about cash values. Lumbering and mining, two of the first large enterprises brought into the region, were "boom and bust" activities. In good times, for instance, the coal mines employed thousands of men, changing mountaineers from farmers to miners. In bad times these men lost their jobs, and their used-up farms could provide them little support. The Depression of the 1930's brought widespread unemployment to the area. Unionization gave miners some security, and the need for coal created by World War II resulted in a brief new prosperity. In the 1940's strip and auger mining came to Appalachia. Operators considered these mining methods more economical because they employed fewer men than conventional coal mining, which involves the sinking of deep shafts at enormous expense. Bulldozers tore away miles of soil and vegetation in the advance of strip mining. As automation further increased unemployment, the region sank back into poverty. In the 1960's shocked Americans began to realize that Appalachia had become one of the nation's most badly depressed areas. The Area Redevelopment Act (1961) was the first of a series of federal measures aimed at rehabilitation of Appalachia.

Reviewed by HENRY J. WARMAN, School of Geography, Clark University

The Teton Range in Wyoming rises above the winding Snake River.

ROCKY MOUNTAINS

The Rocky Mountains are the backbone of North America. Forming a major part of the great North American cordillera, they stretch more than 3,000 miles (4,800 kilometers) from New Mexico to Alaska. At some points the range is as wide as 300 miles (480 km.).

From the sagebrush-covered mesas of Arizona and New Mexico, the land rises sharply upward to form the Southern Rockies of Utah, Colorado, and southern Wyoming. There are more than 50 peaks over 14,000 feet (4,300 meters) in the Rockies. All of them are in Colorado, where even some valleys are a mile (1.6 km.) above sea level. The Middle Rockies form the rugged country of central Wyoming. The Northern Rockies begin in Yellowstone National Park in the northwest corner of Wyoming and continue through Canada and Alaska to a point beyond the Arctic Circle. They include the Teton Range, the forested peaks of Montana, the Bitterroot Range of Idaho and Montana, and the spectacularly beautiful Canadian Rockies. The Canadian Rockies are in British Columbia, western Alberta, and the Yukon and Northwest Territories. The highest peak is 12,972-foot (3,954 m.) Mount Robson in British Columbia.

Conquering the Rockies

The men who first explored the gigantic stone wall of the Rockies were sure that there was a river flowing through the range to the Pacific. The Scottish explorer Alexander Mackenzie—who in 1793 became the first man to cross the continent north of Mexico—found no waterway. Nor did Meriwether Lewis and William Clark find a waterway when, in

1805, they struggled through Montana and Idaho to the mouth of the Columbia River in present-day Oregon. But some pioneers clung to the dream of a "Great River of the West" as late as the 1840's.

Another legend described the entire Rocky Mountain region as a vast desert, a place totally unfit for growing things. This story was spread by Zebulon Pike, the discoverer of Pike's Peak, and was circulated further by Stephen Long in 1820. It had some basis in fact, for much of the Rocky Mountain area is dry. However, it is by no means all desert country. There is adequate precipitation in the northern forests, in the alpine gorges, and on the highest mountain peaks.

The earliest settlers to face the severe water shortages of the Rocky Mountain country were the Mormons. Beginning in 1847, they conquered their stretch of desert land near the Great Salt Lake by creating marvels of irrigation. They provided a pattern of survival for later settlers in the region. The struggle for water in the Rockies has resulted in countless power dams, reservoirs, tunnels to divert streams through the mountains, and squabbles about water rights. Seven states battling over Colorado's water resources finally formed the Colorado River Compact in 1922; other states in the area have followed their example.

Gold in the Hills

Despite water shortages, the Rockies have been a source of wealth and adventure for many generations. The original wealth of the region was founded on the fur trade, especially beaver. From about 1820 through the early 1840's, bearded mountain men trapped along the wilderness streams of the United States and Canada, living off the land as the Indians did. Because they knew the wilderness so well, many of these mountain men and trappers became noted explorers, and others guided immigrants to Oregon and to California.

Gold was the next prize offered to the adventurous by the mountain country. By 1859 the gold fever that struck California in 1849 had spread to Nevada, Colorado, and Montana. Prospectors were not disappointed: over the past 100 years, the Rockies have yielded more than $34,000,000,000 worth of gold, silver, copper, lead, and other metals. In the 1950's, history was repeated when the needs of nuclear research sent uranium prospectors scurrying over the Rockies with Geiger counters.

In the 1870's and 1880's cattlemen were lured to the Rocky Mountain country by an almost limitless range for their herds. Their adventures provided the ingredients for America's favorite story—the Western.

Today's Treasures

For people of today, the great treasure of the Rocky Mountains may well be the same savage wilderness that killed many early settlers. People now go west to escape civilization, to fish in mountain streams, to hunt elk, or to pack along trails in country that looks much as it must have looked to Lewis and Clark. In the United States, vacationers throng Yellowstone Park, first of the national parks, which was founded in 1872, and other parks, including Grand Teton, Rocky Mountain, Mesa Verde, Glacier, Grand Canyon, Bryce Canyon, and Zion. In Canada, visitors are thrilled by the majestic scenery of many national parks, including Banff and Jasper in Alberta, and Kootenay and Yoho in British Columbia.

Reviewed by HENRY J. WARMAN, School of Geography, Clark University

MISSISSIPPI RIVER

MINNESOTA
Lake Itasca
Falls of
St. Anthony
WISCONSIN
St. Paul
Minneapolis
Madison
IOWA
Des Moines
Keokuk
Dam
Nauvoo
Hannibal
Springfield
ILLINOIS
St. Louis
MISSOURI
Cairo
KENTUCKY
TENNESSEE
ARKANSAS
Memphis
Little Rock
Greenville
MISSISSIPPI
Vicksburg
Jackson
Natchez
LOUISIANA
Baton Rouge
Lake Pontchartrain
New Orleans
Mississippi Sound
Breton Sound
Mississippi Delta
GULF OF MEXICO

MISSISSIPPI RIVER

The Mississippi River, called the Father of Waters, begins as a brook a boy can step across. The river's headwaters in the Minnesota forest near Lake Itasca were unknown until an American, Henry Schoolcraft, surveyed the region in 1832. The lower river was sighted in 1541 by Hernando de Soto, a Spanish explorer.

The white man's attempt to conquer the Mississippi really began in 1673, when two Frenchmen, Louis Jolliet and Father Jacques Marquette, discovered the upper Mississippi, and another Frenchman, Robert Cavelier, Sieur de La Salle, explored the river from Illinois to the Gulf of Mexico. In 1682 La Salle claimed all of the Louisiana Territory—a vast stretch of land lying to the east and west of the river—for France.

For many years the northern reaches of the Mississippi bore the canoes of French fur traders. French outposts were built to the south—including a fort at Natchez and a village at New Orleans. However, in 1763 France was defeated in war and lost the rich territory east of the Mississippi to Britain. France also gave up its lands west of the Mississippi —and the city of New Orleans—to Spain. Although the Louisiana Territory had been restored to French rule by 1801, Napoleon I, the ruler of France, considered Louisiana a liability in his continuing war with Britain. Rather than risk losing the territory to Britain, he agreed, in 1803, to sell it to the United States. The Americans called the event the Louisiana Purchase. The Mississippi had become an American river.

The Mississippi River is 2,350 miles (3,780 kilometers) long. It also has hundreds of tributaries: 31 states and parts of Canada are drained by the Mississippi River system. The main tributaries—the Illinois, Missouri, Ohio, Arkansas, and Red rivers—are important in their own right. The combined Missouri-Mississippi river system is one of the world's longest waterways. It is nearly 4,000 miles (6,400 km.) long. The sands of Montana and Pennsylvania mingle in the almost 1-mile-wide (1.6 km.) stream that loops between the levees (man-made earth or concrete riverbanks), on its way to the Mississippi Delta and the Gulf of Mexico.

A ferry crosses the Mississippi near Baton Rouge, Louisiana.

The Upper River

Even today the headwaters of the Mississippi are in wilderness country—a little creek winding through the lakes, wildlife preserves, and swamps of Minnesota and northern Wisconsin. These forests were once the frontier of fur traders and loggers. Timber felled by Scandinavian lumberjacks was assembled on the upper river into log rafts that often measured many thousands of square feet. These were then guided downstream to market. In 1823 the first lumber mill was built on the Mississippi at the Falls of St. Anthony, now in Minneapolis. Below the falls, the Mississippi winds through St. Paul into a deep gorge.

Steamboat Country

From the head of navigation at St. Paul and Minneapolis, the river flows south to St. Louis between sandstone bluffs and around wooded islands. This is the river of Indian legends and steamboat lore. In the 1820's lead mines on its Wisconsin and Illinois tributaries lured miners into the area. They built some of the earliest frontier outposts. Today the river separates Wisconsin dairy land and Illinois farms on the east from the rich grain and livestock lands of southern Minnesota, Iowa, and Missouri on the west. It passes through Nauvoo, Illinois, the Mormon settlement that briefly—in 1841—was one of the river's largest cities. It touches Hannibal, Missouri, the boyhood home of Samuel Clemens, once a steamboat pilot. Under the pen name of Mark Twain, he immortalized life on the river in his famous books *The Adventures of Tom Sawyer, Life on the Mississippi,* and *The Adventures of Huckleberry Finn.* Just above the great modern city of St. Louis, the muddy Missouri River (sometimes called the Big Muddy) enters the Mississippi from the west, doubling the size of the stream. Then, at Cairo, Illinois—a town wedged between rivers and guarded by levees—the Ohio enters from the east, and the Mississippi becomes the mighty "Old Man River" of the South, the Mississippi of story, legend, and song.

Old Man River

Now, instead of flowing below bluffs, the river rides high above its floodplains, confined by levees.

Because there is more high ground on the east bank of the Mississippi than on the west bank, more early settlements developed in Tennessee and Mississippi than in Arkansas and Louisiana. The river passes through Memphis, Tennessee, an important cotton market and the place where the blues were born; through Vicksburg, Mississippi, the scene of a crucial battle of the Civil War; and on to Natchez, where the cotton-plantation culture of the South reached its peak. The river then flows through Baton Rouge, Louisiana, a river port that can be reached by oceangoing vessels. At New Orleans, with its romantic French and Creole past, the legendary Mississippi Delta country of Louisiana begins. About 100 miles (160 km.) from the Gulf of Mexico, the slowing stream begins to deposit soil, yearly adding more land to Louisiana. Finally, the river splits into many "passes," or channels, leading out into the Gulf. Here, among tropical swamps and bayous, rises a great steel forest of oil rigs, the symbol of the great petroleum wealth of the modern delta.

River Traffic

Before the 1840's the Mississippi was a barrier to the east–west expansion of the United States, although the north–south river traffic was a major asset in the country's early development. Freight was first moved on the river on rafts and keelboats. By 1823 steamboat service had been introduced. For the next 40 years the paddle-wheel steamboat was king on the Mississippi and its navigable tributaries. It bore the riches of the southern and central United States to market—at the rate of 10,000,000 tons a year at the height of the steamboat era—and made New Orleans one of the world's largest ports. The spread of railroads after the Civil War caused the decline of river traffic, but during World War I its value was rediscovered. Today barges are lashed together to form huge rafts—often more than 1,300 feet (400 meters) long—which are pushed by powerful diesel vessels called towboats.

Taming the River

The Mississippi would not remain navigable without great engineering feats of dredging and channel maintenance. Engineers have harnessed the river to produce electrical power at the Falls of St. Anthony, Keokuk Dam, and other power-dam sites. But the main thrust of the engineering effort has been to tame the monster that the river can become in flood time. In 1927 a flood killed several hundred people, swept away houses and barns, and in some places widened the river temporarily to 80 miles (130 km.). The Flood Control Act of 1928 was passed as a result of this disaster. Floodways and giant levees were built. But in 1937, despite the new safeguards, the greatest flood in recorded history covered the towns and cities of the Mississippi River and its tributaries with a raging sea.

The battle of men against the river goes on as increasingly effective flood-control systems are developed. People who live on the riverbanks have grown accustomed to the constant shifting of the river. But they continue to hope that the Father of Waters may one day become a safe neighbor.

Reviewed by HENRY J. WARMAN, School of Geography, Clark University

Cathedral of the Assumption, Mexico's largest cathedral.

MEXICO

A colorful tile in a Mexico City restaurant proclaims: "Christian by the grace of God; gentlemen thanks to our Spanish descent; noble lords from our Indian ancestry—we are, then, the Mexicans."

With characteristic Mexican flair, the motto points to the blending of contrasting elements that is the essence of Mexico. Out of a population of about 50,000,000 people, only a tiny percentage are wholly white. Twenty to 25 percent of the population are pure Indian. The remaining vast majority of Mexicans are mestizo, people of mixed Indian and Spanish blood. Although Spanish (spiced with some Indian words) is the national language of Mexico, about 50 Indian languages are still spoken, including Otomi, Tarascan, Zapotec, Mixtec, Mayan, and Nahuatl, the tongue of the Aztecs. Approximately 1,000,000 Indians speak only their own Indian language and know no Spanish at all. About 96 percent of the population is Roman Catholic. However, the Mexican Constitution requires strict separation of Church and State, and the government has at times been bitterly anti-clerical.

Mexico is the only nation in North America with a history that goes back far beyond Columbus. The distance from the modern skyscrapers of Mexico City to primitive Indian villages in the remote parts of Mexico can be measured in centuries as well as in miles. There is an even sharper

contrast between the heated swimming pools, exquisite furnishings, and lush garden patios of the wealthy Mexican businessmen's homes and the tin-can hovels of the city slums or the one-room, thatched adobe shacks of the small farmers. In principle, Mexico is an egalitarian nation, a country where all men are equal under the law. But the vast majority of people still live as primitively as their ancestors did. This is a situation that the government is desperately trying to change through a wide range of economic and political programs.

THE LAND AND THE ECONOMY

The traditional strength, persistence, and endurance of the Mexican farmer come, in part, from the fact that his land is mainly parched deserts and rugged mountains and offers relatively little acreage suitable for farming. He has always had to struggle to raise his crops. Only about 8 percent of the land is under cultivation. Mexico does not really have any equivalent of the amazingly productive Corn Belt that occupies the heartland of the United States or the Wheat Belt that occupies the vast spaces of the Canadian West. Mexico's heartland is the Central Plateau, a region similar geographically to the relatively unproductive plateau sections of the United States Southwest and Rocky Mountain regions.

The Central Plateau. The northern part of the Central Plateau, from the United States border to the vicinity of San Luis Potosí, is generally too dry to be cultivated without irrigation. The southern part of the plateau is generally higher, gets more rainfall, and is more productive. This southern part of the Central Plateau, extending roughly from San Luis Potosí on the north to Guadalajara on the west to the general vicinity of Mexico City, is the richest and most populous part of the country, containing about half of Mexico's total population. Conditions here are generally favorable for agriculture, but even here the yield of the Mexican farmer's favorite crop—corn—is still far less than in the Corn Belt in the United States.

Within the heartland the most developed region is the Valley of Mexico, where Mexico City is located. This is a valley within the larger plateau, a valley thousands of feet above sea level. Fifty miles (80 kilometers) long and 40 miles (64 km.) wide, the Valley of Mexico has mod-

---

FACTS AND FIGURES

THE UNITED MEXICAN STATES—Estados Unidos Mexicanos—is the official name of the country.

CAPITAL: Mexico City.

LOCATION: Southern North America. **Latitude**—14° N to 32° 43′ N. **Longitude**—86° 47′ W to 117° 07′ W.

AREA: 761,602 sq. mi. (1,972,549 sq. km.).

PHYSICAL FEATURES: Highest point—Pico de Orizaba (18,700 ft.; 5,700 m.). **Lowest point**—sea level. **Chief rivers**—Rio Grande (Río Bravo), Santiago, Río de las Balsas, Usumacinta, Pánuco. **Major lakes**—Chapala, Cuitzeo, Pátzcuaro, Laguna Salada.

POPULATION: 49,000,000 (estimate).

LANGUAGE: Spanish (official), Indian languages.

RELIGION: Roman Catholic.

GOVERNMENT: Republic. **Head of government**—president. **Legislature**—senate, chamber of deputies. **International co-operation**—United Nations, Organization of American States (OAS), Latin American Free Trade Association (LAFTA).

CHIEF CITIES: Mexico City, Guadalajara, Monterrey, Puebla, Mérida, Veracruz, Tampico, Cuernavaca, Acapulco, Taxco.

ECONOMY: Chief minerals—silver, iron, petroleum, zinc, lead, sulfur, copper, antimony, coal, gold, manganese, mercury, tin. **Chief agricultural products**—corn, beans, wheat, sugarcane, coffee, cotton, oranges, tomatoes, tobacco, henequen. **Industries and products**—mining, petroleum, drilling and refining, fishing, textiles, cigars and cigarettes. **Chief exports**—silver, lead, zinc, copper, sulfur, cotton, coffee, wheat, shrimp, sugar, corn. **Chief imports**—machinery, electrical appliances, motor vehicles, wool, paper, railway equipment.

MONETARY UNIT: Peso.

NATIONAL HOLIDAY: September 16, Independence Day.

NATIONAL ANTHEM: *Himno Nacional de México* (National Hymn of Mexico).

Ixtacihuatl, a dormant volcano, looms over farmers at their work.

erate rainfall and crisp, sunny, springlike weather all year round. Since ancient times it has been the busiest center of Mexican life. Today, crisscrossed by modern superhighways, the Valley of Mexico has become the center for bustling industrial complexes at Tlalnepantla and other cities. The communities clustering in the valley are rapidly gaining population. Their delightful weather and rapid modernization make them a mecca for tourists.

Mountains. On the east, west, and south, the Central Plateau is hemmed in by three great mountain ranges, all of which are called Sierra Madre. The Sierra Madre Oriental (Eastern Sierras) is probably a southern extension of the Rocky Mountains of the United States. The Sierra Madre Occidental (Western Sierras) is probably the Mexican extension of California's Sierra Nevada. A little below Mexico City these two great ranges come together in a spectacular jumble of enormous volcanic cones. These include the Pico de Orizaba, which at 18,700 feet (5,700 meters), is the third highest mountain in North America, and the fabled snow-clad peaks of Popocatepetl (Smoking Mountain) and Ixtacihuatl (Sleeping Woman), both of which can be seen from Mexico City. South of this volcanic zone, which contains some volcanoes that are still active, is the Sierra Madre del Sur (Southern Sierras), which extends down to the Isthmus of Tehuantepec, separated from the Pacific Ocean by a narrow plain.

Coast, Desert, Jungles.   The great central region of plateau and mountains is rimmed by coastal plains on the east and west, by desert on the northwest, and by jungles on the south.

In the east, the Gulf coastal plain extends all the way from the Texas border to the Yucatán Peninsula. The northern half of the plain is warm and semiarid, and the southern half is wet and clothed in jungles. People have tended to avoid both extremes by clustering in the middle, in the general vicinity of Veracruz. The port of Veracruz also serves as an important outlet for the products of the Central Plateau. The Gulf coastal plain, like its counterpart in the United States, has substantial oil fields, which also are concentrated in the state of Veracruz.

In the west, the coastal plain is much narrower than the Gulf coastal plain and also not as well developed. The northwestern corner of Mexico is occupied by the Sonora desert. In the extreme west is the long, narrow finger of Baja California (Lower California), separated from the mainland by the Gulf of California. Baja California is mountainous, barren, and sparsely populated, although some of its remote fishing villages attract the more adventurous of tourists.

In the south the mountains give way to the low-lying areas of the Isthmus of Tehuantepec. Constituting about two thirds of the isthmus, these low-lying regions consist mainly of swampland and jungle. High rainfall and a hot climate are conducive to the cultivation of sugarcane, bananas, and coconuts. Sap from the *chicozapote*, or sapodilla tree, is

Coastal area of Baja California.

Tiny villages along tidal inlets are a common sight in Yucatán.

collected for the manufacture of chicle for chewing gum. Fish are abundant, and there is oil in Tabasco state. Tabasco's principal city, Villahermosa, is the site of great archeological finds.

The Yucatán Peninsula, with its awesome Maya-Toltec ruins at Chichén Itzá, is another rewarding region for archeologists. Yucatán is formed of very porous limestone rocks, which filter the rainwater and form underground lakes. Wells cut to reach them are the only source of water for the people. The land is not well suited to farming. Sisal fibers harvested from henequen, a plant that can live on these inhospitable plains, are the basis of the economy. Mérida is the main city. The coast of the eastern part of the peninsula, the territory of Quintana Roo, is covered with tropical rain forests. Coral banks surround the peninsula. The islands of Cozumel and Mujeres lie off the coast on the Caribbean side.

Tierra Caliente, Templada, Fría.   Since all of Mexico is either tropical or subtropical, the climate would be almost universally hot if it were not for the mountains. In general, the higher one goes in Mexico, the cooler it gets, even if one is going from north to south. Usually, too, rainfall tends to increase with altitude, even though there are low coastal areas in Mexico—the southern part of the Gulf coastal plain, for example —which are extremely rainy.

The Spaniards, recognizing the importance of mountains to climate

"Tierra caliente": village of San Blas, state of Nayarit, on the west coast.

"Tierra templada": cornfield in the state of Guerrero.

in Latin America, distinguished three altitudinal zones and gave them names that are still used today. *Tierra caliente*—"warm (or hot) land"—includes regions from sea level to 2,000–3,000 feet (600–900 m.). Where there is enough rainfall, as along the southern part of the Gulf coastal plain, heat-loving crops, such as tobacco, sugarcane, sisal, coffee, and bananas, can be grown. But much of the *tierra caliente* in Mexico, such as the Sonora desert in the northwestern part of the country, is too dry for farming, except in rare areas where irrigation can be provided.

At higher altitudes, about 3,000–8,000 feet (900–2,400 m.), is *tierra templada*—"temperate land"—where most of Mexico's good agricultural areas are found. *Tierra templada* comprises the Central Plateau and the intermediate slopes of the various mountain ranges. The average temperatures for January and for July may be only 10 to 15 degrees apart. Mexico City's mean temperature in January is 57 degrees Fahrenheit (14 degrees Celsius), and its mean temperature for July is 63 degrees F. (17 degrees C.); Puebla's January mean is 60 degrees F. (16 degrees C.) and its July mean 63 degrees F. (17 degrees C.); Guadalajara's mean temperature for July is 69 degrees F. (21 degrees C.), and for January it is 60 degrees F. (16 degrees C.). In *tierra templada* there is extensive cultivation of the maguey, or century plant, from which the popular Mexican drinks pulque and tequila are made. Wheat and beans are grown in these regions, and most extensively planted of all is maize (corn), even though optimum conditions do not exist for maize cultivation, summer temperatures actually being a little too cool.

As the land rises above 8,000 or 9,000 feet (2,400–2,700 m.), average temperatures get lower, and there is frost. This is *tierra fría*—"cool (or cold) land"—which above 10,000 feet (3,000 m.) is virtually uninhabited.

Farmers Against the Odds

In all, only about 8 percent of Mexico's total land area is cultivated. But about half the people are farmers. In the United States, on the other hand, less than 5 percent of the population are farmers, even though the percentage of land under cultivation is twice that of Mexico's. One of the basic problems facing Mexico is simply that too many are still trying to earn a living from the land.

At the same time, there is no doubt that the situation of the average Mexican peasant has improved substantially in this century. In 1900, almost 80 percent of the people toiled on the land, and almost all the land was included in great estates called haciendas, owned by a small minority of wealthy Mexicans. Today much of that land has been redistributed either to peasant communes called ejidos or to individual peasant smallholders. Mexican agriculture as a whole has become more productive. Irrigation projects in the north have turned that part of the country into a great cotton-producing area. As a result, Mexico now produces enough cotton not only for its own needs but for substantial foreign export as well. Also, research, training, and federal assistance programs have brought about a general improvement in agricultural methods and in average crop yields. Much remains to be done, however, just to keep pace with the food needs of Mexico's population, which has been increasing at a rate of more than 3 percent a year.

Mexico, then, is faced with this dilemma: it must continue to increase its agricultural production but must do it with fewer farmers.

Bales of raw cotton, Mexico's major export, crowd the docks in Tampico.

Irrigating the land on a small farm in central Mexico.

Actually this is less contradictory than it sounds because the key to increased production lies in replacing the age-old, inefficient farming methods of the peasant with modern, efficient machine agriculture. But the rural Mexican has an almost mystical love for his land. Although urbanization has been progressing rapidly, it is not always a satisfactory answer for the villager whose roots are deep in the community where his ancestors lived.

Mineral Resources

Although agriculture remains the heart of the Mexican economy, Mexico is perhaps more generously endowed with mineral wealth than with agricultural wealth. Mineral wealth, in fact, has been largely responsible for the rapid development of Mexico's economy in this century. And, in the more distant past, it was primarily gold and silver that attracted the Spanish conquerors to Mexico in the first place.

By far the most valuable source of mineral wealth in Mexico today is petroleum. Oil is found in small but rich fields along the Gulf coastal plain, particularly around Tuxpan, in the state of Veracruz, where the largest oil fields are located. Tampico, farther up the coast, is Mexico's principal center for oil refining. Most oil, however, is pumped into tankers in crude form for export, principally to the United States. It is a commentary on the level of Mexico's industrial development that, although it has an abundance of crude oil, it has to import refined petroleum products back from the United States. Mexico's refineries are not adequate for the nation's domestic needs.

Next to petroleum, Mexico's leading minerals, in terms of total value of production, are zinc, copper, and silver. Mexico leads all nations in the production of silver. The nation's biggest mining regions are the northern part of the Central Plateau and the Sierra Madre Occidental.

Industrialization

In large part, Mexico's drive toward an improved standard of living depends on the development of manufacturing industries. Industrialization helps get poor farmers off the land and into more productive work. Workers earn money and thus help create a demand for more manufactured goods, which in turn creates more jobs and industries to produce those goods. And so it goes, in an upward spiral.

Today, Mexico still has to import many vital and costly manufactured products from the United States and other advanced industrial nations. These goods include automobiles and automobile parts, as well as all kinds of machinery for farming, mining, and manufacturing. The country is still not nearly so self-sufficient industrially as its leaders want it to be. But manufacturing has advanced to the point where it contributes considerably more to the national economy than does agriculture. Mexican industrialization received its first big push during World War II, when there was a worldwide shortage of manufactured goods. Even so, as late as the middle 1950's, the agricultural part of the economy accounted for more of the gross national product than the manufacturing part. Today this is no longer true.

The largest industry in terms of employment is textiles. Mexico produces enough cotton textiles for its own needs, but it still has to import some textile machinery and machinery parts from the United States and other nations. Other major industrial products are iron and steel, chemicals, petrochemicals, electrical machinery, glass, and paper.

The Government's Economic Role. In Mexico, the government oversees the growth of the economy and also owns and operates a number of important industries. Petróleos Mexicanos (PEMEX), is the government oil monopoly. The government runs the nation's main railway and telegraph system and owns a majority interest in the private concern that provides over 95 percent of Mexico's telephone service. Also, the production of petrochemicals (chemicals obtained from petroleum and natural gas) is reserved for the government through PEMEX or other state-owned enterprises. Through the state development bank, Nacional Financiera, S. A., the government has part ownership of a large group of enterprises, producing iron and steel, foodstuffs, pulp and paper, industrial chemicals (including fertilizers), coal and coke, railway cars, automobiles, textile machinery, seamless steel pipe. The government

These men work in a tractor engine plant near Mexico City.

Acapulco is one of Mexico's great tourist attractions.

Indian crafts, another popular tourist item.

has also been stressing the Mexicanization of industry. Majority Mexican control is required by law in many fields of economic activity ranging from mining and transportation to soft drink bottling.

Mexico has its vigorous private enterprise sector, too. In fact, privately owned enterprises contribute considerably more to the gross national product than publicly owned enterprises. One of the major reasons for government ownership of industries is to stimulate the growth of private industries. For example, government investments in electrical plants or refineries provide important sources of power for the development of new industry by private investors.

Over and above its direct ownership of vital industries, the government oversees the development of the economy as a whole. It fashions the policies that seek to increase private investment without sacrificing the public interest and to attract money from United States investors without letting them dominate the economy. (Americans, in fact, own a far smaller share of Mexico's economy than of Canada's.) Mexico is a prime example of a nation committed neither to capitalism nor to socialism but simply to whatever works best. The ideal, certainly, is to combine the best elements of capitalism and socialism—capitalist drive and initiative with socialism's concern for the public interest. The result for Mexico over the past few decades has been one of the highest continuous rates of growth for any developing country in the world.

Tourism

Another important aspect of the Mexican economy is tourism. The American dollars that tourists bring into Mexico are important in balancing off the dollars Mexico has to pay for vital manufactured imports. Mexico has about 2,000,000 visitors a year, 90 percent of whom come from the United States.

One important factor in the growth of tourism in Mexico is the development of good transportation facilities. The Pan-American Highway, which runs down through South America, has connecting branches in all major parts of Mexico. Jet airports are located in Mexico City, Acapulco, and other cities. There is also excellent intercity bus service. Improved transportation and the building of modern hotels have, in the course of the past few decades, made life considerably more comfortable for the growing number of tourists who visit this nation every year. For the United States citizen, Mexico is the nearest large country with a truly foreign flavor. In the big cities, improved sanitation has vastly reduced the risk of "turista" or, as it is also known, "Montezuma's revenge," the intestinal disorder that attacks travelers who eat unwashed fruit or drink unboiled water.

Mexican handicrafts also play their part in the tourist trade. Creating objects of beauty is for Mexicans both recreation and a means of earning extra pesos. Mexicans are famous for their folk arts and handicrafts, especially in rural areas, where each village may specialize in particular articles, such as sarapes, pottery, baskets, masks, sleeping mats, wooden bowls, jewelry, and household articles of unique Indian design. Making them is often a sociable community project, and selling them to other villagers at the market is as much a festive social occasion as a business venture. The eagerness of tourists to acquire beautiful handmade objects is an increasingly important source of income for rural artisans

Statue of Columbus at an intersection of Mexico City's Paseo de la Reforma.

CITIES

Visitors who come to cities like Mexico City or Monterrey expecting to find quaint, sleepy towns will be disappointed. The hectic rhythms of modern city life have largely destroyed the peaceful world of Old Mexico —a world where a craftsman could devote a lifetime to the creation of toys or lovingly crafted household items. Many people still live in villages and small towns, where Indian and colonial styles merge, interspersed with an occasional Coca-Cola stand or gas station. But Mexico has thirty or more cities with populations over 100,000. More than half the people of Mexico today live in urban places, and every year the size of the urban majority grows.

Mexico City. The sparkling glass-and-concrete towers of Mexico City, their murals ablaze with Aztec motifs, seem to bring together the fierce strength of Mexico's Indian past and the powerful thrust into the future that is modern Mexico.

Mexico City—known simply as Mexico to the Mexicans—dominates this country as no single city dominates the United States or Canada. About 6,000,000 people (approximately one Mexican in eight) live in Mexico City and the surrounding Federal District. More than a third of the nation's manufactures are produced there.

The oldest and the newest meet in this metropolis of the cool, sunlit Valley of Mexico, where Aztec ruins stand side by side with colonial churches and modern high-rise apartment buildings. Like any great city, Mexico is a place of contrasts. It is fringed by terrible slums but also by luxurious suburbs. There are narrow, twisting alleys and beautiful park-like avenues, noisy city markets and sophisticated shops.

Mexico City is built on the ruins of the Aztec capital Tenochtitlán. The original Aztec city was located on an island in Lake Texcoco. Over the centuries much of the original lake has been drained away, and only a remnant remains, located a few miles east of the city. The city's skyscrapers stand on the mud flats of the ancient lake. Buildings sometimes have developed cracks as they slowly settled into the soft ground, a problem architects have only recently learned to solve. Most newer buildings in Mexico City are built to rest on huge concrete caissons that "float" on the soft ground. This type of construction prevents sinking and also lessens the danger of earthquake damage.

The heart of the old Spanish section of the city is the Zócalo, or, as it is also called, la Plaza de la Constitución. Here the Spaniards erected the magnificent Cathedral of the Assumption, on the site of a demolished

Balloon vendor in Chapultepec Park, where presidents of Mexico once lived.

The celebrated Shrine of the Virgin of Guadalupe is just outside Mexico City.

Aztec temple to the god of war. The National Palace, the main building of the Mexican Government, and other government buildings are also located in the Zócalo.

Westward from the Zócalo, on the broad expanse of the Avenida Juárez, stands the 44-story Latin American tower, which is one of the tallest buildings in Latin America. The Avenida Juárez leads to the Alameda, a beautiful park built in the 16th century on the site of an old Aztec marketplace. At one end of the park is the Palace of Fine Arts, which houses, in addition to art galleries, the National Symphony and philharmonic orchestras, facilities for ballet, theater, and opera, and the National Institute of Fine Arts. Three blocks from the Alameda park, the Avenida Juárez runs into the Paseo de la Reforma, a broad boulevard 300 feet (90 m.) wide, 9 miles (14 km.) long, lined with trees and adorned with historic monuments. The Paseo de la Reforma, one of the most beautiful boulevards in the world, is lined with modern office buildings, fashionable boutiques, embassies, hotels, and restaurants. It extends through the gardens and woods of famous Chapultepec Park with its historical and archeological museums.

The areas outside the city limits also boast many sites of interest. University City, the campus of the University of Mexico, rivals any university campus in the world for sheer architectural beauty. In another suburb the visitor may glide in a flower-decked boat between the floating islands of Xochimilco, where many centuries ago the Aztecs planted flowers on earth-covered reed rafts that became anchored by the roots of tropical plants and eucalyptus trees. Thirty miles (48 km.) from Mexico City is Teotihuacán, an ancient sacred city that contains ruins more than 2,000 years old. The ancient capital of the Toltec Indians, Tula de Allende, is about 45 miles (72 km.) north of the city.

Closer to home, a 15-minute drive from the heart of Mexico City, is the Shrine of the Virgin of Guadalupe, Patroness of Mexico. The shrine is built in the very place where, according to tradition, an Indian named Juan Diego first had a vision of the dark Madonna on December 9, 1531. Three days later in a second appearance she told Juan Diego to pick flowers and take them to the bishop. When he presented them as instructed, the roses fell out of his cape and there appeared suddenly on the cape the painted image of the Lady.

Other Cities. In the mountain valleys south of Mexico City are the picturesque colonial cities of **Taxco**, its narrow streets lined with the shops of silver craftsmen, and **Cuernavaca**, city of gardens, its renowned Cortes Palace glowing with murals by the famous contemporary Mexican artist Diego Rivera. Cuernavaca and Taxco are favorite stopping places for tourists on their way from Mexico City to **Acapulco**. Overlooking the sunny Pacific, Acapulco is the queen of pleasure cities, with lavish nightclubs and luxury hotels.

Guadalajara, northwest of Mexico City, is the nation's second largest

Market in Guadalajara: can supermarkets ever match this?

city, now boasting a population of more than 1,000,000. Rapidly indus- trializing, it has become a major producer of leather goods, glass, pottery, and tequila. Guadalajara is the site of a cathedral dating from the 16th century and of two universities.

Monterrey, the nation's third largest city, is the leading metropolis of northern Mexico. Monterrey, the steel and iron capital of the land, is a powerful, modern industrial center—hot, dusty, and americanized. Mon- terrey also has a large number of breweries, flour mills, and textile plants. Monterrey Institute of Technology and Higher Education, a private, co- educational institution, is located there. Modeled after the Massachusetts Institute of Technology in the United States, the institute has under- graduate and graduate divisions as well as a summer program for students from the United States.

Mexico's two leading ports, **Tampico** and **Veracruz**, are both located on the Gulf coast. Tampico is important for its oil refineries as well as for its shipping. Veracruz, to the south, has been Mexico's major port

Veracruz, Spain's first Mexican settlement. The harbor is in the background.

since the Spanish explorer Cortes landed there in 1519. Veracruz is the chief outlet for the southern Mexico plateau, the most developed part of the country. It also has rail connections to the southern Sierras and to the Isthmus of Tehuantepec and thus draws on the products of a variety of regions. Chief exports from Veracruz are silver and other metals, coffee, bananas, and handicraft products. Major imports include automobiles, machinery, hardware, textiles, and foodstuffs.

Other Mexican cities are known for cultural, artistic, or archeological reasons. **Puebla**, southeast of Mexico City, one of the nation's leading textile centers, is also famous for the beautiful tiles it produces. **Oaxaca** is noted for its coffee, its black earthenware pottery, and its nearness to the archeological marvels of Monte Albán. **Mérida**, the largest city of the Yucatán Peninsula, is located near the Mayan sacred cities of Chichén Itzá and Uxmal, fascinating to archeologists and tourists alike.

WAY OF LIFE

As Mexico moves forward with the rest of the world, new customs slowly come into being. Inevitably the Mexican way of life is influenced by the United States. The modern world makes its incursions, yet an older, deeper heritage remains, too. It is, in fact, the oldest national heritage in North America, for only in Mexico did the conquering European find a civilization in many ways equal to his own. Canada and the United States were vast wildernesses with scattered primitive tribes. In Mexico, the Spaniards found a people who had built great cities and whose society had evolved over centuries. The Spaniards conquered the Indians, but Indian culture survived. The two civilizations—Spanish and Indian—melded together into a Mexican culture.

Religion and Festivals

Even the practice of Roman Catholicism, the nation's dominant religion, is imbued with Indian influences. The Virgin Mary, invoked in Mexico as the Virgin of Guadalupe, is depicted as brown-skinned in pictures and statues. The same is true for the saints of the Catholic Church, who are often venerated in rites resembling the ancient religious rites of Mexico's native Indian peoples.

The saints are a central part of the average Mexican's life. Each person is baptized with a saint's name. Towns, as well as crafts and professions, have patron saints. The calendar is filled with feast days dedicated to the saints. On his feast day the statue of a town's patron saint is often carried around the village at the head of a noisy parade while people throw coins in the basket beside it. They honor the saint with fireworks, the playing of mariachi bands (consisting of stringed instruments, cornets, and gourd rattles), and pageantry. The pageant may include costumed men re-enacting Spanish historical events, such as the Spaniards battling the Moors. Folk dancers carry religious banners, but the aim, as in Aztec times, is to induce the spiritual powers to bring rain for the crops and to protect them from the hazards of fate.

Special festivals mark Holy Week, the Christmas season, and All Souls' Day. On Holy Saturday, before Easter, the traitor Judas Iscariot is burned in effigy. He is represented by a cardboard monster garlanded in firecrackers that Mexican boys ignite with glee, shouting as the enemy explodes and goes up in flames.

Breaking the piñata.

During the 9 days before Christmas, groups called *posadas* (the Spanish word for "inns") commemorate the wanderings of the Holy Family. They knock at a door, ask in song to be admitted, and are refused. The ritual is repeated until they reach a house, decided on in advance, that does admit them. The high point of the evening is the breaking of the piñata, a hanging earthenware or papier-mâché figure gaily decorated and filled with fruits, candy, and toys. Blindfolded, the children take turns striking at it with a broomstick until finally someone breaks it. A cascade of surprises falls out amid flying scraps of pottery, and everyone scrambles for the treasure. All this is accompanied by Christmas carols, painted silvery snow scenes, and "Nativities," miniature representations in clay of Christ's birth in the manger. Families invest much imagination and even money they can ill afford to set up a Nativity scene.

All Souls' Day, November 2, is dedicated to the memory of the dead,

Entertainment in Mexico can be a bullfight, like this one in Mexico City.

Dancers in the state of Veracruz. Dancing is another popular recreation.

Market provides an occasion for socializing as well as buying and selling.

and so it is also called the Day of the Dead. Cities and towns are decked with the yellow flowers offered to the deceased—flowers still known by the Indian name *zempazuchitl*.

The Day of the Dead is not a mournful occasion. It expresses certain uniquely Mexican attitudes toward death, especially a macabre humor. Children devour sugar skeletons with phosphorescent eyes and common names like Maria, Concha, or Lupe inscribed on their foreheads. Toy skeletons execute frantic dances on wires or move their jaws to the accompaniment of wild outbursts of laughter. On church altars covered with gay tissue paper, worshipers place sweets and bread for the hungry in the other world, a survival of an ancient Indian belief that the immortal soul of the deceased still craves creature comforts. Cemeteries have more visitors than on any other day of the year and look almost like gypsy camps. In spite of certain solemn manifestations and much visiting of churches, the Day of the Dead is a time of gluttony and of hidden passions breaking out. The men, picnicking among the gravestones, toasting the departed in fiery tequila, consider themselves released from the strict code of behavior that governs everyday actions.

Perhaps the most exciting festival takes place on September 16, when Mexicans celebrate the anniversary of the first uprising against Spain in 1810. Fireworks are made up in frames, called castles, strung with luminous figures. When they are set off, they look like incandescent kaleidoscopes spinning in the night air. Children play with toys of tissue paper or cardboard. These are fragile, meant only for the celebration, and rarely outlast the carnival period. What is characteristically Mexican about them is the creative talent and loving artistry that go into the making of them. It is almost as if the craftsman enjoys creating them more than the children enjoy playing with them. Like all Mexican carnivals, the days that commemorate revolutionary heroes are marked by tremendous noise, mariachi music, firecrackers, and much festive trading at the market in the plaza, where people from miles around gather to display their goods for sale.

Today, fiestas still have a strong hold in rural areas. But in the cities, old traditions have been diluted as Mexico enters the modern age. Although no one could oppose modernization, Mexicans are sometimes seized with nostalgia when they think of the simplicity of old customs and their magic way of revealing beauty and creating high moments of community joy.

This Indian woman still makes tortillas much as her ancestors did.

Cooking

The waning of tradition threatens also to spread to the art of cooking, as hot dog and Coca-Cola stands begin to crowd the tamale vendors in the plaza.

Mexican cooking began with the Indians, who had developed an impressively varied diet before the Spanish conquerers arrived in the 16th century. The Indians gave the world about 40 foods that were unknown before the Conquest, including maize (corn), squash, sweet potatoes, avocados, peppers, many kinds of beans, vanilla, chile, chocolate, and tomatoes. Maize was the Indian's staff of life, from which they made tortillas, huge flat cornmeal pancakes about a foot wide. Tortillas are still the bread of Mexico. The Indians varied their vegetable diet with wild game, turkeys, and small dogs that were bred especially to be eaten. Chocolate was used to spice game dishes, or mixed with cornmeal and hot peppers to make a fiery drink. The cacao beans from which it came were also a form of currency.

Though the Indian foods were highly original, they could hardly match the sumptuous dishes that mestizo genius contributed in colonial times. The Spaniards brought many additions, including lard, beef, cheese, and onions. In palaces and convents the complicated national menu took shape, a mixture of these foreign ingredients with the Indian foods. Nuns toiled over dishes to please the bishop, and palace cooks devoted all their ingenuity to winning the approval of court ladies. Recipes for the resultant masterpieces were printed in books with engraved covers to grace the libraries of powerful Spaniards.

Vendor of "chicharrones," or fried pork rinds.

One of Mexico's most famous dishes today, mole, is allegedly the creation of a 16th-century nun. Mole is a concoction of turkey or chicken with a sauce of bitter chocolate, nuts, and various hot spices. Complex dishes using chocolate, parsley, Mexican tea, peanuts, vanilla, tomatoes, and omelets of corn fattened the friars and viceroys, while the Indian who grew everything got along on his traditional beans, chile, and tortillas. But new creations were rare after the 19th century.

Popular among Mexican foods today are tacos and enchiladas, both of which consist of meat, chicken, or cheese rolled in tortillas. Tacos have a crisp outside, while enchiladas are softer and are covered with chile sauce. Tamales, another popular dish, are corn dumplings filled with seasoned meat and other ingredients and steamed in corn husks. Quesadillas are a kind of corn-meal turnover filled with cheese, meat, or even squash blossoms and fried in lard. But food is rapidly becoming internationalized, and city restaurants in Mexico now provide the standard dishes of many other lands.

New Social Trends

Change is coming also to the traditional preparers of food, the women. But it comes slowly, and the high-status career woman is still a rarity. Before the Revolution of 1910, which laid the basis for the present Mexican state, the only work the Mexican woman did outside the home was in convents, where she might do some teaching or nursing. Co-education was looked on with disfavor. The coddled upper-class señorita might have private lessons, but she was expected to be mainly "ornamental," an object of romance. Since the Revolution, changes have come slowly, and today more and more women are entering the working world as office workers, teachers, professionals, and civil servants. Women have had full political rights in Mexico since 1953. Women's organizations work effectively on problems relating to health, welfare, nutrition, and unwed mothers.

But winning legal rights is not always the same as achieving full equality. By tradition, submission is characteristic of Mexican women. Among the poor and uneducated the cult of *machismo* has flourished. *Machismo* is a kind of belligerent pride in manliness that has developed over centuries among Latin American men in general. In part, *machismo* expresses the extraordinary importance Mexicans attach to pure physical courage, an importance reflected in the great popularity of bullfighting in Mexico. But *machismo* is also an expression of frustration. A man who dares not raise his voice at work to protest injustice may relieve his feelings at home by shouting at his wife and daughters and maintaining arbitrary dictatorship over them. *Machismo* justifies him in spending his miserable wage drinking at the cantina, neglecting his dependents. It inspires mocking disdain for tenderness and human life. In large part, *machismo* is a reaction to hardships he feels powerless to alter.

Today, however, social reforms are beginning to give the Mexican man a chance to hope that he really can improve his lot. Information from the outside world and the rapid spread of education are beginning to free the humble Mexican home from *machismo*—to free men from their despair and women from complete control by men.

Education. The most fundamental agent of change is education. Before the Revolution of 1910, nearly 80 percent of the Mexican people could neither read nor write. Illiteracy is now down to about 30 percent and dropping fast. Free and compulsory education for all was an essential principle of the revolution and was embodied in Article 3 of the Constitution of 1917, which also provides for the separation of schools from Church control.

Education got a special boost from President Manuel Ávilo Camacho's all-out attack on illiteracy, starting in 1944. He asked every literate Mexican to teach another Mexican to read and write, with the result that 700,000 became newly literate in the first year of the campaign. Minister Jaime Torres Bodet, who launched the project, later undertook an 11-year program aimed at giving Mexico all the schools and teachers it needed—a herculean task, for the nation's population increases by about 3.5 percent a year.

Education of all children up to the age of 15 is required by law in Mexico today. However, a survey in the 1960's showed that while 6,000,000 children were in school, another 3,000,000 were not, because of a shortage of schools. Heroic efforts are being made to remedy this, and school classrooms have been built recently at a rate of one every 90 minutes. One ingenious device is the prefabricated school, which villagers themselves can erect under the guidance of a federal engineer. Prefabricated schools are a great source of pride in many a small village today. At one time, the rural Mexican resented the invading schoolteacher, but today his attitude has changed completely, and he now demands a proper school for his children, even if he still may see no reason why he should not sometimes keep a daughter home to tend the babies or a son to help harvest the corn.

The secretary of public education co-ordinates the activities of federal, state, local, and municipal agencies. According to recent statistics, the federal educational budget averages well over $1,000,000 a day, and states contribute additional funds. The National Commission for Free Distribution of Books tries to supply sufficient free textbooks to all elementary schools.

Pre-school education is provided in kindergartens that give children their first contact with the real world outside their homes. Elementary schools concentrate on "the three R's." When the young Mexican knows how to read and write, he can then begin to learn the history of his country and many other subjects as well. Mexico also has training schools, which provide excellent vocational training on a slightly lower level than the professional training offered by the nation's universities. These special vocational schools include normal schools to train teachers, technical institutes, and agricultural schools where students learn the new farming methods that are rapidly increasing the nation's agricultural output.

The University of Mexico is the nation's foremost institution of higher learning. Founded in 1551, it is the oldest university in North America. Today about 100,000 students, paying very low tuition, are studying in the University of Mexico to become the scientists, lawyers, doctors, and artists of Mexico's future. The university's modern campus, completed in 1954 in the suburb of Mexico City called University City, is one of the architectural marvels of the world, with its superb modernistic buildings and its magnificent murals by Mexico's leading artists. And today the university's academic prestige has begun to equal its archi-

Students at the Monterrey Institute of Technology and Higher Education.

This famous mural by Siqueiros adorns a building of the University of Mexico.

tectural reputation. One of the bulwarks of this growing scholarly excellence is the fact that academic freedom in Mexico is guaranteed by law.

Flowering of the Arts

In addition to the great boost it gave to education, the Revolution of 1910 produced a brilliant flowering of artistic activity. Mexican art burst into bloom like a sudden blaze of poinsettias against a gray mission wall. This is the period when Mexican muralists moved the entire world with their bold use of color and sensual design. In keeping with the great revolution that had changed all of Mexican life, they depicted Indians with sympathy and produced biting caricatures of wicked foreigners. Their art, springing from pre-Columbian roots, looms as monumental, as flamboyant, and sometimes as fierce and forbidding as ancient Indian idols and temple carvings.

Like their ancestors, post-revolutionary artists believed art was for the people and for the expression of the nation's passionate beliefs. Unlike their ancestors, their art was no longer devoted to a pantheon of idols but was channeled now into faith in the Revolution. So they

One of Diego Rivera's many celebrated murals, National Palace, Mexico City.

sought popular, historical, and social themes, and their genius was almost entirely devoted to decorating public places and transforming buildings into objects of beauty.

The big three of the revival of Mexican art were Diego Rivera, José Clemente Orozco, and David Alfaro Siqueiros. Among them, Rivera stands out for his great imagination and fidelity to the origins of the people. Like the others, he felt that "only a work of art can elevate the taste of the masses." With full government support but tiny wages, he covered the walls of the Secretariat of Public Education, the National Agricultural School, the National Palace, and other public buildings with a glowing documentation of his country's struggle. Orozco's gaunt masses overwhelming their oppressors and Siqueiros' heroic farmers battling aristocratic army officers express the same themes.

Today, though Mexican painting remains mostly in the fresco tradition, it is no longer devoted solely to social significance. Mayan and other native themes still appear, but the art itself is international. Rufino Tamayo, Juan Soriano, and José Luis Cuevas seek, as Cuevas puts it, "...broad highways heading out to the rest of the world rather than narrow trails connecting one adobe village with another." They are not simply "Mexican" artists, but brilliant members of the world's art community.

Tamayo, a descendant of the Zapotec Indians, is a fantastic colorist and a bitter enemy of the "social realism" school, with its emphasis on political and social themes. Comfortable about being Mexican, he is no chauvinist and does not adopt slogans for his subjects. In his work he takes apart reality and recreates it in startling oil paintings that seem to be bathed in light. The monumental architecture and mosaic art of Juan O'Gorman, exemplified in the striking library building of the University of Mexico, also combines pre-Columbian motifs with a spirit that is of the future even more than of the present.

Modern Music and Literature.   In the public mind the pre-eminence of fresco and architecture tends to overshadow the great achievements of Mexicans in other art forms. The folk spirit of Mexican music finds expression in composers like Carlos Chavez and dancers like Amalia Hernandez. Achievements in the field of philosophy include the works of Samuel Ramos, author of *Profile of Man and Culture in Mexico,* in which Ramos analyzes forces in the life and mind of his country. Octavio Paz is another author who has delved with insight into the question of the Mexican national character.

In the field of literature, Alfonso Reyes (1889-1959) personifies the man of letters and represents the virtues of a great humanist. His far-ranging intellectual curiosity has brought him a lasting and well-deserved prestige. Among contemporary Mexican novelists mention must be made first of all of Mariano Azuela, because of his contribution in the field of the revolutionary novel. His novel, *Los de Abajo (The Underdogs)* is notable for its clean-cut style, its acute psychological observations, and its sharp delineation of customs and manners. Azuela is one of Mexico's most frequently translated authors. But it is Agustín Yáñez, with novels such as his much acclaimed *Al Filo Del Auga (Edge of the Storm)* who brings us, through his sharp and condensed characterizations, signs of a new style of novel, a novel that no longer describes manners and customs but reflects the complex inner problems of man.

Ancient monument to the rain god Tlaloc, anthropological museum, Mexico City.

Toward the beginning of the 1950's, two outstanding prose artists appeared. One is Juan José Arreola, an intellectual who in a detailed style traces diagrams of a complicated world of the imagination. The other, Juan Rulfo, writes of the native misfortune in language that borders on magic. Somewhat later, Carlos Fuentes, Sergio Galindo, and Gustavo Sainz emerged as important novelists.

As for Mexican verse, the modern poets who stand out include José Gorostiza, Carlos Pellicer, and Xavier Villaurrutia. Gorostiza wrote his impressive poem *Muerte Sin Fin (Death Without End)* in the late 1930's. Another major poet, Octavio Paz, uses surrealist imagery.

In the theatre, the names of Emilio Carballido and Sergio Magaña, come immediately to mind as modern playwrights of undoubted creative vitality.

All of these literary achievements in the theater, poetry, novel, and essay point to an increasingly complex, stimulating, and mature body of work.

ANCIENT MEXICO

Time and modern man have destroyed much of pre-Columbian Mexico. A veil of mystery separates the modern Mexican from his ancient culture, though he may speak one of the tribal dialects and grind his maize on metates, or milling stones, as his ancestors did before the birth of Christ. Many puzzles are unsolved, and research is constantly changing the interpretation of data. Study of the amazing Mayan civilization is still hampered by inability to understand their hieroglyphics.

Most scholars believe the Indians migrated from Asia across the Bering Strait about 30,000 years ago, spreading southward until they peopled both North and South America. They were hunter-gatherers who had mastered fire and the art of chipping flints for stone weapons, but little else. Eventually the Indians reached Mexico. There, beginning about 5,000 B.C., they gradually moved from gathering wild plants to growing their own food plants, thus taking the first crucial step toward civilization, the cultivation of maize. As farmers they had to settle down in one spot and study the seasons. In time this led to property rights, mathematics, the calendar, and a complex ritual designed to win the favor of the gods so that the harvest would prosper. A priestly caste, temples, and idols evolved.

Before 1000 B.C., ceramic vessels and graceful figurines began appearing in what is now Mexico. These were buried with the dead in accordance with the belief that the surviving spirits wanted food and beautiful objects. Towns developed. By then tools, pottery, and agricultural techniques such as irrigation had already come into wide use.

One of the ancient peoples of Mexico was the Olmecs, whose influence appeared in southern Mexico around 1000 B.C. Theirs was a magician culture. The Olmecs were people of mysterious rites and frightening idols, worshipers of a god half-human, half-jaguar, perhaps a rain or fertility deity. They were fine artisans, particularly fond of jade, and they knew how to process rubber and fibers, including cotton. The great moon-faced, Buddhalike carvings of the Olmecs date from this era. They have been found mainly in the present-day states of Veracruz and Tabasco.

Mexico's Classic Period. During the preclassic period (650 B.C.–A.D. 150) the Valley of Mexico became densely populated, and a priestly caste came to power. The priests created stable governments and built temple cities.

Several of Mexico's archeological marvels, undertaken in this preclassic period, were brought to peak splendor in the classic period (A.D. 150–900). One is the Zapotec center, **Monte Albán**, in Oaxaca. It is the earliest known archeological site in Mexico, where written numbers and carved stone calendars with hieroglyphic writing have been found. Another architectural marvel was the **Cholula Pyramid**, near Puebla. It is bigger, overall, than Egypt's Great Pyramid. The grandest undertaking of all was the ceremonial city of **Teotihuacán** in the Valley of Mexico, which at its peak may have had 100,000 inhabitants. Its Sun Pyramid was second in size only to Cholula Pyramid. Teotihuacán also contained the temples of the rain god Tlaloc and the plumed serpent Quetzalcoatl; a Moon Pyramid; and a Temple of Agriculture, intricately decorated with flower and shell designs. These monumental structures were erected by people who had not developed the wheel or metal tools and who did not have beasts of burden. Teotihuacán's trade influence extended as far as what is now Guatemala.

During the classic period, Mexico's Golden Age, the Mayan peoples of the Yucatán Peninsula and Isthmus of Tehuantepec developed a high civilization which included superb architecture, astronomy, the concept of "zero," hieroglyphic writing and record-keeping on stone pillars (stelae), and a calendar more accurate than Europe's. The calendar is still in use today among Maya and determines times for planting, harvesting, and religious holidays. The Maya also produced sculpture that shows an original vision and profound religious sensibility. The famous English art critic Roger Fry has drawn attention to a similarity between Mayan

This pyramid was part of the Mayan city Uxmal, in Yucatán, built about A.D. 1000.

and Hindu sculpture. He asserts Mayan work is more stylized and artistically superior.

In the same period, in central Mexico, the Teotihuacáns, Mixtecs, Tarascos, Zapotecs, and others built well-planned cities served by drains and aqueducts and graced by temples, pyramids, markets, and ball courts. The ball courts were probably used for ceremonial games. Losing a game was a sign that the player had lost favor with the gods and was to be sacrificed to appease them.

Toltecs. The classic period began its decline with the downfall of Teotihuacán around A.D. 750. The city may have been sacked or may simply have gone bankrupt. As temple cities were abandoned, their people migrated. Towns became isolated. The interaction between them that had sparked progress no longer took place. Into the power vacuum of this "dark age" came warriors from the north, the Toltecs, who began their expansion around 900. They were the vanguard of a group of peoples that spoke the Nahuatl language, a group that included the Aztecs. New tribes always adopted some of the ways of the people they invaded, and the Toltecs fell heir to classic Teotihuacán culture. They played an important role in the evolution of myths surrounding a major Teotihuacán diety, Quetzalcoatl.

Quetzalcoatl was the Plumed Serpent, able to crawl and fly—a benevolent creator-god who taught farming and the arts, who demanded highly moral behavior, and forbade human sacrifice. In the polytheistic

Indian religion, gods took on the characteristics that social needs dictated, so Quetzalcoatl meant different things to different tribes. To some, such as the Olmecs, he was a manifestation of the morning star, Venus. To the Aztecs, he was a savior-deity embodied in a human figure.

In the 10th century a Toltec chieftain-priest, also named Quetzalcoatl, tried to get his people to follow the god's humane code. But the banning of human sacrifice seemed a heresy because of the belief that the gods were nourished on human blood. Unless they were fed they would perish and so would the universe. Chief Quetzalcoatl was betrayed and fled into exile. The legend arose that he would return in the year Ce-Acatl, a year in the Aztec calendar relating to the appearance of Venus as the morning star. In the Aztec calendar, the year Ce-Acatl fell in the years 1363, 1467, and 1519. In time people confused the priest with the god himself, who was supposed to be blonde and bearded. Thus, when the bearded, fair-skinned Cortes appeared in the year Ce-Acatl (1519), many believed this marked the god's return.

Around A.D. 1000 the Toltecs extended their power southward from the Valley of Mexico to the Mayan centers in Yucatán. The Maya were said to have sheltered the exiled Quetzalcoatl. Revenge for this may have motivated the attacks of the warrior Toltecs on the peace-oriented Maya. Chichén Itzá, a major city in Mayan country, shows great Toltec influence.

By 1500, wars had torn the Yucatán society apart. By this time, too, conflicts between pro- and anti-Quetzalcoatl factions had weakened the Toltecs and broken their control of subject tribes.

Aztecs.   The Nahua tribes, the last to arrive in the Mexican highlands, inherited the extensive cultural complex of the region. One of these tribes was the Mexica-Aztecs, or Aztecs. At first the Aztecs were an upstart tribe battling on the fringes of the territory. They were followers of a bloodthirsty warrior god, Huitzilopochtli. During their wanderings as outsiders the Aztecs were sometimes reduced to dressing in plant leaves and eating insects. But adversity toughened them and eventually they became politically and militarily the best-organized society in central Mexico.

In about 1325 the Aztecs came to the spot where Mexico City now stands. It was then a complex of marshy lakes and little islands. On an island in Lake Texcoco the Aztecs are reputed to have seen an eagle with a serpent in his mouth perched on a cactus. Seeing this as a magical omen, the priests declared the island had been chosen for the Aztecs by their gods. Upon it they built Tenochtitlán. They extended their city by making rafts of interlaced twigs and reeds covered with soil and plants. In time the vegetation took root in the shallow lake bottom and anchored the islands. The city was divided into four neighborhoods and crossed by water canals where small boats loaded with fruits and vegetables passed on their way to market. Three causeways connected Tenochtitlán to the mainland. By the time of the Conquest (1519) the city was a dazzling Venice of plazas, temples, and floating gardens.

The Aztecs were not innovators and had little to offer culturally except in military matters. But in the 2 centuries after the founding of their city, they combined the superior cultures of the established civilizations around them and remnants of classic culture. They subdued their neighbors by armed might, and eventually their dominion reached as far north as San Luis Potosí and southward to Mayan territory.

Fishermen with butterfly nets on Lake Pátzcuaro, where Indian kings vacationed.

Aztec society was rigidly divided into classes. The priest-warrior caste was at the top, and slaves were at the bottom. In between were the free worker-artisan class and, slightly higher, the merchant class. The latter traveled among neighboring tribes and served as spies. The least offense against these merchants was severely punished by the army. Subject tribes had to pay tribute to the Aztecs in the form of gold, jewelry, slaves, cacao, maize, beans, and other products, so that everything drained into Tenochtitlán, making it splendid at the expense of other peoples.

The center of commercial activity was the *tianguis,* a very active market held in a huge central plaza. Lumber, household goods, pots, mats, obsidian knives, pheasants and other game, foodstuffs, and cotton dresses were paid for with various currencies, which included shells or luxury feathers, or cartridges filled with ground cacao or gold.

Among the crops grown by the Aztecs was the maguey, or century plant, such an all-purpose supplier that the Spaniards called it the Indians' "green cow." The leaves of the maguey were used as fibers for cloth or thatch to roof adobe houses. Its center yielded pulque, an intoxicating liquor, which contributed to the decline of groups using it too freely. (Pulque, incidentally, is still a very popular drink in Mexico.) The thorns of maguey could be pulled off with plant fiber attached, providing a ready-made needle and thread. The hard and prickly thorns also served to test the courage of young men. In the Calmecac, the Aztec school for boys of the priest-warrior caste, the teachers used them in character-training. The Aztecs' extremely rigid moral code demanded respect for elders, obedience to parents, temperance in food and drink, courage, and fidelity in marriage.

But being "moral" for the Aztecs did not mean being humane. No one honored the code of Quetzalcoatl. The Aztecs' main god, Huitzilopochtli, was the bloodthirstiest deity in their pantheon of gods. Even Tezcatlipoca, the god of spring, demanded human sacrifice. Each year a young boy was chosen for him, and for that year the boy lived like a prince. Dressed like the god he represented, with golden bells on his sandals and white feathers in his headdress, he paraded among the people; and everyone, even the king, knelt down before him. On the day of sacrifice he walked up the steps of the temple and was offered as food to the god of spring. Being sacrificed was considered an honor, not a punishment.

Huitzilopochtli, in particular, was so voracious that on special occasions thousands were sacrificed to him in a single day. Long lines of victims toiled to the top of the pyramid where relays of priests seized each in turn and cut his heart out with an obsidian knife, presenting it warm and bleeding on the god's altar stone. For such massive offerings, the Aztecs could not depend on volunteers, so they sent frequent raiding parties into the surrounding territory to capture victims.

At the peak of Aztec dominion, Tenochtitlán was the center of increasingly bloody ceremonials. Sacramental banquets of human flesh, flaying ceremonies, mortifications even in the home, and other rites combined to create a life overshadowed by symbols of death. The Aztecs were as fiercely hated by their helpless neighbors as any people in history.

THE CONQUEST

This was the situation when the Aztec chieftain-priest Montezuma began hearing rumors of "floating mountains bearing fair gods" in the Gulf of Mexico. The Spanish had touched on Yucatán in 1517 and explored as far as Veracruz the following year. But it was in 1519, the year when the priests had predicted Quetzalcoatl's return, that Hernando Cortes landed on the coast with a large expedition consisting of 11 ships, some 500 men, and 16 horses. In Tabasco, Cortes received 20 women as a gift. One of them was named Malinche and was called Doña Marina by the Spaniards. She spoke the Mayan and Aztec languages, learned Spanish, and became Cortes' wife, guide, and interpreter.

When Cortes landed, messengers confirmed Montezuma's worst fears: the strangers were indeed white-skinned and bearded, and must be emissaries of their enemy-god Quetzalcoatl. At first Montezuma hoped to buy them off, so he sent them magnificent presents, which Cortes shipped back to King Charles I of Spain. When the European artist Albrecht Dürer saw Montezuma's jewels, including huge gold and silver plates, he declared they were as exquisite as any art in the world. Of course this treasure only whetted Cortes' appetite, and he pressed inland. As he went he picked up many recruits among the Tlaxcala and others who craved revenge on the Aztecs. With his forces thus vastly augmented, Cortes reached Tenochtitlán in late 1519. Montezuma received him courteously in the palace. Cortes promptly took the King hostage and ruled the city from behind his throne.

Hearing that an expedition was coming from Cuba to replace him,

Cortes went to fight them, leaving his lieutenant Pedro de Alvarado in command. Alvarado committed such atrocities that the Aztecs rebelled, besieged the palace, and stoned Montezuma to death. Cortes, who had returned by then, tried to get his troops out of the city, but the Aztecs breached the causeways and hundreds of Spaniards, loaded with loot, fell into the lake and drowned, while the Aztecs slaughtered the panicked troops who jammed together trying to escape. Cortes himself fled, but this defeat, the "sad night," cost him three quarters of his men.

Then the Aztecs were decimated by smallpox, previously unknown. One victim was the new chief, Cuitlahuac. His successor, Cuauhtémoc, swore never to surrender to the Spaniards. But Cortes recruited other Indians, and the culture of obsidian knives could not withstand steel weapons. In August, 1521, 150,000 hungry, besieged Indians surrendered their city to Cortes, who then proceeded to level it. Cuauhtémoc was captured and executed. Today many monuments honor him, but in all Mexico there is no statue of Cortes.

Spanish Rule

For nearly three centuries after the conquest, Mexico was ruled by Spanish viceroys who lived like kings. Catholic friars spread through the

Taxco's silver mines made it one of Mexico's most prosperous colonial towns.

Like Taxco, San Miguel de Allende (founded in 1542) retains much historical flavor.

land establishing missions. Guided by the Spaniards, talented Indian craftsmen learned new skills, including glassmaking, working with bronze and forged steel, and the art of wax portraits. Ancient ceramic art reached high levels, especially in Puebla, where elaborate kitchen utensils covered with glass designs were made. European styles and embroidered fabrics appeared, utilizing silk produced by the silkworms the Spaniards had introduced into Mexico. The Spaniards also introduced sugarcane, the wheel, and domesticated beasts of burden such as the horse, the ox, the donkey, and the mule.

Spain's cultural contributions to Mexico went far beyond those of agriculture and simple craftsmanship. In 1551, Spain issued a decree creating the University of Mexico. Much later, in 1792, a school of mines opened, and among its professors were Fausto de Elhuyar, discoverer of tungsten, and Andrés Manuel del Rio, discoverer of vanadium. Architecture, a major art form under the Indians and in modern Mexico, was also important in colonial days. The Cathedral of the Assumption, largest in Latin America, is an outstanding example of the earliest architectural style, the classic. The cathedral was begun in 1573 and finished in 1667. Additions have been made in later styles. For example, the Metropolitan Shrine, which is connected to the cathedral by a wall of *tezontle* (native reddish stone), is done in the highly ornamented baroque style that flourished in Europe into the 18th century.

Colonial Mexico produced its scholars and artists as well. They included Francisco Javier Clavijero, author of *Ancient Mexican History*, Mateo Aleman, author of the novel *Guzmán de Alfarache*, and Francisco Javier Alegre, a noted authority on Latin. Perhaps the best-known play of the era was *The Truth Suspected (La verdad sospechosa)* written by Juan Ruiz de Alarcon, the Mexican dramatist, who, together with the Spaniards Lope de Vega, Tirso de Molina, and Calderón de la Barca, represents the highest level of the Spanish classical theater. Noteworthy, too, are Bernardo de Balbuena, the poet, and Sor Juana Inés de la Cruz, who would have been considered a great poetess in any period, in or out of America. Also Bernardino de Sahagún, perhaps the most talented historian the colonies produced; the Indian historian Fernando de Alva Ixtlilxochitl; the Valencia-born sculptor Manuel Tolsa; Fray Pedro de Gante, who introduced painting to Mexico; the painter Miguel Cabrera, a native of Oaxaca—all of these made up a brilliant panorama of contributions to the culture of colonial Mexico.

The Spaniards settled about 100 towns in Mexico and expanded their realm into what is now California and the American Southwest. Their society, like that of the Aztecs, was rigidly stratified. At the top were men born in Spain—*gapuchines,* or wearers of spurs. Criollos—persons of Spanish blood, but Mexican-born—came next. Intermarriage with Indians produced the present major ethnic strain, the mestizos. Other crosses—such as Spanish-black (mulatto) or Indian-black (zambo)—were of minor importance. All mestizos had very low status, but were still superior to Indians, who made up half the population and were virtually slaves. The gap between aristocrat and lowly Indian peon was astronomical. Spaniards owned vast haciendas and mines and dominated all government posts, the Church, and the military. Wealth was drained from the land and siphoned to Spain or to the baronial estates of bishops and other *gapuchines,* and the lower classes were brutally exploited.

INDEPENDENCE—THE FIRST CENTURY

The late 18th century was a great period of new, liberal ideas both in Europe and the Americas. It was also a revolutionary era, the time of the American and French revolutions. These various developments had their effect in Mexico. Criollo and mestizo intellectuals began to dream of overthrowing the Spanish tyranny and of creating a republic.

In the town of Querétaro, one such group of criollos established a literary and social club in which they discussed ideas of independence. One member of the group was Father Miguel Hidalgo, a parish priest from the nearby village of Dolores. Hidalgo, a man widely read, was a humanitarian who had won the love of his Indian parishioners through his efforts to help them. In violation of law, he had taught the Indians to plant various crops and to make new kinds of pottery and leather.

The Querétaro group hoped to lead a bloodless revolt of criollos

Guadalajara: a central plaza faced by the cathedral was typical of Spanish style.

Guanajuato, perhaps Mexico's most beautiful version of colonial style.

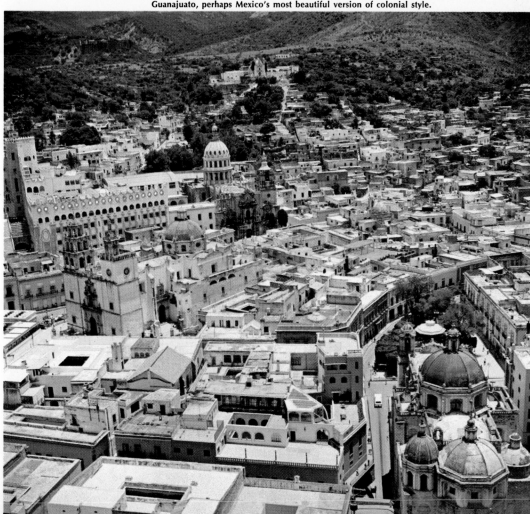

against the *gapuchines*. Their plans were discovered, however, and in September, 1810, orders were issued for the arrest of the leading conspirators. Now Hidalgo turned for help to the Indians. On September 16, 1810, he summoned his parishoners and, in an impassioned speech, called upon them to free their land of Spanish tyranny. He concluded, "Viva la Virgen de Guadalupe! Viva México!" Today this "Cry from Dolores" still echoes across the nation on September 16.

Mexico erupted like one of its own volcanoes. The insurgents fighting under the Virgin's banner were defeated in 1811, and Hidalgo was stripped of his priesthood and beheaded. But his pupil, Father José María Morelos, picked up the banner and led the rebellion. Morelos, Mexico's first mestizo hero, is honored as a farsighted patriot who, looking beyond revolution, called for basic social reforms. He was executed in 1815. In 1820 Agustín de Iturbide, formerly a general of Spanish troops, made a deal with insurgent leader Vicente Guerrero. They proclaimed Mexican independence, and Iturbide took over as emperor of Mexico.

Between 1821 and 1876, Mexico was ruled by two emperors, 40 presidents, and several provisional governments. Civil war and conflicts between Church and State were nearly continuous. Emperor Iturbide held power until 1823, when forces under General Antonio López de Santa Anna overturned his government and declared Mexico a "republic." The criollo leader Santa Anna was a tragicomic figure, a strutting little tyrant, sometimes liberal and sometimes reactionary, who ruled the country several times on and off into the 1850's.

The Mexican War.   Santa Anna's incredible stupidity worked against Mexican interests. He was responsible for the massacre of Texans at the Alamo, after Texas had declared its independence from Mexico in 1836. Later when he was captured, he gave up Texas in return for his personal freedom. In 1846, after the United States annexed Texas (whose independence Mexico had never recognized), war broke out, and the United States invaded Mexico. Because of Santa Anna's lack of skill as a general, Mexican forces fared badly. When General Winfield Scott reached Mexico City, heroic cadets called *Los Niños* ("the boys") died defending Chapultepec. Santa Anna fled, and the Americans were victorious. By armed might the United States took from Mexico more than half its territory, including most of what is now California and the Southwestern States. Later, to pay his debts, Santa Anna sold the United States the Mesilla Valley, now part of New Mexico and Arizona, for $10,000,000.

Benito Juárez and Maximilian.   In 1855 the liberals managed to exile Santa Anna. Their leader was a Zapotec Indian, Benito Juárez, born in the state of Oaxaca. The liberals promulgated the landmark Constitution of 1857, which confiscated Church lands, called for free state-sponsored education, and declared freedom of religion, seeking thus to break the power of the Church and end feudalism in Mexico. In the resulting War of the Reform (1857–61) the liberals won, and Juárez entered Mexico City as president in 1861.

But the country was bankrupt from years of war, and Juárez had to suspend payment of debts to Spain, England, and France. Reactionaries used this failure as a pretext to persuade Napoleon III of France to take over Mexico, In 1862–64 French troops invaded and conquered the country with the support of reactionary elements, who restored the royalist form of government. Napoleon III gave the crown to Archduke Maximilian of Austria and his wife Carlota. Emperor Maximilian proved to be a weak, although well-meaning and surprisingly liberal, monarch. Because he was liberal, he disappointed his reactionary followers. At the same time, he was opposed by Mexican liberals because he was a foreigner. Napoleon withdrew French troops in 1867, and Maximilian, now deserted by all, was executed. Carlota, who had escaped to Europe, was insane for the rest of her life.

Juárez again took over as president. In his brief regime, until he died in office in 1872, he laid the groundwork for the development of industry, transportation, communications, and public education and began at last the process of forging Mexico into a nation.

Porfirio Díaz. In 1876 Porfirio Díaz, one of Juárez's officers, seized the presidency, initiating over 30 years of stability known as the Porfirian Peace. He brought "law and order" to his troubled land by establishing a military dictatorship. Díaz tended to think of himself as a stern father who knew what was best for his unruly children.

The institutions that the reformists had dreamed about and embodied in the Constitution of 1857 were now trampled upon. Díaz restored to the army and the aristocrats all their old privileges and made peace with the Church, returning their vast estates. To develop the land, he encouraged unregulated foreign investment. Through the co-operation of foreign capitalists and wealthy Mexicans, he started the oil industry, built railroads and harbors, and improved agricultural production. Dissent was rigorously suppressed. Díaz dealt with banditry by putting the bandits in uniforms and labeling them *rurales,* rural police. Offices and state governorships went to the wealthy, light-skinned elite. One percent of the population controlled and exploited the rest, so that most of the people were worse off than ever, while the aristocrats lived lives of Parisian elegance.

Under the protection of the Porfirian Peace, landed estates (haciendas) did not need high walls to give them the appearance of medieval fortresses. The estates comprised a big house, which was the home of the landowner, a house for the administrator, a house or houses for employees, the company store, the church, and the jail. Working a brutal daily schedule, the Indian peon was forced to go into debt to the company store. He never got out of debt. Debts became hereditary, insuring virtual slavery. Nevertheless, the regime looked appealing to foreign investors who saw only the ornate opulence of the new buildings in Mexico City and the splendid broad avenues. After all, like Mussolini later in Italy, Díaz made the trains run on time and abolished "civil disorder."

But just as Indian stoicism beneath the Spanish spur had reached its limits a century before, so again Mexico was seething under the surface. The Díaz regime had brought about an intolerable state of affairs, and the rigid facade of the Porfirian Peace began showing cracks as the new century opened. In 1908 a mild, scholarly dreamer, Franciso I. Madero, published *The Presidential Succession of 1910,* which strongly suggested it was time for a democratizing change. Madero, a wealthy cotton planter who fed his workers' children at his own table, was personally a pacifist. Yet, precisely a hundred years after Hidalgo's "Cry from Dolores," the message of his book became a battle cry for insurgents ushering in a decade of unprecedented violence and bloodshed.

THE MODERN MEXICAN NATION

Although Mexicans have lived with revolution throughout their history, when they speak of the Revolution they mean two things. First, they mean the violent revolution that began in 1910 and lasted until 1920. During this ordeal, with their blood, with turmoil and devastation that cost 1,000,000 lives, they bought their liberation at last. But by the Revolution they also mean the continuing peaceful revolutionary change process that still goes on and must go on tomorrow. Its principles are embodied in the Constitution of 1917, which has proved sufficiently flexible and humane to endure the grinding stress of transition into the modern world and is still in force. The idea of revolution is still embodied in the very name of Mexico's one major political party, the Institutional Revolutionary Party.

The Revolution's fighting started with uprisings in the north under Pancho Villa, a cattle bandit turned guerrilla fighter, and in the south under Emiliano Zapata, a tough Indian leader whose one demand was land for his people. Díaz was forced out in 1911, and Madero was subsequently elected president of Mexico. But Madero was politically inexperienced and temperamentally unsuited for high political office. He could not ride out the hurricane. In 1913 the ruthless General Victoriano Huerta, commander of government forces, betrayed Madero and made himself president by force. Madero was imprisoned and then killed while in prison, supposedly while trying to escape.

This federal project, built in Mexico City in the 1960's, houses 80,000 people.

Now the full fury of the Revolution broke over the land, and the hungry people hurled themselves in irresistible hordes against Huerta's tyranny. Before order could be restored in 1920, Mexico had 10 presidents, one of whom lasted less than an hour. All Mexico was a scene of warring armies, burning haciendas, and daily acts of incredible brutality.

One hopeful event, however, did pierce the darkness of these years. Venustiano Carranza, a state governor and general who became leader of the country in 1916, called the convention that drafted the Constitution of 1917. It revived the Juárez principles of free education, separation of Church and State with State control of Church property, and civil liberties. In addition, it introduced the 8-hour workday, fixed minimum wages, and gave workers the right to unionize and strike. Under the Constitution all land and national resources could be reclaimed by the government.

In 1920 Carranza was deposed and, like Madero, assassinated. Other revolutionary heroes who met the same fate were Pancho Villa and Zapata. But out of the maelstrom the leader of the Yaqui Indians, a Sonora rancher named Álvaro Obregon, emerged unscathed except for the loss of his right arm, and he took over the presidency of the nation in 1920.

Since that time, no president has been overthrown by force, nor has Mexico suffered major civil strife. In 1920, exhausted but free of dictators and war, Mexico began the long struggle to build a modern, progressive nation.

The Peaceful Revolution

In effect the Mexican Revolution emerged from the plains and ranches with one hand on the Constitution of 1917 and the other on a gun. Preventing further disorder and healing the terrible wounds of war were the first necessities. Next came the stage of turning the Revolution's principles into practical goals, and then the tremendous task of making the goals become reality.

A Unique Form of Government.   The government that took up this challenge is sometimes called one party democracy and sometimes the presidential system. Uniquely Mexican, it combines elements of strongman rule with elements of real democratic participation. The nation it controls is organized on federal principles, with states headed by governors. At the national level, the president is elected by popular vote for a 6-year term and cannot succeed himself. He appoints his cabinet. There is a 60-member senate and a larger chamber of deputies, elected by the people. The judicial branch is headed by a supreme court, with justices appointed for life who in turn appoint district and circuit court judges.

This is the official system. Unofficially, almost all power is in the hands of the president and his ministers, who are leaders of the only political party with real power, the PRI (Institutional Revolutionary Party). Before 1929, there was no political organization but the army. In that year Plutarco Calles, Obregon's comrade in arms and his successor as president, formed what became the PRI.

All kinds of people—peasants, workers, lawyers, intellectuals, businessmen, students, housewives—belong to the PRI and support it, although they represent a wide range of ideologies. By custom the president chooses his successor, who is duly nominated by the party. Although this candidate's election is a foregone conclusion, he nevertheless stumps the country, addressing huge rallies, as strenuously as if he were the underdog in a tight contest. Masses of voters turn out on election day to give him their blessing. To outsiders the system sounds undemocratic, but it has worked well because of the wide participation in the PRI and the dedication of most presidents to achieving the goals of the Revolution.

The Revolution in Practice. Obregon and Calles guided the nation through its first 14 years. Obregon, president from 1920 to 1924, initiated programs of free public education and land distribution and encouraged labor to organize unions. He chose Calles, his minister of the interior, as his successor. Calles began as a reformer, founding the Bank of Mexico and advancing revolutionary aims, although later he grew conservative. His efforts to implement the Constitution brought him into collisions with foreign oil companies and the Roman Catholic Church. During these years the dissatisfied clergy and generals constantly came up with new plans to sink the Revolution. Labor unions showed hardly any signs of life. Paper money was almost as worthless as confetti. The Church repudiated the Constitution and went "on strike" (1926–29), refusing to hold services. This caused consternation among the devout and plunged the country into brush-fire conflicts between rebel Cristeros and anti-clerical government forces.

With the country thus torn, the leaders believed that no one but Obregon could hold Mexico together, and so the Constitution was amended to allow his re-election in 1928. But before he could take office a fanatic assassinated him. Over the next 6 years Mexico had three presidents serving 2 years each, but the real ruler was Calles. Many felt that Mexico was slipping backwards from its revolutionary aims toward the old corruption and exploitative capitalism.

In this atmosphere Lázaro Cárdenas, "the conscience of the Revolution," was elected in 1934 to serve a term fixed at 6 years. The most leftist of Mexico's presidents, he expropriated oil properties owned by British and American companies and undertook a vastly stepped-up program of school-building and distribution of land to impoverished villagers. About 40,000,000 acres (16,000,000 hectares) of land were placed in the hands of peasants by Cárdenas. He also exiled Calles and his friends. Cárdenas and his more moderate successor, Manuel Ávila Camacho (president 1940–46) managed to make peace with the Church without restoring its political power.

Following the mandate of revolutionary principles expressed in the Constitution, Camacho (1940–46) instituted radical educational reforms. His successor, Miguel Aleman (1946–52), although criticized for corruption, established social security and initiated extensive economic development. Under the regime of Adolfo López Mateos, 1958–64, Mexicans engaged in scientific research aimed at collective improvement of Mexican life. These men and their successors have maintained a generally consistent policy from one administration to the next. They have kept the country on a course of industrialization, increased influence of the middle class, improved communications and transportation, and heightened Mexico's importance in the family of nations.

ANTONIO MONTES DE OCA, University of Mexico

Tourists and Bermudians enjoy lovely Hamilton Harbor.

BERMUDA

Bermuda, a tiny British colony in the Atlantic Ocean, has little in the way of raw materials, agriculture, or industry. It prospers simply by being itself—a place of glorious flowers, perpetual springlike weather, and beautiful beaches of pink coral sand. These attractions help bring about 250,000 tourists to the colony every year. Bermuda has a permanent population of about 50,000 people. Approximately 60 percent of the people are black and of African descent.

The Land

The islands that make up Bermuda are coral islands. They were formed over many centuries by the accretion of coral on the peaks of a great, dormant, underwater volcano. Located about 600 miles (965 kilometers) east of North Carolina, the islands are not, strictly speaking, tropical islands. The average temperature for January is about 63 degrees Fahrenheit (17 degrees Celsius), which is a bit cool for swimming. The year-round temperate climate does produce a wealth of flowers rivaling that of any Caribbean island. Bougainvillea and hibiscus splash brilliant colors against white walls or over pink and blue limestone houses. Flowering trees, tropical plants, and prickly pears flourish, as well as the Easter lilies that are Bermuda's hallmark and one of its few exports.

There are, all told, more than 300 islands, islets, or just plain big rocks in the Bermudas, the overwhelming majority of which are uninhabited. The name "Bermuda" usually refers to the 7 main islands of the group, which curve around to resemble a giant fishhook. These main islands are connected by causeways and have a total area of about 21 square miles (54 square kilometers). The largest island, Bermuda Island,

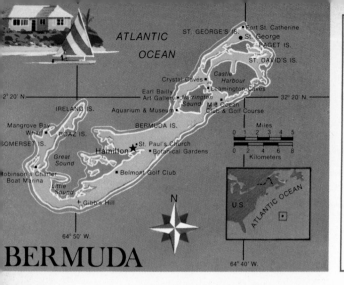

accounts for about two thirds of the total area of the island group. It is the site of **Hamilton**, Bermuda's capital and largest town.

Way of Life

In style, Bermuda still retains some of the old-fashioned attitudes associated with British colonialism. Appearing in skimpy bathing suits or in short shorts anywhere but on a beach is frowned upon, as is the custom of wearing hair curlers in public. But there is plenty of style and color in Bermudian life, too. Dancers, calypso singers, and steel bands enliven the nightclubs, and at Christmas and Easter people called Gombey dancers put on gaudy costumes and dance in the roads. The bobbies (policemen) wear Bermuda shorts.

History and Government

Bermuda is named after the Spanish explorer Juan de Bermúdez, who discovered the islands in 1503. Since the islands were obviously not rich in natural resources, the Spaniards made no attempt at colonization. It was not until 1612 that the first permanent settlement was established. Sixty British colonists founded St. George in that year. St. George still has the appearance of a 17th-century town.

Because of their limited natural resources, Bermudians have always lived more or less by their wits, taking advantage of their strategic position in the Atlantic. For many years the island economy was based on shipbuilding and ship repair. Bermuda provided facilities for the repair of British naval vessels and other ships far from their home port. Bermudians have also, at different times, been privateers and slave traders. During the American Civil War, some Bermudians worked as blockade runners, helping Confederate ships penetrate the Union blockade of Southern ports. The islands' tourist industry got into full swing in the Prohibition era (1920–33) when the manufacture and sale of alcoholic beverages were outlawed in the United States. The islands became a favorite oasis for thirsty Americans—who also enjoyed Bermuda's lovely beaches. During World War II, Bermuda became an Allied military base.

Bermuda is an internally self-governing colony. Most political power resides in the colony's House of Assembly, whose members are elected by the people.

Reviewed by BERMUDA GOVERNMENT TRAVEL INFORMATION OFFICE

BAHAMAS

When Christopher Columbus first touched land in the New World on October 12, 1492, it was in the Bahamas—a group of islands southeast of Florida and north of Cuba. He probably landed on the tiny island that is now called San Salvador.

Columbus found the Indians of the Bahamas friendly, and he took some of them aboard his ship as guides. They were able to help him reach the big island of Cuba. By 1508 all the Bahamas had been depopulated by the Spaniards for whom Columbus had claimed the islands. The peaceful Indians were transported to the Spanish settlements on Hispaniola (the island where the nations of Haiti and the Dominican Republic are now located) and on Cuba, and were forced to work as slaves. Thereafter the history of the Bahamas reads like an adventure story. For about 150 years the islands were a favorite hiding place for pirates, shipwreckers, and smugglers. Now the Bahamas are a place where tourists go to enjoy mild temperatures and white, palm-fringed beaches, as well as some of the best yachting and deep-sea fish-

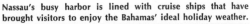

Nassau's busy harbor is lined with cruise ships that have brought visitors to enjoy the Bahamas' ideal holiday weather.

ing in the world. Skin diving and spearfishing are also excellent in the islands and attract many visitors annually.

Pirates to Tourists

In the early 16th century ships laden with rich cargoes began to cross from the New World to Europe. These ships soon became targets for pirates. The Bahamas were a natural base for pirates, who could lie in wait for ships coming through the nearby Straits of Florida. And the tricky channels of the Bahamas could provide sanctuary for pirates in case they were pursued by heavily armed vessels, which could not navigate the shallow waters and coral reefs.

Pirates excepted, there was nothing in the way of a settlement in the Bahamas until the second half of the 17th century. Although Columbus had claimed the islands for Spain, the Spanish are not known to have attempted any settlement there. British explorers were also familiar with the islands, and since the Spaniards had not colonized them, Great Britain laid claim to the Bahamas in the 17th century. In 1648 the Eleutherian Adventurers, a small group of settlers from Bermuda and England, established a colony on the island of Eleuthera. Settlement of the Bahamas proceeded slowly until after the American Revolution, when several thousand British Loyalists migrated from the United States with their slaves. The arrival of these newcomers more than doubled the population of the islands. But there was little further settlement, for the islands lacked valuable minerals and did not have soil suitable for large-scale agriculture.

Only recently has the islands' pace of development changed—and the change has been dramatic. Beginning in the 1950's jet travel brought the Bahamas within a few hours of major American cities, and soon tourists were crowding the islands as never before. Hotels went up everywhere, and tourism increased 25 times in less than 20 years. More than 1,000,000 tourists visit the Bahamas every year.

The Land

The Bahama Islands constitute a great archipelago just north of the Caribbean Sea in the Atlantic Ocean. The land has much the look of the coasts and keys of southern Florida. The islands are generally flat and do not rise to more than 400 feet (120 meters) above sea level. Mangrove swamps, fine white beaches, and coral reefs abound. Winter temperatures in the Bahamas average in the 70's Fahrenheit (20's Celsius), and summer temperatures are usually in the 80's F. (30's C.). The pleasant climate of the islands is due in part to the Gulf Stream, which passes the islands. One of the delights of the islands' climate is that flowers bloom there throughout the year.

All of the true islands of the Bahamas are inhabited. There are, however, many tiny bits of land scattered over the archipelago where no one lives at all. The inhabited islands number about 30. In addition there are about 670 uninhabited islets, or cays (keys), as well as more than 2,000 uninhabited pieces of land so small that they are called rocks. The islands, cays, and rocks of the Bahamas are spread over a vast arc of some 750 miles (1,200 kilometers). Andros Island, the largest island, is 104 miles (167 km.) long and 40 miles (64 km.) wide at its broadest part.

FACTS AND FIGURES

THE COMMONWEALTH OF THE BAHAMAS is the official name of the country.

CAPITAL AND CHIEF CITY: Nassau.

LOCATION: Archipelago off the coast of Florida. **Latitude**—20° 50′ N to 27° 25′ N. **Longitude**—72° 37′ W to 80° 32′ W.

AREA: 5,380 sq. mi. (13,935 sq. km.).

POPULATION: 190,000 (estimate).

LANGUAGE: English.

RELIGION: Christian.

GOVERNMENT: Constitutional monarchy. **Head of state**—British monarch, represented by governor-general. **Head of government**—prime minister. **Legislature**—parliament. **International co-operation**—Commonwealth of Nations, United Nations.

ECONOMY: Chief agricultural products—vegetables, fruits, dairy and poultry products. **Industries and products**—tourism, textiles, paper, rubber goods. **Chief exports**—cement, rum, pulpwood, salt.

MONETARY UNIT: Bahamian dollar.

NATIONAL HOLIDAY: July 10, Independence Day.

NATIONAL ANTHEM: "March On, Bahamaland."

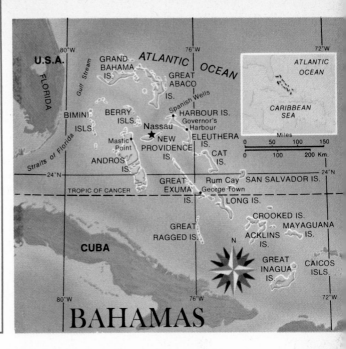

BAHAMAS

The capital—and by far the most important city in the Bahamas—is Nassau, on New Providence Island. Actually, the city proper is fairly small, and constitutes only a fraction of a large residential and resort district that stretches for about 8 miles (13 km.) along the northern coast of New Providence Island. About 100,000 people—or nearly 60 percent of the entire permanent population of the Bahamas—live in or near Nassau. It is a city of winding streets, pink stucco cottages, and whitewashed Anglican churches. More tourists come to Nassau than to any other town in the islands, and its bustling harbor is the busiest in the Bahamas. Nassau is also a center of international finance, for the tax laws of the Bahamas have encouraged the growth of international banking. Nassau's importance in the Bahamian scheme of things is so great that all the islands other than New Providence Island are called out islands, and their inhabitants are called out islanders.

Government

On July 10, 1973, the Bahamas became a fully independent country. However, it maintains its allegiance to the British Crown. The two-house parliament consists of the popularly elected House of Assembly and the Senate, whose members are appointed. Most of the governmental authority resides in the House of Assembly. The head of government is the prime minister, who is head of the majority party in the Assembly.

About 85 percent of the islands' population is black; most Bahamians are descendants of slaves brought to the islands in the 17th and 18th centuries. Until recently most political power in the Bahamas, as well as most of the wealth, was held by the white minority. In 1967, however, a virtually all-black party—the Progressive Liberal Party—gained control of the Assembly, and the islands' first black prime minister, Lynden O. Pindling, took office.

Reviewed by WILLIAM H. KALIS, Chief of Government Information Services
Bahamas News Bureau

The hills of St. Lucia, Windward Islands, rise from the sea.

CARIBBEAN SEA AND ISLANDS

The group of islands—or archipelago—called the Antilles are actually the summits of a submerged mountain range. High and green, the archipelago curves in an arc from Florida to Venezuela. It marks the limits of the Caribbean Sea.

The archipelago is divided into two main groups of islands. The Greater Antilles lie to the north and comprise the four sizable islands—Jamaica, Cuba, Hispaniola (an island shared by the nations of Haiti and the Dominican Republic), and Puerto Rico. The Lesser Antilles form the eastern boundary of the Caribbean Sea and include islands off the northern coast of South America as well. Most of the Lesser Antilles are still linked in some way with the former colonial powers of Europe. A group of islands in the northern half of the Lesser Antilles are called the Leeward Islands. A group in the southern half are called the Windward Islands. All of the Antilles are known popularly as the **West Indies**.

The islands of the Caribbean lie within the tropics, but because of

Island fishermen empty their nets as they have for generations.

A safe anchorage off Tortola, in the British Virgin Islands.

the northeast trade wind the heat is generally not oppressive. Hundreds of thousands of vacationers arrive from the north and from Europe every winter to enjoy the balmy climate. There is a good deal of rain, but a completely sunless day is as rare as a totally rainless day. Climatic conditions are ideal except during the worst part of the hurricane season in August and September. The soil is fertile. During the 17th and 18th centuries the islands of the Caribbean were known as the Sugar Islands. This was the time when the islands brought the greatest profit to the European nations that ruled them as colonies.

Most of the inhabitants of the islands are darkskinned and of African descent. The first African inhabitants of the Caribbean were brought there as slaves by the European plantation owners. There has been a great deal of intermarriage with Europeans, and many of the people are more brown than black. A certain number of East Indians, as people from India are called in the Caribbean, came there, beginning around the middle of the 19th century, as indentured laborers. They were brought mainly to Trinidad, which the British gained by treaty from Spain in 1802. Spain had brought relatively few slaves to Trinidad, and the island had an inadequate labor force for cultivating sugarcane on any large scale. After Parliament voted to abolish slavery in the British Empire in 1833, East Indians from Britain's vast empire in India were contracted to work in Trinidad, as well as in other islands.

Today most of the people of the Caribbean—black, brown, and white alike—live in sovereign nations, independent of colonial rule. There are seven independent nations in the Antilles: Cuba, Haiti, the Dominican Republic, Jamaica, Trinidad and Tobago, Grenada, and Barbados. The first three became independent nations before the present century, and the last four only recently. The newest of the Caribbean nations is Grenada, which became independent in 1974. Among the people of all these nations the desire is strong to be truly independent, to decide their own destinies without interference from the world's big powers. This is even true of Communist Cuba, which has maintained a middle course between the two giants of world Communism—China and the U.S.S.R. All of these small nations are wary of domination by the United States, even while aware that American wealth can benefit them in many ways. It is certainly true that American tourism is an important factor in the economy of the Caribbean.

To be free of outside domination is perhaps the strongest wish common to the small nations of the Caribbean today. But in a sense the peoples of the Caribbean are virtually all outsiders. All are descendants of people who came originally from some other part of the world, whether it was Europe or Africa or Asia. Freely or in chains, the different peoples were brought together by the colonial nations of Europe as they thrust into the New World.

DISCOVERY OF THE CARIBBEAN

The Caribbean and its islands were discovered by Christopher Columbus in 1492. He probably landed first at San Salvador in the Bahamas. On his first voyage he also visited Cuba and Hispaniola. Columbus was looking for a western route to the Orient, and he carried with him letters of introduction to the Great Khan of China. But the calculations on which his trip was based were inaccurate. He knew that the world was

round, but he did not know how big it was. He believed that Cuba was part of the Chinese mainland.

Indians. Columbus was charmed by the native islanders. They altered the shape of their heads by depressing their skulls in childhood with a wooden frame. The islanders were tall and moved gracefully, and they had fine dark eyes and friendly smiles. They were a benign, happy, and pleasure-loving people. Their principal foods were cassava, a starchy root, and maize, or corn. The islanders' favorite game involved kicking a ball over their shoulders with the back of their heels. A skillful player was able to keep the ball in the air for long periods of time. Columbus said of them in his report to King Ferdinand and Queen Isabella of Spain, "So lovable, so tractable, so peaceful are these people that I swear to your Majesties that there is not in the world a better nation nor a better land. They love their neighbors as themselves and their discourse is ever sweet and gentle and accompanied by a smile." These were the Arawaks, an Indian people now extinct in the Caribbean, except for a few descendants in Puerto Rico.

There was, however, in the area—in the Windward and Leeward islands—another very different people, the Caribs. Columbus was to encounter them on his second voyage.

The Caribs were described as tall and brown, with long, shiny black hair, which they dressed daily with great care. They only cut their hair short when in mourning. Like the Arawaks they altered the shape of their heads, but in an opposite manner. In childhood, they placed boards on the forehead and on the back of the head, so that their heads came to have a boxlike look. They scarred their cheeks with deep incisions, which they painted black. Around their eyes they inscribed black and white circles. Many of the Caribs perforated their noses and inserted fish bones or pieces of tortoiseshell. They made bracelets for their arms and ankles out of the teeth of their dead enemies. Carib boys were taught the use of the bow and arrow by having their food suspended from a tree out of reach, so that they would have to go hungry until they had learned to shoot it down.

Unlike the gentle Arawaks, the Caribs loved fighting. They had come from South America and were slowly working their way up the Caribbean islands, killing off the men of other tribes and keeping the women as slaves. They were cannibals. In Guadeloupe (Leeward Islands), Columbus, to his horror, found human limbs hanging from the rafters of Carib huts and the remains of a young man being boiled in a stew.

The Caribs were implacably belligerent, and in the Windward Islands they waged bitter and relentless war against the European invaders. On the island of Grenada some 40 of them leaped from a high cliff rather than fall into enemy hands. The cliff is now called Carib Leap, and the name of the village nearby is Sauteurs, which means "jumpers" or "leapers" in French. Resistance did not really cease until the end of the 18th century, by which time there were practically no Caribs left. A small, now peaceable, colony of them remains in a settlement on Dominica in the Windward Islands.

SPANISH COLONIZATION

In large part the different development of the various islands in the Antilles depended on which nations colonized them. The first European nation to establish colonies was Spain.

The Spaniards who sailed with Columbus on his second expedition had three things on their minds—God, glory, and gold. They wanted to convert the heathens to Christianity, they wanted to earn favor for themselves; and they wanted to bring home gold nuggets. Unfortunately there was little gold or silver in the Antilles, and the Spaniards did not recognize the commercial possibilities of agricultural development in the area. Seventeen ships set out with Christopher Columbus on his second voyage. They brought with them many kinds of seed to grow crops that would feed settlers. The settlers grew wheat, barley, and sugarcane, as well as oranges, melons, and lemons. They also raised domestic animals, including cattle, goats, horses, and poultry.

Although the Spaniards recognized what the islands needed if the white man was to make a home there, they did not recognize what the islands had to give the white man. For instance, on Columbus' first voyage an envoy sent into the interior of Cuba reported that he had seen men carrying flaming branches. They placed these stalks in their mouths, he said, inhaled the smoke, and then blew it into the air. In fact, these men were smoking tobacco. But Columbus did not recognize Cuban tobacco as a potential source of wealth. He was only interested in gold.

He forced the Arawaks to dig for it. These idle and gracious people resisted authority, and they were sometimes hanged for their disobedience. They sought relief in mass suicide. Within a very few years there were virtually no Arawaks left. The Spaniards were too busy to care. They had found in Central and South America the gold and silver they had come to the New World to find. Now they were concerned with the organization of the great gold and silver fleets that filled the coffers of Seville with bullion.

Pirates and Treasure. During the 16th century the might, majesty, dominion, and power of the Spanish Empire reached its peak and excited the envy of other European powers, who felt themselves unjustly excluded from the wealth of the New World. Pirates began to plunder Spanish ships and hold Spanish towns for ransom. The Englishman Francis Drake was the greatest of these adventurers who challenged the power and took the wealth of Spain. To some extent Drake was given official backing; at any rate he was knighted by Queen Elizabeth when he re-

St. George's, Grenada, is a typical West Indian town.

The Dutch brought their own style of architecture to Curaçao.

turned from a voyage around the world in his ship the *Golden Hind*. But many of the other adventurers were little more than brigands.

Spain's difficulty in the New World was that it had bitten off more than it could chew. Losing interest in the Antilles as soon as gold and silver were discovered in South America, Spain concerned itself exclusively with the sailing of the two annual treasure fleets that took the riches of the New World back to Spain. Under this system the island of Hispaniola was valuable to Spain as an administrative center; Havana was valuable as a port; and Puerto Rico was useful as a fort and garrison. The other islands of the Caribbean were useless for Spain's purposes. Yet Spain was not prepared to relinquish any part of its total claim to the Antilles.

French, Dutch, and British sailors, however, were not willing to allow Spain to enjoy what it could not protect. Beginning in the 16th century a phrase, "beyond the lines," came into use in Europe. It meant that European nations only considered themselves responsible for enforcing peace treaties north of the tropics and east of the Azores—that is, in the general area of Europe. Beyond these lines—an area that included the Caribbean—it was a free-for-all.

Among those who welcomed this freedom to maraud were the buccaneers, who flourished in the mid-17th century. Their name was derived from the French word *boucanier,* which referred to one who cured meat on a *boucan,* a wooden grill used over an open fire. These buccaneers were riffraff—homeless, rootless men, with families long since forgotten. They were mutineers, escaped prisoners, and shipwrecked pirates who eventually settled in Tortuga, a small island off the north coast of Hispaniola. The buccaneers also established themselves at Port Royal on the southern coast of Jamaica after the British captured the island from Spain in 1655. The buccaneers were also known as the Brethren of the Coast. Much is known about them because they had in their number a Dutchman named Esquemeling, who acted as their biographer and historian.

The buccaneers wore a common uniform: a small, peaked cap, a jacket of cloth, breeches that came halfway to their knees, and a loose-fitting shirt bound by a belt that held a bayonet and knives. Their muskets were usually taller than the men. On their feet they wore moccasins made of oxhide or pigskin. As soon as the animal was dead they would cut away the skin that covered it, put their big toes where the animal's knee had been, and bind the skin with a sinew. The remainder of the skin was pulled to a point a few inches above the heel and tied there until the skin dried. When an impression of a man's foot was made in soft leather in this fashion, the leather kept its shape.

Food was plentiful on the island of Tortuga. There was a profusion of yams, bananas, pineapples, and other fruit. On Hispaniola hordes of wild boars were to be found, as well as flocks of pigeons. The buccaneers also sold the cured meat of wild cattle to homebound vessels. They were, in fact, self-supporting. It was boredom and the desire to take revenge upon society, rather than necessity, that drove them on their plundering expeditions.

The buccaneers flourished into the 1670's. By that time they had

A traditional way of life: a Jamaican poles his raft downstream.

Workers cut sugarcane. Sugar is still a vital Caribbean product.

outlived their usefulness to England and France, which had previously encouraged the buccaneers to harass Spain's New World colonies.

The Spanish had come to recognize the facts of their position in the Caribbean. Their former enemy, the Dutch, had declined as a Caribbean power. But in the face of British and French enterprise, Spain could not hold possessions it did not need. Spain needed Cuba, Puerto Rico, and the eastern part of Hispaniola. But Jamaica, which Spain had ignored, was ceded formally to England in 1670. Trinidad remained under Spanish control primarily because neither England nor France was interested in it. As for the Windward and Leeward islands, Spain left the English and the French to fight out that issue between themselves. And, indeed, the Caribbean became for a century and a half the cockpit for the imperial ambitions of France and Britain, with most of the islands in the Windward and Leeward groups changing hands at least once.

SUGAR AND SLAVERY

The Spaniards had neglected the Caribbean islands because they were primarily interested in silver and gold. But the French and British recognized their immense agricultural possibilities. Europe needed sugar, and the soil and climate of the Caribbean were perfectly suited to its production. In the 17th century Europeans had begun to realize the delights of tea, coffee, and cocoa. Sugar was usually included in the preparation of these drinks. By the 18th century the demand for sugar was universal.

The word "creole" was used to describe anyone born in or anything native to the islands. Because of the sugar boom, the phrase "rich as a creole" was soon in general use. The immense value of the islands may be gauged from the following incident. In 1763, after the Seven Years War, England sat down at a conference table with France and Spain to decide which of the possessions acquired by England on the battlefield should be returned to their original owners. For England there was a choice between the island of Guadeloupe and Canada. After some indecision, England chose to return Guadeloupe and retain Canada. But the fact that it was a difficult choice shows how important the Caribbean islands were.

There was, however, one difficulty in the conduct of the sugar trade. Few white men were willing to work in the canefields beneath the blazing tropical sun. There was no longer a native population to work the fields, since virtually all the Arawaks and Caribs had either been killed or died out. A labor force had to be recruited somehow, and the Europeans turned to importing slaves from the western African coast.

The Spaniards had imported the first slaves from Africa as early as 1510, and by the late 16th century the slave trade had become a substantial operation. The initiator of the major phase of this nefarious business was the Elizabethan mariner John Hawkins, whose first voyage started in 1562. He transported several hundred Negro slaves to the Caribbean from the Guinea Coast of Africa. The slave trade increased in the 17th century and reached its greatest volume during the 18th century. It is now universally agreed that the slave trade was one of the greatest crimes ever committed by the human race. Men today are still feeling the consequences of that trade. But in the 16th and 17th centuries (which were, nevertheless, the age of Shakespeare, Milton, Cervantes, and Rembrandt) few people thought it wrong. Quite the contrary—in 1663 a coin was struck at the order of King Charles II to be used in the slave trade on the Guinea Coast. It immediately came to be called the guinea.

The French converted their slaves to Christianity and believed that they had saved their souls. The English were less concerned about their slaves' spiritual welfare. They argued that Christians should not be slaves to justify not converting them. It was left largely to Baptist and Methodist missionaries in the 19th century to teach Christianity to the black people of the British islands. The Spanish were generally not involved to a major degree in the slave trade, in part because they did not own any of the African coast. They were ready to take advantage of the bad deeds of their less scrupulous rivals, however, and they bought slaves freely from French, Dutch, and English traders. But the fact remains that today in the Caribbean the Spanish-speaking islands have predominantly white and mulatto populations.

The dimensions of the slave trade may be measured by its extent at the outbreak of the French Revolution in 1789. There were then 40 European forts on the Guinea Coast and many more slave-trading posts, which were known as factories. Here the European traders made their bargains with local African chieftains for slaves, frequently instigating tribal raids from which prisoners were shipped to the barracks on the coast. The 40 forts were divided among the Dutch, British, Portuguese, Danish, and French. The average annual consignment was roughly 75,000 slaves. Not all of these slaves went to the Caribbean. The tobacco planters on the North American mainland—in Virginia, for instance—

An island handicraft: this woman is drying leaves from the pandanus tree, which she will use in making hats.

took their share. In 1790 there were about 750,000 slaves in the southern states of the newly independent United States.

The crossing of the Atlantic was known as the middle passage. During the campaign for abolition of slavery in the late 18th and 19th centuries, gruesome pictures were drawn of the confined quarters into which the manacled slaves were herded. The English Privy Council, which investigated the slave trade, estimated that in 1789 about one eighth of the slaves transported from Africa died during the journey.

Most of the present inhabitants of the Caribbean islands are the descendants of the slaves who survived the middle passage. On their arrival their new owners were careful to separate members of the same tribe, so that there should be no common language in which the slaves could plot an uprising. Eventually they were taught their owners' language, so that today English is spoken, for example, in Barbados, Trinidad and Tobago, and Jamaica; Spanish in Cuba, Puerto Rico, and the Dominican Republic; and French in Haiti, Martinique, and Guadeloupe. In all these places, nevertheless, the European languages have undergone changes, and in the French islands particularly, the great majority of people speak a Creole patois that is considerably different from the language of France. In Dominica, Grenada, St. Vincent, and St. Lucia—British islands that were originally French—a similar Creole patois is also spoken in the back country.

Africa did survive in the culture of the people and also in the religion. It is true that the black people of the Caribbean did adopt the creeds of the Europeans. In the French and Spanish islands they became Roman Catholic. In the British islands they usually became Methodist or Anglican. But the blacks also retained the ceremonies of their ancient African religions. Today voodoo, which derives largely from these religions, is still alive in the Caribbean, most notably in the Haitian countryside. The West Indian Negroes also had their witch doctors, who were called obeah men.

In time, because they constituted a great majority, the Negro slaves came to see themselves as the real inhabitants, or the true people, of the Caribbean islands.

REVOLUTION AND ABOLITION

Throughout the 18th century the slaves toiled in the canefields. Much has been written of the ill treatment to which they were subjected, and there is no doubt that grim acts were perpetrated, especially on estates that were run by overseers in the absence of the landlord. Slave rebellions occurred throughout the century. But in the thinking of the white colonists, the greater potential source of trouble was the mulattoes, or "colored men." They were the offspring of slaves and their white masters. More often than not, they were free men. Many were well educated, particularly in the French islands, where young men of mixed black and white parentage were often sent to Paris to study. On their return they sometimes became involved in revolutionary groups.

Then in 1789 came the French Revolution. The revolutionary parliament in Paris announced that the slaves in French colonies were free. When the planters argued that the plantations could not be maintained without slave labor, Robespierre, the famous leader of revolutionary France, replied that it was better to lose a colony than betray a vital principle of the revolution.

Before long, however, the principles of the revolution were quite thoroughly betrayed in Paris itself, and in the end France lost only one colony. That was Saint-Domingue (Haiti). Trouble there had been expected from the mulattoes, but it was primarily the black slaves who made the Haitian revolution, rising in massive rebellion against their masters in 1791. After many years of fighting, an independent black nation, Haiti, was finally established in 1804. But that was much against the will of France's new ruler Napoleon Bonaparte, who tried unsuccessfully to subjugate the blacks again, both in Haiti and on the other French islands in the Caribbean as well.

Napoleon did manage to re-impose slavery in Guadeloupe, where it had previously been abolished by a revolutionary French governor amidst much bloodshed. In Martinique, a third major French colony, the revolution had almost no impact at all. Martinique was captured by the British shortly after the revolution, and it remained under British control for most of the post-revolutionary period, before being returned to France in 1816. Under the British the original owners remained in possession of their estates, and indeed their descendants—hardly more than a handful of families—still own most of the island today. Slavery was not abolished in all the French islands until 1848.

Ironically the British islands, which were largely unaffected by the revolution's democratic tidal wave, abolished slavery first. The late 18th century in Britain saw a rising outcry against the barbarousness of slavery. By act of Parliament the slave trade was prohibited in all British colonies in 1807. A little more than a quarter of a century later, in 1833, Parliament passed an act to abolish slavery in all the colonies. That process was completed in 1838.

As is always the case in major decisions of this sort, considerations other than moral ones played a part. In the early 19th century the British had acquired new sugar-producing colonies in the West Indies as well as in Asia. It was not unusual now for Britain to find itself supplied with more sugar than it needed. And about this time sugar beets were first being grown in Europe. The beet, which was cheaper to cultivate, gave promise of supplanting cane as a source of sugar. Because of this increased competition, sugar prices were often low, and the phrase "rich as a creole" no longer had much meaning. The West Indian planters lacked both the economic and political influence to withstand the campaign for abolition of slavery. And the hateful institution disappeared forever from the islands.

CHANGE AND CHALLENGE

Partly because of the abolition of slavery, the 19th century and early 20th century were largely a period of economic recession for the French and British islands of the Caribbean. One by one, the old landowners returned to Europe. Agents mismanaged estates, which were eventually sold on a falling market. In the British islands a considerable sum of money was paid to the planters in compensation for their freed slaves, but the planters, for the most part, took the money back to England with them rather than investing it in their plantations. The big houses were abandoned and the windmills crumbled. In 1887 the historian J. A. Froude made a tour of the British West Indies and wrote on his return a depressing account of the general collapse that he saw everywhere. Indeed, the high, proud days were over. There was no longer a challenge there for enterprising young Europeans.

However, there was a challenge in the islands for the brown and black descendants of the people who had been shipped across the Atlantic from the factories on the Guinea Coast. In large part, the white man was going or had gone. It was for the Negroes now to develop the democratic heritages of the colonial powers for their own ends. The road to self-government was to be long and hard, and only after World War II did Britain and France begin to liquidate their colonial empires in earnest. France ended the colonial status of its Caribbean possessions in 1946, when the colonies of Martinique and Guadeloupe became overseas departments of France. Today the inhabitants of the various islands included in those former colonies have the same rights enjoyed by every Frenchman, including, of course, the right to elect deputies to the French Assembly. On the British side, the largest colonies became completely self-governing nations, with solidly democratic governments. Jamaica and Trinidad and Tobago became fully independent nations in 1962. Barbados achieved independence in 1966. Grenada, one of the smaller islands, got its independence in 1974.

THE SPANISH ISLANDS AND THE UNITED STATES

The former Spanish islands have had a history quite different from that of the French and British islands. Spain was a considerably weaker

This gracious house is a reminder of early colonial days. It is now part of Codrington College, Barbados.

The sound of the 20th-century Caribbean: a steel band.

nation than Britain and France in the 19th century. By the end of the century Spain had lost all of its Caribbean colonies. Trinidad had been ceded to Britain at the very beginning of the century (1802) and quickly lost its Spanish atmosphere and traditions. The other three Spanish colonies—Santo Domingo (Dominican Republic), Puerto Rico, and Cuba—have retained the Spanish language and much of their traditional Spanish culture to this day. The Dominican Republic declared its independence of Spain in 1821, later placed itself under Spanish rule again briefly, and then regained its national independence in 1865. But it was a woefully weak nation. Meanwhile, Spain's decline was accompanied by the rise of the United States as a hemispheric power. Spain lost Cuba and Puerto Rico in the Spanish-American War, between Spain and the United States, in 1898. Puerto Rico became a possession of the United States. Cuba became an independent nation.

The history of all three of these former Spanish colonies has been dominated by the United States in the 20th century. Whether American policy has been mainly for good or for ill is a matter of debate. Puerto Rico has certainly benefited from its ties with the United States. It enjoys a higher per capita income than any other nation in the Caribbean, and it also has a truly democratic government. In Cuba's case, it was American money that made Cuba the greatest sugar-producing nation in the world. But there is no question that the people of Cuba and the rest of the Spanish Caribbean have been exploited by American business interests and that most of the people remained poor. The United States has repeatedly intervened militarily in the affairs of Caribbean nations. The Dominican Republic (as well as its neighbor on Hispaniola, Haiti) was actually ruled for years by a United States military government. In the 1960's anti-Americanism in the Caribbean reached new heights in Cuba, where, under the government of Fidel Castro, United States-Cuban diplomatic relations were broken and a Cuban Communist state was established.

Today the United States continues to wield vast power and influence in the Caribbean, possibly more than any of the colonial nations of the past. American business interests are extensive there, and American tourists come in droves. And there remains, too, the power of the American military. As recently as 1965 the United States dispatched troops to the Dominican Republic to prevent Communists from taking any possible advantage of a chaotic situation then prevailing there. The American intervention was widely interpreted to mean that the United States would tolerate no more Communist states like Cuba in the Caribbean. On the other hand, this military intervention probably evoked more opposition in the United States itself than any similar operation in the past. Very possibly the day is past when even the United States can dictate the future of the independent and freedom-loving people of the Caribbean.

Today, after a long history of colonial domination, the Caribbean people are probably freer than ever before to work out their destinies for themselves. Each island has a slightly different background; each has to face different problems. The story of the Caribbean today is not so much the story of one area as of a number of separate and individual nations.

ALEC WAUGH, Author, *A Family of Islands*

Beautiful Havana harbor is still the gateway to Cuba.

CUBA

Shaped somewhat like a crocodile in repose, its head pointed toward the Americas in the west and its tail toward Africa in the east, the island of Cuba stretches lazily under the tropical skies of the Caribbean. The Republic of Cuba includes not only the largest single island in the West Indies but also a vast archipelago of over 1,600 smaller islands, islets, and keys.

When Christopher Columbus first sighted Cuba on October 27, 1492, during his first voyage of discovery, Cuba became the gateway to the New World. The island's geographic location between the Atlantic and the Caribbean, as well as its closeness to both the mainland of the United States and Mexico, made Cuba the logical jumping-off point for the Spanish conquistadores bent on new adventures. A close neighbor of Haiti to the east (the narrow but dangerous Windward Passage separates them) and Jamaica to the south, Cuba rapidly became an important maritime and trading center in the West Indies. Columbus died convinced that Cuba was a continent. Although it proved not to be, the island Columbus discovered did lie across the great trading routes of the Atlantic and the Caribbean: it was to have a remarkable future.

Blessed by the fertility of its soil, Cuba developed into a rich country. The nation's wealth was not always properly distributed and put to the best possible use for the benefit of the people. This situation was, in fact, one of the causes of the Cuban revolution of 1959, led by Fidel Castro Ruz, and of the island's eventual transformation into the Western Hemisphere's first Communist republic.

THE LAND

Cuba's strategic location was the foundation of the island's key role in the history of the Western Hemisphere. Cuba's natural resources also contributed to its importance. Cuban sugar, tobacco, and minerals made the island a coveted prize for Spain. The Spanish ruled the island for nearly 4 centuries. These same resources attracted the rapidly growing United States in the 19th and early 20th centuries when American influence began to spread to the south into the Caribbean and Latin America.

For one thing, Cuba is extremely accessible. It is only 100 miles (161 kilometers) from Havana, the capital, to Key West. The distance from Cuba's Cape San Antonio (which is the tip of the crocodile's nose) to the Yucatán Peninsula of Mexico is 120 miles (190 km.). On a clear day, from Pico Turquino (Cuba's highest mountain) in the Sierra Maestra range, one can see the famous Blue Mountains of Jamaica, 85 miles (137 km.) away. From Cape Maisí, the tip of the crocodile's tail, it is less than 50 miles (80 km.) to Haiti. In a sense, then, the crescent of Cuba forms the northern boundary of the Caribbean Sea.

If Columbus had been a geologist, he might have been pleased with his conclusion that Cuba formed part of a continent. Cuba's geological history, going back about 150,000,000 years, suggests that Cuba is part of a submerged North American mountain range that forms many of the Caribbean islands. Massive movements of the earth's crust beneath the sea gradually made the mountains surface, and the mountain slopes and peaks became islands.

Cuba's geological history inevitably affected its topography and also gave the island breathtaking natural beauty. In the southeast, there are the Sierra Maestra mountains and, on the northern side of the island, the lower Sierra del Cristal.

Cuba has about 200 rivers and thousands of creeks. These streams flow through the island's mountains, often cascading down waterfalls like

Cuban workers gather sugarcane on a co-operative farm.

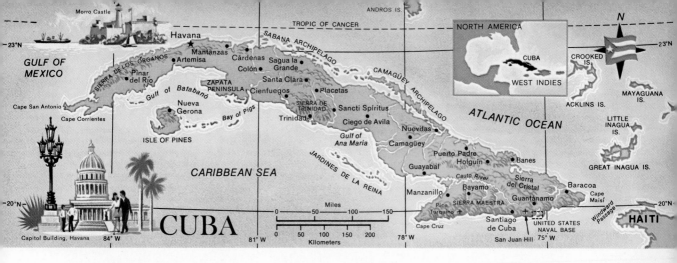

FACTS AND FIGURES

REPUBLIC OF CUBA—República de Cuba—is the official name of the country.

CAPITAL: Havana.

LOCATION: North America (an island in the Caribbean Sea). **Latitude**—19° 49' N to 23° 17' N. **Longitude**—74° 08' W to 84° 57' W.

AREA: 44,218 sq. mi. (114,524 sq. km.), including the Isle of Pines.

PHYSICAL FEATURES: Highest point—Pico Turquino (6,560 ft.; 2,000 m.). **Lowest point**—sea level. **Chief river**—Cauto.

POPULATION: 8,250,000 (estimate).

LANGUAGE: Spanish.

RELIGION: Roman Catholic.

GOVERNMENT: Communist republic. **Head of state**—president. **Head of government**—premier. **Legislature**—council of ministers. **International co-operation**—United Nations; Organization of American States (OAS), active membership suspended, 1962.

CHIEF CITIES: Havana, Santiago de Cuba, Camagüey, Santa Clara, Matanzas, Pinar del Río.

ECONOMY: Chief minerals—manganese ore, nickel, chromium. **Chief agricultural products**—citrus fruits, tobacco, sugar, coffee, rice. **Industries and products**—sugar refining, cement, gasoline. **Chief exports**—sugar, inorganic chemicals, tobacco. **Chief imports**—machinery, crude oil, cereals.

MONETARY UNIT: Cuban peso.

NATIONAL HOLIDAY: January 1, Liberation Day.

NATIONAL ANTHEM: *Himno de Bayamo* ("Hymn of Bayamo").

Caburni Falls, Toa Falls, and Agabama Falls. Cauto River in the east, Cuba's principal inland waterway, is about 150 miles (241 km.) long.

The mountains, the rivers, the plateaus, and the lowlands of Cuba contribute to making it an island of both great beauty and great contrast. There is the lushness of the hot eastern provinces where most of the Cuban sugarcane grows and the more severe landscape of the savannas (grassy plains) of the central and western portions of the island. It is in the savanna regions that the famous Cuban tobacco grows. The island's great cattle ranches are located on the savannas, too.

Climate.   Situated immediately south of the Tropic of Cancer, Cuba is essentially a subtropical country. A stranger to winter, the island has an average annual temperature of about 75 degrees Fahrenheit (24 degrees Celsius), although the thermometer sometimes rises to 100 degrees F. (38 degrees C.) in the summer in the eastern provinces and in the Havana region on the northern coast.

Cuba is frequently the victim of destructive hurricanes. The great annual hurricanes are spawned south and east of Cuba every autumn, and they move across the island, like a scythe, toward the North American mainland. The tropical downpours that accompany the storms cause rivers like the Cauto to flood the Cuban countryside.

City and Country

Traditionally Cuba has been a blend of urban and rural societies. Each of its six provinces—stretching from east to west they are Oriente,

Camagüey, Las Villas, Matanzas, Havana, and Pinar del Río—has one or more major cities.

Santiago de Cuba, an old town reminiscent of Spanish colonial days, is the capital of Oriente. This province also has the trading centers of **Holguín** and **Bayamo**. In Camagüey province, the city of **Camagüey** and **Ciego de Ávila** are the main urban centers. In Las Villas, the capital is **Santa Clara** and it, too, brings back memories of Spanish colonial days, with its ancient churches, narrow streets, and old houses. **Matanzas**, a city that has importance as a port but is somewhat less than beautiful, rules the province of the same name. **Havana**, the capital of the country and of Havana province, still is a major American metropolis, even though the Castro revolution took away much of its former brilliance. **Pinar del Río**, a quiet town, is the capital of Pinar del Río province.

Havana.   Cuba's capital, with a population in the city proper of close to 1,000,000 people, is one of the oldest cities in the Western Hemisphere. It is the largest city in the West Indies.

Despite the scars of revolution and economic problems, Havana remains a fascinating city. This is due in part to the natural setting of the capital. Havana has been built along a gently curving harbor. Many of the city's modern buildings have exceptional views out over the harbor and beyond—toward Key West.

Havana also has the unique appeal of being a very old city by New World standards. The harbor is guarded by El Morro, an imposing fortress that the Spanish built in the 16th century to protect the city from pirates and invaders. The oldest district of Havana, which lies west of the harbor, looks very much like a Spanish city. It has narrow streets, tile-roofed houses, and handsome old churches.

The national Capitol in Havana resembles its American model.

Many of Cuba's former luxury hotels stand almost empty now.

Beyond old Havana are the country's Capitol—which resembles the Capitol of the United States—and other government offices. Havana's modern business district lies beyond the government center. The newer districts of Havana once had many luxury hotels. Many of these buildings were converted to other uses by the government after the Castro revolution. The great flood of tourists from the United States and other Western countries had stopped.

Havana is still the all-important center of Cuba's economic life. Sugar, tobacco, rum, minerals, and many other export items are still shipped from the busy harbor. In the past, most of this extensive trade and commerce was with the United States. Now ships from the Soviet Union and many of the other Eastern European countries are a common sight at Havana's docks.

THE PEOPLE

Close to 8,250,000 people live in Cuba. This is a remarkable increase from the 6,000,000 estimated in 1955—especially in the light of the fact that over 500,000 Cubans fled their homeland in the decade following the victory of the Castro revolution. In comparative terms, this means that the density of population in Cuba is more than three times higher than that of the United States. Cuba's 8,000,000 people live in a territory of about 44,218 square miles (114,524 square kilometers), of which a good portion is sparsely populated mountain country.

The history of the Cuban people began in 1511, when Diego Velázquez landed at Baracoa, on Cuba's northeastern tip, to take control of the island from its Indian inhabitants. The conquerors met little opposition and settled their new colony so rapidly that within 4 years of Velázquez' arrival, they had founded Havana and several other towns. The Roman Catholic spirit of the Spanish conquistadores was evident in their naming of some of the new towns—Santiago (St. James), Sancti-Spíritus (Holy Spirit), Trinidad (Trinity). But there were also political reasons for naming other places. When Columbus sailed past the southern coast of Cuba, he named the archipelago stretching along it Jardines De La Reina ("queen's gardens"), in tribute to Queen Isabella who financed his voyages of discovery. Not to be outdone, Diego Velázquez christened the archipelago facing the northern coast Jardines del Rey ("king's gardens"), in honor of King Ferdinand of Aragon, Isabella's husband.

On their arrival in Cuba, the Spaniards found the island inhabited by tribes of tall Indians whose skins had a copper hue. The Indians were an intelligent, mild people who farmed the land. The conquerors promptly put the Indians to work in their fields and in the mines as slaves. Although the Indians were formally emancipated around 1550, they became virtually extinct as a race. Many of them died of diseases that were brought in by the white man and to which they had no natural immunity. But memories of the Indians live on in the names of many Cuban mountains, rivers, and towns—the name "Cuba" is derived from the Indian word *cubanacan,* which means a "center" or "central place."

Cuba was colonized by Spaniards and Creoles (people of Spanish parentage born in the New World). But in the centuries that followed the earliest settlements, Negro slaves were brought to the island in large numbers to work as cheap manpower. They established the island's present-day Afro-Cuban culture, which has had such a strong influence on Cuban music and folklore. The large number of Spanish immigrants who came to Cuba, mainly from the Canary Islands, in the opening years of the 20th century served to even out the racial balance. Nowadays, the whites account for slightly over half of all Cubans; most of the rest are blacks and mulattoes (people of mixed white and black parentage). There is also a Chinese minority in Cuba.

HISTORY

In 1516 the Spaniards started a shipbuilding industry in Cuba, and Hernando Cortes used the island the following year as the starting point for his conquest of the Aztec empire in Mexico. In 1539 Hernando de Soto sailed from Cuba to capture Florida for the Spanish Crown. Neither Cortes nor De Soto, to be sure, had to sail very far to reach his objective. Nevertheless, Cuba thus won its fame as the gateway to the New World.

Cuba existed in relative tranquility under the Spanish rule of captains-general, named by the Crown, until 1762 when the British captured Havana. But a year later they traded it back to Spain for Florida. (A detailed account of the early history of the Caribbean islands can be found in the article CARIBBEAN SEA AND ISLANDS.)

Serenity returned to Spanish Cuba. It was not disturbed again until the unsuccessful wars of independence in the latter part of the 19th century. The Cuban patriots—those Cubans who wanted independence from Spain—failed in their first two attempts. However, it was inevitable that independence would come eventually. The Spanish Empire was rapidly breaking up, and such influential revolutionary leaders as José Martí knew it was only a question of time and opportunity before independence came. In addition to being a revolutionary leader, Martí was also a poet and a great hero to the Cuban people.

Both the time and the opportunity for revolution came with the Spanish-American War in 1898. The American involvement in the war was touched off when the United States battleship *Maine* was mysteriously blown up in Havana harbor. The war with the United States cost Spain Cuba and Puerto Rico, as well as the Philippines and Guam. However, the war did not bring true independence to Cuba. For all practical purposes, Spanish influence in Cuba was replaced by American influence.

To be sure, Cuba was granted formal independence in 1902. However, Cuba was allowed formal independence only after accepting the so-called Platt Amendment as part of the new Cuban constitution. This amendment established United States military bases on the island (including the famous base at Guantánamo, which the United States still holds). It also provided the following conditions: "The government of Cuba consents that the United States may exercise the right to intervene for the protection of Cuban independence, the maintenance of a government adequate for the protection of life, property and individual liberty. . . ."

The Platt Amendment, in fact, turned Cuba into something quite close to a dependency of the United States. The United States never hesitated to apply pressures based on this privilege. The conditions of the Platt Amendment were also underlying causes of the Castro revolution 57 years later.

For over half a century, the United States made its political and economic influence profoundly felt in Cuba. The young republic had a series of uprisings, coups d'état, and every other imaginable form of internal struggle. The 1920's brought the dictatorship of Gerardo Machado y Morales. The Machado government was overthrown by revolutionaries led by a young sergeant in the Cuban army named Fulgencio Batista y Zaldívar. The overthrow of the Machado regime brought Ramón Grau San Martín to the presidency. However, Batista was able to take over the government as dictator in 1934. Batista's government won American support. In 1944 Batista's regime was replaced, and for a relatively brief period of time Cuba had a representative democracy. This was not to last for long. A new coup returned Batista to power in 1952. In a way, the stage was again set for revolution.

Castro. On July 26, 1953, a young Havana lawyer named Fidel Castro, the son of a Spaniard from Galicia, attempted to storm the Cuban army barracks in Santiago. He was captured, tried, and sentenced to prison, but not before he told the court in what was to be the first of his marathon speeches, "History will absolve me." Batista subsequently freed Castro. He lived to regret it. The young lawyer, who used his time in prison to expand his vast knowledge of history and politics by devouring one book after another, left for Mexico where he proceeded to organize an invasion of Cuba. In December, 1956, he landed with a small band of companions in Oriente province and set up his base in the Sierra Maestra, near Pico Turquino. Castro then began a guerrilla war against the Batista government. He attracted to his side peasants as well as students, intellectuals, and liberals from the cities. His chief lieutenants were his brother Raúl Castro and Ernesto (Ché) Guevara, an Argentine revolutionary physician with strong sympathies for Communism.

It took Castro 2 years to bring about Batista's downfall as a virtual civil war developed in Cuba. There was extensive sabotage, occasional military clashes, and a reign of terror against Castro and his followers by Batista and his police. Nationwide unrest deepened. Batista fled Cuba on December 31, 1958, and 3 days later Castro, the bearded guerrilla leader, swept into Havana to take over the government.

The revolution changed virtually everything in Cuba. Above all, it changed the Cuban people. In the heyday of the revolution, Castro had most Cubans behind him. He was a hero to peasants and students, to bankers and lawyers, to women and children—to almost everyone in Cuba. Before his break with the liberals, Castro was probably the first leader ever to unite the nation. Cubans, who traditionally tended to be easygoing, fun-loving, and cynical, suddenly became serious about their country. They became excited about social justice, economic development, and neighborhood improvements. A sense of purpose swept the country.

But, somehow, Cubans managed to retain their fondness for the pleasures of life. In the first months of the victorious revolution—before Castro began to establish a Communist state and to set up his own brand of dictatorship—the Cuban nights were alive with the sounds of the islanders' favorite dances, guarachas and Afro-Cuban *pachangas*. Having inherited the love of baseball from the Americans, the Cubans filled the baseball stadiums. Even Castro came out occasionally to pitch against professional batters. For others, the evenings were filled with cockfights, another favorite Cuban sport. The roulette wheels whirred in the casinos of Havana, and beautiful dancing girls performed in elaborate nightclubs to the music of the rumba. Ernest Hemingway, the famous American writer, loved Cuba second only to Spain. He lived in a Havana suburb and let it be known that he, too, was for the revolution. Castro and the Cuban people were having a delightful honeymoon.

CUBA UNDER CASTRO

In 1970, the Cuban revolution was more than a decade old. The Castro government had survived the Bay of Pigs invasion mounted by Cuban exiles and directed by the United States in 1961. A year and a half later, the Castro government emerged unscathed from the missile crisis, which erupted when the Soviet Union began installing on Cuban territory nuclear weapons that were aimed at the United States. The confrontation that followed between John F. Kennedy, the President of the United

States, and Soviet Premier Nikita Khrushchev threatened not only to engulf Cuba, but to plunge the world into a nuclear war.

Castro had to ally his government with the Communist world. He also had to call himself a Communist. In this way Cuba became eligible for massive economic aid from the Communists and was better able to survive the severing of all its ties with the United States. It has been estimated that it costs the Soviet Union $1,000,000 a day to keep Cuba going economically. In addition, the Soviets have had the expense of equipping and training the Cuban armed forces to become the third largest and strongest army in the Western Hemisphere, after those of the United States and Canada.

In a sense, Castro's achievements have been noteworthy. He smashed the old political, economic, and social order. He nationalized $1,000,000,000 worth of American investments in Cuba, enforced a drastic land reform, and geared Cuba to a Marxist- or Communist-style economy. Building a new order, he created agricultural collectives and co-operatives; put industry and most of commerce in the hands of the government; and filled the country with schools, hospitals, child-care centers, and recreational facilities for underprivileged Cubans—and the underprivileged were the great majority of the population.

But the price Cubans paid for these reforms was equally great or greater. Although the standard of living rose, Cubans had to go through years of shortages and deprivations. Castro created a police state in order to make sure there was no opposition to his revolution. There were arrests, trials, prison sentences, and executions. About 500,000 Cubans —many of them badly needed professionals—fled the country, mostly to the United States.

An advance of the Castro government—a modern school for boys.

The Economy. The inexperienced army officers and revolutionary leaders whom Castro put in charge of Cuba's economy committed costly blunder upon blunder. It soon became evident that, in a sense, Cuba's dependence on the Soviet Union and other Communist countries was even greater than its former dependence on the United States. The Soviet Union supplied all of the petroleum consumed by Cuba as well as food, industrial equipment, and consumer goods. The Soviets bought Cuban sugar at artificial prices, high above the world levels. Cuba's economy had become entirely subsidized from abroad and went on operating in this rather artificial way. At the same time Castro, an impatient man, implored his fellow citizens to work hard and learn the modern techniques required to carry out his crash program for the modernization of Cuba. He scored a success in the limited field of poultry production. However, he failed, in 1969, to produce the promised record sugar crop of 10,000,000 tons. In preceding years, he barely matched the prerevolutionary production levels despite new harvesting machinery and the massive use of soldiers and civilian volunteers to cut the sugarcane. Castro personally spent long hours cutting cane with his machete to set the example for other Cubans.

Way of Life. In a curious way, the revolution benefited the countryside at the expense of the cities. The *guajiros*, the straw-hatted Cuban peasants, earned better wages than ever before. A certain amount of decent housing was made available to replace the miserable huts they had lived in. For the first time in Cuban history, the children of the *guajiros* had access to free elementary, secondary, and college education as well as to modern medical care. All of the *guajiros* were given a sense of dignity and identity they never before possessed.

In a country where the average age of the population is under 22 years—and where children under 14 account for nearly 40 percent of the total population—Castro has brought up a whole new revolutionary generation. More than half of the present population either had not been born before the revolution or had no clear recollection of the past. Regimentation replaced the former individualism of the Cubans. But Castro could still claim that his peasants had never had a better life.

In contrast, the cities bore the brunt of the national sacrifice. Castro may have cleaned Havana of theft, prostitution, and other weaknesses that in his eyes demoralized the society. And he has made a striking effort to encourage the arts and make them available to all. But Havana, the country's beautiful capital on the sea, has become a dilapidated city. The old automobiles can hardly operate because of a shortage of spare parts. The buildings have been allowed to deteriorate. Despite shortages of clothes and cosmetics, Cuban women remain attractive because of their innate sense of elegance. Although the *guajiro* is incomparably better off nowadays than a decade ago, urban living standards have plummeted.

The Future. Cuba remains potentially wealthy. Castro does not have to worry about national bankruptcy. For one thing, he can remain certain that the Soviet Union cannot afford politically to let him down as far as economic help is concerned. After his first 10 years in power Castro admitted that it had been an error to sacrifice Cuba's agricultural development in the period just after the revolution in order to industrialize the country at a breakneck speed.

Cuba's most famous luxury product, the legendary Havana cigar, is still rolled by skilled craftsmen in the traditional way.

Cuba's resources remain considerable. Notwithstanding Castro's early contempt for "king sugar," he is now pushing sugar production more and pushing industrialization less. Tobacco—the raw material of the famous Cuban cigars—is a source of income from abroad. Manganese and nickel, Cuba's principal metals, are also important to the island's economy. The fishing industry, which was once as primitive as it frequently is in the rest of the Caribbean, has been improved. There are new fishing boats and better methods of processing fish. Fish has become a major source of food supply in Cuba, and it is also sold abroad.

The question that faces Castro is how to use Cuba's natural resources most efficiently for the good of the nation without letting them be wasted in politically oriented experiments. The related question is how long he can retain his spellbinding influence over the Cuban people. It does not seem likely that any leader can maintain his own popularity and that of his government at a high pitch indefinitely. And, finally, what would happen if Castro were to vanish from the scene? There are, of course, no precise answers to these questions.

Meanwhile, Cuba—once the gateway to the New World—remains isolated from most of the countries of the Western Hemisphere. Canada and Mexico are the only meaningful trading partners Cuba has in the New World. Aside from the United States airlift from Havana to Miami to bring out thousands of refugees, Cuba's only air link with the Americas is by way of Mexico.

Yet, it must be remembered, Cuba has always been known as the "cork island," because since prehistoric times it has been tossed on the waves of the seas that surround it—and survived. The island has survived invasions, wars, revolutions, epidemics, hurricanes, and earthquakes. Therefore, it seems possible that the island nation may overcome its current problems.

TAD SZULC, Diplomatic Correspondent, *The New York Times*

El Morro, built in 1539, watches over San Juan harbor.

PUERTO RICO

The story of Puerto Rico is the story of its people. Although the island itself is beautiful, it has almost no natural resources. However, it does have a rich variety of terrains. There are lush rain forests, long, sandy beaches lined with palm groves, small but rugged mountain ranges that cross the center of the island from east to west, and in the southwest corner there is a semi-arid region with salt mines and the famous Phosphorescent Bay. And there are people everywhere: people living in small villages cradled within the central mountains; people living in the coastal towns amid the flatlands, which are covered most of the year by sugarcane; and people living in the big and growing cities. Puerto Rico's cities are concrete monuments to the island's phenomenal economic and social progress.

Puerto Rico is the smallest island of the Greater Antilles; it is also the farthest east. It is one-fourteenth the size of Cuba and one-ninth the size of Hispaniola. Only 3,435 square miles (8,900 square kilometers) in area, the island sustains a population of close to 2,800,000 people. If Puerto Rico were a state of the Union, it would rank 25th in population. (However, it would only rank 49th in area.) But Puerto Rico, although its people are United States citizens, is not a state. It is a semi-autonomous commonwealth under the protection of the United States.

Cristo Street, in Old San Juan, could be a corner of Spain.

The relation of little land and few natural resources to a big population is the single most important factor in the history of Puerto Rico in the 20th century. These lacks have been, at the same time, Puerto Rico's greatest problem and greatest challenge.

THE PEOPLE

The Puerto Rican people have had a long history. Christopher Columbus discovered the island on November 19, 1493, on his second trip to the New World. Thus, when the Pilgrims landed on Plymouth Rock, Puerto Rico had already been a Spanish possession for 127 years.

The culture of Puerto Rico is Latin American. Spain is the mother country and Spanish the mother tongue of the people of Puerto Rico. English is the island's second language and is taught in all public schools. About 80 percent of the people are Roman Catholics. In recent years Protestant churches have steadily increased throughout the island. The vast majority of the people are of Spanish descent, but centuries of intermarriage with Indians, Negroes, Latin Americans, other Europeans, and North Americans have virtually erased racial lines. Racial harmony, although not perfect, exists in Puerto Rico at a higher level than in most countries of the world.

Puerto Ricans are a particularly healthy people. This is reflected not only in the statistics (life expectancy, for instance, averages 70 years), but in the people's vitality, mobility, and, above all, their ambition and impatience for a better life.

Compared to the standard of living in the United States, most Puerto Ricans live in poverty. They live in hundreds of small towns and villages, which dot the entire island. Each town follows the traditional Spanish pattern of the plaza at the center, the white plastered church at one end, and the *alcaldía* (city hall) at the other. Agriculture is still the economic mainstay of the small towns. Sugarcane is grown on the coastal plains. Some of the sugar is refined and some is made into rum. Puerto Rican rum is world famous. Cattle, coffee, tobacco, and citrus fruits are raised in the mountains. But more and more, the government of Puerto Rico has encouraged the growth of industry near the small towns. As factories are built, the way of life of the people changes, too.

Factories bring jobs, and jobs bring money. Wooden houses are replaced by concrete houses. On Saturday afternoons the plazas of many Puerto Rican towns buzz with shoppers buying clothing, furniture, and electrical appliances. And in an ever-growing number of these towns, the small, shady streets, designed years ago for horse-drawn carriages, are becoming jammed with bumper to bumper automobile traffic. The horn blowing of impatient drivers pierces what for centuries was the silence and serenity of rural Puerto Rico.

But there are not enough factories and not enough jobs. The young people are often unwilling to wait for them. In recent years the govern-

Bottles of Puerto Rican rum are sealed for worldwide shipment.

ment has brought schools to every region of Puerto Rico. Almost every Puerto Rican young person has had at least a taste of classroom education. For an industrious and healthy people, just a taste of education creates a big appetite for more learning—and for more of everything else. The result has been the great migration of people from the rural areas to the cities. And hundreds of thousands of Puerto Ricans have gone one giant step farther—across the ocean to the United States mainland.

Cities

For all Puerto Ricans, the capital city of **San Juan** is synonymous with progress. It is a beautiful city that has become the commercial, industrial, and cultural hub not only of Puerto Rico, but of a large part of the Caribbean. San Juan offers something for everyone. The old part of the city is surrounded by the huge fortresses and walls that were built by the Spaniards to protect the island from armed invasion and from pirates. El Morro, San Cristóbal, San Jerónimo, and La Fortaleza are fortresses where visitors suddenly find themselves transported to a lost world, the world of Spain's colonial empire. La Fortaleza is still the seat of Puerto Rico's government and the residence of the island's governors.

Not far from the Old City is San Juan's Gold Coast. This "gold" is

La Fortaleza (rear), the residence of Puerto Rico's governors.

San Juan's Condado Beach is lined with luxury hotels.

not the type the conquistadores were seeking, but it attracts about 1,000,000 tourists a year. The Gold Coast is an area of huge luxury hotels, many of them on San Juan's beaches. They are gradually extending west to Dorado and east as far as Fajardo.

The Hato Rey area, San Juan's business district, is the place where the visitor can best see San Juan's great prosperity. There are tall, modern buildings in Hato Rey, which house banks, airlines, large industries, and government offices.

Directly south of the Hato Rey, in the Río Piedras district, is the main campus of the University of Puerto Rico. Established in 1903, the university now has some 30,000 students in all fields. The Río Piedras campus has buildings designed in both traditional Spanish style and in the most modern styles of architecture.

Around San Juan are sprawling housing developments called *urbanizaciones*. These communities have brightly colored concrete houses surrounded by flower gardens and citrus trees. The *urbanizaciones* show, dramatically, how many of the migrants from rural areas have climbed into the middle class. But not all of the rural migrants have succeeded financially. There are also sprawling slums in San Juan—thousands of wooden houses, with rusted tin roofs, tightly packed together along the canals that wind through the center of the city.

There are other urbanized areas in Puerto Rico: **Ponce** on the south coast and **Mayagüez** on the western tip of the island. But they are still far from competing with San Juan.

Each of these small cities has its own distinct personality. The people of Ponce are trying to preserve Puerto Rico's traditional Spanish architecture and customs. The second largest city on the island, Ponce is also an important seaport. The people of Mayagüez hope to keep alive the island's agricultural tradition. Ponce offers not only its beautiful tree-lined plaza, but also the island's most important museum of art, El Museo de Ponce. This fine museum has an excellent collection of classical European and modern Puerto Rican and Latin American art. Mayagüez is the home of the island's College of Agriculture and Engineering, a branch of the University of Puerto Rico. The surrounding plains and soft rolling hills are among the most fertile in Puerto Rico.

Way of Life

Ponce, Mayagüez, and rural Puerto Rico are so different from metropolitan San Juan that many people say that there are really two Puerto Ricos. Each is characterized not only by the different stages of physical development, but also by different styles of living.

The Puerto Rican outside San Juan continues to be essentially a family-oriented person. His basic diet consists of the traditional rice and kidney bean stew, codfish, and roast pork. The head of a household works hard and is something of an authoritarian in his relations with his

This is the striking foyer of Ponce's excellent art museum.

A traveling theater brings Spanish plays to the countryside.

wife and children. He goes to bed soon after sundown and is up at sunrise. He is generous and convinced that his life and the lives of his family are controlled by fate, but he is also convinced that fate will be generous to him and to his family.

The Puerto Rican in San Juan has had his traditional family life greatly altered. A wife may leave the house with her husband in the morning to go to her own job. In fact, if the family can afford it, the wife may have her own car. The family eats what is on sale at the big supermarkets located in shopping centers. The food is not much different from that eaten in New York or Los Angeles, but it is a little costlier. The family stays up late watching many of the same television programs seen in the mainland United States, except that the voices have been dubbed in Spanish.

The head of a family in San Juan spends a good deal of his income on improving his house or apartment. He saves very little. Credit is readily available in Puerto Rico, and a family often spends more money than it earns. But on most weekends the father of a San Juan household packs his family in the car and heads out into the other Puerto Rico—into the country or to one of the smaller cities—where it is still green, relaxed, and informal. They visit relatives and for a few hours relive a kind of life that they have probably given up permanently.

But there is a third Puerto Rico—the 1,000,000 or more people that left the farm and went up to New York and other large cities on the United States mainland. The existence in New York (and other cities) of jobs requiring little or no skill, and offering good salaries compared with those in Puerto Rico, was the decisive factor in this massive movement northward. Almost all of the Puerto Rican migrants went to live in New York's worst slums. Many of them were subjected to ethnic and racial

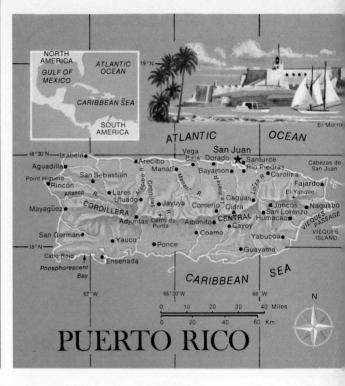

PUERTO RICO

prejudice. None of them were really prepared to live in a cold climate and in a culture that they did not understand.

It shocked many mainlanders to see so many Puerto Ricans leaving their beautiful, warm, friendly island for the cold harshness of mainland urban slums. But the Puerto Rican migrant was sustained by a personal dream. He wanted more than just a good-paying job; he dreamed of returning one day to Puerto Rico to live a good life. Many fulfilled that dream. The peculiar thing about the migration of Puerto Ricans is that there is also a return migration. In some years, when there are fewer jobs in New York and other mainland cities, more Puerto Ricans return to the island than leave it.

PUERTO RICO AND THE UNITED STATES

All of this movement—indeed, all of the progress in Puerto Rico—is made possible by Puerto Rico's unique political association with the United States. Puerto Ricans are United States citizens. As such, they move to and from the mainland just as mainlanders move between states. The island is officially a commonwealth; in Spanish, an *estado libre asociado* ("free associate state"). Puerto Rico forms part of the United States federal system—very much like a state of the Union. But there are two important differences. Puerto Ricans living on the island are exempt from all federal taxes, and they do not vote for the president of the United States or have voting representation in the United States Congress. However, Puerto Rico has more governmental and financial autonomy than the states in the Union. The island elects its own governor and legislature. Laws made by Congress generally apply to Puerto Rico. The island has one representative in Congress, called a resident commissioner. He participates in all the work of Congress, but does not vote.

Many visitors to Puerto Rico wonder how the island evolved this unique relationship with the United States. Many ask why Puerto Rico, being so close to the United States, does not ask for entry into the Union as a full-fledged state. Others ask why the island, having a Latin American culture and desiring to preserve it, does not become an independent republic as have so many other Latin nations in the Western Hemisphere. Puerto Ricans themselves have debated this question for many years. What Puerto Ricans call the status issue has in fact monopolized island politics.

The majority of the people favor continuing commonwealth status. A large minority favors statehood. A much smaller minority favors independence. In 1967 the question was put directly to the people in a referendum, and 60 percent voted for commonwealth, 39 percent for statehood, and 1 percent for independence.

The long history of Puerto Rico reveals why the island's people have sought an unusual solution to their political problems.

HISTORY

According to legend (only partially verified by documents) Christopher Columbus considered Puerto Rico the most beautiful of the Caribbean islands he visited. However, for the adventurous Spaniards who accompanied Columbus and for those who were to follow his path over the next 3 centuries, the striking thing about the island was not so much its beauty as its lack of valuable natural resources and the quietness of life there. Juan Ponce de León became the island's first governor. But if Ponce de León expected to make his fortune in Puerto Rico he was doomed to disappointment; he had to roam far from the island to find either gold or adventure.

The Indians whom Ponce de León found living in Puerto Rico were few in number and generally peaceful. It was not long, however, before the native population had practically disappeared. In fact, less than 50 years after Ponce de León colonized Puerto Rico, authorities reported that almost all Indians had died either in war or of disease or had fled to neighboring islands. It is known, however, that some fled to the island's central mountains, and among many Puerto Ricans one can still see Indian racial characteristics.

Puerto Rico's major problem in the 16th century was preventing total depopulation of the island. Since there was neither great wealth nor great adventure to be found there, as there was in Mexico or Peru, for instance, few Spaniards wanted to stay. However, Spain considered the island of great strategic importance as the gateway to its vast colonial empire. So did Spain's enemies—especially the British, Dutch, and French. At one time or another all sent ships and troops to take Puerto Rico away from Spain. All expeditions failed, due to the marvelous Spanish fortresses protecting San Juan—and due to the bravery of the island's defenders. But despite the island's strategic importance, the Spaniards living on Puerto Rico dreamed of going to places like Mexico and Peru, where fabulous wealth awaited them. Through the centuries, many did leave. In 1800, after 300 years of Spanish rule, the island's population was only 155,426.

But things did begin to happen in the 19th century, as they happened everywhere else in the Spanish Empire. Just as Latin Americans were asserting for the first time a national identity distinct from Spain, the Puerto Rican people were saying that they were not "overseas Spaniards," but Puerto Ricans. It was a century of upheaval in Spain, and as the Spanish Government became somewhat more liberal at home, its policies in the New World also became more liberal. Early in the 19th century Puerto Rico sent its first representative, Ramón Power y Giralt, to the Spanish parliament. Power was an outstanding speaker, and he achieved important improvements in internal government and trade regulations for Puerto Rico. But when politics in Spain went back to absolutism, some of the old repressive policies were again imposed on the Spanish colonies. These restrictions merely served to increase the passion of the Latin Americans for freedom from Spain.

There was a desire for freedom in Puerto Rico, too, but with two distinguishing characteristics. First, Puerto Ricans wanted change, but they rejected violence. There was never a revolution on the island; the only attempted uprising, in 1868 near the small town of Lares, collapsed almost immediately because of lack of support from the people. The second difference was that Puerto Ricans wanted freedom, but not independence. The Puerto Rican goal was to achieve personal freedom, the abolition of slavery, and full self-government, but without breaking its bonds with Spain. Champions of this autonomist movement were such political leaders as Ramón Baldorioty de Castro and, towards the end of the century, Luis Muñoz Rivera. Finally, in 1897, Muñoz Rivera got a liberal Spanish government to agree to the Charter of Autonomy for the island. The following year Puerto Rico's first local government was organized, with Muñoz Rivera as prime minister. But there was to occur, within a year, an abrupt and unexpected change in the entire course of Puerto Rican history.

United States Involvement. In 1898, as one of the conditions to ending the Spanish-American War between the United States and Spain, Spain was forced to cede Puerto Rico to the victorious United States. Before the end of the war, American troops had landed on the island's south coast and had moved up all the way to San Juan without resistance from the Spanish garrison. Strangely enough the Americans were welcomed warmly by the Puerto Rican people, who saw in the United States flag a symbol of freedom and prosperity. Under the new sovereignty, however, Puerto Rico reverted back to a purely colonial government. But now there was a difference. Whereas the United States Government showed no great desire to give Puerto Rico self-government, it did demonstrate concern for the island's overwhelming problem—the extreme poverty in which all but a handful of the Puerto Rican people lived.

The Puerto Rican political leadership was dazed by the events of 1898. Their immediate reaction upon seeing how the people welcomed the Americans was to ask for statehood. But soon after, the leadership divided itself into the three familiar camps—those wanting complete independence, those wanting assimilation into the United States, and those wanting something in between, autonomy. Muñoz Rivera, who was elected Puerto Rico's resident commissioner in the United States Congress, continued as leader of the autonomist movement. In 1916 he convinced Congress to increase the island's self-government and to extend United States citizenship to all Puerto Ricans.

United States officials, more concerned about improving the miser-

Barranquitas is a small Puerto Rican town nestled in the hills.

able lot of the people of Puerto Rico than in getting involved in island politics, carried out programs for the building of schools, hospitals, and roads. In the 1930's President Franklin D. Roosevelt attempted to extend his New Deal program to the island, with several welfare and development projects. Some progress was made. Private investment came to the island to develop the sugar industry, but the industry was so small that it hardly touched the lives of the great majority of people. The problem now was a too-large population growing too fast. But it was also that the local political leadership seemed to be obsessed with its status issue and to have little inclination to deal with the more pressing problems of economic and social improvement.

The turning point in island history came in 1940 when Luis Muñoz Marín, only son of Muñoz Rivera, came to power, winning election to the Puerto Rican legislature by a very narrow margin. Only the legislature was then elected by the people; the governor was still named by the president of the United States. Muñoz Marín became president of the Puerto Rican senate and carried out a broad program of economic reform. He insisted that the island's problems of poverty, unemployment, bad housing and health, and terrible educational facilities have priority over the status issue. His efforts to attack these human ills got the support of the people and of the United States Government.

In 1941 President Roosevelt named Rexford Tugwell governor of

Puerto Rico. An experienced administrator with progressive ideas, Tugwell worked closely with Muñoz Marín to begin what was to become Puerto Rico's "peaceful revolution." In 1948 Puerto Rico was given the right to elect its own governor. Muñoz Marín, as expected, was elected by a large majority.

It was not long before Muñoz and his government made one fundamental discovery. All the reform laws and all the speeches about equality and social justice were not going to do much to lift the island from 4 centuries of economic misery unless there was large-scale industrialization. The assignment of promoting the industrialization of the island was given to Teodoro Moscoso, a former aide to Tugwell. Moscoso organized Operation Bootstrap, which proved remarkably successful, finally putting the island on the road to prosperity.

The status issue, however, still lurked in the background, and Muñoz Marín decided to tackle it. All of his mature life he had been an *independentista* (an advocate of independence). But his political career

A new house goes up because of government aid—and hard work.

had taught him that the people then, as during the previous century, rejected nationalism and political separation. And his governmental career had taught him that independence would kill any hope of rapid industrialization. The experience of Operation Bootstrap had proved that capital investment was coming to the island because Puerto Rico was under the United States flag. Goods produced on the island had free entry into mainland markets. On the other hand, tax exemption was the big inducement to attract industries. Statehood would mean ending tax exemption. Thus, Muñoz also decided that statehood was economically impossible.

In 1952, after Congress had approved appropriate legislation and Puerto Rico had drafted and approved its own Constitution, commonwealth status was officially proclaimed. Under this new status the islanders retained both United States citizenship and tax exemption. Commonwealth status also did much for the dignity of Puerto Rico. It lifted the island from colonial status to a position of full self-determination. For the first time since the landing of United States troops in 1898, Puerto Rico had the status that the majority of its people wanted.

Historians have come to call the years 1940 to 1964 the Era of Muñoz. During those years he and his Partido Popular Democrático (PDP) received great support from the people. Particularly among the rural people, the *jíbaros*, Muñoz Marín was the object of intense loyalty and affection. He had not only helped to give the island one of the world's fastest growing economies (a growth rate of 10 percent a year) and provided an answer to the status issue, but he had also encouraged the people to use their new prosperity wisely, creating a good civilization in spiritual as well as in material values. In the mid 1950's he named this goal Operation Serenity.

In 1964, at the age of 66, Muñoz Marín declined the nomination of his party to run for a fifth consecutive term as governor. He personally selected his chief assistant, Roberto Sánchez Vilella, to run for the governorship, and the party won again by a large margin. The exit of Muñoz from the seat of power, however, divided the party into warring factions. Governor Sánchez Vilella left the PDP, and in 1968 the division produced the defeat of the party. Luis A. Ferré, a leading industrialist and Statehood Republican Party (SRP) candidate for governor in three previous elections, won the governorship. However, Ferré won the governorship as head of his own party, the New Progressive Party, not as a candidate of the SRP.

The new party in power was also committed to statehood for Puerto Rico—a major departure from the policies of the Era of Muñoz. However, Puerto Rico's great need to continue industrialization was a strong indication that even the New Progressive Party would not pressure either the people or Congress for a rapid change in status. The Muñoz administration had made it very clear that statehood would cause many problems in the industrialization program. As evidence of this the PDP candidate, Rafael Hernandez Colon, was elected governor in 1972.

Puerto Rico is still one of the poorest areas under the United States flag. The island still has a long road ahead to catch up. But the people of Puerto Rico, who have come such a long way in such a short time, are as restless and impatient as ever. There is every reason to believe that their peaceful revolution will continue.

ALEX W. MALDONADO, associate editor, *El Mundo*, San Juan, Puerto Rico

DOMINICAN REPUBLIC

The Dominican Republic is the largest Caribbean country after Cuba. Sharing the island of Hispaniola with Haiti, the Dominican Republic occupies approximately the eastern two thirds of the land area. With its rugged mountains and fertile valleys, Hispaniola is very beautiful.

The people of the Dominican Republic and those of Haiti have little in common except the island they share. They speak different languages (Spanish in the Dominican Republic and French and Creole in Haiti); they have widely different cultures; and they have fought many times across their common border. The racial heritage of the two nations is also different. Haiti is largely a black nation, with a deep racial consciousness and a history that has been scarred by racial violence. The Dominican Republic is a mulatto country. Nobody knows for sure what the exact percentage is, but probably about 60 or 70 percent of its 4,000,000 people are of mixed black and white ancestry. Dominicans have experienced little racial conflict. Yet the Dominican Republic's history has been mainly an unhappy one, marked by repeated armed invasions from abroad and by poverty, dictatorship, and division at home.

THE PEOPLE

Christopher Columbus discovered the island of Hispaniola for Spain on December 5, 1492. Columbus' initial landing was on the part of the island now included in Haiti, but the first permanent settlements

The ruins of a 16th-century Spanish building in Santo Domingo.

were made in the Dominican part of the island, which the native Indians called Quisqueya. The first words of the Dominican Republic's national anthem are *Quisqueyanos valientes* ("courageous Dominicans"). Although many places in the country still have Indian names, the Indians have had little influence in Dominican history.

Following the discovery of Hispaniola, the Spaniards quickly established settlements in the eastern part of the island. These included Santo Domingo, which was founded in 1496 and became the seat of Spanish colonial government in the New World. The Spaniards lost no time in taking gold from the native Indians, most of whom belonged to the friendly Taino tribe. The Spaniards repaid the Tainos' friendship by murdering and enslaving them. By 1550 the Indians had all but disappeared from the island. Long before that time, the Spaniards had begun to replace the Indian workers with slave laborers from Africa. The Dominican people are descended from the Spaniards and African slaves.

A Mulatto Culture. The Dominican Republic has the distinction of being the only predominantly mulatto nation in the Americas. It is mixed culturally as well as racially, since it is enriched to about the same degree by its Spanish and African heritages.

Spanish is the country's language and Roman Catholicism is the predominant and official religion. But African-derived music and dancing often find their way into religious observances. The African influence, in fact, is apparent in much Dominican music.

But the customs and culture of old Spain are still very much alive in the republic, too, especially in the country's great central agricultural region, the Cibao. The Cibao is the most Spanish part of the Dominican Republic, the home of the nation's oldest and most powerful families. Medieval and Renaissance words and turns of phrase, which disappeared long ago from modern Spanish, are still part of the daily vocabulary of the people of the Cibao. The reciting of Spanish Renaissance couplets and the dancing of traditional Spanish dances are still favorite pastimes there.

The average Dominican lives in a simple house or cottage, usually built of wood and often roofed with thatch. The favorite piece of furniture is the rocking chair. Even poor families frequently have several wooden rockers for the various members of the family and for guests. They use them in the house and on their front porches, where they sit to catch the trade winds.

The most popular dish in the average Dominican home is *sancocho*. *Sancocho* is a rich stew that usually includes potatoes, yucca, plantains, and whatever meats are available. Goat is the usual meat included in the stew, but pork, beef, chicken, pigeons, and on rare occasions, even parrots or egrets are included as well. It is cooked for several hours in a big iron pot.

Although there are many instances of Spanish and African influences in Dominican life, the United States has inevitably had an influence, too. The national pastime of the country is baseball, and many wealthy Dominicans send their children to American schools and colleges.

Light Skins, Dark Skins. Compared with its neighbor, Haiti, the Dominican Republic had a mild experience of slavery in colonial times. Haiti (or Saint-Domingue as it was called under French rule) was ceded to France by Spain in 1697. Under French rule it developed into the rich-

FACTS AND FIGURES

DOMINICAN REPUBLIC—República Dominicana—is the official name of the country.

CAPITAL: Santo Domingo.

LOCATION: North America (eastern two thirds of the island of Hispaniola in the Caribbean Sea). **Latitude**—17° 36′ N to 19° 58′ N. **Longitude**—68° 19′ W to 72° W.

AREA: 18,816 sq. mi. (48,734 sq. km.).

PHYSICAL FEATURES: Highest point—Pico Duarte (10,417 ft.; 3,175 m.). **Lowest point**—sea level. **Chief rivers**—Yaque del Norte, Yaque del Sur, Yuna.

POPULATION: 4,029,000 (estimate).

LANGUAGE: Spanish.

RELIGION: Roman Catholic.

GOVERNMENT: Republic. **Head of government**—president. **Legislature**—national congress. **International co-operation**—United Nations, Organization of American States (OAS).

CHIEF CITIES: Santo Domingo, Santiago de los Caballeros.

ECONOMY: Chief minerals—nickel, bauxite, limestone, gypsum, salt. **Chief agricultural products**—sugar, coffee, cacao, tobacco, plantains, rice, maize (corn), groundnuts (peanuts), livestock. **Industries and products**—sugar, cement, textiles, glass bottles, paper and cardboard. **Chief exports**—sugar, coffee, cacao, tobacco. **Chief imports**—chemical and pharmaceutical products, foodstuffs, automobiles, petroleum.

MONETARY UNIT: Dominican peso oro.

NATIONAL HOLIDAY: February 27.

NATIONAL ANTHEM: *Quisqueyanos valientes* ("Courageous Dominicans").

est European colony in the New World. But the economy of Saint-Domingue (Haiti) was a plantation economy based on the harshest exploitation of hundreds of thousands of Negro slaves. In neighboring Spanish Hispaniola (now the Dominican Republic) the economy was based on raising cattle for export to richer, more populous Saint-Domingue.

By its very nature, the cattle industry worked to soften relations between the races. Spanish master and African slave would go out together to watch over the herd, and both men would have to be armed. This made for a relationship strong in trust and camaraderie. Under Spanish law it was comparatively easy for slaves to buy their freedom, and many did. In contrast to Haiti, the Dominican Republic has escaped the ravages of racial strife throughout its history.

That fact notwithstanding, it is also true that wealthy Dominicans today are usually white and that black Dominicans are usually poor. In part, the Negro's continuing poverty derives from the sheer lack of economic opportunity. But racial prejudice operates here, too. A black Dominican is likely to have a harder time finding a good job than a light-skinned person with the same qualifications. A kind of snobbery exists even among very poor Dominicans, who commonly refuse to work in the sugar fields, considering cane cutting to be degrading work. The Dominican Republic is a nation in which unemployment is one of the major problems; yet thousands of workers must be brought in from across the border in Haiti to cut the Dominican sugar crop.

HISTORY

In 1795, after being routed by French armies in Europe, Spain ceded its Hispaniola colony, Santo Domingo, as well as other colonial territories, to France. At that time the population of Spanish Hispaniola was from 100,000 to 150,000, at least half of whom were whites and freemen of mixed blood. Neighboring Saint-Domingue (Haiti) had a total of about 50,000 or 60,000 whites and free non-whites, and about 500,000 black slaves.

In 1791 the Negroes of Saint-Domingue (Haiti) had risen up in rebellion against their masters. The French were eventually driven out entirely, and in 1804 Haiti became an independent nation. Santo Domingo remained in French hands until 1809, when it became a Spanish colony again. Dominican historians refer to this second period of Spanish rule as the reign of *España boba* ("foolish Spain"), because it was characterized by such utter incompetency. In 1821 the Dominicans shipped the colonial governor back to Spain and proclaimed their independence. However, within a matter of weeks the armies of neighboring Haiti marched across the border and brought the whole island under Haitian rule. So it remained for 22 years, a cruel and oppressive time that Dominicans still think of with bitterness.

In 1844 Haitian rule was overthrown, and the Dominican Republic was proclaimed. Unfortunately, the new nation was beset by the internal conflict and corruption that have characterized the politics of the Dominican Republic for most of its history. The republic had its honest and liberal leaders. But since there was no strong democratic tradition to rally the nation behind these men, Dominican politics became a welter of corruption and betrayal, plots, coups, and assassinations. Unscrupulous Dominican politicians kept trying to barter their country away for their own profit.

Fear of a new Haitian occupation led the Dominican Government to arrange for the country's re-annexation by Spain in 1861. Independence was regained in 1865. In 1869 the entire Dominican Republic was offered, by treaty, to the United States. The treaty was not ratified by the United States Senate; if it had been, the Dominican Republic might now be part of the United States.

By the early 20th century irresponsible leaders had placed the Dominican Republic deeply in debt to American and European investors. In 1905 the United States took over the collection of Dominican customs to insure the payment of the nation's debts. From that point, the United States took an increasingly active role in the Dominican Republic's affairs until finally, in 1916, the United States Marines occupied the country and a United States military government was established. In part, the American take-over was dictated by United States concern over the course of World War I and the fear of possible German influence in Hispaniola. The American military occupation continued until 1924. Following the occupation, there were 6 years of relative democracy under the presidency of Horacio Vásquez. However, in 1930 the most powerful of the nation's dictators, Rafael Leonidas Trujillo Molina, became president.

The Trujillo Era.   Rafael Trujillo was the son of a small businessman from San Cristóbal, an inland town about 15 miles (24 kilometers) west of Santo Domingo. In the 1920's Trujillo had risen through the ranks of the Dominican police. In 1928 the police force became the national army and he was named chief of staff. In 1930 he engineered the overthrow of the Vásquez government and had himself elected president in an obviously rigged election. Trujillo then went on to rule the Dominican

Republic for 31 years, either holding the presidency himself or arranging for the election of a puppet president of his choosing. He not only ruled the nation; he also dominated every aspect of its life. He renamed the capital city of Santo Domingo Ciudad Trujillo, or "Trujillo city." (After Trujillo was assassinated in 1961, the city was called Santo Domingo again.) Statues and photographs of the dictator appeared everywhere, as did signs that read *Dios y Trujillo* ("God and Trujillo"). Meanwhile, Trujillo virtually transformed the nation into his private estate.

To be sure, there were some accomplishments during the long Trujillo era. The United States customs receivership was finally ended; sanitation was improved; and sugar, banana, coffee, and cacao production were increased. Trujillo also rebuilt the capital after most of it was destroyed by a hurricane in 1930. As a result, Santo Domingo is one of the most modern cities in the Caribbean. But the gains that were made under Trujillo carried little benefit for most Dominicans.

THE LAND

At the end of the Trujillo era in 1961, the Dominican Republic was still a very poor nation. It remains so today. Fortunately it is also a nation rich in economic potential. Its soil is fertile, and its mountains contain stands of pine, mahogany, and other valuable woods. With just under 1,000 miles (1,600 km.) of coastline, there is a scarcely tapped potential for a sizable fishing industry. For tourists there are fine beaches, beauti-

A rural village. Most Dominicans are still small farmers.

ful mountains, and places of considerable historical interest. But because of its unstable governments and lack of tourist facilities, the country attracts virtually no tourists today.

The Dominican Republic, 18,816 square miles (48,734 square kilometers) in area, has a generally mountainous terrain. It is a tropical country with warm temperatures all year. The average yearly temperature range is 75 to 85 degrees Fahrenheit (24–30 degrees Celsius). Geographically as well as politically, this is a divided country. Many Dominicans are entirely ignorant of regions of the country other than their own. The largest mountain range, the Cordillera Central, practically divides the country in half, extending from the Haitian border westward for almost the entire length of the island. An extension in the east is called the Cordillera Oriental.

To the north is a smaller range, the Cordillera Setentrional, which runs parallel to the Cordillera Central and ends east of Samaná Bay. The two ranges enclose La Vega Real ("the royal valley"), a rich and fertile valley; La Vega Real is the eastern portion of Cibao, a broad lowland extending eastward from Monte Cristi. This is the most prosperous part of the Dominican Republic, a region of flourishing farms and bustling cities such as Santiago and La Vega. The bulk of the rice, corn, and beans grown for domestic consumption is produced in the Cibao, which is called the food basket of the nation. Most of the nation's cacao, tobacco, and coffee—crops grown principally for export—are produced in the Cibao, too.

The Dominican Republic's largest cash crop is sugar, most of which is grown on great estates, or plantations, in the southern and southeastern parts of the country. The coastal plain that covers that region is also suitable for cattle raising. In the west and southwest the country is generally dry, with large stretches of desert.

A new public housing project goes up in the nation's capital.

A modern courtyard at the University of Santo Domingo.

Dominicans are principally an agricultural people. What industry there is in the Dominican Republic is largely involved in food processing. Agricultural products account for about 85 percent of the value of the country's exports, and sugar products alone account for more than 50 percent. Most of the produce for export comes from a relatively small

Santo Domingo's Centro de los Héroes rises beside the Carribbean.

number of farms. The typical Dominican farmer, however, owns a very small farm and raises little more than he needs for himself and his family. And many Dominicans have no land of their own and have to make their living by working for large landholders.

CITIES

In the absence of land reforms, many poor and landless Dominicans are migrating to Santo Domingo and other cities in search of opportunity.

Santo Domingo, the capital, is by far the republic's largest city, with a population of more than 575,000 people. It is the principal port and commercial center of the nation. It also has the distinction of being the oldest city in the Western Hemisphere. Buildings of the first half of the 16th century, when Santo Domingo was the center of Spanish life in the New World, are still standing today. They include the Cathedral of Saint Mary the Minor, which contains a tomb believed by some historians to hold the remains of Christopher Columbus. (Other historians believe Columbus is buried in Seville.) Another relic of the 16th century is the Alcázar de Colón ("castle of Columbus"), which was the home and head-quarters of Diego Columbus, the explorer's son, when he was governor of Hispaniola. Santo Domingo is also the home of the University of Santo Domingo, the leading institution of higher learning in this still largely illiterate nation.

Santiago de los Caballeros, or Santiago, is the republic's second largest city. With a population of over 100,000, it is the largest city of the Cibao region and also its commercial center. It was initially settled in 1504.

GOVERNMENT

Following the assassination of Trujillo, the nation's first democratic election in almost 40 years was held in 1962 and resulted in the election of Juan Bosch to the presidency. Bosch had enemies among the Dominican Communists on one side; among the landholding, business, and professional classes on another side; and among the military on a third side. Within 7 months after he was inaugurated as president, Bosch's government was overthrown by a military coup.

In April, 1965, the three-man government that had replaced the Bosch government was also overthrown by the military. Fighting then broke out between different factions of the military. As the situation became chaotic, the United States dispatched more than 20,000 Marines to Santo Domingo with the stated purpose of restoring peace and preventing any possible Communist take-over of the nation. Subsequently, the Organization of American States (OAS) dispatched a peacekeeping force to Santo Domingo, into which the American troops were incorporated. In 1966 a free election was held under OAS auspices. Joaquín Balaguer defeated former president Bosch for the presidency. All OAS forces were subsequently withdrawn from the country.

Today the Dominican Republic is governed under the provisions of a constitution adopted in 1966. The executive power is vested in a president and vice-president, elected by direct popular vote for 4-year terms. Legislative powers are exercised by a congress made up of a senate of 27 members and a house of deputies of 74 members.

MARCIO VELEZ MAGGIOLO, University of Santo Domingo, Dominican Republic

Haiti's legendary Citadelle towers above the jungle.

HAITI

Haiti, which occupies the western third of the island of Hispaniola, is a land of romance, adventure, and mystery for everyone but the Haitians. Its artists, dancers, and drummers are world-renowned. Its beautiful, inaccessible beaches and waterfalls have lured many tourists from their hotel pools and over the most bone-rattling of roads. To an outsider, Haiti's voodoo religion, with its torchlight ceremonies, seems more spectacular than a circus—which it in fact sometimes resembles. But to most of the more than 4,500,000 Haitians, many of whom are starving or hungry in this land of eroded mountains, their country is a nightmare from which there is no escape. This is the tragic irony of the Caribbean's oldest republic, the nation that outlasted the French armies of Napoleon I to win its independence.

HISTORY

The Caribbean island of Hispaniola, which Haiti shares with the Dominican Republic, was discovered by Christopher Columbus—sailing for Spain—on December 5, 1492. By the 17th century Hispaniola had become a haven for buccaneers, or pirates, many of whom were Frenchmen with a violent hatred for Spain. The buccaneers made the little island of Tortuga, off the northern coast of Hispaniola, their stronghold. In 1697, when a treaty was signed by France and Spain that, in effect, set off the area where their pirates could operate, France was given the western third of Hispaniola, which today is Haiti.

Saint-Domingue. There followed for the French 90 years of prosperity, perhaps unequaled before or since in the Caribbean. By 1780 the colony of Saint-Domingue, as Haiti was then called, was producing most of the coffee and sugar for Europe. Half a million black slaves worked the canefields and the coffee plantations. They were so overworked and so weakened by disease that every generation almost their whole number had to be replaced. The whites, numbering about 25,000 in all, administered the colony with ruthless efficiency and reaped princely profits for themselves.

Living uneasily between whites and blacks were the mulattoes, a free people of mixed black and white parentage. Mulattoes were given the freedom to own land and have slaves, but they were not accepted socially by the whites and they were not permitted to hold political office or even practice professions. The mulattoes, quite understandably, hated and envied the whites. They also despised and feared the blacks.

Revolution and Independence

The inevitable explosion in Haiti was touched off by the French Revolution (1789). The revolutionary Constitution of France provided that important new civil rights be extended to mulattoes. The white colonists in Haiti refused to comply. Late in 1790 a force of armed mulattoes marched on Cap-Haïtien (then called Cap-Français). The insurrection was put down, and the mulatto leaders were executed. This occurred early in 1791.

In the following months the whites and mulattoes of Saint-Domingue maneuvered against each other. But it was the forgotten blacks who made the Haitian revolution, rising against their masters (August, 1791) in a wave of killing and burning. Years of fighting followed. Alliances were formed and reformed in endless combinations among whites, blacks, and mulattoes.

Mulattoes sided with blacks in some parts of Haiti and with whites in other parts. Whites even sided with blacks in areas where the mulattoes were particularly strong. White leaders themselves split into factions, supporting or opposing the revolutionary government in France. To complicate matters further, Spain and Britain went to war with France in 1793 and sent troops into Saint-Domingue. But in the end, to everyone's surprise, Spain and Britain were driven out of Hispaniola, the mulattoes were defeated, and the entire island was unified in 1801 under the remarkable black leader Toussaint L'Ouverture.

Pierre Dominique Toussaint L'Ouverture. Toussaint was a former slave. He was a small, homely man, who possessed the shrewdness to play off nations and factions, one against another, and the boldness to win final control of the revolutionary forces in Haiti. Unfortunately he had, by prevailing in Hispaniola, won himself no less an enemy than the great French military leader Napoleon Bonaparte, who then ruled France.

Although Hispaniola remained a French possession, Napoleon wanted complete control—and he wanted to re-impose slavery. He mounted a huge amphibious military expedition against Haiti, with his own brother-in-law, Charles Leclerc, in command. Toussaint's slave armies were defeated. Toussaint was seized and sent into exile and prison in France, where he eventually died. But the great victory in Hispaniola amounted to nothing for France. The dread Caribbean yellow fever killed General Leclerc and the better part of his army. Toussaint's most trusted lieutenants, Jean-Jacques Dessalines, Henry Christophe, and Alexandre Pétion, drove the remnants of the French army from the western part of the island.

On January 1, 1804, the former French colony of Saint-Domingue became the Republic of Haiti—the first sovereign nation in the Caribbean. In his first act as president, Jean-Jacques Dessalines tore out the white section of the French tricolor flag. He announced that henceforth Haiti's flag would be red and black—the traditional blue of the tricolor becoming black to symbolize the people of Haiti.

Poverty and Misfortune

Haiti was beset by poverty and misfortune from the start. The flourishing economy of the country had been virtually destroyed by war and revolution. Dessalines managed to hold the new nation together by sheer terrorism. However, he was assassinated in 1806, and Haiti was split in half. The north was ruled by Henry Christophe. The south was ruled first by Alexandre Pétion and later by Jean Pierre Boyer, both mulattoes.

Henry Christophe was an extraordinary man. He crowned himself King Henry I and built a magnificent royal palace (Sans Souci). On a peak near the palace he built Citadelle La Ferrière, a fortress of stupendous grandeur, even though it was virtually useless militarily. Christophe was able to restore prosperity to his kingdom by means of harsh dictatorial policies. He committed suicide in 1820. At Christophe's death, Haiti was re-united once and for all under Jean Pierre Boyer, the leader of southern Haiti.

Both Boyer and his predecessor Alexandre Pétion were easygoing leaders who set the pattern for the political corruption that has been part of Haitian politics since their time. They also unwittingly laid the basis for Haiti's extreme poverty by dividing up the land among the peasants in such small parcels that large-scale commercial agriculture—which is usually the most prosperous kind of modern farming—still remains all but impossible in Haiti.

Throughout the 19th and into the 20th century, Haiti sank deeper and deeper into sloth and helplessness. The land was subdivided into increasingly smaller units. Agriculture remained undeveloped and the black farmers remained poor and illiterate. In an overwhelmingly black nation, black politicians usually held the presidency. The mulattoes controlled what little commerce and industry there were, and also formed a social and cultural elite with a monopoly on education.

The mulattoes eventually had the opportunity to control politics as well as commerce and culture. In 1915, during World War I, the United States Marines began a long occupation of Haiti. By that time Haiti's condition approached complete political anarchy. Between 1912 and 1915 one president had been blown up in the national palace, a second had been poisoned, a third, fourth, and fifth had been overthrown by coups, and a sixth had been killed by an angry mob in the main square of Port-au-Prince. The United States, fearing that pro-

Gros-Morne, with its tin-roofed houses, is a typical small town.

Haitian farmers must cultivate every inch of their small plots.

FACTS AND FIGURES

REPUBLIC OF HAITI—République d'Haiti—is the official name of the country.

CAPITAL: Port-au-Prince.

LOCATION: Western third of Hispaniola, Caribbean Sea. **Latitude**—18° N to 20° N. **Longitude**—71° 35′ W to 74° 30′ W.

AREA: 10,714 sq. mi. (27,750 sq. km.).

PHYSICAL FEATURES: Highest point—Morne La Selle (9,000 ft.; 2,743 m.). **Lowest point**—sea level. **Chief river**—Artibonite.

POPULATION: 4,674,000 (estimate).

LANGUAGES: French (official), Creole (Haitian dialect).

RELIGION: Christian (predominantly Roman Catholic).

GOVERNMENT: Republic. **Head of government**—president. **Legislature**—house of assembly. **International co-operation**—United Nations, Organization of American States (OAS).

CHIEF CITIES: Port-au-Prince, Cap-Haïtien.

ECONOMY: Chief minerals—limestone, bauxite, copper. **Chief agricultural products**—bananas, coffee, sisal, sugar, cacao. **Industries and products**—refined sugar, cement, sisal rope. **Chief exports**—coffee, sugar, bauxite, sisal. **Chief imports**—foodstuffs, cotton fabrics, motor vehicles, industrial machinery.

MONETARY UNIT: Gourde.

NATIONAL HOLIDAY: January 1, Independence Day.

NATIONAL ANTHEM: *La Dessalinienne* ("Song of Dessalines").

German forces might take advantage of the chaos, decided to step in. (They intervened in the Dominican Republic the following year.) The American occupation of Haiti lasted until 1934, long after the threat of a German take-over had vanished. During their occupation of Haiti, the United States Marines found it easiest to work with the mulattoes. They backed a succession of mulatto puppet presidents.

The Americans did a considerable amount of road building and modernized Haiti in various other ways during the occupation. The improvements, however, had little effect on the lives of Haiti's impoverished black masses.

After the Marines left Haiti the mulattoes continued to govern benevolently, but corruptly, until 1946. In 1946 there began a succession of black presidents, who also governed benevolently and corruptly. Then, in 1957, François Duvalier, a black physician, was elected to the presidency. He continued as president, ruling harshly and with absolute power, until his death in 1971. He also brought the government and economy to their worst state of dilapidation since the 19th century. Duvalier was succeeded in office by his son, Jean-Claude Duvalier, who became president for life.

THE LAND

The Haitian landscape bears marks of the people's unhappy and impoverished history. The country has many naked, eroded hillsides, where the farmers have cut down the trees for firewood. Since agriculture in Haiti is primitive, there is little notion of maintaining the fertility of the soil. Instead, when the land is exhausted, the farmers traditionally burn down the trees on adjacent land and plant there, leaving a waste of scrub growth behind. As the land was stripped of trees, severe flooding and soil erosion became common in Haiti. The rainy season—which occurs between April and June and again during October and November—is an especially bad time of flooding and soil erosion. In some places along the Dominican border, it is actually possible to tell where the border is by the bareness of the land on the Haitian side. On the other hand, some areas of Haiti are still thickly forested, and there are parts of the mountainous country as lush and untouched as the remote jungles and forests of Africa and South America. The island of Hispaniola is also subject to violent hurricanes, which occur in the fall of the year. A number of hurricanes in the past have caused severe destruction and loss of life.

Anyone who has been lucky enough to visit Haiti for the first time by ship gains a sense of the country's over-all beauty. Blue-black mountains, range upon range visible from far out at sea, present a brooding, mysterious, and strikingly beautiful vista.

Haiti is even more mountainous than its neighbor, the Dominican Republic, with which it shares the island of Hispaniola. Eighty percent of the Haitian landscape consists of rugged mountain ranges or elevated plateaus. The island's highest mountain is Morne La Selle in the southeast; it is just under 9,000 feet (2,700 meters). Several large plains lie between the mountains. The most notable is the Cul-de-Sac plain, lying northeast of Port-au-Prince. Well irrigated, it is the most productive region of Haiti, furnishing most of the country's sugar crop. It is the country's most densely populated area.

Haiti has two large peninsulas, which are separated by the Gulf of Gonâve. The southern peninsula, which is 50 miles (80 kilometers) long, is the more densely populated of the two. It points toward Jamaica. The northern peninsula, which is shorter than the southern and largely very dry, points toward Cuba. Between them in the Gulf of Gonâve lies the island of Gonâve. Although it is of considerable size—it is larger, in fact, than the islands of Barbados or Grenada—Gonâve does not have a developed harbor or road, or even a real town with shops to serve the people who live there.

North and South.   Northern Haiti is the birthplace of Haitian independence. During the United States occupation, northern Haiti was the scene of sporadic guerrilla activity against American occupation forces. More than a century before that the north had been the focus of the Haitian revolution. The former French colonial capital, Cap-Haïtien, is in the north. Henry Christophe proclaimed north Haiti's independence in Cap-Haïtien. In some ways north Haiti is rather like Christophe himself—independent in spirit, theatrical in manner, and oriented in style toward Europe. The two most famous monuments to Christophe's reign, his royal palace, Sans Souci (now in ruins), and the magnificent and forbidding Citadelle, stand near Cap-Haïtien.

In contrast to northern Haiti, southern Haiti has always been soft and sensual in mood, less rebellious, and more taken up with voodoo. The Caribbean towns of Jacmel, Les Cayes, and Jérémie have always been ports for exporting coffee. Indeed, the ease in picking coffee berries compared with the fierce exertion required to cut cane and sisal, the major crops in the north, may account for many of the subtle differences between north and south Haiti.

The busy Iron Market, with its fantastic towers and crowds of shoppers, is one of Port-au-Prince's best-known landmarks.

The Artibonite, Haiti's only sizable river, rises in the western part of the Dominican Republic and flows to the Gulf of Gonâve between the two peninsulas. (Haiti has many rivers, but most of them are actually little more than short, swift-flowing streams.) South of the Artibonite Valley is Haiti's only real city, Port-au-Prince. About 250,000 people live in Port-au-Prince, making it more than eight times as large as the second largest city, Cap-Haïtien. Port-au-Prince is the national capital and the business and cultural center of Haiti, as well. The city and the nearby mountain resorts of Pétion-Ville, Kenscoff, and Furcy are centers of such tourism as Haiti has managed to attract in recent years. However, the amount of tourism has been quite small.

THE PEOPLE

If Haiti's history has often resembled a nightmare, it is also true that the Haitian people have survived that nightmare. They scoff at fate with wild, mocking humor. They draw upon seemingly bottomless reserves of joyous vitality and refuse to admit despair. They carry on in the lives that they must lead by identifying themselves with the gods of their voodoo religion.

Voodoo

Voodoo is part of the lifeblood of Haiti. It is a religion that was derived originally from the tribal religions of the Africans brought to Haiti as slaves. It was the unifying and inspirational force of voodoo that made possible the massive revolt of the slaves against their French masters in 1791.

As the African tribal religions were mixed together in Haiti, certain gods or spirits called *loa* came to predominate. Some of the *loa* of voodoo originated in Hispaniola itself. Some are actually Christian saints who have been taken into the religion. Many Haitians who participate in voodoo also consider themselves Christians, and various symbols, ceremonies, and outward forms of Christianity have been incorporated into voodoo rites. The cross, for example, doubles as the sign for Baron Samedi ("Baron Saturday"), one of the most powerful and dreaded of the *loa*. Voodoo is more changeable, less abstract, and less systematic than the major world religions. Laws and beliefs in voodoo are unwritten, and more than in other religions, religious practices and rites are developed as they are needed.

Voodoo ceremonies may be held at any time an individual or community needs help and is willing to pay for the services of the *houngan*, or priest. The whole purpose of a voodoo ceremony is for the participant to become possessed. Having an emotional seizure, he temporarily loses his earthly identity and takes on the identity of the *loa* whom he has invoked. Which *loa* it happens to be depends on the participant's problem. For problems of the heart or romance, for example, the *loa* invoked would probably be Erzulie Fréda Dahomey, goddess of the home, of purity, and of love. When the participant feels himself to be possessed by the *loa,* he is cleansed of his worries.

Possession is brought about by a combination of means. Most voodoo ceremonies take place at night. The dark, crowded *tonnelle,* or gathering place, is illuminated by wicks floating in kerosene, and the eerie setting helps to convince the participant that he has entered a world remote from his own, where anything can happen. The ceremony begins. The thunderous beating of drums, played in batteries of three, helps break down the participant's conscious inhibitions, as do the dancing—face to face but never touching—and the *vever,* a very intricate abstract design that the *houngan* draws with flour or ashes on the earthen floor of the *tonnelle*. Finally, the blood sacrifice of a chicken, goat, pig, or bull serves to remind the participant of the African past, where human sacrifices were made, and religion was a matter of life and death.

Down through the years voodoo, which is essentially well-intentioned, has become entangled with black magic, which is not well-intentioned. Sometimes the *bocor* (sorcerer) and the *houngan* (priest) are one person. The *bocor's* activities include preparing love potions and death-charms, finding buried treasure, turning enemies into werewolves, or resurrecting the dead to work the fields as zombi slaves. All of this, of course, is done for a price. Today voodoo has become so infiltrated with black magic that it is difficult to see a ceremony with any semblance of its original purity.

A Rich Cultural Life

With a rich voodoo folklore on the one hand, and an educated elite on the other hand, Haiti has a cultural life that is surprisingly full for a nation that is so poor in material things.

Painting and Sculpture. Haitian primitive painting and sculpture became world-famous in the decade following World War II. Before that time Haiti's rich heritage of folk culture had been expressed almost entirely in music and in dance. Then, in 1944, an American painter named DeWitt Peters opened the Centre d'Art ("art center") in Port-au-Prince. This was an art school as well as an outlet for selling the

Many people consider these murals in the Episcopal cathedral in Port-au-Prince the crowning achievement in Haitian folk art.

works of Haitian artists. The decision was wisely made to let self-taught Haitian folk artists develop largely on their own, with a premium placed on high standards of craftsmanship and taste. The result of this policy was to help develop the first school of self-taught artists anywhere.

Among the most impressive examples of the resulting art are the murals of the Episcopal Cathedral of the Holy Trinity (Saint-Trinité) in Port-au-Prince. They were painted by the Haitian artists Philomé Obin, Castera Bazile, Wilson Bigaud, Rigaud Benoit, and others between 1949 and 1951. (The author of this article initiated the mural project.) The Centre d'Art also developed great Haitian sculptors. These include, most notably, Jasmin Joseph and Georges Liautaud.

One of the first painters to achieve worldwide fame through the Centre d'Art was the late Hector Hyppolite, a voodoo priest. The best of the present generation of Haitian painters, André Pierre, is also a voodoo priest.

Literature. Unlike much of the best Haitian painting, Haitian literature has been, by and large, about voodoo rather than a direct expression of the religion. Literature has been almost exclusively the art of the largely mulatto Haitian elite. The great mass of people are illiterate and speak Haitian Creole, a dialect formed mainly of French and some African words and phrases. (It also includes elements of English, Spanish, and Dutch.) Creole is not a literary language, and so Haitian literature is in French.

Actually Haiti has a rather sizable body of literary work. More books have been produced per capita in Haiti than in any American country except the United States. The flowering of Haitian literature occurred in the 1920's and 1930's during the United States occupation of the country. Before that time Haitian writing had been little more than an extension of French literature. However, during the long American occupation, Haitian intellectuals became newly aware of themselves as Haitians. The result of this movement was a vigorous and original literature. It included the poetry of Emile Roumère and Magloire St. Aude and the novels of the Marcellin brothers—Philippe Thoby-Marcellin and Pierre Marcellin—work that is largely pre-occupied with the role of voodoo and of superstition in Haitian life.

THE FUTURE

With a per capita income estimated at about $70 a year, Haiti is the poorest country in the Americas. Its population, which now numbers over 4,500,000, continues to rise every year. With two thirds of the land area of Haiti too rough and too mountainous to be cultivated, Haiti would undoubtedly have a severe food shortage even if Haitian agricultural methods were not as backward as they are. The United States provides some food, medical supplies, and other materials, but only on a small scale because of its disapproval of the government. On the other hand, the United States continues to maintain diplomatic relations with the Haitian Government.

With or without its present government, Haiti's problems are deep ones. Even if a progressive government were to come to power, it would only mark a first step for this beautiful but poor country, with its rich and strange history.

SELDEN RODMAN, Author, *Haiti: The Black Republic*

Visitors to Jamaica find guest houses on lovely, sheltered coves.

JAMAICA

Christopher Columbus discovered Jamaica in 1494 and thought it was the most beautiful of the West Indian lands he had seen. This central Caribbean island, south of Cuba, is still known for its extraordinary natural beauty. *Xamaica*, the Indian word from which the island takes its name, means "land of wood and water." Jamaica has many rushing rivers and streams. But Jamaica is even more a land of mountains, and spectacularly beautiful mountains many of them are—luxuriantly overgrown, towering up into the clouds, the play of light over the slopes giving them an unearthly bluish hue.

The highest and steepest mountains of Jamaica are actually called the Blue Mountains; they occupy most of the eastern third of the island. From there, the land tapers off into less rugged hill and plateau country, including the largely inaccessible area known as Cockpit Country. There the erosion of the limestone plateau has produced numerous gorges in the shape of inverted cones, called cockpits. Only about 20 percent of Jamaica could be called flat or gently rolling. Most of the coast is flat, and there are plenty of fine beaches. Many large hotels have been built for tourists, particularly on the northern coast, at Montego

The Jamaican landscape is dominated by the Blue Mountains.

Bay, Ocho Rios, and other places. About 400,000 tourists a year now visit Jamaica to enjoy the warm surf and a climate that is mild winter and summer. It is a lush island, still something of a tropical paradise.

Despite its beauty and many natural advantages, Jamaica has a number of very real problems. After 300 years as a British colony, Jamaica became an independent nation in 1962. The transition to independence has been smooth, but Jamaica is still a poor nation with a rapidly growing population and a continuing severe shortage of jobs. The growing tourist trade can help this situation, but much also has to be done to develop the economy and to provide the improved standard of living the people demand. Many Jamaicans still do not know how to read or write. New industries are needed to provide jobs. Agriculture has to be made more efficient, as well as more responsive to local demands. One of the strange facts about this apparently lush country is that Jamaica still has to import much of the food it consumes.

THE LAND

Jamaica is the third largest island of the West Indies, but it is still not a very large island. It has an area of 4,232 square miles (10,962 square kilometers). The mountainous nature of much of the terrain tends to reduce the amount of land that can be cultivated profitably and thereby further limits living space. It is a crowded—some people say overcrowded—nation with a population that is increasing all too rapidly. About 250,000 Jamaicans have left the island for the United Kingdom since 1950, although immigration into the United Kingdom was sharply curtailed in the early 1960's. Other Jamaicans have chosen to go to the United States.

Kingston. Many rural Jamaicans have come to Kingston, the capital city and commercial center of the island. About 500,000 people, or one fourth of Jamaica's total population, live in or near Kingston, many of them recent arrivals from the Jamaican countryside in search of improved job opportunities. New industries have been developed, but many newcomers to Kingston remain unemployed. Shantytowns of flimsy shacks have grown up on the western edge of the city. Otherwise, Kingston is a large commercial city, a place mainly for doing business—government business, commercial business, and shopping. The city has its lively side, too. It has one of the largest natural harbors in the world, and there is plenty of activity around the docks, where merchant ships and seamen from all over the world gather.

Farming the Land

Despite the recent tendency among Jamaicans to migrate to Kingston and other cities, Jamaica is still a predominantly rural country. The majority of the rural population are independent farmers working small farms. About three fourths of all Jamaican farms are 5 acres (2 hectares) or less, and perhaps half of these are less than ½ acre. The small farmer in Jamaica may barely eke out a living for himself and his family at something close to the subsistence level.

Many poor Jamaicans subsist on a relatively unvaried diet of yams, sweet potatoes, breadfruit, and other easily obtainable foods, such as bananas and beans. Malnutrition among infants and young children, resulting from a lack of protein, is still fairly widespread. But a Jamaican's diet may be quite varied, too. It may include corn, pork, white potatoes

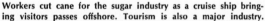

Workers cut cane for the sugar industry as a cruise ship bringing visitors passes offshore. Tourism is also a major industry.

Bauxite from Jamaica's mines is loaded on a ship at Ocho Rios.

and sweet potatoes, land and sea crabs, chickens, eggs, curried goat, and a wide range of fish and shellfish, besides pepper pot (a highly spiced soup of meat, spinach or calaloo, and other vegetables) and salt cod mixed with the fruit of the ackee tree.

Large-Scale Agriculture. At the other end of the spectrum from the small farms are the great corporate estates of up to thousands of acres, many of which are foreign-owned. Today about 56 percent of all farmland in Jamaica is taken up by only .7 percent (or less than 1 percent) of all the landholdings. There is an obvious need for more equitable land ownership, and the government has taken measures in that direction. On the other hand, Jamaica's agricultural problems are complicated and are not to be solved simply by redistributing the land.

Sugar and bananas are Jamaica's leading export crops. Sugar is Jamaica's oldest staple crop; bananas were first grown commercially in the late 19th century and for a long time were the leading staple crop. The sugar industry is dominated by about 20 large companies. The company-owned farms, or estates, generally occupy the best of the land once occupied by slave-operated plantations.

Cane cutting today remains the hard and poorly paid work it has always been. Employment is generally seasonal, lasting from December to May, the months in which the cane is harvested. The cane cutters are likely to be idle the rest of the year. The estate-owning companies process all the cane raised on the island, either refining it as sugar or making it into molasses or rum. But about half the cane is grown by more than 20,000 independent farmers, from whom the companies are obliged to purchase it for processing. Thousands of small farmers grow bananas too, sometimes marketing as little as a stem or two a week.

Jamaica also exports citrus fruits, pimientos, and coffee. The most notable of these exports, however, is the coffee grown in the Blue Mountains. Some coffee experts prefer Blue Mountain coffee to the best South American varieties. Other export crops include cacao, tobacco, and coconuts.

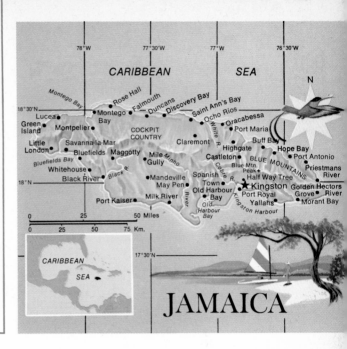

JAMAICA

New Uses for the Land

For a long time Jamaica's economy was almost entirely agricultural, based largely on sugar, rum, and bananas. Today this is no longer true. In the 1950's large American and Canadian companies began to exploit Jamaica's considerable reserves of bauxite, the ore that is the chief source of aluminum and its compounds. Because Jamaica has lacked the vast amounts of cheap hydroelectricity needed for the final stage of aluminum production, much of the bauxite is exported unrefined, particularly to the United States. Some of it is refined into alumina, the white powder from which aluminum is made. Today Jamaica is the world's leading exporter of bauxite and alumina and supplies about half the ore consumed by the entire United States aluminum industry. The value of bauxite and alumina exports is about equal to that of all of Jamaica's agricultural exports combined.

Then there are the tourists. For a long time Jamaica's tourist trade was small, but in the 1960's the Jamaican Government undertook an energetic campaign to expand tourist facilities as well as to improve the atmosphere for tourism. By the late 1960's tourism had risen to about double what it was when Jamaica achieved its independence in 1962.

THE PEOPLE

"Out of many, one people" is the motto on Jamaica's official coat of arms. In its long history Jamaica has been a country of different races and peoples. Altogether, more than 90 percent of Jamaicans have some African ancestry. Of these, about one out of five is of mixed ancestry, leaving the majority to be described by the census bureau simply as Africans. More than 250,000 Jamaicans are classified by the census as Afro-European, which means they are of both white and Negro ancestry. In addition, various other races and nationalities have settled in Jamaica, including Indians—or East Indians, as they are sometimes called in the Caribbean—Chinese, and a small number of Lebanese.

Many island families still live quiet lives in the countryside.

More than 30,000 Indians and a smaller number of Chinese were brought to Jamaica as contract laborers in the decades following the abolition of slavery in 1838. Many stayed beyond the years specified in their contracts. The Chinese in particular frequently started their own small businesses. Most of the Lebanese immigrated to Jamaica early in the 20th century and generally became shopkeepers or restaurant proprietors. The new groups mingled with the Negro majority, and today Jamaica has about as many Afro-East Indians as East Indians, about as many Afro-Chinese as Chinese.

The nation's mixed heritage shows itself in many ways. Jamaica's official language is English, but in fact the majority of people talk a kind of shorthand dialect sometimes called Jamaica talk, which contains elements of Elizabethan (16th-century) English and of African languages. It can be quite difficult for British or American visitors to understand.

The nation's African heritage is also very evident in the folklore and in some of the religious cults and folkways. Some of the old beliefs are centered on evil spirits called duppies, who according to tradition lived in the roots of cottonwood trees. There was also the legendary Rolling Calf, which was supposed to breathe fire from its nostrils and was said to haunt country roads. A mere glimpse of it was supposed to be fatal.

In the peasant world of yesterday, religion included the Christian church and also, less obviously, the obeah man. This word is derived from *obayifo,* a word of the Ashanti tribe of Africa, which means "wizard." The obeah man was a kind of witch doctor.

As education has improved, the old superstitions have declined. The differences between races have become less pronounced. Still, gaps do remain. White persons constitute less than 1 percent of Jamaica's population, but their wealth is much greater than their numbers. On the other hand, there is marked poverty among black and brown Jamaicans. Despite the relative harmony among the races, a legacy of bitterness exists from the days of slavery. The distribution of wealth among the races is one of the major challenges facing Jamaica today.

HISTORY

The first inhabitants of Jamaica, as far as anybody knows, were neither white nor black. They were the cave-dwelling Ciboneys—Indians who came from Florida, lived on fish, and painted themselves with red or yellow dye. They were quietly dispossessed by the Arawaks, a peaceful Indian people who came from Venezuela.

After Columbus' discovery of Jamaica in 1494, Spain annexed the island, drove out or exterminated the Arawaks, and imported Negro slaves from Africa.

The Spaniards raised cattle and planted sugarcane in Jamaica, although not in very great quantity. When Spain's colonial rival England captured the island in 1655, no more than a few thousand Spaniards and slaves were living there. Spain formally ceded the island to England by the Treaty of Madrid in 1670.

The Maroons.   During the years in which the Spanish settlers were fighting a guerrilla war against the English invaders, they armed their Negro slaves with muskets and used them as allies. The freed slaves joined slaves who had previously run away. They were joined later by slaves escaping from British settlers. Groups of these runaway slaves made settlements of their own in inaccessible places in the mountains. They were called Maroons, a contraction of the Spanish word *cimarron*, which means "wild" or "unruly." Before long these excellent guerrilla fighters were coming from the hills to raid plantations.

Attempts to subdue the Maroons failed. Finally, in 1738, the British signed a treaty with the Maroons granting them land and various rights, including the right to punish their own people for crimes they committed. There are still about 1,500 Maroons in Jamaica, most of them living in the Cockpit Country. They are indistinguishable from the other Jamaicans, but they retain some of the privileges conferred on them in the 1738 treaty. Their leader is called the colonel.

Pirates.   Meanwhile, about the time the trouble with the Maroons was first starting, Jamaica became a headquarters of the buccaneers, the pirates who terrorized the Caribbean in the 17th century. The pirates centered their activity in Port Royal, which quickly became the greatest center of wealth in the Caribbean. Merchants swarmed over from England to purchase at low prices the treasures plundered by the buccaneers from other colonies. For a while, the British authorities left the buccaneers alone and even encouraged them. But in the 1670's the government began to suppress piracy. In 1692 a great earthquake followed by massive flooding struck Port Royal and all but destroyed the city. That event in turn occasioned the building of a new commercial center, Kingston, on the opposite side of the harbor.

Slavery and Its Abolition.   At this time, too, sugar planting was being greatly expanded in Jamaica. The British planted on a far greater scale than the Spaniards had done previously, importing thousands of slaves from Africa every year to do the work. By 1750 Jamaica was Britain's leading sugar colony, using over 300,000 slaves on its plantations. Sugar planting continued to be enormously profitable until the early 19th century, when a series of internal and international developments combined to bring about its decline. One of the final blows was the abolition of slavery, partially in 1834 and totally in 1838.

After emancipation, many former slaves were unwilling to remain field workers, even for wages. They went into the hills to farm their own lands. Many of the people of Jamaica were desperately poor and were subject to exploitation by those in authority. Discontent exploded in a short-lived Negro uprising against the government at Morant Bay on Jamaica's southeastern coast. The uprising was quickly put down, but many of the island's property owners and professional people, almost all white or of mixed ancestry, now feared the rising power of the Negroes, particularly the educated Negroes. Up to this time, Jamaica had always had a large measure of self-government through the elected membership of the Jamaican House of Assembly. Now the colony's leadership was willing to trade that element of self-government for the security of tight British control. In 1866, therefore, the Assembly voted to abolish itself and petitioned Queen Victoria to assume entire management and control of the island's affairs. Jamaica became a crown colony, with virtually all power residing in the British-appointed governor.

Toward Independence. The system of government established in 1866 remained in effect, with a few modifications, until 1944. By that time there were many signs of a growing political consciousness among Jamaica's black majority, and a new constitution was proclaimed providing for a measure of self-government as well as for full adult suffrage. In 1959 another constitution granted Jamaicans full internal self-government and placed the colony one step away from complete independence. The year before, Jamaica had joined with other British colonies in the Caribbean to form the Federation of the West Indies, which was scheduled to achieve independence in 1962. But in 1961 the Jamaica electorate voted to secede from the federation. Jamaica became a fully independent nation on August 6, 1962. Sir William Alexander Bustamante, a Jamaican who had first emerged as a public figure in the 1930's, became the nation's first prime minister.

GOVERNMENT

Officially Jamaica is a monarchy under the sovereignty of the Queen of England and her appointed governor-general. Actually, their powers are merely ceremonial, and most real power is vested in the lower house of Parliament, the House of Representatives, which is elected by popular vote. The prime minister is the head of the majority party in the House of Representatives and the Senate, the upper house of Parliament. The Senate has 21 members, who are appointed by the governor-general, 13 of them on the advice of the prime minister and eight on the advice of the head of the opposition party. The Senate has the power to reject a bill sent up from the House, but the House can still make it law by passing it a second time.

Reviewed by PHILIP SHERLOCK, Vice Chancellor, University of the West Indies

A friendly cricket match on a Barbadian beach.

BARBADOS

Like a sentinel Barbados stands alone, farther out to sea than any other Caribbean island. Barbados, with an area of 166 square miles (430 square kilometers), is one of the smallest nations in North America. Because the population of the island exceeds 250,000, it is one of the most densely populated nations in the world. Overpopulation is a problem in this former British colony. The economic pressures brought about by overpopulation have led many islanders to emigrate to Trinidad, Guyana, Central America, the United States, Canada, and Great Britain.

THE LAND

Geologically, Barbados is not part of the chain of islands known as the Lesser Antilles. Those islands are the above-water portions of a submerged mountain range. Barbados is an island formed by the accumulation of coral on a separate base of ancient rock. The landscape of Barbados is gentle in comparison to the characteristic Antillean contours of jagged mountains and deep valleys. The highest point on the island, Mount Hillaby, is only about 1,104 feet (336 meters) above sea level.

There are no rivers to speak of on Barbados. The ground absorbs rainwater quickly, the water draining away into subterranean basins. Summer lasts all year, and the two seasons in Barbados are the wet season and the dry season. The dry season lasts roughly from December to May. During that time the people call a shower of rain a "blessing." They know that a drought can cut back the production of sugar, the crop on which their livelihood largely depends. The temperature ranges from 75 to 80 degrees Fahrenheit (24–27 degrees Celsius) all year round, with trade winds that moderate the heat of the sun blowing steadily from the north-

Policemen (center) wear 19th-century seamen's garb at Bridgetown harbor.

east. Perhaps because Barbados' climate is so equable, islanders use the word "weather" to mean bad weather only. A stormy sky means that the island is "in for some weather."

Barbadians mark the seasons as "crop time" or "planting time." They also speak of the times to harvest certain crops—for instance they speak of "yam time" or "mango season." But basically Barbados is a one-crop island: seven eighths of the cultivated land is planted in sugarcane. Therefore, "crop time" means March and April, when the workers move through the dense canefields of the sugar estates slashing at the roots of the high, tough stalks of cane. Planting time follows crop time, and the green of the cane stalks gives way to the brown of stubble and then the black of tilled earth. The trees break into a glory of flowers. There is the wide-spreading flamboyant tree with its gorgeous orange and scarlet flowers; the cordia and the cassia trees with flowers like apple blossoms or like showers of gold; and the frangipani with flowers of bronze, scarlet, and white. Christmas is the season of the red poinsettia.

An Orderly Land, An Easy Pace

Whatever the season in Barbados, the impression is of an orderly, tended land. The northeast coastal area is the exception, with its eroded rocks and steep cliffs. Elsewhere the land is well-used. About two thirds of the land, a very high percentage, is under cultivation. Great estates owned by members of the small minority of white Barbadians comprise four fifths of the cultivated land. Black and brown landowners own smaller parcels of land. The more prosperous of these smallholders grow sugarcane and food crops and raise cattle, goats, and sheep. Barbadian sheep, incidentally, are raised to be eaten, and only a trained eye can distinguish them from the local goat, because they have no wool. Some smallholders have plots that are not big enough to support them. They find work where they can or migrate from the island.

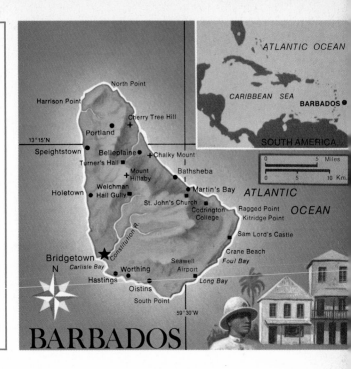

FACTS AND FIGURES

BARBADOS is the official name of the country.

CAPITAL: Bridgetown.

LOCATION: Caribbean Sea. **Latitude**—13° 02' to 13° 21' N. **Longitude**—59° to 59° 12' W.

AREA: 166 sq. mi. (430 sq. km.).

PHYSICAL FEATURES: Highest point—Mount Hillaby (1,104 ft.; 336 meters). **Lowest point**—sea level.

POPULATION: 253,000 (estimate).

LANGUAGE: English.

RELIGION: Anglican.

GOVERNMENT: Constitutional monarchy. **Head of state**—British monarch represented by governor-general. **Head of government**—prime minister. **Legislature**—parliament. **International co-operation**—Commonwealth of Nations, Organization of American States (OAS), United Nations.

CHIEF CITY: Bridgetown.

ECONOMY: Chief agricultural product—sugarcane. **Industries and products**—sugar refining. **Chief export**—cane sugar. **Chief imports**—consumer goods.

MONETARY UNIT: Barbados dollar.

NATIONAL HOLIDAY: Nov. 30, Independence Day.

NATIONAL ANTHEM: "In plenty and in time of need."

A typical Barbadian landscape might be this: a checkerboard of neat fields; the parish church of stone with its square tower, sheltered behind a screen of casuarinas or mahogany trees; an old plantation house secure behind a wall of whitewashed limestone. All this derives from a way of life that originated more than 3 centuries ago. Still part of the landscape, too, are the old round windmills of stone that once supplied the sugar factories with power and the workers' wooden cottages huddled together on the fringes of the sugar estates. In Barbados, the winds of change have not blown hard. This remains true even now that Barbados is an independent nation.

A Way of Life

The past and its habits and traditions have a hold on the islanders. This fact accounts for much of the charm Barbados has for tourists. A visitor is warmly welcomed to Barbados. But if he should decide to stay, he may not have become a "belonger" after 20 years.

Barbadians, or Bajans, as they are called for short, have their own identifiable way of life in which they take pride. They have a special way of speaking English with broad "a" and "o" sounds. Nouns are transformed into verbs, as in, "They been friendsing for a long time." There are proverbs suited to an island of sun and sea, like the Bajan rendering of "snake in the grass" as "shagger [sea crab] in the seaweed." Their speech reveals the Barbadians as a prudent people who do not intend to be misunderstood, even if it means repeating themselves. And so they don't simply say "ram" but "ram-sheep," not simply "rooster" but "fowl-cock," not simply "bull" but "bullcow." More importantly, Barbadians have the highest literacy rate of any Caribbean people; indeed, they have one of the highest literacy rates in the world. They enjoy this advantage because they have a fine school system, modeled after Great Britain's.

Barbados, in fact, is the most British of the Caribbean islands, an island where there seems to be a positive affection for things British. Bridgetown, the largest town on the island, has a miniature Trafalgar Square, modeled after London's famous square. As in the London square, there is a statue of the great British naval hero Lord Nelson (1758–1805). The statue is built to scale to conform with the smaller dimensions of the Bridgetown square. Harbor policemen dress like the sailors of Nelson's day, with bell-bottom trousers, neckerchiefs, and flat straw hats.

HISTORY

Barbados was the only major Caribbean island that was never colonized or ruled by any European nation other than Great Britain. Before the British came to the island, it was inhabited by the Arawaks, American Indians who migrated from the South American mainland and settled on islands as far north as the Bahamas and Cuba. Some of their artifacts, mainly trinkets of shell, have been found on Barbados. But the Arawaks themselves had abandoned the island before the arrival of the first Europeans.

Spanish and Portuguese explorers are known to have made landings on Barbados in the 16th century. In February, 1627, 80 English settlers arrived on Barbados to become the island's first European settlers.

With its gentle climate and fertile soil, Barbados quickly attracted more settlers, and by 1640 there were about 40,000 people living on the island. They were mostly from the British Isles and grew tobacco, cotton, and indigo for export. Cheap labor was obtained from indentured servants as well as from African slaves. The indentured servants were often beggars or thieves or debtors from Britain, people given a chance for a fresh start in the West Indies. They usually contracted to serve masters for a period of 5 years before they became free settlers themselves.

Sugar and Slavery.   In the 1640's competition with the North American mainland colony of Virginia for tobacco markets was hurting the Barbados planters. The islanders turned to sugar. In so doing, they inaugurated a new phase in the history of Barbados. The commercial growing of sugar demanded capital. The sugar planter had to have large tracts of land, a large labor force, and herds of animals for pulling carts. Planters with a lot of capital bought out the smallholders.

More than 30,000 people migrated from Barbados around this time to settle elsewhere in the Caribbean or in Virginia and the Carolinas. Thousands of Africans were brought in as slaves, and blacks became a great majority on the island. By the middle of the 18th century there were about 60,000 black slaves on Barbados and about 16,000 whites.

Slavery finally came to an end in Barbados and in the entire British Empire following the passage of an act of emancipation by the British Parliament in 1834. But the structure of economic and political power remained much as it had been before. A white minority controlled an enormously disproportionate share of the island's land and wealth and controlled the island's politics as well. The former slaves, meanwhile, had no place to go. There was no back country on this tiny island to move to. And so the Negroes on Barbados provided a large pool of labor at a time that other West Indian colonies had to import labor from the Orient.

Toward Independence.   In Barbados, as throughout the English-speaking Caribbean, the 1930's were a dividing line between an earlier period of white minority rule and a period of popular pressure for con-

Opulent Sam Lord's Castle, built by a 19th-century brigand, is now a hotel.

stitutional reform and independence. Constitutionally, Barbados had had a system of representative government from its earliest years. But voting was always limited to a few. Then, in the late 1930's, a black Barbadian lawyer, Grantley Adams, organized a political movement that finally led, in 1950, to granting the right to vote to all adults. Barbados became an internally self-governing colony in 1961 and became a fully independent nation in 1966. The new nation's first prime minister was a black Barbadian lawyer, Errol Barrow.

MODERN BARBADOS

The energies set free by independence have been used to exploit Barbados' natural advantages. One advantage is location. Bridgetown is 500 miles (805 km.) nearer than Kingston, Jamaica, to London. It is the first port of call for many ships entering the Caribbean, and with its modern deepwater harbor it has become an important commercial center for the Lesser Antilles. The island's excellent beaches are also an important natural resource. The government has worked energetically to increase Barbados' tourist trade. The government has further sought to diversify the economy (perhaps too much dominated by the sugar industry) by encouraging the growth of new industries.

Government

Barbados is a member of the Commonwealth of Nations. Officially it is ruled by Queen Elizabeth of England and her appointed governor-general. Actual political power rests with the Barbadian Parliament, principally in the House of Assembly, the members of which are elected by the people. The majority party in the House of Assembly selects from its number the nation's prime minister. There is also a second legislative house, the Senate, which is a largely honorary body.

PHILIP SHERLOCK, Vice-Chancellor, University of the West Indies

The magnificent harbor of St. George's, capital of Grenada.

GRENADA

"Sweet Grenada, a lovely place is Grenada" are words from a popular Calypso song, and an increasing number of tourists as well as the 100,000 Grenadians agree that Grenada is indeed a lovely place. White beaches, flowing streams, green valleys, and the vivid color of tropical flowers are part of the island's charm. Grenada calls itself "the isle of spice." It has been said that sailors in the old days could find Grenada by the fragrance that wafted out to sea from the island's nutmeg trees.

THE LAND

The most southerly of the Windward Islands of the West Indies, Grenada lies on the eastern rim of the Caribbean Sea. Its nearest neighbor is the island of St. Vincent to the northeast. Between the two is a group of islets called the Grenadines. A few of the islets belong to Grenada; the others are part of St. Vincent. Including the Grenadines, Grenada has an area of 133 square miles (344 square kilometers).

Grenada is of volcanic origin. The island is dominated by a ridge of thickly forested mountains running from north to south and rising to a height of 2,749 feet (848 meters) at Mount St. Catherine. High in the mountains lies Grand Etang, a lake formed in the crater of an extinct volcano. Cold weather is unknown in Grenada. There are only two seasons—a wet and a dry one. The average temperature is 80 degrees Fahrenheit (27 degrees Celsius) and even in the rainy season the humidity is rarely uncomfortable.

St. George's, with a population of about 7,000, is Grenada's capital and the only town of any size. It has a magnificent sheltered harbor surrounded by green hills on which cluster brightly roofed houses.

Grenada is the only island in the West Indies that produces nutmeg and mace, spices that are particularly important to the island's economy.

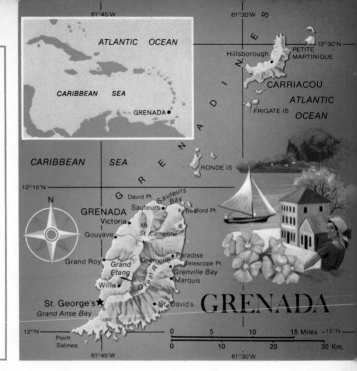

Bananas and cocoa are also grown commercially. Limes and cotton are grown on Carriacou, the largest of the Grenadines.

THE PEOPLE

Grenada's original inhabitants were Carib Indians who were wiped out in the colonization of the island. Today the majority of the people are of African ancestry, descendants of the slaves brought to the island in the 18th and 19th centuries. Most of the people are Roman Catholic, though there are Protestant churches throughout the island. The language of Grenada is English richly laced with expressions common to the West Indies. A French patois, or dialect, handed down from the early French settlers, is still spoken in some parts of the island.

HISTORY AND GOVERNMENT

Grenada was discovered by Christopher Columbus on his third voyage in 1498, but it was more than 100 years later that the first attempt to settle the island was made by a group of Englishmen. The fierce Carib Indians managed to drive off all would-be settlers until 1650, when the French succeeded in establishing a colony. The island changed hands several times. In 1783 Grenada was ceded finally to Great Britain.

During its early colonial days sugar was the chief product of the island, and slaves were imported to work the large plantations. The freeing of the slaves in the 19th century and the decline of sugar prices ended the plantation system. Grenada has since been a land of small farms.

In 1967 Grenada became self-governing as a West Indies Associated State. Great Britain remained responsible for the island's defense and foreign affairs. Grenada achieved complete independence in 1974. The government consists of the governor-general, who represents the British Crown; the cabinet, which includes the prime minister and ministers; and the Parliament, which is composed of the House of Representatives and the Senate.

Reviewed by GRENADA TOURIST INFORMATION OFFICE

TRINIDAD AND TOBAGO

Trinidad, the southernmost of the Caribbean islands, and its small neighbor Tobago have been united politically since 1889, first as a British colony and later, since 1962, as a fully independent nation within the Commonwealth. About 97 percent of this new nation's population of more than 1,000,000 live on Trinidad, which is by far the larger of the two islands. Trinidad, an emerald-green island, is known for its lush tropical vegetation, its oil wells, Pitch Lake, steel bands, calypso, and Carnival. Most of all it is known for the Trinidadians themselves, as diverse and colorful a people as one is likely to find anywhere. Tranquil, cigar-shaped Tobago is known for its glittering beaches of white sand, its sanctuary for birds of paradise (on Little Tobago islet), and its unusual species of birds, fish, and shells.

THE PEOPLE

Trinidad has a variety of peoples extraordinary even for the ethnically mixed West Indies. Persons of African descent do not constitute an overwhelming majority here, as they do on Tobago or on some of the other islands of the Caribbean. Trinidad had a comparatively short experience of slavery. When the British abolished slavery in the 1830's, the island's economy was still relatively undeveloped, and the slave population numbered only about 21,000. The island of Barbados, with less than one-tenth the

Scarborough, a typical Caribbean town, is on Tobago Island.

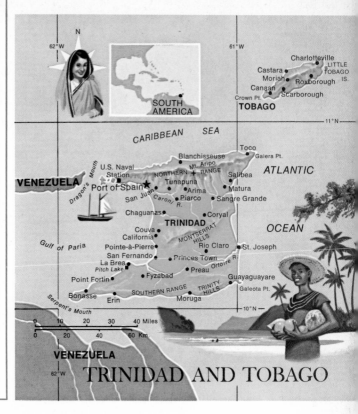

TRINIDAD AND TOBAGO

area—to choose only one example—had about four times as many slaves. Large numbers of field laborers subsequently had to be imported to work Trinidad's sugar fields, the great majority coming from the Bengal section of present-day India and Pakistan. Most of the East Indians, as they are called in the Caribbean, remained in Trinidad after the expiration of their contracts. Today their descendants constitute about 38 percent of the nation's population. About 40 percent of the population is classified by the census as Negro, and about 16 percent as being of mixed descent. The remainder of the population is descended from people of many nationalities, including English, Irish, Portuguese, Spanish, French, Chinese, Syrian, Lebanese, and Venezuelan.

Trinidad's various ethnic groups, though economically interdependent, traditionally tended to go their own ways. The two largest groups, Negroes and East Indians, retained distinct social patterns, with different diets, religions, cultural traditions, and ways of family life. Although the distinctions are not as sharp today as they once were, they are still easily seen. East Indians live largely among themselves on small farms, in villages, or on the sugar estates. They have a reputation for hard work and thrift, and many have saved their money, bought land, and prospered. East Indians have also become businessmen and entered the professions. The people of African descent have tended to congregate in the towns or at the oil fields, where they constitute most of the labor force in the oil industry, the nation's economic mainstay. Negroes have traditionally formed the backbone of the nation's civil service.

In general, the different peoples have lived in harmony. However, racial antagonisms are not unheard of, particularly between the Negroes

Left: Workers lift chunks of natural asphalt from Trinidad's Pitch Lake.
Right: Muslims in Port of Spain celebrate the festival of Hosein with
drums and an elaborate replica of a mosque.

and East Indians. Race and religion do play important roles in the politics
of this young nation. But traditional interracial differences are also breaking down. Contrasting styles of dress among different peoples, for example, have all but disappeared.

Port of Spain. Nowhere is the diversity of the island's population
more apparent than in this capital city of more than 100,000 people. Walking down Port of Spain's narrow streets, one is likely to hear snatches of
conversations in any number of languages. Here, a Muslim mosque, a
Benedictine monastery, and a Hindu temple can be visited within a few
minutes' drive of one another. This noisy, crowded, colorful city, the nation's largest, is also its commercial and administrative center and its
largest port.

Way of Life

Slavery existed on more than a negligible scale for only about 50
years in Trinidad, a relatively short time for the Caribbean. Even during
that time there was no great number of slaves. There is no oppressive
legacy of bitterness here. On the contrary, Trinidadians are a characteristically exuberant people, gay, fond of a fete and of Carnival, lovers of
music, quick to poke fun in their calypso songs and in their vivid Trinidad
talk. Music, in fact, is more than entertainment in Trinidad—it is almost a
way of life. Calypso singers may give themselves extravagant names like
Mighty Sparrow, Lord Kitchener, and Lord Pretender, but their songs are
very much down to earth—topical, witty, often openly political.

Besides calypso, Trinidad's other great musical creation is the steel
band, in which the instruments, or "pans," are made from discarded oil
drums. Steel bands originated as recently as the 1940's. Since that time the
pans have been refined by scoring the metal into sections and tuning it

with heat, so that a player striking the different sections with rubberized drumsticks can produce the fine liquid notes that are the essence of the steel band.

Carnival.   Every year, beginning at 5 A.M. of the Monday before Ash Wednesday, Trinidadians in every kind of costume take to the streets of Port of Spain and other towns to celebrate Carnival. For about a month before Carnival, Trinidad's leading calypsonians rehearse in tents or halls, delighting large crowds with their latest creations. Steel bands practice in yards in crowded settlements. Some of the bands that "play Carnival" have hundreds of members and followers dressed in colorful, dramatic costumes. For 2 days the Queen's Park Savannah, Port of Spain's huge park, and the streets of the island's towns and villages echo with music and overflow with dancing crowds. Young and old of every color and class shuffle, jump, and sway to the rhythm of the music. Just before midnight on Tuesday everyone hurries to join the "las' lap." On the stroke of midnight the dancing stops, the music dies away, and the fun of Carnival gives way to the solemn mood of Lent.

THE LAND

Trinidadians are fortunate in inhabiting a land rich in natural resources. Most valuable of those resources is oil, which was first extracted in sizable quantities in 1909. Oil is obtained from southern Trinidad and from the Gulf of Paria, which separates Trinidad and Venezuela. In addition, crude oil is imported from Colombia, Venezuela, and the Middle East for processing at Trinidad's huge west-coast refineries. Petroleum and petroleum products account for about 85 percent of the value of all the nation's exports. They constitute the principal reason that Trinidad and Tobago has the highest per capita income of any Caribbean nation. It is also true, however, that a large part of the profits goes to foreign investors. The national government has expanded its role in the industry, sometimes in partnership with private foreign interests.

Farming occupies about 20 percent of the work force in Trinidad. The land is largely flat or gently rolling, with the major exception of three narrow belts of highland crossing Trinidad from east to west. The prevail-

Farmers on Trinidad still use oxen to plow their rice fields.

ing warm and moist tropical climate is well suited for the cultivation of sugarcane, which is Trinidad's largest cash crop. Other crops grown in Trinidad and Tobago include cacao, coconuts, bananas, citrus fruits, and coffee. Tobago, largely undeveloped until recently, is building up an important tourist industry based on its fine beaches and great natural beauty.

Trinidad also has two highly unusual exports. Natural asphalt is dug out of Pitch Lake, which is a virtually inexhaustible deposit of asphalt in the southwestern part of the island, and also possibly one of the hottest places on earth. Angostura bitters, a flavoring agent, is made by a company in Port of Spain from ingredients said to be known to only four men.

Although Trinidad and Tobago boasts a relatively high standard of living for the Caribbean, this young nation is not without its economic problems. Unemployment is high, and the entire economy is highly dependent —overdependent, it is feared—on oil and sugar. The government has worked energetically to improve this state of affairs and has instituted programs to encourage crop diversification and to foster new industries. One hopeful development was the discovery in the late 1960's of a large natural gas field off Trinidad's southeastern coast, an important potential source of power for the island's industrial growth. Trinidad has a larger overseas trade than any other Commonwealth Caribbean country. Its chief trading partners are Britain, Venezuela, the United States, and Canada.

HISTORY

Despite its abundant natural resources, Trinidad was virtually ignored by the colonial powers of Europe for several centuries. Christopher Columbus discovered the island during his third voyage to the New World in 1498. He called it Trinidad after three landmark hills—the so-called Three Sisters or Trinity Hills—in the southeastern part of the island. Spain claimed the island on the basis of Columbus' discovery, but for centuries did next to nothing to develop the island. Then, in 1783, Spain opened the island to colonization by foreigners. This led to the first substantial settlement of the island, principally by sugar planters from French possessions in the West Indies, who brought their slaves with them. Many of the planters were refugees of the French Revolution, but others were simply attracted by the abundance of virgin soil in Trinidad and the rarity of hurricanes. Up to this time the native people of the island, the Arawak Indians, survived in some numbers, but few traces of them now remain. By 1797 the European and African population on the island numbered about 17,000. Of these about 10,000 were Negro slaves and most of the rest Frenchmen. In that year the island was captured by Britain, which was then at war with Spain. Trinidad was formally ceded to Britain by treaty in 1802.

Tobago may have been sighted by Columbus on his third voyage, but there is no evidence that he landed there. This tiny island occupied a highly strategic position in the Caribbean, and during the 17th and 18th centuries it was captured and recaptured by the English, French, and Dutch. Even the Latvian duchy of Courland entered the picture during the 17th century, for the Duke of Courland claimed Tobago on the basis of a grant from the King of England. The British regained control of the island in 1793 and, except for a brief period of French control in 1802 and 1803, governed the island thereafter.

Trinidad and Tobago were administered as separate colonies by Britain for most of the 19th century, but the two islands were put under

Tobago's miles of peaceful beaches attract holiday visitors.

a single administration in 1889, largely in order to cut administrative costs. Tobago retained a certain measure of control over its local affairs at the time, but 10 years later the two colonies were merged completely.

Thereafter self-government came slowly. The governor was appointed from London and was in no way responsible to the people of Trinidad and Tobago. A change was made in 1925, when a legislature was elected, but only a very small proportion of the population was eligible to vote. Universal suffrage was achieved in 1946, and the colony was granted full internal self-government in 1961. The increase in the pace of constitutional reform was due to the founding of a political party, the People's National Movement, under the leadership of the eventual first prime minister of Trinidad and Tobago, Dr. Eric Williams.

In 1958 Trinidad and Tobago became a part of the Federation of the West Indies. The federation, which included islands that were formerly British colonies, was dissolved in 1962. On August 31 of that year Trinidad and Tobago became a fully independent nation.

GOVERNMENT

Trinidad and Tobago accepts the British monarch as its sovereign, and the governor-general represents the sovereign, but complete legislative authority rests with the Parliament of the country. Parliament consists of two houses, the House of Representatives, which is wholly elected, and the Senate. Senators are appointed by the governor-general on the advice of the prime minister or the leader of the Opposition. The prime minister is the leader of the majority party.

Trinidad and Tobago plays a leading role in encouraging regional cooperation, especially among other Commonwealth Caribbean countries. It is a member of the Caribbean Community and Common Market, which includes as members a number of Commonwealth countries of the Caribbean. Trinidad and Tobago is also one of the chief supporters of the Caribbean Development Bank, which is associated with the organization.

Reviewed by PHILIP SHERLOCK, Secretary-General
Association of Caribbean Universities and Research Institutes

ILLUSTRATION CREDITS

The following list credits, according to page, the sources of illustrations used in volume 5 of LANDS AND PEOPLES. The credits are listed illustration by illustration—top to bottom, left to right. Where necessary, the name of the photographer or artist has been listed with the source, the two separated by a dash. If two or more illustrations appear on the same page, their credits are separated by semicolons.

346 Lisl Steiner
348 Jane Latta
350 Eric L. Ergenbright—Lenstour
352 Jane Latta
353 Carl Frank
355 Harrison Forman; De Wys, Inc.
358 Carl Frank
361 Bermuda Government Travel Bureau
362 Mulvey-Crump Associates, Inc.
363 Bahamas News Bureau
365 George Buctel
366 De Wys, Inc.
367 Leon Deller—Monkmeyer Press Photo Service; Cathleen FitzGerald
369 George Buctel
371 Williams—De Wys, Inc.
372 Scheier—Monkmeyer Press Photo Service
373 Harrison Forman
374 Harrison Forman
376 Leon Deller—Monkmeyer Press
379 Bradley Smith—Photo Researchers; Harrison Forman

381 Ron Laytner
382 Henri Cartier-Bresson—Magnum Photos
383 Frank Schwarz—Lee Ames Studio
384 Ron Laytner
385 Ron Laytner
389 Henri Cartier-Bresson—Magnum Photos
391 Ron Laytner
392 Joyce Deyo
393 Joyce Deyo
394 Joyce Deyo
395 Joyce Deyo
396 Joyce Deyo
397 Puerto Rico Information Service
398 Commonwealth of Puerto Rico
399 George Buctel
402 Fran Hall—Photo Researchers
403 Puerto Rico Information Service
405 Lisl Steiner
407 George Buctel
409 Jerry Frank
410 Lisl Steiner
411 Lisl Steiner

413 Henry C. Burrows
416 Henry C. Burrows; Gloria Karlson
417 George Buctel
419 Editorial Photocolor Archives, N.Y.
421 Henry C. Burrows
423 Jamaica Tourist Board
424 Jamaica Tourist Board
425 Jamaica Tourist Board
426 Jamaica Tourist Board
427 George Buctel
428 Jamaica Tourist Board
431 Baum—Monkmeyer Press Photo Service
432 Pan American Airways
433 George Buctel
435 Theodore C. Hines
436 Suva—DPI
437 George Buctel
438 Trinidad-Tobago Tourist Office
439 George Buctel
440 Trinidad-Tobago Tourist Office
441 Trinidad-Tobago Tourist Office
443 Trinidad-Tobago Tourist Office